POWER MISSES II

CINEMA, ASIAN AND MODERN

Avant-gardes will not endure, and the most fortunate thing that might happen to them is, in the full sense of the term, that they should have served their times.
   Guy Debord

or he were a Jew or a
Welshman
   William Carlos Williams

POWER MISSES II

CINEMA, ASIAN AND MODERN

DAVID E. JAMES

British Library Cataloguing in Publication Data

POWER MISSES II: CINEMA, ASIAN AND MODERN

A catalogue entry for this book is available from the British Library

ISBN: 0 86196 747 6 (Paperback))
ISBN: 0 86196 976 0 (ebook-EPUB)
ISBN: 0 86196 977 7 (ebook-EPDF)

Cover: Frame enlargement from *Two Stage Sisters* (*Wutai Jiemei*), 35 mm film directed by Xie Jin, Shanghai Tianma Film Studio, 1965.

Published by
John Libbey Publishing Ltd, 205 Crescent Road, New Barnet, Herts EN4 8SB, United Kingdom   e-mail: john.libbey@orange.fr; web site: www.johnlibbey.com

Distributed Worldwide by
Indiana University Press, Herman B Wells Library—350, 1320 E. 10th St., Bloomington, IN 47405, USA. www.iupress.indiana.edu

© 2020 Copyright John Libbey Publishing Ltd. All rights reserved.
Unauthorised duplication contravenes applicable laws.

Printed and bound in the USA.

Contents

	Acknowledgements	vii
	Foreword	ix
Chapter 1	Im Kwon-taek: Korean National Cinema and Buddhism	1
Chapter 2	Im Kwon-taek's Use of Nativist Korean Culture as Allegories of Cinema: *Ch'unhyang*, *Chihwaseon*, and *Hanji*	29
Chapter 3	The Name of a Desire: Recollections of Socialist Realism in East Asian Art Cinema	45
Chapter 4	Tradition and the Movies: The Working-Class Asian American Avant-Garde in Los Angeles	67
Chapter 5	The Sons and Daughters of Los: Culture and Community in Los Angeles	87
Chapter 6	Toward a Geo-Cinematic Hermeneutics/The City as Means of Production: Representations of Los Angeles in *Killer of Sheep* and *Water and Power*	103
Chapter 7	Expanded Cinema in Los Angeles: The Single Wing Turquoise Bird	127
Chapter 8	L.A.'s Hipster Cinema	153
Chapter 9	Film as an Instrument of Thought, Cinema as an Augury of Redemption: Ken Jacobs' *The Sky Socialist*	173
Chapter 10	"Apotheosis Into Tragedy": Catoptrics of Self in Andy Warhol's *Lupe*	201
Chapter 11	Letter to Paul Arthur (Letter With Endnotes)	215
Chapter 12	Agricultural Revelation: Land, Labor, and Voice in Three Films About Laxton	229

Acknowledgements

During the extended period in which these essays were first published, I was sustained by many friends and colleagues. I cannot begin to mention them all, but nor can I omit noting my gratitude for assistance in these specific projects to P. Adams Sitney and to Paul Arthur, Catherine Elwes, John Ganim, Adam Hyman, Branden Joseph, Chuck Kleinhans, Scott MacDonald, Michele Pierson, Martha Ronk, Patrick Tarrant, and Dale Wright. As always, my obligation to Joann Edmond is absolute. Sophia Serrano assisted me in the preparation of the text with all her customary joy and efficiency. My thanks to John Libbey for his continued support.

Earlier versions of these essays appeared as follows. My thanks to the respective editors: "Im Kwon-taek: Korean National Cinema and Buddhism", *Film Quarterly*, 54, 3 (Spring 2001); "Reflexive Ethnography: *Hanji* and Im Kwon-taek's use of Nativist Korean Culture as Allegories of Cinema", Lee Byung-hoon, ed., *Fly High, Run Far: The Making of Korean Master Im Kwon-taek* (Seoul: Korean Film Archives, 2013); "The Name of a Desire: Recollections of Socialist Realism in East Asian Art Cinema", *Grey Room* No. 26, (Winter 2007), reprinted courtesy of The MIT Press; "Tradition and the Movies: Minor(ity) Literature and Film in Los Angeles, with Special Reference to Asian Americans", *Studies in Language and Literature* (Taipei) 6 (1994); "Introduction: The Sons and Daughters of Los", David E. James, ed., *The Sons and Daughters of Los: Culture and Community in L.A.* (Philadelphia: Temple University Press, 2003); "Expanded Cinema in Los Angeles: The Single Wing Turquoise Bird", *Millennium Film Journal*, 43-44 (Fall 2005); "L.A.'s Hipster Cinema", *Film Quarterly*, 63, 1 (Fall 2009); "Towards a Geo-Cinematic Hermeneutics: Representations of Los Angeles in Non- Industrial Cinema – *Killer of Sheep* and *Water and Power*", *Wide Angle*, 20, 3 (1998); "*The Sky Socialist*: Film as an Instrument of Thought, Cinema as an Augury of Redemption", Michele Pierson, David E. James, and Paul Arthur, eds., *Optic Antics: The Cinema of Ken Jacobs* (New York and London: Oxford University Press, 2011); "Close-Up: The Mirror and the Vamp: David E. James on Andy Warhol's *Lupe*", © *Artforum*, 54, 5 (January 2016); "Letter to Paul Arthur (Letter With Footnotes)", *Moving Image Review & Art Journal* (London), 1, 1 (2012); reproduced with the kind permission of Intellect Books and the editors; "Agricultural Revelation: Land, Labour, and Voice in Three Films About Laxton", *Moving Image Review & Art Journal* 7:1 (2018) ; reproduced with the kind permission of Intellect Books and the editors.

I would like to thank the following for permission to reproduce illustrations: poster by John Van Hamersveld for Pinnacle Productions concert, Shrine Exposition Hall, Los Angeles, 1968, courtesy of and © John Van Hamersveld, all rights reserved; poster for Single Wing Turquoise Bird performance, Santa Barbara, 1969, courtesy of and © Michael Scroggins, all rights reserved; Single Wing Turquoise Bird performance announcement, 1970, courtesy of and © Michael Scroggins; all rights reserved; Single Wing Turquoise Bird performing in *The Baby Maker*: frame enlargement, annotations by Michael Scroggins, courtesy of and © Michael Scroggins, all rights reserved; Single Wing Turquoise Bird performing in *The Baby Maker*, photograph courtesy of and © Larry Janss, all rights reserved; Single Wing Turquoise Bird performing in *The Baby Maker*, Michael Scroggins at liquid overhead projector with strobe and color wheels, photograph courtesy of and © Larry Janss; "Echo Park Film Center audience, 22 May 2008", courtesy of Echo Park Film Center; Lawrence Weiner screening, Museum of Contemporary Art, Los Angeles, 14 June 2008, courtesy of Jessica Youn; REDCAT Theatre, courtesy of Heika Burnison and Anthony Rzeteljski, all rights reserved; Black Dice in performance at the Echo; photo © David E. James; Mike Kuchar, *Sins of the Fleshapoids*, Afterall screening, Westin Bonaventure Hotel, 21 August 2008, courtesy of and © Stacey Allan; Mark Toscano working on restoration at AMPAS, photo credit, Brian Meacham; Nancy Buchanan, *3 Fates*, photo © Doug Wichert, Liza Simone, and Phantom Galleries; Nokia Plaza, Andrew Bernstein, Bernstein Associates, courtesy of Aeg, permissions, Cara Vanderhook for Nokia Theatre L.A. Live; Milford Zornes "Master Bridge", linoleum block print after a 1936 painting, photo courtesy of and © Bill Anderson; Ken Jacobs, Charles S. Cohen, M.M. Serra, Carolee Schneemann, Jonas Mekas and Jeffrey Deitch at the Pacific Design Center, 15 October 2010, Evans Vestal Ward/Pacific Design Center; "Ploughing at Laxton in the early seventeenth century, illustration from Mark Pierce's map (1635)", Shelfmark: MS. C17: 48 (9), Courtesy of the Bodleian Libraries, University of Oxford.

Foreword

The Sun has left his blackness, & has found a fresher morning
And the fair Moon rejoices in the clear & cloudless night;
For Empire is no more, and now the Lion & Wolf shall cease.
   William Blake, *America: A Prophecy*

The essays collected here were written since the publication of my *Power Misses: Essays Across (Un)Popular Culture* in 1996. The cinemas with which they are concerned range across many modes of film production and from the 1960s almost to the present; they move generally from east to west, from China, Taiwan, and Korea to Los Angeles and New York in the U.S., and finally to England. Though their heterogeneity can hardly be subsumed to the unity of a monograph, nevertheless, like the earlier volume, this one is concerned with vanguard cultural activity that is rooted and flowers in the working classes. The forms of culture it privileges are those whose aesthetic achievements revolve around their own contestatory position in class relations, if not their direct representation of class conflict. In this, they are *a priori* anathema to the corporate capitalist commodity culture industries.

A quarter century ago, concern with the cultural self-production and self-consciousness of working-class people ran counter to the two interdependent controlling orthodoxies in the U.K. and U.S. study in the humanities: identity politics and what was then known as "cultural studies". Together these had almost entirely displaced consideration of class.[1] The former supposed that sexual, ethnic, and other forms of identity had a greater determinacy over life possibilities than did position in the economic and social hierarchies of capitalism and so should be the focus of political activism and hence of cultural analysis. The second, as it mutated from the study of working-class culture into affirmative approaches to capitalist culture, mitigated critiques of the latter by proposing liberatory elements within it that were supposed to empower its consumers, whether or not this was achieved by acts of deliberate reading "against the grain". Both methodologies reflected and contributed to the repression of working-class self-consciousness in the academy and so to the repression of Socialist thought in the U.S. intellectual environment generally, then ordered by the collapse of the Soviet Union and the apparent absence of any alternative to the global Pax

Americana, enforced by a military whose budget was larger than that of the next seven nations combined.

Since that time, if not in a clear direction, many things have changed, militarily, economically, and culturally. On the one hand, the catastrophe of the U.S. invasion of Iraq and the ongoing chaos wrought by U.S. policies in Afghanistan, Iran, Syria, and other countries in the Middle East have revealed the destitution of its imperialist pretentions. On the other, the 2007–08 financial crisis and the subsequent global recession exposed the reality of neo-liberal economic policy. The next decade saw the election of reactionary incompetent governments in U.K. in 2010 and the U.S. in 2016, quickly followed by the ascendancy of fascist oligarchies in China, India, Hungary, Poland, Brazil, and elsewhere. Rather than improving the situation for the U.S., British, or Russian people, let alone the global working class, the end of the Cold War produced only the increased immiseration of all but financial oligarchs. In the U.S., for example, where the Great Compression of 1937–67 had seen a dramatic fall in the gap between the rich and everyone else, Reaganomics introduced a shift in tax policy that over the next decades made income inequality in the U.S. greater than anywhere else among the wealthy nations. In 1996, the top 10% owned 61.75% of the national wealth; by 2019 it held 70.2%. In 1996 the combined wealth of the top 1% was $8.18 trillion to the bottom 50%'s $1.24 trillion. By 2019 the poorer portion had indeed become richer, with the bottom 50% increasing its wealth to $1.66 trillion; but by then the wealth of the top 1% had risen to $36.8 trillion, an increase in disparity of over 350%. Globally, the situation became equally dire: by 2015, the richest 1% owned half the world's wealth.[2]

Over the same period technological developments transformed the sphere of industrial culture. The emergence of the World Wide Web in the mid-1990s and the previously unimaginable expansion of digital communications since then have created new relations between popular creativity and the exertion of corporate or state control over it. These developments have not been without moments of populist intervention, especially the utopian invocations of an uncontrolled public sphere with mass political leaderless organizations capable, as in the short-lived Arab Spring, of generating local resistance and revolutionary insurrection. But even these radical digital communities can only exist within the structures of the internet, which overall has created new regimes of the exploitative administration of human knowledge, agency, and culture. The hegemony of theatrically-consumed feature motion pictures, of television programs viewed on the traditional family set, of record albums, and of other previously dominant forms of industrial culture has been eroded, almost to the point of disappearance.

The cultural autonomy of broadcast television, for example, was always illusory; embedded in and beholden to advertising (the form of programming that sustained it), whatever moments of empowerment that interrupted its ideological regime were always purchased by the consumption of advertisements and the *weltanschauung* they collectively enshrined. But the multiplication of viewing platforms developed since the turn of the century and the advent of streaming services have produced an unprecedented omnipresence of corporate entertainment and its assimilation to new forms of authoritarian control. Google's signal transition from being merely a search engine into a surveillance system for mining and monetizing user information was quickly imitated by Facebook, Amazon, Netflix, Microsoft, and so on. Now, as we use our phones, pads, and laptops indiscriminately for intimate personal texts and emails, for keeping up with tv and movies, for internet searches, for YouTube videos, or to book a ride on Uber, we are no longer watching corporate power: corporate power is watching us. In this new historical phase of "surveillance capitalism" the important extractive industries are not coal or iron ore, but personal and social data, our very humanity.[3]

These developments have generated resistance in both independent activism and national electoral politics, often indeed mobilized by digital communications: on the one hand, Occupy Wall Street, Black Lives Matter, the #Me Too movement, popular resistance to police violence and so on; and on the other, the interventions of Jeremy Corbyn and the Momentum movement in the U.K. and of Bernie Sanders' campaigns in two U.S. presidential elections. All these reveal that (to appropriate the title of one of the essays below) Socialism still lives even if only as "the name of a desire" – the desire to see the fulfillment of the program announced by the Social Democratic Party of Germany at their meeting at Erfurt a hundred and thirty years ago to end "not only the exploitation and oppression of wage-earners, but every kind of exploitation and oppression, whether directed against a class, a party, a sex, or a race". The essays below speak to particular instances of that desire, whether specifically in class terms or in more general attempts to create cultural communities outside and opposed to corporate exploitation.

Half of them concern the cultural activity of people of various nationalities, ethnicities, and gender, whose cultural work has been associated directly with the working class. These include South Korean women (Chapters One and Two); Chinese women in the vanguard of the 1949 Liberation, Korean men and women, and Chinese students, male and female together (Three); Korean American women and a Chinese American gay man (Four); autonomous African American and avant-garde filmmakers in Los Angeles (Six); and Jewish American bohemian filmmakers in New York (Nine). The others focus on the cultural activities of people who, while never totally outside the cultural hegemony of capitalist media, nevertheless have created forms of commonality, sustaining resistance across class, sexual, and racial categories. These include grass-roots attempts in Los Angeles – the capital of the culture industries – to create communities outside it (Five), to organize community cinemas (Eight), and to inaugurate the communal composition of projected light accompanying the euphoric era of popular music (Seven); and a gay filmmaker in New York (Ten). Chapter Eleven describes the activities of the community of curators, programmers, and historians of avant-garde cinema in Los Angeles and London. And the final chapter considers the question of cinema and community in a macro-historical form, the maintenance of the *commons* in a very literal sense in attempts by filmmakers to aid the inhabitants of the last remaining common-field farming village in Britain to resist its enclosure. Over the centuries, along with other forms of dispossession and sequestration by landlords, the enclosure and privatization of what had been communally worked and controlled common land anticipated the catastrophic forms of monetization and theft of the public commonweal in the advanced form of capitalism we know as neoliberalism. It also anticipated the hyper-expansive exploitation of extra-human nature that has culminated in the climatological, environmental, and ecological crises of our time: global warming, the depletion of animal species, the poisoning of the air and oceans – all for the sake of limitless economic growth, the imperial enrichment of the already wealthy, and the immiseration of the remainder of human kind.

The globally-networked regimes of capital that exploit both human and non-human resources have come to be known as *Empire*. Looking back on the way the different emancipatory cultural struggles against Empire sketched here *served their times* in the past may encourage us to work toward a time when Empire will be no more. Indeed, it is a distinct privilege to be writing this preface in June 2020 at a historical moment when proto-fascist governments world-wide, not least in the U.K. and the U.S., are being challenged by unprecedented multi-racial, anti-fascist, working-class mobilizations against the Lions and the Wolves.

Endnotes

1. On the exclusion of class from academic film studies in this period, see my "Is There Class in This Text?" in David E. James and Rick Berg, eds., *The Hidden Foundation: Cinema and the Question of Class* (Minneapolis: University of Minnesota Press, 1996).

2. U.S. figures are from the Federal Reserve Board: see https://www.federalreserve.gov/releases/z1/dataviz/dfa/distribute/chart/#range:2004.4,2019.4;quarter:121;series:Net%20worth;demographic:networth;population:1,7;units:levels. Accessed 28 February 2020. Global figures are from Credit Suisse's global wealth report, see "Half of World's Wealth Now in Hands of 1% of Population, *The Guardian*, 13 October 2015. https://www.theguardian.com/money/2015/oct/13/half-world-wealth-in-hands-population-inequality-report. Accessed 28 February 2020.

3. Shoshana Zuboff, *The Age of Surveillance Capitalism: The Fight for a Human Future at the New Frontier of Power* (Public Affairs: New York, 2019).

Chapter One Im Kwon-taek: Korean National Cinema and Buddhism

In 1926 Han Yong-un, an eminent Buddhist master and leader in the movement to free Korea from Japanese occupation, published a collection of poems, *Silence of Love* (*Nim ŭi ch'immuk*) in which he assumed the persona of a woman abandoned by her lover. In the title poem, she looks out across the mountains and the path through them by which he left her; but, with the dialectical logic of Buddhism, she finds in her loss the implication of its opposite, and so concludes by affirming her anticipation of re-union with him. *Silence of Love* is usually read allegorically simultaneously in religious and political terms, with the absent lover figuring both the void at the heart of Buddhist ontology and the Korean national homeland abducted by the Japanese invaders.

Twenty years later, a similar scene occurs in Yun Yong-gyu's film *Home is Where the Heart Is* (*Maum ŭi kohyang*, 1948), one of the few Korean films from before the civil war that survives to us. In this film the erotic metaphor is oedipalized. To-song, a young boy being raised by the monks at Chongnam temple, desperately awaits the return of his mother who abandoned him and who now lives in Seoul. He asks an old woodcutter if his mother is beautiful, and when he hears that she is, he raises his eyes to the mountains that surround him, to the peaks and the forests, which we see from his point-of-view. As these figure both his mother's beauty and her absence, To-song's scopophilic gaze, like Han's lyric voice, makes palpable and present that which is missing – a function that has been proposed as fundamental to the cinematic signifier and its Oedipal operation, and one that the film's narrative will confirm by bringing him a surrogate mother who is nevertheless invested with all the erotic intensity of a lover.

Thirty years later, the same motifs of loss and restoration begin to pass obsessively through the films of Im Kwon-taek. In his mature work, Im explored precolonial cultural forms in order to engage the question of Korean national identity, especially as it has been alienated and thrown into crisis by the multiple forms of colonization to which the country has been subject. Of the traditional cultural vocabularies Im interrogated, Buddhism will be the one considered in detail below. Like Han and Yun, he mobilized the resonant metaphors of eroticism and

1

landscape that Buddhism contains, though the quite different historical conditions of the three artists ensured that those metaphors would be differently inflected. But before turning to Im's use of Buddhism, we must consider his confrontation with what, for a filmmaker, is an especially immediate form of alienation, that is, a national cinema subject to neocolonial political control and censorship and marginalized by the global hegemony of the U.S. capitalist culture industries. We begin, then, with Im's attempt to turn the colonized Korean film industry into the vehicle of a national culture.

I. Korean National Cinema: Im Kwon-taek as Auteur

Although the theoretical status of the concepts of the art film, national cinema, and the director-as-author has been largely undermined, practically they continue to organize scholarship. Even so, to approach a Korean auteur and a Korean art cinema committed to national reconstruction in the general terms they demarcate demands at the outset some justification in an account of the material conditions of film production in South Korea. Designating a number of locally-specific variants either within or on the edges of studio production, the concept of the art film mediates between the division of labor of the industrial feature film and the personal expressivity associated with authorship in avant-garde or independent films. Although the South Korean film industry centered in Seoul's Ch'ungmuro district has been consistently market-driven (rather than government subsidized in the manner of, for example, the German or Taiwanese New Waves), its structure has been unstable, oscillating between the proliferation of small, more or less independent studios and government attempts to control these by forcing them into conglomerates. The absence of a stable infrastructure is commonly bemoaned by Korean critics, in terms such as "over the course of its 70-year history … the Korean film industry has not established a systematic or organized industrial structure for itself",[1] especially since government censorship inhibited whatever ideological flexibility or variety the dispersion of production might otherwise have allowed. The first break in this control occurred in the mid-1980s, during the *Minjung* movement, when a populist alliance of workers, peasants, and factions of the middle class joined to oppose the authoritarian state, leading to a liberalization of the political climate and eventually to a democratically elected government.[2] The cultural component of minjung included a generation of young filmmakers who emerged from the university cine clubs to create an underground, agitational cinema, known as the "small-film movement" (*chagŭn yŏnghwa undong*). Some of these activists subsequently founded their own small companies, allowing them to explore political themes in the often very illustrious features that have gained international recognition as the Korean "New

Wave": Park Kwang-su's *To the Starry Island* (*Kŭ sŏme kago sipda*, 1993) and *A Single Spark* (*Arŭmdaun ch'ŏng'nyŏn Chŏn T'ae-il*, 1995) are outstanding examples.³ The authorial expressiveness allowed by this mode of production emerged, however, in the shadow, and often within the stylistic vocabularies of Im Kwon-taek's earlier auteurist attempt to fashion a Korean art cinema capable of addressing national issues, one that was made under entirely different and fundamentally circumscribed industrial conditions.

Im has only occasionally had anything like the autonomy of the New Wave directors. During the 1960s and 1970s, he worked for small, usually short-lived studios that were dependent on immediate market returns, and generally not able to sustain long-term commitments of the kind that allowed an innovative directorial style to mature.⁴ But still, they had more in common with the director-driven period of the silent American cinema than with the producer or package-driven systems that replaced it. In the productive system where Im learned his craft, once topics were approved by the studio, directors generally had immediate and more or less complete responsibility for all stages in production – writing, photography, and editing, as well as directing. In this situation, where industrial genre production itself to some degree resembled Western art cinema, Im was able to develop the range of skills that makes the idea of authorship credible later in his career when he was able to choose his own topics.

Other specifically Korean conditions shaped his development. A revision to the motion picture law in 1973 giving the producers of a "quality" film more privileges in importing Hollywood money-makers coincided with Im's desire to shift the direction of his work, and he quickly became known as a director of "quality" films. And the relaxation of censorship in the 1980s allowed him to raise, if not deeply to probe, previously-proscribed political issues, though typically in historically-distanced allegorical form: the story of the nineteenth century Tonghak nativist uprising, *Fly High, Run Far* (*Kaebyŏk*, 1991), for example, was read as referring to the contemporary student movement. But undoubtedly behind Im's emergence as a singularly prolific and distinctive director was the length and success of his studio work and the unusual range of responsibilities it centralized in one person. He had already made fifty features in this system when, in 1973, a crisis of conscience set him on the path to the art film. "One day I suddenly felt as though I'd been lying to the people for the past 12 years. I decided to compensate for my wrongdoings by making more honest films".⁵

After this crisis, which Im has described in several interviews, he envisaged his subsequent career in two streams. In return for his continuing to make genre works for mass consumption, his producers would allow these to subsidize his "honest" films, without expecting them all necessarily to make a profit. The distinction between the two streams turned out to be anything but categorical. The very profitable genre action film, *The General's Son* (*Chang'gun ūi adūl*, 1990) and its sequels contain many motifs in common with the art films considered here, while Im's "honest" films still mobilize the hoariest melodramatic effects. And *Sopyonje* (*Sŏp'yŏnje*, 1993), Im's masterpiece and the most fully realized of his personal undertakings, which he never expected to be a commercial success, turned out to be the most profitable domestic film in Korean history until the blockbuster *Shiri* (*Swiri*, Kang Je-gyu, 1999). But the arrangement did allow Im to clarify for himself a specific project: in the "honest" films he would confront the manifold traumas of Korean history, and in doing so he would create a specifically Korean art film style.

Since World War II, national art film styles have been conceived in the interplay between deconstructions of the languages of the classic Hollywood cinema and some combination of primarily two other frames of reference. First, the languages of cinemas constructed against capitalism, notably the socialist realisms adopted from the Soviet models in the People's Republic of China, Viet Nam, and North Korea or the socialist modernisms developed especially in Latin America. Second, the languages of precolonial domestic cultural practices as adapted to the medium of film. The first alternative was categorically unavailable in South Korea in the Park Chung-hee [Pak Chŏnghui] regime in the 1960s and 70s when Im was coming to maturity. During the consolidation of his stylistic strategies and indeed of his fundamental conception of what a film could be, domestic repression, militant anti-communism, and the demonization of North Korea, anathematized any gestures toward socialist realism or the revolutionary Third Cinemas. By the minjung era, when loosening censorship allowed both directions to be explored in the short-film underground, Im was already fifty years old, and successfully entrenched in his own project that had perforce been organized in quite different terms. Of necessity, those terms had been developed out of the other possibility. With no access to a direct critique of capitalist culture per se, Im's address to Korean modernity was negotiated in respect to precolonial national culture.

For East Asian cinemas generally, traditional theater has been the most important of such resources. The very first film made in China, for example, *Dingjun Mountain* (1905), was an adaptation of scenes from a Beijing opera. More recent Chinese films, otherwise as disparate and made in as radically different political conditions as *The Red Detachment of Women* (Xie Jin, 1961), *Two Stage Sisters* (Xie Jin, 1964), *Peking Opera Blues* (Tsui Hark, 1986), *Woman Demon Human* (Huang Shuqin, 1987), *Good Men, Good Women* (Hou Hsiao-hsien, 1995), and

Farewell My Concubine (Chen Kaige, 1993) attest to opera's ability to supply stylistic alternatives to U.S. narrative forms. Though *Sopyonje* concerns a traditional operatic form and though precolonial dramatic and ritual forms were refurbished during the minjung cultural movement, theater has not generally supplied such a fundamental resource for Korean cinema. Im's *oeuvre* as a whole is, then, notable for his search through non-theatrical pre-cultural forms to ground the language of a modern Korean cinema, and in several of his best films traditional cultural practices supply metaphors and models for his own aspirations.

Of Im's films about art, *Sopyonje* is the most comprehensive. The *p'ansori* singer, Yu-bong, and especially his adopted daughter, Song-hwa, are proposed as exemplary Korean artists, who attempt to sustain a specifically Korean culture against its debasement, neglect, and the encroachments of foreign media. In *Mandala* (1981), the protagonist expresses his dissatisfaction with the indifference to worldly suffering that he perceives in traditional Buddha images by carving his own primitive, agonized figure. And in *Festival (Ch'ukche*, 1996), Im's negotiation between Confucian tradition and contemporary culture is explicitly inscribed in the two roles of the protagonist, Chun-sŏp: on the one hand, he is a novelist who has made his career by writing about his family; on the other, a dutiful son who, on his mother's death, presides over the rituals of a traditional funeral, which the film presents in elaborate ethnographic detail. Bringing together the several narrators who recount the widowed mother's heroic story of raising her seven children, these rituals restage the national question in the form of an allegory of the family, one that explores the terms by which its black sheep may be reintegrated into it. And the funeral ceremonies are interwoven with further dramatizations of the family in other mediums: Chun-sŏp composes a children's story of his mother's aging that is presented in a highly artificial film-style utilizing digital technology; and his exploitation of his family in his own art is explored in critical reviews by a young journalist from a literary magazine.[6]

Such a use of multiple narrators subtends Im's distinctive formal innovations. Omniscient linear narration is replaced by extended, sometimes multiply nested, subjective flashbacks to produce a structural sophistication matched only by Hou Hsiao-hsien of contemporary fiction filmmakers. In Im's best films, especially *Mandala, Sopyonje,* and *Festival,* the subjective narrators do not contradict each other and thereby mobilize some humanist ontological uncertainty in the manner of, say *Rashomon* (Akira Kurosawa, 1950), the *locus classicus* of this technique. Rather they fragment the narrative into tesserae that in editing the filmmaker recombines to make thematic arguments, turning narrative into argument, *histoire* into *discourse*. But Im's use of the figure of the artist to investigate questions of national identity was first developed in a formally simpler film, one made at a low point in South Korean cinema mid-way between the golden age of the 1960s and the mid-1980s renaissance. In *The Genealogy* (*Chokpo*, 1978) – the work in which he himself believed he first successfully "reflected a personal style"[7] – he turned to ceramics, one of the mediums of Korea's greatest cultural achievement, to limn the terms of a postcolonial cinema.

The Genealogy is set in the late-1930s during the most oppressive phase of the occupation, when attempts to extirpate cultural difference included forcing all Koreans to take Japanese names. Believing in the sanctity of his family line, Sŏl Chin-yŏng, a Confucian clan patriarch, refuses to dishonor his ancestors by denying his Korean name. The negotiations between him and the colonial administration are carried out by a young Japanese, Dani, who is also a gifted artist. Recognizing the accomplishment of Dani's genre painting in classical styles, Sŏl welcomes him into his home, more as a son than as an invader, and the signs of a romance between Dani and one of Sŏl's daughters, Ok-sun appear. Dani also experiments in modern idioms; he makes a pencil sketch of Ok-sun, and she accompanies him as he tries to paint the Korean countryside in oils (see figure 1.1). Meanwhile Sŏl attempts to solve his predicament by a linguistic sleight; he simply takes the name that is the Japanese pronunciation of the Chinese characters that form his Korean name. But the Japanese see through his strategy. Increasing the stakes, they torture his prospective son-in-law, thereby ruining his other daughter's marriage opportunity; then they draft Ok-sun into the Japanese army support unit, and Dani only narrowly manages to save her from becoming a comfort woman.

Sŏl's realization that he must choose between compromising his lineage and committing suicide comes to a crisis when his grandchildren demand Japanese names. After hearing their request, he turns to his collection of ceramics, and the film cuts to a non-diegetic interlude in which the camera scrutinizes a series of exquisite vases, while in a voiceover Sŏl quotes a Japanese theorist of Korean aesthetics, Yanagi Muneyoshi:

> Whoever reads the history of Chosŏn cannot but feel gloomy at its dark, miserable, and sometimes frightful history. This is the reason why they discuss the quality of solitude in aesthetics, and the aesthetic quality of solitude. That is, its suppressed destiny sought consolation in unspeakable loneliness and longing. The aesthetic of Chosŏn is … delicately imbued with the people's indescribable rancor, sorrow, or longing. Where else in the world could you find such beauty with so much sorrow? … Chosŏn is a country that might be weak outside, but is strong inside in its art.

1 – Im Kwon-taek: Korean National Cinema and Buddhism

Figure 1. *The Genealogy*: Dani with Ok-sun, painting the landscape.

"So Yanagi Muneyoshi has written", Sŏl concludes, "but I wonder what he would think about the suffering of Chosŏn that even forces people to change their names?" And as the camera passes over the elaborately wrought ceramic tiles of a Korean roof, the diegesis is restored and we see Sŏl walking to his final confrontation with the Japanese and his suicide. The film concludes with Dani and Ok-sun together watching his funeral procession move through the countryside.

As well as experimenting with non-linear narrative forms (for example, after Dani learns of Sŏl's death there follows a series of subjective interludes in which he imagines himself attacking his superiors in the occupying forces), *The Genealogy* assembles the terms of Im's mature project. Traditional Korean ceramics supply a referential aesthetic model; they embody an essential form of Korean culture, their rounded, hollowed forms making them readily apposite for female-gendered conceptualizations of the nation, and in them is inscribed the trauma of Korean history. The central concept expressing this trauma is *han*.[8] Taken by Koreans to be the essential national experience, han is constituted from sentiments of loss and rage at the severance of wholeness and continuity between self and history. The accumulated emotions of sufferers (and, inevitably in a strict Confucian patriarchy, especially of women), han may be projected onto any political ordeal, but in the twentieth century it was especially the lived response to devastating colonial occupation and national division. The han sedimented in Sŏl's ceramics thus refers to the present, but the artworks themselves do not hold practical answers to present political problems. Any art that aspires to address Korea's modern traumas has to be rooted in tradition like ceramics, but also adapted to modern, colonial mediums like film. In *The Genealogy*, such an art is suggested in Dani's turn away from classical ink painting to experiments in western art forms; his oil painting of the countryside and his pencil drawing of Ok-sun exemplify the confrontation with modern mediums that can allow the modern story to be told. But Dani's artworks also announce what in his subsequent films Im will mobilize as the two privileged symbols on which the historical trauma of the nation is re-enacted: the body of the Korean landscape, especially its spectacular mountains, and the bodies of Korean women, especially those of the working-class.

Both tropes are constructed from the position of patriarchal specularity, but beyond that, the relationships between them are multiple, and reconstructed within the narrative possibilities of each film. Generally they oscillate between parallel and complementary functions. On the one hand, beautiful images of women and landscape signify a precolonial and so pre-lapsarian Korea. As such they are mutually equivalent and interchangeable with each other; and in films about the modern period they both typically appear in a violated or degraded form, with the metaphoric equivalent of the desecrated woman's body being the antithesis of the natural landscape, that is, the metropolis, Seoul. On the other hand, the two tropes can also displace each other, with the natural landscape used to represent the nation in its pristine precolonial state and the ravaged female body its recent historical fate. Ubiquitous in Im's work, these two motifs probably reflect his own unconscious, unresolved Oedipal drives, and the personal resonances they carry must be rich and complex. But both are also deeply traditional.

Landscape is the core of precolonial Korean painting, and the parallel literary traditions are informed by the rigid sexual codes of Confucian patriarchy. One of the master-myths of Korean culture is the all-but sadomasochistic *Story of Ch'unhyang* (*Ch'unhyang'ga*), a fable about the daughter of a *kisaeng* (courtesan) and so a member of the lowest class (*ch'ŏnmin*) in Chosŏn society, who is cruelly tortured during the prolonged absence of her *yangban* (aristocratic) husband; the story was the subject of the first Korean talkie in 1935, it has been filmed a dozen times since then, with spectacular success by Lee Kyu-hwan in 1955, and most recently by Im himself.[9] One of the most famous and often-reproduced of Korean paintings, "Women on Tano Day" by Sin Yun-bok (1758–?) (figure 1.2), itself an innovation against classical Chinese painting, combines the motifs of both the female body and the landscape, while its depiction of furtive male spectators also foregrounds the voyeuristic transactions of patriarchal specularity.[10]

Given this genealogy, any contemporary use of the two motifs must be deeply ideological, inhabited by all the cultural structures of precolonial feudalism as

1 – Im Kwon-taek: Korean National Cinema and Buddhism

Figure 2. "Women on Tano Day" by Sin Yun-bok (1758–?).

well as by their adaptation to the requirements of colonial and neocolonial capitalist development. However traditional it might be, the idealization of the Korean landscape is for the domestic spectator overdetermined by the industrialization and urbanization that (as at the inception of industrialization and modern landscape art in England at the end of the 18th century) cause the rural world to appear as the location, not of agrarian labor or deprivation, but of recreation and spiritual renewal. For the foreign spectator, an equivalent attraction is fueled by the imbrication of the cultural tourism of cinema with the global politics of the tourist industry, a prostitution of its spectacular natural landscape in which South Korea has conspicuously engaged in its attempt to attract international recognition.

Korean feminism and film theory have presented fully-developed analyses of the relations between both Confucian patriarchal and contemporary capitalist exploitation of women and their roles in the post-colonial literature and Ch'ungmuro film industry.[11] The central argument has been that the metaphoric use of women to represent the violation of the nation by Japanese and U.S aggressors can never be merely metaphoric, but also renews the ideological conditions for the ongoing

9

exploitation of women. The feminist argument is clearly applicable to the phylum of Im's brutalized heroines: Ok-sun in *Mandala*, Se-yŏng in *Ticket* (*Tik'et*, 1986), Ok-nyŏ in *Surrogate Mother* (*Ssibaji*, 1986), Adada in *Adada* (1988), Song-hwa in *Sopyonje*, Yong-sun in *Festival*, and so on. In these films, Im represents the historical exploitation of working-class women through graphic images of sexual victimization that also provide quasi-pornographic sadistic pleasure for the spectator. *Adada* is especially problematic in its use of both motifs: the scenes of Adada's sexual intercourse with her *yangban* husband before he is corrupted by capital and with her peasant lover before his greed causes her death are all powerfully erotic, turning her rape into titillating spectacle. And the sympathetic reflection of her tragedy in images of the countryside completes the aestheticization of the environment; whether they represent the fecundity of her youthful purity in spring and harvest time or, in winter, the devastation to which she is victim, the scenes are always ravishing.

However the multiple social and cultural pressures that produce it are understood, the insistent narrative positioning of both women and nature as objects of a masculinized national subjectivity cannot be disregarded nor simply ascribed to a self-conscious play with the expectations of a reifying, self-orientalizing gaze. And neither Im's own reiterated explanation of the historical grounding of his use of the trope of the victimized woman, nor its ubiquitousness in other cinemas can mitigate its role in reproducing the ideological conditions that sustain the exploitation of proletarian women in Korea and everywhere else. A progressive cinema will, to be sure, find its own accommodation between (to use Mao's terms) the "raising of standards" and "popularization"; but, short of re-engaging the utopian gesture of early feminism and jettisoning cinema as a whole with nothing "more than sentimental regret",[12] any cinema that aspires to a wide social influence will have to work within the terms that constitute national subjectivity.

But in fact, while the two motifs consistently form the basis for Im's symbolic vocabulary, across his oeuvre their positions in the thematic structure of his narratives are not mechanically fixed. Rather, a range of local variations in different films opens out to varying degrees of self-consciousness and critique of the main combinatory. Such indeed has already been instanced in *The Genealogy*, where the invasion is enacted on the *patriarchal* body, and Ok-sun is *saved* by a *Japanese* from being *raped* by the *Japanese*. But even where, as is most common, the nation is gendered as female, the oppression of women is commonly linked, not simply to the oppression of Korea by invaders, but specifically to the oppression of the working class. This use of women to symbolize the working class is made possible either by virtue of the class-location of the women themselves (Ok-nyo in *Surrogate Mother*, or Yong-sun in *Festival*) or by allegorical identification, as in the case of Adada, whose expulsion from the *yangban* household allows her intradiegetic affiliation with the landless peasantry and her extradiegetic association with the labor movements of the winter of 1987–88. Im's metaphoric use of gender difference allowed him to imply class issues at times when censorship prohibited any explicit address to labor unrest. It is noteworthy that in none of the cases of the sexual brutalization of women mentioned above is the male a foreign invader; he is always Korean, a "bad" Korean to be sure, who acts as the agent of an internal structural social inequality. Furthermore, in Im's two remarkable films starring actress Kim Ji-mee [Kim Chimi], the class/gender parallels are extremely complicated. In *Gilsottum* (*Kilsottŭm*, 1985) Kim plays an exemplary Im-heroine/victim who has suffered all Korea's trials in the last half-century; but when she finds the son she lost during the civil war, she rejects him because his lumpen behavior and attitudes manifest a class difference she now finds unacceptable. In *Ticket*, Kim's character is a divorced woman who survives by managing a brothel. As a madam, she collaborates with capitalist patriarchy in extracting surplus value from the young women who work for her; but the contradictions between her oppression of them and the oppression she as a woman herself experiences – between her roles as the agent and as the victim of exploitation – finally drive her insane.

Further to illustrate the flexibility and nuance with which Im has mobilized these motifs, I now turn to his two films about the modern existence of one of the most ancient components of Korean culture, *Sŏn* Buddhism, whose philosophic structures would appear categorically to inhibit the identification of the nation's geographical body and the bodies of its women. One was made before and the other after the minjung movement that transformed the possibilities of Korean political and cultural expression.

II. Buddhism: Eroticism and Landscape in *Mandala* (1981) and *Come, Come, Come Upward* (*Aje aje para aje*, 1989)[13]

Several schools of Mahayana Buddhism were transmitted from China to Three Kingdoms Korea around the end of the fourth century, and with the Silla unification in 668 the religion became closely associated with the autocratic monarchy. By the end of the seventh century, *Sŏn*, the Korean form of the *Ch'an* schools that emphasized individual attainment of enlightenment through meditation rather than through the progressive accumulation of merit by sutra study, ritual acts, or good works, was established as the Nine Mountain Schools (*Kusan Sŏnmun*).[14] Solidifying its relation with state power, *Sŏn* had by the ninth century become the dominant force in Korean Buddhism, and hence the dominant cultural force in Korea. Despite seminal attempts to syncretize the schools by Ŭich'ŏn and by Chinul in the eleventh and twelfth centuries respectively, tensions between Sŏn and other schools of Buddhism, especially the *Kyo* schools that emphasized doctrinal study, were continuous, though Sŏn was generally dominant. During the Chosŏn dynasty, Buddhism was persecuted by the Neo-Confucian bureaucracy; monastic lands were confiscated and most temples, including all those in metropolitan areas, were disbanded. Not until the Japanese occupation did Buddhism begin to reconstruct its former prominence; in 1935 Sŏn and Kyo were merged into a single order, called *Chogye*, and since then both forms have been practiced side by side in all Korean temples. The restoration process has continued in the South since the liberation and partition, with the Buddhist hierarchy also renewing its relations with state power.[15]

Throughout this history, in Sŏn thought the natural world and sexuality have been antithetical. On the one hand, since the time of Nine Mountain Schools the monasteries have always been built in remote mountain areas, and Sŏn has been so fundamentally associated with the mountains that the Korean vernacular for "to become a monk" is *ipsan*, "to enter the mountains". Celibacy is similarly fundamental. Following the *Vinaya Pitaka*, the foundational disciplinary text of Buddhism, the third of the ten precepts that the novice monk commits to during the ordination ceremony is the promise not to engage in sexual intercourse, and doing so is one of four *parajikas*, offenses that can incur expulsions from the order.[16] In Sŏn thought, then, Im's two dominant tropes – the landscape and erotic relations – are both prominent, but as the mutually exclusive terms of a binary: the monastic celibacy of the mountains is the antithesis of sexuality and the city. Im's two Buddhist-themed films force the disjunction between the semiotic structure of Sŏn and that of his own characteristic themes into a productive interaction, and rather than mechanically reproducing either system, they construct their narratives across the tensions between them.[17]

Both *Mandala* and *Come, Come, Come Upward* explore the same question: what is socially at stake in the choice between a pure ascetic life in the mountains and a life of active participation in the world's affairs. The films are structurally parallel, each narratively focused on a pair of Sŏn monks in mountain temples; in both, one monk makes a commitment to meditational retreat but the other leaves to live in the world; and in both, the latter option is followed as a result of expulsion from the monastery for infraction of the prohibition against sexual relations. But in the former film, the monks are both males, and in the latter, both females. The dynamics of sexuality, including the power and scopic relations

Figure 3. *Mandala*: Pŏb-un and Chi-san in the world.

constructed within it, appear then in antithetical, reversed formulations. *Mandala* exhibits a substantial reconfiguration of Im's usual gender positionings, but in the later film, *Come, Come, Come Upward* where the protagonists are women, they are spectacularly reconstructed. Though the primacy of suffering in Buddhist ontology universalizes han in these films, presenting loss as intrinsic to the human situation rather than exclusively a condition of Korean history, nevertheless Buddhism's responsiveness – or lack of it – to the trauma of national catastrophe is Im's real concern in both. But since one was made at the beginning of the 1980s and the other at the end, the question is broached at opposite points of the radical transformation of Korean society.

Mandala, an adaptation of a best-selling novel,[18] concerns a young monk, Pŏb-un, who meets an older monk, Chi-san while both are on the road during the free period between winter and summer meditation. Chi-san, an obstreperous drunk, tells the story of how he was seduced, not unwillingly to be sure, by Ok-sun, a teenage girl vacationing near his temple. Soon after, her girlfriend was raped and Chi-san was accused; though he was acquitted after a semen test, the scandal of his relations with Ok-sun caused him to be expelled from the temple. Still wearing his robes, he left with Ok-sun for a period of indulgence in Seoul's bars and discos. But, as Chi-san tells Pŏb-un, dealing with sexual desire by confronting it rather than evading it did not bring enduring pleasure; sex temporarily reconciled subject and object, or self and the world, but in the end "stacking up two bodies was a futile attempt indeed". After a week, Chi-san arrived "at a peak of emptiness" and, realizing that his vocation was still that of a monk, he left Ok-sun and became an itinerant. Later, Pŏb-un encounters Chi-san again and travels with him, eventually back to the red-light district in Seoul where, now several years later, Ok-sun is a prostitute. Pob-un returns to meditation in his home temple, where he meets Su-gwan, a monk who tries to gain enlightenment by burning off his fingers. Then he meets Chi-san yet again, travels with him to the mountains in the winter, and accompanies him when he is called on to consecrate a small temple. But, after a night of drunkenness, Chi-san freezes to death in the snow. Pŏb-un builds him a pyre, and then goes back to Seoul where he briefly meets his own mother who had abandoned him as a child. Bidding her farewell, he sets out on the road again.

Chi-san is one of the artist figures who model Im's own project. As mentioned above, on one occasion when Pŏb-un's discipline and abstinence seem ineffective, he comes across Chi-san carving a Buddha that, unlike traditional images, is crude and grotesque, tortured rather than serene. As the visuals cut to non-diegetic images of traditional smiling Buddhas, Chi-san argues that since Gautama was a human, not a god, he could not have kept smiling when the poor and the weak were "suffering under oppression by the privileged", and so his image should "bear expressions of agony, grief, sorrow, and rage". Against Sŏn's lack of social engagement and the dispassion of conventional Buddhist images, Chi-san's art summarizes the compassion of his socially-engaged practice, and his concern with the oppression of the lowly by the privileged. These are the issues that Im wants his own art to address; Chi-san's Buddha image and the han it expresses figure a socially responsible cinema that can narrate the han of Korean history and critique contemporary Korean society, while still retaining a dialectical continuity with traditional cultural forms. Conversely, Im's endorsement of Chi-san's humanist revision of Sŏn that brings Buddhism closer to social problems also obliges him to reconfigure the deep structures of his own iconography.

The film's most crucial doctrinal issues revolve around Chi-san's sexual indulgence. Initially his doubts and his drunken licentiousness mark him, as he admits, as a degenerate apostate, a *ttaengch'o*, "an unworthy monk, a disgrace to others". His subsequent rehabilitation demands that these sexual transgressions be not merely absolved but proven to constitute a practice superior to monastic renunciation. The narrative argues such a critique of Sŏn orthodoxy first by demonstrating the limitations of asceticism, and second by revealing a soteriological

1 – Im Kwon-taek: Korean National Cinema and Buddhism

Figure 4. *Mandala*: Chi-san in the temple; Chisan and Ok-sun drinking in Seoul; Su-gwan burning his finger; Pŏb-un; Chi-san painting the Buddha's eye; Pŏb-un says bids his mother farewell.

implication in Chi-san's sexuality. The narrative elements that make these points are both entirely absent from the novel, and Im's fabrication of them indicates their importance to his film's argument. The first is introduced via Su-gwan, a character not even present in the novel; he impugns his head monk's insight and, although he has already burned off two of his fingers, he burns off a third, in an act of symbolic castration that Im photographs in excruciating detail.[19] But later, when Su-gwan meets Pŏb-un on the road, he tells him that though his critique of the master still stands, he has realized the futility of self-mortification and

15

indeed of meditation itself. From now on, Su-gwan affirms, he will be guided by the Buddhist precept that there is no distinction between self and others, his route to salvation will be via service to others, and he consigns himself to Kwanseŭm (Avalokitesvara), the Bodhisattva of Compassion. Questioned further by Pŏb-un, he describes how he has been inspired by a heroic monk who, during a plague on Chukto, a remote island off the south coast, devoted himself to the sick without regard for his own safety. The monk's name, he declares, was Chi-san.

The film immediately cuts to Chi-san in meditation; a shot of a flock of birds rising in the air symbolically indicates his enlightenment and prefigures Pŏb-un's,[20] and the narrative returns to the latter as he comes to meet Chi-san for the final movement of the film. From this point on, Chi-san's story unfolds exclusively in the mountains, and here he is finally recognized as a master. Called on to light the eyes of a Buddha in a mountain temple, he delivers his final sermon emphasizing, not doctrinal correctness, but the awakening of the heart to Buddha. And here he achieves his fiery apotheosis. In these scenes, Im gives full-reign to cinematographer Chŏng Il-sŏng's most extravagantly beautiful snow-covered landscapes of Mount Sŏrak, which now read as evidence of Chi-san's enlightenment.[21]

Though in Sŏn, meditational practice is absolutely superior to social benevolence, this is not the case in other forms of Mahayana Buddhism. Chi-san's final position and Su-gwan's decision to emulate him have a long genealogy in Mahayana's privileging of the bodhisattva who forgoes personal attainment of nirvana for deliberate rebirth in the cycles of *samsara* in order to save all sentient beings; Avalokitesvara and Manjusri are the most celebrated examples of such bodhisattvas. Indeed, Mahayana emerged in antithesis to the self-centered practice of early Buddhism that, in this respect at least, Sŏn reproduces. Similarly, though Sŏn history does record cases of "unconstrained conduct" (*muae haeng*) – that is, unorthodox practices against the constraints of monastic discipline that resemble Chi-san's – the most important Korean instances are outside Sŏn. The most famous is the monk, Wŏn-hyo (617–86) who, as well as writing some 240 works on Buddhism and creating one of the five major schools of early Silla, named his trousers "No Obstacle" and justified his visits to *kisaeng* on the grounds that "It's not good for a monk to live in heaven all the time. He must also visit hell and save the people there, who are wallowing in their desires".[22] However much it may recall Wŏn-hyo's, Chi-san's sexuality is fundamentally different (as indeed it is different from practices of ecstatic sexuality in Tantric traditions) in that it is undertaken, not in a state of enlightenment but in one of desperate suffering. In any case, the narrative claim that Chi-san's licentiousness reflected his correct recognition of the sterility of meditational isolation and so was necessarily propaedeutic to his enlightenment is constructed across the very weak bridge of his service to the plague victims of Chukto – an instance of social responsibility that is not present in the novel, not represented in the film except in Su-gwan's account, and so not developed as a component within Chi-san's characterization. This benevolent service is an arbitrary and dramatically-unconvincing addition, adduced *ex machina* to link Chi-san's "love" for Ok-sun with his "love" for humanity, just as the cycles of sexual desire and emptiness he experiences with her teach him the meaning of the parallel cycles of death and rebirth generally. The strain in the narrative structure reflects the tension between the novel's vision of Buddhism and the demands of Im's own thematic concerns and iconographic system.

The final images of Chi-san in the mountains also resolve the discursive use of landscape in the narrative. Where the sexuality-enlightenment antinomy is resolved by authorial fiat, the parallel mountain-city binary of the tradition is reconfigured through the introduction of a third spatiality: the intramontane plains of everyday village life and human labor. The importance of this spatiality is indicated at the beginning of the film where, after the opening scenes of meditation in the mountain temple, a very long stationary shot shows a desolate and empty winter agricultural landscape, in which the only activity is a bus moving down a primitive road at the edge of the frame. This is clearly one of the shots that Im has spoken of as his ideal, that is, completely static shots that articulate the "Korean traditional concept known as chŏngchungdong … meaning … motion (or action) within stillness" – an ideal with obvious correlatives in Buddhism.[23] But unlike the long takes at the beginning of *Gilsottum* and especially the celebrated long take in *Sopyonje*, which are occupied by human actors and given elaborate thematic depth by the other art forms they each contain (respectively, the plangency of the North-South reunions in the television program and the *p'ansori* recitation), here the only movement in the frame is the bus that will bring Chi-san and Pŏb-un together. In this liminal space between Seoul and the mountains, Chi-san wanders, performs his ministry, and finds the way to his salvation. Its thematic role is made explicit when, at the nadir of his agony, Chi-san asks where he can go. Pŏb-un tells him to go to the mountains, that is, back to the conventional practice of Buddhism. But Chi-san – whose name means "one who knows mountains" – replies this is not possible for him, setting into play the narrative's task in these everyday places, which is to equip him for precisely his movement across Im's key icons, to return him to his true self by transforming him into "one who knows mountains" from, so to speak, "one who knows women".

POWER MISSES II: CINEMA, ASIAN AND MODERN

Figure 5. *Mandala*: Pŏb-un finds Chi-san dead in the snow.

Chi-san's odyssey in this liminal space occupies the bulk of the film, sustaining the implication that the work of the true Buddhist is done in the midst of everyday life. The theme is dramatized in Chi-san's own narrative, and also via his effect on other characters: on Su-gwan, on Ok-sun (who, when she has become a prostitute, devotedly receives him as a holy man), and especially on Pŏb-un. Since generally Pob-un's peregrinations follow Chi-san's, the landscape motif is articulated in parallel terms; the world in which Pŏb-un must find his own way between sexuality and asceticism is that of everyday life, between Seoul and the mountains. But certain aspects of the articulation of the two motifs are in Pŏb-un's case even more complex.

Like Chi-san, Pŏb-un is tormented by erotic desires that threaten his practice. Primarily he yearns for his college girlfriend Yŏng-ju, whom he left to become a monk, and the agony of his desire for her makes him a sympathetic interlocutor for Chi-san. But fueling that situation is an unresolved Oedipal desire that recalls *Home is Where the Heart Is*. In fragmentary flashbacks we learn that when he was a child his mother abandoned him to go to Seoul, driven by her own sexual desires after her husband was murdered. Traumatized by the loss of his mother, Pŏb-un continues to have an inordinate amount of affect around her and, after he is enlightened by Chi-san, it is she (not Yŏng-ju who had appeared to reclaim their love) whom he visits before he takes his final leave of human relationships. In the film's concluding scenes, Pŏb-un journeys to Seoul to meet her, and his parting from her supplies the film's most powerful visualization of liberation from earthly attachments.

But though Pŏb-un does not imitate Chi-san's exploration of sexuality, his torment is still illustrated via Im's dominant tropes. During his initiation, for example, when the master reads the precept against sexual intercourse, Im inserts, entirely without diegetic justification, a single shot of a fruit-tree in full bloom. Though non-diegetic metaphors are not impossible within the terms of Im's realism, the caprice here suggests that whatever reading we might adduce – that the blossom represents Pŏb-un's realization that religious interdictions fall on life's fairest flowers, perhaps – is as much a function of Im's subjectivity as of Pŏb-un's own. Pŏb-un does not live the tension between the two tropes as fully as Chi-san does, so it surfaces only in fragments like this, cinematic versions of slips of the tongue that voice repressed desire. But in one instance the expression is extraordinary.

During the brothel scene, after Chi-san retires with Ok-sun, Pŏb-un goes to sleep in an unused room. While he is sleeping, a woman who is known to the other prostitutes for liking sex with monks, enters the room and fellates him, a reversal of the violation of women by men so common in Im's *oeuvre*. Though it does not entail the violent physical penetration and invasion of personhood of a real rape, when he awakens in the middle of it, Pŏb-un experiences the fellation as a horrifying defilement. But before he wakes, he dreams: a rapid alternating montage of his face and the back of the prostitute's naked body builds up, cut through by a series of traveling shots across a lush green forest. These are further intercut with a scene that has *no* narrative justification or explanation whatsoever, in which Pŏb-un rapes his old girlfriend, Yŏng-ju; he tears at her clothes, she resists, and as the act is consummated, Im cuts to a shot of her purse laying in the grass. In this nightmare, the film's unconscious generates a condensed figure for Im's fundamental thematics, reasserting them even at the moment of their most drastic reversal.

Where the novel emphasizes the corruption of the orthodox Buddhist community, Im's rewriting of it as a critique of Sŏn's meditative asceticism allows him to re-affirm the humanism of his historically self-conscious art cinema as a whole, and also to foreground the oppression of working-class women and the redemptive power of their sexuality. Like Im's reworking of Buddhist symbolic topography, both themes are incommensurate with Sŏn doctrine. But though the tensions between Sŏn and the structuring combinatory of Im's *oeuvre* appear as ruptures in the thematic architecture of *Mandala*, they also generate the film's emotive power. By incorporating sexuality and spectacular landscape photography in a complex narrative so profoundly fixed in an integral component of the national culture, Im achieves a film with immense resonances for both domestic-popular and international art film audiences. Its affective force does not come from its critique of Buddhism, but from its presentation of Buddhism as a national cultural treasure, the epitome of humanist social responsibility yet also intrinsically exotic and indeed erotic – in a word, "orientalized".[24] *Mandala*'s authority rests on its sublimity, a sublimity in which soaring Buddhist chants hallow sublime Buddhist temple architecture, sublime Buddhist ritual, and even – as in the case of Su-gwan's finger burning and perhaps the "rape" of Pŏb-un – sublime Buddhist anguish.[25]

During the 1980s, the decade after *Mandala*, political liberalization and increased attention to the exploitation of the working class within the Korean economic miracle accompanied a relaxation of censorship laws that allowed filmmakers to address these issues more directly, and also allowed them a new, often exploitative graphicness in the representation of sexuality. In this context, Im made detailed studies of working-class exploitation in *Gilsottum*, *Ticket*, *Surrogate Mother* and *Adada*, all focusing on victimized women. In 1989 he returned to a Buddhist-themed narrative, structurally parallel to *Mandala*, but with the radical difference that its main protagonists were all women. To frame the narrative possibilities that, along with the transformation of the Korean cultural environment between the two films, this change allowed, we may suggest a somewhat more formalized model of the underlying semiotic structure of both films.

Im's turn to Buddhist themes in *Mandala* allowed him to mobilize his personal symbolic system and its underlying Oedipal drives within the terms of Korea's richest iconographic traditions, but one that nevertheless imposed its own regulations on his favored images. Though certain discrepancies between Im's personal themes and Sŏn's discursive structures generated the local emboli in *Mandala*'s narrative we have noted, their general isomorphism allowed him to employ as the vehicle of his own narrative the primary structures of Buddhist dialectics, that is, the dualisms of mind/body, self/other, thought/no thought, and so on. Since these must be the underlying elements of any Buddhist narrative, in Im's Buddhist-themed films his figures of mountains and women are coherent signifiers, not simply as themselves the primary units of narrative meaning (or semes, in structuralist terminology), but as the form of appearance of the more fundamental structures. These and hence the narrative grammar of the films they generate may be represented in the form of a semiotic square:[26]

In this, S1 (mind) and S2 (body) are contraries, or the fundamental binaries of Buddhist philosophy; S, their dialectical sublation, is a condition of enlightenment itself. As we have seen, in *Mandala* these concepts are mobilized in verbal

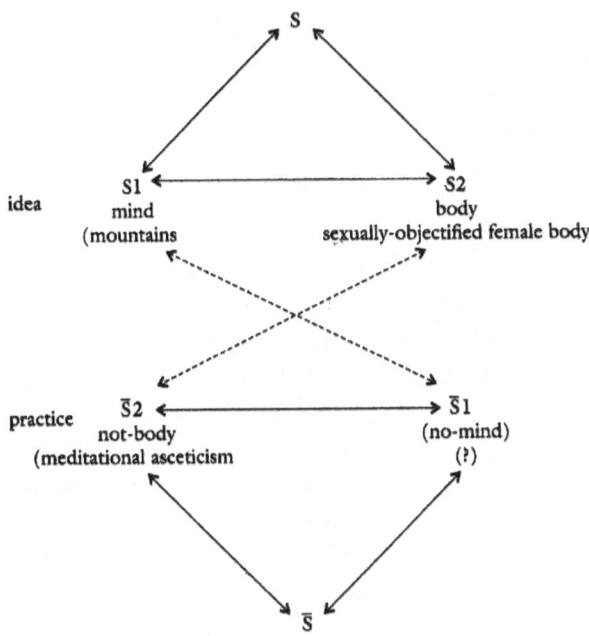

debates about Buddhist doctrine, but they also appear as semes in the narrative and, in symbolic form, in the geographical environment in which narrative unfolds. When such semes are mobilized in human activity, narrative is generated, but only within the constraints they dictate; so, S2 produces the contradictory, $\bar{S}2$ or Sŏn meditation which, though it is a physical practice, aims to transcend the body, as well as any sensuous, social engagement outside the sangha, the community of monks. For Im – from a Confucian background, uninterested in Buddhism before the popular success of the novel *Mandala* and committed to a cinema that would contribute to progressive social reform by representing exemplary responses to the social injustices of neocolonial Korea – $\bar{S}2$ alone is a priori unacceptable. Hence his critique of conventional Sŏn: it appears as political disengagement, with debilitating associations with quietism, if not with collaboration in political repression, and so affirmation of it is an unacceptable narrative resolution. In parallel, $\bar{S}1$ will represent its contrary, a "thoughtless" or spontaneous social activity, directed by compassion but in accord with reality as it immediately presents itself. In Buddhist terms this means the renunciation of personal attainment of nirvana, and the sharing of all accrued merit with other sentient beings, that is, the activity of a bodhisattva like Kwanseŭm. But beyond this general principle, more concrete terms for $\overline{S}1$ are not given in advance. How should we properly live in this world of suffering is precisely the question that Im's "honest" films confront, and so the narrative's task is to generate a model of unselfish Buddhist social action, compatible with Im's overall humanism and his rejection of ideology. If such could be found, its dialectical reconciliation with $\overline{S}2$, would then produce, $\overline{S}$ that is "enlightenment" as a social condition, or a non-exploitative, redeemed society.

Mandala presents Chi-san as having achieved $\overline{S}1$; but the film's weakness, we argued, was that the manifestation of his bodhisattva activity in his service to the plague victims of Chukto was dis-articulated from its narrative links with eroticism; the result was a thematic rupture, for the implied association between sexuality and social service was not dramatized or otherwise persuasively presented. While *Come, Come, Come Upward* downplays *Mandala*'s orientalizing spectacularization of Buddhist ritual and architecture, as well as lacking Chŏng Il-sŏng's ravishing landscape photography, it more fully elaborates the semiotic resources of Im's combinatory, and demonstrates in both narrative and visual terms the relationship between erotic love and social compassion that is so flimsy in *Mandala*. It also allows Im to take advantage of the relaxed censorship situation and, since the main protagonists are women, female sexuality becomes to an unprecedented degree proactive. Women appear as themselves possessed of sexuality and as the agents of historical transformation rather than merely the passive objects of male violation and historical trauma. The foregrounding of female sexuality in *Come, Come, Come Upward* allows Im more forcefully to critique Sŏn, and to affirm Mahayana Buddhism's compassionate social activity and his own humanism. But now his "non-ideological" humanism is distinguished against the more explicitly "ideological" politics of minjung, and the more radical New Wave filmmakers who had come to maturity during the decade.

Come, Come, Come Upward is primarily the story of Sun-nyŏ, a young nun who has entered a temple as a novitiate. Despite her fervent desire for a life of meditation, she is several times refused ordination, and the head nun Ŭn-sŏn mysteriously tells her that the study she needs is not to be found in the monastery, and that rather than joining the *sangha* she should accept herself and the mission that she already knows is hers. The scenes of Sun-nyŏ's early days at the temple are punctuated by a series of extended flashbacks to her life as a schoolgirl that associate her with a strong sexual energy and also with some of the most traumatic events in Korean history; they range from the defeat of last king of Paekche by Silla and Chinese forces, through the Tonghak rebellion, to Korea's neo-colonial

Figure 6. *Come, Come, Come Upward*: Sun-nyŏ is ordained.

dependency on the United States represented by the Gwangju massacre and Korean participation in the invasion of Viet Nam.[27] These flashbacks, all of which involve some combination of sexual and national politics, preoccupy the first half of the film. Though justified in terms of Sun-nyŏ's characterization, they do not primarily function to reveal her psychological motivation or establish the importance of her subjectivity; in fact, as the narrative unfolds these latter are revealed as irrelevant, entirely subordinated to her karma. Rather, the flashbacks operate analytically and, organized by the compositional strategies Im had perfected over the previous decade, they generate a thematic crisis. By the mid-point of the film Sun-nyŏ has become invested with all the han of Korean history and contemporary politics, and the film has produced Im's summary thematic issue: how can traditional culture be used to confront the han of present-day Korea, and here specifically, what part can Buddhism play in that confrontation? The second half of the film answers this question by again contrasting orthodox Sŏn practice, represented by another young nun, Chin-sŏng, with the unconventional, extra-monastic benevolent practice into which rejection by the head nun precipitates Sun-nyŏ. So where the first half of the film is an alternating montage of Sun-nyŏ's monastic life and the previous experiences that invest her with Korea's han, the second half is an alternating montage of Chin-sŏng's and Sun-nyŏ's contrary practices of Buddhism.

Sun-nyŏ is eventually accepted into the order, but no sooner has she taken her vows, than the full weight of her karma crashes down on her. A petty criminal whose life she inadvertently saves when he attempts suicide becomes obsessed with her, and his attentions are so scandalous that, despite all her appeals, Sun-nyŏ is expelled from the temple. But before she leaves, Ŭn-sŏn implies that one day she might be allowed to return and gives her a *hwadu* or koan that restates the primary dialectics of Sŏn in terms of her own situation: "Between your spirit that stays here and your body rambling around in the world, which one is real?" Sun-nyŏ's experience of her body rambling in the real world leads her to a life of benevolent self-sacrifice among the working class that includes sexual relations with men. Initially she gives herself to the man who caused her to be expelled, and though he rapes her, she reforms him, and they both become very happy, especially when she becomes pregnant; but he is killed in a mining accident and Sun-nyŏ loses her baby. She continues her practice, becoming an itinerant nurse, and working heroically through a cholera epidemic on a remote off-shore island, an event that (unlike its equivalent with Chi-san on Chukto in *Mandala*) is extensively represented and integrated into the narrative. During the epidemic, Sun-nyŏ becomes involved with an ambulance driver named Song, caring for him and his baby son. All the while, her bodhisattva practice of spontaneous benevolence in the real word is counterpointed with the career of Chin-sŏng, who manifests none of Sun-nyŏ's social commitment. Even when she encounters the 1987 democratization riots during a period of university study in Seoul, she dismisses the activist student who reproaches her unconcern with the city-workers' and farmers' struggles. But Chin-sŏng's meditational practice fails to develop, and she too sets out wandering.

The two practices reach their crisis in two paired scenes that conclude the film. In the first, a surrealistic sequence parallel to Pŏb-un's nightmare but also recalling Su-gwan, Chin-sŏng's quest has led her to a remote cave. While she is meditating there, she is assaulted by a monk who has castrated himself in a vain attempt to transcend his own sexual desire and so free himself from obsession and anxieties. He seizes her and undoes his clothes as if he would rape her, but all he can do is force her to look at his wound. The scene is extraordinary, without parallel in any cinema I know. Beginning as if it will again act out the violation of a woman by a man, it categorically inverts patriarchal power and scopic relations. It is the man, not the woman who is positioned as the object of the gaze, and when the woman looks, what she sees is the mark of his castration, his lack of a phallus that figures the impotence of meditational asceticism and self-mortification.

The film then returns to Sun-nyŏ's ministry; she continues her heroic work and

1 – Im Kwon-taek: Korean National Cinema and Buddhism

Figure 7. *Come, Come, Come Upward*: Sun-nyŏ learns of the traumas of Korean history; Ŭn-sŏn expels Sun-nyŏ from the temple; Sun-nyŏ in the world with her husband; Chin-sông in the world, rejecting the militant students; Sun-nyŏ as a nurse on a distant island; Ŭn-sŏn welcomes Sun-nyŏ's return.

the epidemic is eventually contained. After the doctors and nurses have a party to celebrate their success, she and Song go home together, and in a very graphic scene, she passionately makes love to him. But he dies during his orgasm. Again the film cuts, this time back to the mountain temple; Chin-sŏng has broken the impasse in her practice, but Ŭn-sŏn is on her deathbed. Sun-nyŏ hurries to Ŭn-sŏn, who welcomes her and indicates that she – Sun-nyŏ not Chin-sŏng – has

Figure 8. *Come, Come, Come Upward*: the attempted rape of Chin-sŏng.

fulfilled her mission. While watching Ŭn-sŏn's cremation, Sun-nyŏ finally realizes the answer to her hwadu. Recognizing the Buddha-nature that was, as Ŭn-sŏn implied, already hers all along, she collects fragments of the abbess's bones, planning to build a thousand pagodas, each with a bone at its heart. The film ends with her setting out once again to save the masses from their struggle in illusion.

Together, Sun-nyŏ's and Chin-sŏng's diametrically opposite practices – respectively $\overline{S}1$ and $\overline{S}2$ on the square – catalogue the Im combinatory as it is articulated through contemporary Buddhism and figured in extreme forms of sexuality. The tension between the mountains and the metropolis is again resolved by centering the narrative in small provincial towns, but this time more richly and completely than in *Mandala*. The resultant spatiality appears as the location of industry, ordinary social life, human relations, and of course, epidemic illness; it mediates between mountain isolation and the polemically-political, Marxist-influenced politics of Seoul, where by this time, the small-film movement's confrontation with Korean social injustice was filmically and politically more radical than Im ever sought to be. Oscillating between the extremes of Seoul and the mountain cave, Chin-sŏng's itinerary links these spaces, denigrating both radical politics and asceticism as opposite sides of the same coin. Sun-nyŏ achieves enlightenment in the liminal geographies between them; her sexual munificence is metonymic for her general social ministry and it is the source of her own spiritual development. This allows the film to assert a redemptive humanism, founded in female sexuality and defined in contradistinction to both meditational asceticism in the mountains and the ideological models of violent social change taking place in the -dominated metropolis. Sun-nyŏ's sexual self-sacrifice is, of course, on one level a sado-masochistic Confucian male fantasy, and the scene where the intensity of her sexuality kills Song echoes with the motifs of soft-core pornography and exploitation genre films (for example, cult filmmaker Kim Ki-yŏng's sexually voracious "Killer Butterfly" women). But Sun-nyŏ's love is also the benevolence of an enlightened bodhisattva, and we may surmise that if the ecstasy with which she delivers Song from this incarnation does not gain him Nirvana, then nothing will.[28] Concluding her work in the epidemic, her act is the fully-expressive climax of her overall spiritual itinerary, and the peripety of a narrative in which Im negotiates the conventions of both popular melodrama and Korea's richest pre-colonial heritage to argue a compelling cultural allegory: rather than merely representing the ravished, colonized nation, a working-class woman becomes both symbol and agent of its redemption.

Notes

1. Huh Chang, "Anatomy of the Korean Film Industry", *Koreana* 3, no. 4 (1989): 4.
2. On the minjung period, see Hagen Koo, "The State, Minjung, and the Working Class in South Korea", in *State and Society in South Korea*, ed. Hagen Koo (Ithaca, N.Y.: Cornell University Press, 1993), pp. 131–162, and Kenneth M Wells, ed., *South Korea's Minjung Movement: The Culture and Politics of Dissidence* (Honolulu: University of Hawaii Press, 1995).
3. The definitive account of this generation of directors is Kyung Hyun Kim's *The Remasculinization of Korean Cinema* (Durham, N.C.: Duke University Press Books, 2004).
4. In the late 1950s, when Im was serving his apprenticeship and the industry was producing about a hundred features a year, there were seventy-two companies; in 1973, the motion picture law reduced the number of these companies from seventy-one to sixteen; see Lee Young-Il, "A Thumbnail Sketch of Korean Film History", in *Im Kwon-Taek: Filmemacher aus Korea/A Korean Filmmaker*, ed. Klaus Eder (Munich: Munich Film Festival, 1990), p. 72.
5. Quoted in Gina-Yu Gustaveson, "Im Kwon-Taek: Filmmaker and Humanist", in *Im Kwon-Taek: Filmemacher aus Korea*, p. 30. The film with which Im attempted to move from merely commercial filmmaking was *The Deserted Widow* (*Chapch'o*, 1973). Another account of Im's personal crisis is recorded by Tadao Sato: "It was the fruit of an intense feeling of wanting to throw off the mask that I so fondly wore when entertaining my audiences. I wanted to escape from those blatant lies ... the best way to bring out the truth, I thought, was to depict the life of my own mother"; see Sato's "Tradition and Transition: Im Kwon-Taek", *Cinemaya* 12 (1991): 63.
6. The list of artist-protagonists who are surrogate for the director himself also includes the journalist in *Hidden Hero* (*Kippal ŏmnŭn kisu*, 1979), and his writer's block. Foreshadowing Adada's muteness in *Adada* (1988), he figures Im's narration of the impossibility of telling the Korean story. A parallel complex of issues revolves around language, with the tensions among Chinese, Japanese and Hangŭl representing the fragmentation of national identity, somewhat in the manner of Hou Hsiao-hsien's use of linguistic dispersal in his films about the colonial period in Taiwan. The name changes the Japanese impose on the patriarch in *The Genealogy* is an especially condensed instance; see the discussion below. Adada's imminent degradation is similarly prefigured by her husband's attempts to treat her muteness by teaching her to pronounce Japanese letters. Parallel issues recur with the prostitutes in *The Hidden Hero* who learn English to work the occupying GIs.
7. Quoted in Klaus Eder, "Conversation with Im Kwon-Taek", in *Im Kwon-Taek: Filmemacher aus Korea*, p. 30.
8. On han, see Choi Kil-Sung, *Han'gugin ŭi han* (*The Koreans' Han*, Seoul: Yechonsa, 1991). Korean Americans have

superimposed the fact of exile from the homeland on the inherited resonances of han; see, for example, Juli Kang, "Stories Behind the Han", *KoreAm Journal* 9, no. 3 (March 1998): 20. *Sopyonje* contains Im's fullest elaboration of the aesthetics of han, articulated in Dong-ho's teaching and dramatized in Song-wha's performance.

9. Im's *Chunhyang* (2000) was chosen for the Official Competition Section at the Fifty-fifth Cannes Film Festival, the first time ever that a Korean film had been so honored.

10. Sin, the first Korean artist to paint *kisaeng*, was eventually expelled from the Bureau of Painting because of his erotic themes. See Marjorie Williams, "Five Hundred Years of Korean Painting", *Orientations* 12, no. 1 (January 1981): 10–13.

11. For the "violence" of sexualized representations of the nation; see You-me Park, "Against Metaphor: Gender, Violence and Decolonization in Korean Nationalist Literature" in *In Pursuit of Contemporary East Asian Culture*, eds. Xiaobing Tang and Stephen Snyder (Boulder, Colo.: Westview Press, 1996), pp. 33-48; for the ideological function of the Korean "women's film" and for avant-garde feminist critiques of it; see Kim So-young, "Questions of Woman's Film", in *Post-Colonial Classics of Korean Cinema*, ed. Chungmoo Choi (Irvine, Ca.: University of California, 1998); and for the cultural reverberations of the double oppression of post-colonial Korean women, see Chungmoo Choi, "Nationalism and Construction of Gender in Korea", in *Dangerous Women: Gender and Korean Nationalism*, eds. Elaine H. Kim and Chungmoo Choi (New York: Routledge, 1998), pp. 9–30.

12. Laura Mulvey, "Visual Pleasure and Narrative Cinema", *Screen* 16, no. 3 (Autumn 1975): 18.

13. *Aje aje para aje* are the opening syllables of Korean form of the Sanskrit mantra, *Gate, gate, paragate, parasamgate, bodhi svaha*, that concludes the *Heart Sutra*.

14. Deriving from the Chinese Ch'an, Sŏn is the meditational form of Buddhism known as Zen in Japanese. For English language accounts of Korean Buddhism, see especially Robert E. Buswell, "Buddhism in Korea", in *The Encyclopedia of Religion*, ed. Mircea Eliade (New York: Macmillan, 1987), vol. 2, pp. 421–426; *Tracing Back the Radiance: Chinul's Korean Way of Zen* (Honolulu: Hawaii University Press, 1991); and *The Zen Monastic Experience: Buddhist Practice in Contemporary Korea* (Princeton: Princeton University Press, 1991). See also Peter Lee, ed., *Lives of Eminent Korean Monks* (Cambridge, Mass.: Harvard University Press, 1969); Stephen Mitchell, ed., *Dropping Ashes on the Buddha: The Teaching of Zen Master Seung Sahn* (New York: Grove Press, 1976); Keel Hee-Sung, *Chinul: The Founder of the Korean Sŏn Tradition* (Seoul: Po Chin Chai, 1984); Mu Soeng Sunim, *Thousand Peaks: Korean Zen – Tradition and Teachers* (Berkeley: Parallax Press, 1987); and J.C. Cleary, ed., *A Buddha from Korea: The Zen Teachings of T'Aego* (Boston: Shambala, 1988).

15. Buddhism was actively supported by both the Syngman Rhee and Park Chung-hee administrations, and after Roh Tae-woo's government put him on trial for the Kwangju Massacre, Chun Doo-hwan took refuge in a Buddhist temple. Until the mid-1970s, neither the Buddhist sangha or the Christian church were actively involved in the social and political movements of the time, and a "Minjung Buddhism" did not emerge until several years after *Mandala*.

16. In only one period was this celibacy qualified. During the Japanese occupation, following the Japanese custom, monks were permitted to marry. Believing that Buddhism had to secularize if it was to regain its contact with the lay population, Han Yong-un (1878–1944) vigorously proposed this, circumventing the Vinaya prohibition by employing the notion of "the unimpeded interpenetration of all phenomena" (*sasa muae*), a "quintessential doctrine of interfusion" (Buswell, *Zen Monastic Experience*, p. 27) that he invoked to argue that celibacy and marriage were really no different. The project was initially successful, but in the post-liberation era, hostilities – and sometimes physical conflict – between married and celibate monks for possession of the monasteries flared up. Government intervention eventually secured the dominance of the celibate Chogye Order, which it presently retains.

17. By contrast, the Korean film about Buddhism best known in the west, *Why Has Bodhi-Dharma Left for the East? (Dalma ka tongjjok ŭro kan kkadak ŭn*, Pae Yong-gyun, 1989), simply reproduces them; it is set in the mountains, and women are all but entirely excluded.

18. Kim Song-dong, *Mandala: A Novel*, trans. Ahn Jung-hyo (Seoul: Dong-suh-Munhak-sa, 1990). The two monks have different kinds of relationships and with more women in the novel, and the film makes other substantial changes, some of which are discussed below.

19. On finger burning in Sŏn, see Buswell, *Zen Monastic Experience*, pp. 195–197.

20. A major component in Sŏn meditation revolves around a koan (Korean: *hwadu*) that the master assigns to each novice. Pŏb-un's is the question about how to remove a bird trapped in bottle without breaking the bottle, and his progress towards solving it is regularly raised in his discussions with the abbot. Placed between scenes involving Chi-san and himself, the unmotivated image of the birds suddenly rising from the ground suggests that Pŏb-un has solved his hwadu and links Chi-san's breakthrough to his own.

21. Chŏng Il-sŏng's photography has contributed substantially to Im's overall achievement. As well as *Mandala*, he shot *Gilsottum, The General's Son, Fly High, Run Far, Sopyonje, Adada*, and *The Taebaek Mountains (T'aebaek sanmaek*, 1994) – all of them distinctly alike, distinctly unlike Im's film's with other cinematographers, and also unlike Chŏng's

cinematography for other directors (such as Kim Ki-yŏng). In all cases the distinctiveness of the landscape photography raises the issue of Im's relation to the language of classical Chinese painting. (Chŏng was in fact trained in classical painting, before he turned to photography.) Korean landscape artists of early Chosŏn dynasty were strongly influenced by Chinese models, especially of Northern Sung – the same era whose art has been most influential on Chinese cinema since the rejection of Socialist Realism. But by the eighteenth century, Korean styles and themes were being modified in the direction of greater realism, especially by Chong Sŏn (1676–1759), the first Korean painter to advocate painting directly from nature rather than previous works. This movement, called "landscape painting of actual scenes" (*chin'gyong sansu*) also affected genre painting of the same period, including Sin Yun-bok (Williams, "Korean Painting", pp. 10–13). Despite these modifications, it is clear that the multi-perspectival pictorial organization of panoramic views with only the tiniest of human figures, the use of extremely high horizons that flatten visual space, the inclusion of large areas of unpainted surface, and similar properties of Sung landscape inform Im's work, and the result is to affirm an East Asian (if not a specifically Korean) visual language. But in the case of *Mandala*, the formal parallels with Sung painting are less important than the Taoist – and hence Ch'an – epistemological principles they manifest, specifically the lack of a fixed position for the viewer and the limitless extension of space that figure the subjectivity of a consciousness that rejects the distinction between self and object in its embrace of the void. The transposition of these principles to photography informs the visual composition of the temple photography (especially the placement of figures in geometrically demarked sections of the frame, otherwise entirely occupied by a monochrome or black "void"), and especially the photography of Sŏrak-san in winter at the climax of *Mandala*, where the snow and mist allows Chŏng to disassemble the mountains into quasi-autonomous fragments that resemble the composition of Sung landscapes.

22. Mitchell, *Dropping Ashes*, p. 62; see also Mu, *Thousand Peaks*. Buswell notes that the last Sŏn master to practice unconstrained conduct was Ch'unsong sunim (1891–1978), a disciple of Han Yong-un whose most notorious act was to make reference to the vagina of Park Chung-hee's wife during the first lady's birthday celebration; see Buswell, *Zen Monastic Experience*, pp. 127–128. More clearly in the novel than in the film, Chi-san invokes Won-hyo, but as a nihilist, rather than a justification for his own profligacy; see Kim, *Mandala*, p. 108.

23. Quoted in Eder, "Conversation", p. 34. Im continues, "My ideal camera is static. To be honest, my mobile shots, tracking and panning, are only expressions of my fear and insecurity in not having found my ideal static shot." The parallel with Mizoguchi is obvious, but indicates, not his direct influence, but their origin in a common East Asian aesthetic derived ultimately from Chinese Buddhism. Other elements of camera-style in *Mandala* and Im's films of this period generally that reflect the same aesthetic include the positioning of figures in a small portion of the screen with the rest occupied by, for example, a flat wall; the effect is to place human subjects in a visual void, again a specifically Buddhist trope.

24. Western fascination with Buddhism, including the vogue for Tibetan Buddhism in Hollywood, is undoubtedly nourished by the same kind of sliding erotic/aesthetic affectivity that Im develops. Cross-cultural confusions, of course, follow; then Cardinal Joseph Ratzinger (later to become Pope Benedict XVI), designated by the *Los Angeles Times* as "the Vatican's chief guardian of doctrine" for example, attacked Buddhism as "'an erotic spirituality' [that] would replace Marxism as the church's greatest challenge by 2000"; see John Dart, "Vesak Festival Celebrates Life of Buddha", *Los Angeles Times*, 5 May 1997, B3.

25. For an enormously insightful reading of *Mandala* as a critique of Sŏn, see Dale Wright, "The Awakening of Character as an Image of Contemporary Enlightenment" in *What Is Buddhist Enlightenment* (New York: Oxford University Press, 2016). In this essay I have been careful to avoid the assertion that these are in any categorical sense "Buddhist" films, rather proposing that in their narratives about Buddhism, the affirmation of certain spiritual and cultural principles pertaining to Buddhism and the use of Buddhist iconography and aesthetics are held in a productive tension with the critical interrogation of Buddhism's contemporary social role. In doing so, I have elided what must surely be the fundamental question for all study of the relationship between Buddhism and cinema, that is the degree to which Buddhist principles may supply a film's formal properties, rather than its thematic concerns. Stated baldly, is it possible for a film in some sense to *be* Buddhist or to perform Buddhist functions, irrespective of whether its narrative is *about* Buddhism? Or, can the Buddhism be a function of filmic rather than profilmic or diegetic codes? For a Korean argument that Buddhist teachings are built into the process of making Buddhist art, see Dojin, "Built-in Buddhist Teachings: The Invisible Through the Visible", *Lotus Lantern* (Seoul) 1, no. 1 (Spring 1999), pp. 12–13. The possibility that Buddhist meaning may reside in the cultic events a film organizes rather than in its discursivity is raised by certain western avant-garde abstract films – James Whitney's *Yantra* and Jordan Belson's *Samhadi*, for example – that may be understood as involving processes correlative to *dhyana*. Presumably parallel issues are raised by other Western media that display meditational functions, either demanding them in the process of their manufacture or inducing them at the point of reception; Ad Reinhardt's all-black paintings, together with his admiration for the putatively timeless perfection of Buddhist art, are an especially apposite instance; see his essay, "Timeless in Asia", *Art News* 58, no. 9 (January 1960): 33–35. Conversely, given the history of Buddhism's syncretism, it is not likely that any essentially or limitingly Buddhist properties in traditional Buddhist culture will be categorically distinguishable from the more generally Asian aesthetic forms in which they inhere, and presumably the same syncretism allows Buddhism to operate in sympathetic Western culture of entirely different origins. Nevertheless, the question is an important one, for its own sake, and also to allow for the notice of films which may deal in

Buddhist iconography without having any real commitment to Buddhist values – though this is not the case with Im, as I take it. Fran Cho's study of *Why Has Bodhi-Dharma Left for the East*, "Imagining Nothing and Imaging Otherness in Buddhist Film" in *Imag(in)ing Otherness: Filmic Visions of Living Together*, eds. S. Brent Plate and David Jasper (Atlanta: American Academy of Religion, 1999), is an exemplary exploration of the relation between diegetic and filmic expression of Buddhist principles.

26. The following is loosely based on Algirdas Greimas, "The Interaction of Semiotic Constraints" in *On Meaning: Selected Writings in Semiotic Theory* (Minneapolis: University of Minnesota Press, 1987).

27. In the first, when questioned by Ŭn-sun, the abbess at her temple, Sun-nyŏ says she comes from Kwangju, the site of the U.S. supported massacre of democratic activists in 1980. In the second, she finds a monk visiting her mother with whom she lives after her father abandoned them. Conniving to meet the monk, she later travels with him towards his temple, and as they walk together across bleak snowy mountains, he tells her about her father; after serving in Viet Nam, he became a monk but, when it was too late, he realized that the most precious things are achieved, not by solitary meditation, but by suffering with the starving masses. And in the third, still as a schoolgirl, she develops a crush on her teacher. Although he claims to have a wife and a child, she comes across him lonely and drunk in the city streets at night. Again she connives to travel with him and learns that in fact his wife was killed at the Kwangju massacre, when she was eight months pregnant. The two visit the famous cliff, Nakwha Am, where the teacher recounts the story of the defeat of last king of Paekche by Silla and Chinese forces, and the suicide of his 3,000 concubines; but, he asserts, since history is always written by the victors, the king should be recognized as a patriot and his dissoluteness forgotten. And he tells Sun-nyŏ that he promised his wife he would write an epic poem about both the end of Paekche and the Tonghak rebellion. (Sun-nyŏ accidentally comes across this book, just before her final sexual encounter discussed below.) Finally, in an incident that recalls Chi-san's Buddha icon, Sun-nyŏ overhears a tour guide explaining that the large Buddha images in the grounds of her temple are visually ambiguous, resembling traditional images but also ordinary people.

28. Though Sun-nyŏ's sexual benevolence clearly reflects generic requirements and the structures of Korean patriarchy generally, it is not without precedent in the Korean Buddhist tradition. The contemporary Sŏn master, Seung Sahn, for example has made reference to a prostitute called "Pass-a-million", who during the Buddha's time used sex to teach Buddhism; all the men she had sex with became enlightened. See Mitchell, *Dropping Ashes on the Buddha*, p. 65.

Chapter Two   Im Kwon-taek's Use of Nativist Korean Culture as Allegories of Cinema:
Ch'unhyang, Chihwaseon, and *Hanji*

Born on May 2, 1936, in Changsŏng, Chŏllanam-do, Im Kwon-taek is the most important and celebrated filmmaker in South Korea. Amid the poverty and chaos of the aftermath of the Korean War, he moved first to Busan and then to Seoul, where he found work as a production assistant in the embryonic film industry. Having directed his first feature, *Farewell to the Duman River* (*Tuman'ganga Charitkŏra*), in 1962 and his most recent, *Revivre* (*Hwajang*), in 2014, his career spans more than half a century. During this time he has produced an astonishing oeuvre of more than one hundred films that have made him popularly known as the "father of South Korean cinema". Many of these films, especially the earlier ones, were formulaic genre quickies for small, usually short-lived, studios that were dependent on immediate market returns. He had already made fifty popular entertainment features of this kind when, in 1973, a crisis of conscience that he has described in several interviews set him on the path to the art film. "One day I suddenly felt as though I'd been lying to the people for the past 12 years. I decided to compensate for my wrongdoings by making more honest films." Generally funded by the continuing popularity of his action films, these "more honest" art films brought him international acclaim, earning him the Best Director award at the Cannes Film Festival in 2002. Of them, a dozen concern nativist, premodern Korean culture.

I. Nativist Korean Culture

Though various in their narrative strategies, *The Genealogy* (*Chokpo*, 1978), *Mandala* (*Mandara*, 1981), *Surrogate Mother* (*Ssibaji*, 1986), *Adada* (1987), *Come Come Come Upward* (*Aje Aje Para Aje*, 1989), *Sopyonje* (*Sŏp'yŏnje*, 1993), *Festival* (*Ch'ukche*, 1996), *Ch'unhyang* (*Ch'unhyangdyŏn*, 2000), *Chihwaseon* (*Ch'wihwasŏn*, 2002), *Beyond the Years* (*Ch'ŏnnyŏnhak*, 2007), and, the latest to date, *Hanji* (*Talbin kirŏolligi*, 2011), all dramatize with ethnographic detail and accuracy ancient customs or art forms, and several also explore their precarious survival into the present. *Mandala*, for example, very beautifully dramatizes the traditional customs and art of Korean *Sŏn* (Ch'an or Zen) Buddhism as it narrates the stories of two monks who differently attempt to reconcile their religious faith and insight with their desire to live in the modern world. These films sometimes include quasi-documentary interludes that interrupt the diegesis and pedagogically elaborate the elements of the nativist culture in question, but more frequently they dramatize such material in popularly accessible and often spectacular narrative forms that exploit the conventions of film melodrama that Im had mastered during his earlier work as a journeyman director.

Their resistance to global capitalist culture's homogenizing erasure of the past and cultural difference in its promotion of a totalized corporate postmodernism marks the overall importance of these historical retrievals. But, beyond this, their specifically Korean significance can hardly be overemphasized, given the devastation inflicted on the nation and nativist culture in the twentieth century: the Japanese annexation that lasted until the end of World War II; the brief "day of freedom" before the division of the country between the subsequent U.S. neocolonial occupation of the South and the communist dictatorship in the North; the civil war; and then in the South the series of U.S.-maintained military dictatorships that endured until the free election of a civilian president in 1992. This history of trauma and chaos jeopardized the continuity of much of Korea's unique cultural heritage as it had coalesced during the half millennium of the Chosŏn dynasty (1392–1897), when, instead of being divided and ravaged by foreign intruders, Korea was unified, largely in isolation from the outside world. The rituals and customs of this period, its forms of civic organization and judicial administration, and its architecture, pottery, music, painting, and dress matured into distinctive integrated forms, a unique cultural economy. Preeminent within it was *Han'gungmal*, the singular Korean language that many linguists believe has no genetic relationship to any other, and *Han'gŭl*, the writing system designed exclusively for it – a unique visual language.

In respect to the renewal and reassertion of specifically Korean culture, Im's ethnographically oriented features had three main functions.[1] First, their dramatization of neglected and endangered cultural traditions pedagogically displayed their aesthetic value and affirmed their social function, reeducating a population on whom for a century the presumptive superiority of Japanese and then US capitalist culture had been imposed. Second, the domestic box office success of some of them (especially *Sopyonje*, whose acclaim ignited an extraordinary revival of popular interest in the traditional folk opera, *p'ansori*) and the recognition they achieved in festivals abroad fostered the growth and international prestige of Korean cinema generally, opening the way for the younger filmmakers of the New Korean Cinema and for a revival of interest in neglected older ones. Third and most important, the narrative focus on art and artists provided the basis for Im's allegorical exploration of the present state of Korean culture and especially of his own filmmaking. The representation of a specific traditional artist, art form, or cultural practice in any given film generated reflexive patterns of similarity and difference between it and Im's film about it, providing him with a vocabulary through which the possibilities of his own art could be explored.[2] The possibilities and limitations of the artists he depicted, their artwork, and its social existence provided a model in respect to which Im himself, his films, and their social function could be imagined. He made them into allegories of cinema.

Such a reflexive allegorical use of the past to investigate the possibilities of contemporary Korean culture was not without contradictions. While their aural and visual exoticism made the spectacular elements in Chŏson culture well suited for cinematic reproduction, other aspects complicated allegorical use of it. Whether aristocratic or folk, its almost entirely artisanal mode of cultural activity differed fundamentally from the industrial mode of production of capitalist cinema and the specific forms of alienation intrinsic to its consumption. Other difficulties appeared in two recurrent motifs by which Im elaborated the cultural past: images of women and images of the natural landscape, most often brilliantly photographed by Im's virtuoso cinematographer, Chŏng Il-sŏng.[3] Many of them, *Adada*, *Sopyonje*, and *Ch'unhyang* most notably, were thematically and visually pivoted on images of the violation and exploitation of beautiful women, often set in the context of the Korean Peninsula's mountains, valleys, and shores, variously enhanced by sunshine, mist, or snow. As figures for the nation, the women and their tragedies were offered as a vocabulary by which the suffering and the spirit – the *han* – of the distant past could frame, if not diagnose, the traumas of the present, while the beauty of the natural landscape conversely proposed an ideal to which the nation might be restored. Im has typically justified the cruelty inflicted on his heroines by pointing out that in Confucian society women were sequentially subjected to fathers, husbands, and sons, and so did indeed bear a disproportionate share of hardship and suffering. But in a period when feminists radically retheorized gendered visual codes, such representations, it was argued, also reproduced the conditions that allowed for the continued subjection of women. Similarly Im's celebration of Korea's uninhabited, unworked spaces mobilized an essentially touristic nostalgia that could hardly provide a generative metaphor for social renewal amid the rapid industrialization of the late twentieth century and the state-enforced vicious exploitation of the working class. Severely hierarchical and without a middle class, the rural agricultural Chosŏn era could only vaguely parallel modern urbanized Korea, and the forms of resistance available to feudal peasantry bore little relation to the democratic mobilizations of the Minjung movement. Intrinsic to the disparities between Im's present and the received Confucian cultural heritage, such aporia in his project could never be fully resolved. But his great achievement was to work with and through them, setting them in different contexts and manipulating them in different permutations to make them the narrative, thematic, symbolic, and especially affective materials of his cinema.

Three of these reflexive allegorical ethnographies, made in the twenty-first century when the directions of Korean culture had shifted away from the narrative filmmaking of the New Korean Cinema toward television, pop music, and other forms of digital consumer culture, are especially important: *Ch'unhyang*, *Chihwaseon*, and *Hanji*. The two that earned Im most acclaim were the costume dramas, *Ch'unhyang* and *Chihwaseon*. They were concerned with two of the major cultural forms of the Chosŏn era, folk music in one and aristocratic painting in the other. *Hanji*, which was neither a popular nor a critical success, was concerned with the manufacture of traditional Korean paper.

II. Ch'unhyang and *Chihwaseon*

Dating from the seventeenth century, the *Ch'unhyang ga* (Legend of Chunhyang) derives from a shamanistic ritual of the Namwŏn area, less than a hundred kilometers from Im's birthplace. A version of the story composed in the 1870s (immediately after the peasant uprisings dramatized a decade earlier in *Fly High, Run Far* [*Kaebyŏk*, 1991]) provides first existing the text of the *p'ansori*. The story recounts the relationship instigated by Yi Mong-nyong, the son of a local governor, with Ch'unhyang, the daughter of a *kisaeng* and a former governor who abandoned her upon returning to Seoul. Ch'unhyang initially resists Mong-nyong but gives herself to him when he promises fidelity, writing his oath on her dress and informally – and illegally – marrying her. When his family is called back to Seoul, he leaves her, and the next governor, Pyŏn Hak-to, viciously exploits the peasants and commands Ch'unhyang to submit to him. Arguing that, just as a subject can have only one king, a woman can have only one husband, she refuses, thereby breaking the law and effectively condemning herself to death. She is cruelly tortured, but on the day of her execution Mong-nyong, having been successful in his examinations and sent by the king to investigate the administration of the provinces, returns to save her and punish the evil governor.

Figure 1. *Ch'unhyang*: the *p'ansori* reciter; Mong-nyong sees Ch'unhyang; Ch'unhyang with her friends; Mong-nyong writes his undying love for Ch'unhyang on her dress.

The more than a dozen films of the *Ch'unhyang ga*, several of them made in North Korea, all celebrate Ch'unhyang's virtue, but they each emphasize different aspects of the story and differently negotiate the conflicts among her Confucian responsibilities, most crucially her faithfulness to her husband and her disobedience to the governor.[4] In Im's version, Ch'unhyang initially appears imperious, invoking her father to assert her social superiority; but by the last act, the parallels between Pyŏn's cruelty to her and his exploitation of the peasants have made her a folk heroine and hence a figure for populist resistance. In order to allow Mong-nyong to be a correct governor but also to be identified with Ch'unhyang and with the peasants, the film has to tread a fine line through Confucian ethics. For example, when Ch'unhyang reproaches Mong-nyong for needlessly prolonging her sufferings by failing to reveal himself when he first returns, he explains that he had promised the king not to do so. But when he reproaches Pyŏn for his harsh treatment of Ch'unhyang, the other replies with impeccable logic: "Class has a definite order. A daughter of a courtesan becomes one naturally. She didn't disobey just me, but she disgraced the law and committed treason." Mong-nyong's reply – that the explanation was Ch'unhyang's "will to being a human" – wrenches Confucian logic to fit it to the ideology of Im's populist humanism.

But these intricacies of Confucian legal dialectics are subordinate to Im's larger concern with an idealized ethnography of the period and of late Chosŏn culture.

Im's celebration of Ch'unhyang as a faithful wife and a folk heroine is achieved through his documentation of a performance of the *Ch'unhyangga* by singer Cho Sang-hyŏn and his drummer Kim Myŏng-hwa, who appear at the film's beginning and ending as well as periodically throughout. But for most of the performance, Im replaces their musical recitation with the spectacular audiovisual richness of a melodramatic narrative film. He uses the resources of an industrial cultural form to represent and affirm the pleasures of *p'ansori* and to propose that traditional art can be, rather than an artificially sustained elite culture, a truly popular, indeed "folk", culture.

As the film opens, the musical narrative plays behind the title, and the first visuals introduce the performers on a bare stage, with Cho, dressed in white before a black screen, moving his fan for dramatic emphasis as he sings an address to Ch'unhyang. The second shot cuts to a street scene in Seoul showing a group of fashionably dressed teenagers entering the theater and reluctantly taking their seats for what is revealed to be a school assignment. One of them tries to leave but is restrained by another who declares that traditional art has never disappointed her. Then Cho, standing before a traditional hand-painted screen, asks the audience to encourage him so he can do his job well during the five-hour performance, thus positioning them not as passive cultural consumers but as participants in the drama. As he continues his introduction, the film cuts to the ornate pavilions of the governor's home and then to the Chŏllabukto countryside. Though occasionally Cho's voice is heard over the visuals, subsequently the film alternates between brief shots of his stage performance and the extended cinematic dramatization of his narrative. Filmed with virtuoso brilliance by Chŏng Il-sŏng [Jung Il-sung], it is an audiovisual feast: the splendor of the architecture, costuming, handwriting, music, and rituals of aristocratic *yangban* culture; the equally picturesque costumes and dances of the peasants; the colors and textures of the landscapes; and the ethereal beauty of Ch'unhyang herself. Reflecting the relaxation of censorship, the erotically graphic depiction of the young couple's lovemaking is unprecedented for Im, though the scenes of her torture recall the worst of the sadism inflicted on, for example, the namesake character of *Adada* or the unfortunate heroine of *Ssibaji*.

As the film moves to its climax at the Kwanghallu pavilion, where Ch'unhyang is to be flogged to death, Cho is heard describing the scenes that we simultaneously see: the entry of the regional nobles into the main hall, the rich folkloric details of the luxurious food, the elaborately costumed dancers and the kisaeng,

Figure 2. *Ch'unhyang*: governor Pyŏn Hak-to arrives; he demands that Ch'unhyang submit to him; Ch'unhyang in prison; Ch'unhyang vindicated.

and outside the masses of angry peasants among whom Mong-nyong and the king's troops are concealed. After the dénouement, with the evil nobles tied up and Ch'unhyang in her husband's arms, Cho's narrative voice in Seoul is taken over by the people in the *p'ansori's* filmed narrative, notably Ch'unhyang's mother, who, surrounded by the other peasant women, sings the song of celebration that the *p'ansori* assigns to her, a mother's celebration of her daughter. When Cho resumes the narrative for the coda, the film returns to him on stage in Seoul, but this time the camera angle is reversed: instead of facing him, the camera is placed at the rear of the stage, looking out between the two musicians to the audience, who are now applauding in rhythm with the song, several of them dancing and all encouraging him as he had initially asked them to do. In its closing scenes, then, the *p'ansori* recitation has dissolved into both the narrative and the audience. The filmed performance has become a nexus uniting the seventeenth-century peasants with the contemporary theatergoers into an idealized homogenous folk community. By implication, this commonality extends to and includes audiences for the film, for whom it has both documented Cho's performance of the *p'ansori* and dramatized it as a cinematic spectacle. Cho is thus an ideal model of Im's own art: the filmmaker teaches his public the ethical meaning of Ch'unhyang's life and the aesthetic significance of the *p'ansori* that it inspired and that preserves it for future generations.

Chihwaseon, Im's free adaptation of the life of Chang Sŭng-ŏp (1843–1897), a painter who lived through the collapse of the Chosŏn dynasty, is more overtly an allegory of his own attempt to create an aesthetically superior yet socially responsible cinema, generating patterns of analogies between the two artists, their personal qualities, and their life's work but also patterns of disanalogies and contradictions. It is divided between the success of Im's cinematic recreation of the painter's art and the narrative's pessimism about the possibility of the artist's ever finding a productively engaged social role.

Chang's desire to ally his art with popular politics is hindered by his birth into the lowest social stratum of feudal Korea, a social position into which Im, the son of a landowning family, was precipitated only by conflicts between left and right in the post-liberation period. Chang's ambitions are focused on painting, the summary and most important medium in late Chosŏn society, but also a ritual, a performance in which the practice of art mediates the external world into a model of correct human and social behavior. To perform these functions, he must master the classical Chinese rules of representation but also transcend them to achieve a superior expression of his individual sensibility and of the national Korean identity and also to become the agent of a harmonious Korean social order – all of which anticipates Im's own project.

The aesthetic competition between Chinese suzerainty and Korean independence in painting reenacts the macro-political struggles of the 1894–1895 Sino-Japanese War when Korea became the battleground between collapsing Chinese power and an aggressively modernizing, proto-imperialist Japan. The film shows the impotent monarchy, corrupt nobility, and exploited peasantry, among which the government is torn between a conservative faction that sees China as the best ally for their attempt to retain Confucian social organization and a progressive faction hoping to reform and modernize Korea by linking notions of human equality introduced by Catholic missionaries to Japanese economic and military power. The privileged cultural status of painting draws Chang into this struggle, generally on the side of the proto-democratic possibilities of the reform party. But the conflicts between his headstrong temperament and his extraordinary abilities and those between his lowly origins and his aristocratic patrons prevent him from fulfilling himself as either an artist or a political agent. Chang is tormented equally by the demands of his aesthetic sensibility and by the apparently insoluble task of making his painting contribute to democratization, an end to domestic exploitation, and the defense of the nation against foreign invaders.

2 – Im Kwon-taek's Use of Nativist Korean Culture as Allegories of Cinema

Figure 3. *Chihwaseon*: Chang Sŭng-ŏp painting for his aristocratic patrons.

Unable in his art to harmonize the individual creative act with its social context, his career is riven by contradictions, and he finally commits suicide in a pottery kiln, itself a furnace of the most sublime Korean nativist culture.

The impossibilities that consume Chang reflect the historical situation of late Chosŏn painting. Dependent on aristocratic patronage for his education, Chang is displaced from his own class and obliged to work in a medium monopolized by the ruling class, who attempt to exploit him both for their own aggrandizement and for gifts that will appease foreign intruders, both Chinese and Japanese. The only way common people can benefit from his art is by vicariously identifying with his reputation and social mobility, and the only political function for the common people that Chang himself can envisage for his work is quietist. Translated into modern terms, Chang's tragedy is that he is superlatively gifted in the dominant art form of the time but cannot make it the vehicle of a progressive aristocratic public sphere, and especially not of a proletarian public sphere.

Though these impossibilities allow Im to create Chang as a dramatically complex protagonist, *Chihwaseon* subordinates the momentum of his personal drama in an episodic structure focused rather on the political issues his life manifests, making the film a transparent allegory of parallel issues in contemporary South Korea. Questions about painting translate fairly directly into questions about cinema, which during the Korean New Wave of the early 1990s was still intellectually and politically engaged. As the privileged cultural practice, cinema provided a public sphere where political issues were mobilized and where a progressive Korean artist could feel that his or her work might contribute to the struggles for a freely elected government and liberation from foreign influence.

The contemporary equivalent for the overwhelming authority of Chinese painting is the Hollywood film industry, which, as instanced by the success of *Shiri* (*Shwiri*, Kang Che-gyu, 1999) released several years earlier, appeared to be recolonizing Korean cinema. Struggling to maintain itself in a global corporate culture dominated by Hollywood, Im's ambition to create an authentic Korean quality cinema that also contributes to democratic modernization parallels Chang's desire to combine supreme aesthetic achievement and popular political significance in painting. And many of the ancillary qualities of Chang's practice recur in Im's own, often mystical, sense of his vocation; for example, his frequent remarks that while making his films he sometimes feels possessed by a power outside himself echo Chang's claim that his "brush was moved by some mysterious force".

On the other hand, differences between the two artists suggest that Chang is an idealized rather than an accurate self-portrait, a model of Im's ambition. The steadfastness of Chang's rejection of official favor, for example, contrasts with Im's acquiescence to politicians during the long night of the military dictators. In other respects, Im appears to be using Chang to justify the contradictions in his own oeuvre and his failure to address social issues directly: for example, when Chang's mentor, a senior in the reformist party, accuses him of having been blinded by his popularity and having strayed from the authentic realism of Korean genre painting by failing to depict the people's suffering, he replies that, despite its exaggeration, his art offers them consolation. And in other cases, the identification between Im and Chang is routed via Chŏng Il-sŏng. *Chihwaseon* is made persuasive as a film equivalent for Chang's art by virtue of Chŏng's virtuosity in creating moving-picture photography as magisterial as Chang's painting. The magnificence of Chŏng's landscape photography is emphasized in a series of key montages in which the film passes back and forth between shots of Chang's work – a landscape or a sky full of swirling birds – and Chŏng's photography of a virtually identical scene. Recalling the painting contests within the narrative, these sequences suggest that Im is using Chŏng to display the modern medium's parity with the ancient one, perhaps even the superiority of the movies over painting.

III. *Hanji*

With *Beyond the Years*, Im returned to the short story upon which *Sopyonje* was based, but failed to achieve either popular or critical success. Then four years later he released another art film: *Hanji*. A remarkable work, it both continued the reflexive ethnography and significantly transformed the conventions that appeared to have coalesced into a quasi- generic stability.

Hanji centers on P'ilyong, an inept government bureaucrat who, hoping for a promotion, joins a project to revive the production of *hanji*, a Korean paper made from the *tak* tree (Paper Mulberry) and a hibiscus shrub, both native to Korea. As early as the Three Kingdoms period, *hanji* was recognized as the finest paper in the world, and the industry flourished through the Chosŏn period. But during the Japanese occupation and since, it so radically declined that – like Buddhism, ceramics, temple architecture, and many other cultural practices that were introduced to Japan from Korea – the Japanese have appropriated it so that the best *hanji* is known internationally as "Japanese paper". So complete is the loss that (according to the film's conceit), only one man, a drunken Chang Tŏk-sun, still knows the secret of its production. The immediate cause of the demand for real *hanji* is for the restoration of a copy of 47 of the 1,893 volumes of *The Annals of the Chosŏn Era*, that in 2006 were returned from Japan to Chŏnju, again a city in Chŏllabukto and less than seventy kilometers from Namwŏn. In the somewhat elliptical and meandering narrative, P'ilyong's administrative responsibilities oblige him to organize a competition among small firms to make a paper good enough for the restoration. This entails cajoling the dishonest and conniving papermakers to undertake what is a financially unrewarding project. He eventually completes his task, the *Annals* are restored, and the film's dramatic arc seems complete. But instead of ending there, *Hanji* launches into a remarkable coda, in which P'ilyong and Chang Tŏk-sun go off to the mountains to make the real Goryeo *hanji*.

Throughout this narrative, P'ilyong also has to manage two women, Hyo-kyŏng and Chi-wŏn. The former is his wife, now incapacitated by a stoke supposedly caused by his extramarital affair, as a result of which their son lives with his parents; her power over her guilt-ridden husband is strengthened by her ancestry in an ancient papermaking family. The other is a troublesome filmmaker who, unable to make the features to which she aspires, is reduced to documentaries, specifically one about *hanji*. The social tensions among P'ilyong, the government bureaucracy, the papermakers, and the two women who flank him, along with several structuring image patterns, notably one involving reflected moonlight, are developed with an intricacy that recalls the multi-dimensional integration of the fibers in *hanji*. But again the nuances of film's realism are assimilated into allegory and the combination of the usual elements of Im's reflexive ethnographic films: a Korean cultural form, once internationally preeminent but now lost; not one, but two broken families as figures for the broken nation of Korea, two beautiful women, one of them traumatized; and a drunken genius artist and other cultural workers who stand in for the filmmaker himself. In this instance, however, Im transforms the organization and interaction of his motifs. The traditional culture of the feudal past is brought into the present of the industrialized Korean economy and its elaborate bureaucracy; despite Hyo-kyŏng's suffering, both women are empowered by their different relations to *hanji*, and neither is made the object of the male sadistic erotic gaze; one of them, Chi-wŏn, is an artist who represents Im, if only in a finally qualified fashion; and the relations between documentary and fictional narrative are manipulated with great finesse. Since all social relations are inflected by aesthetic issues, the paper-making narrative inevitably projects itself as another allegory of the medium of film and the institutions of cinema. But in this case, the relations between fiction and documentary are especially subtle.

The dramatic narrative of Chi-wŏn's administrative struggles includes extended quasi-documentary interludes as when, for example, government officials specify the arcane and exacting details for the paper's correct manufacture or when a celebrated calligrapher demonstrates its unique properties. But it also contains fragments of actual documentaries, a television program about the *Annals* that P'ilyong watches while exercising with his wife, for example, and especially Chi-wŏn's film. Assigned to assist her, P'ilyong initially struggles with her intrusive willfulness and skepticism about *hanji*'s uniqueness; but eventually the two develop a working relationship, and as the competition he organizes and her film proceed in parallel alongside each other, a romance between them seems to bud, certainly enough to re-ignite Hyo-kyŏng's jealousy. Their relationship comes to head when she invites him to her apartment to watch a rough cut of her film, also titled *Hanji*; though mostly a straightforward educational documentary, it also contains a fictional dramatized interlude about a *yangban* returning to his wife in the moonlight. At this point, P'ilyong abruptly kisses her and they passionately embrace. But instead of continuing with the erotic scene, Im breaks his tradition of depicting a rape by abruptly cutting to her documentary and bringing its video frame into his full 35 mm film frame. Im's *Hanji* becomes one with Chi-wŏn's *Hanji*, and the incipient sexual union is displaced by an aesthetic one. As, within Im's film, Chi-wŏn's video ends, Im cuts to an audience of officials, revealing them as the audience at the premiere of her completed documentary, with its concluding peroration, "The preservation of our ancestors has been through and we have to promise that our records will be preserved for the next one thousand years". Rather than being made a sadistic spectacle, Chi-wŏn's sexuality is sublimated into the cultural responsibility that her *Hanji* articulates.

The generic development is made especially resonant by the fact that Chi-wŏn is acted by Kang Soo-yeon [Kang Suyŏn], a great beauty who starred in two of Im's films about traditional culture focused on victimized women, *Surrogate Mother* (for which she won Best Actress award at the 1987 Venice International Film Festival) and one of Im's greatest films, *Come, Come, Come Upward* (*Aje aje para aje*, 1989). This generic reversal fundamentally reconstructs women's role in Im's previous films, replacing the earlier sexual objectification with a symbolic elevation that in this case makes Chi-wŏn a surrogate for Im himself. Her comments on her documentary, "I feel the need to tell about things that need to be told", speak for Im himself. Furthermore, Tŏk-sun's unique traditional craftsmanship that allows him to recover authentic *hanji* is matched by Im and Chi-wŏn's contemporary craftsmanship, neither of which entails any attempt to disguise itself as unalienated folk art. But the parallels between Im and Chi-wŏn – and between them both and Tŏk-sun – are also problematized by the singular quality of *hanji*, the Thousand Year Paper.

Along with the softness, beauty, and propriety for handwriting that make it superior to all other papers, *hanji*'s durability is unmatched. Seen in Chi-wŏn's documentary, the *Great Dharani Sutra of Immaculate and Pure Light* (Mugujŏnggwang Taedaranikyŏng), for example, was printed on *hanji* in 706 and is still legible. This durability makes *hanji* both a cultural object and the best means of sustaining and preserving other cultural practices: painting, but also writing and printing, whether of Buddhist texts or Chosŏn government proceedings, and within them records of the human activity that constitutes history. In this it resembles film, especially Im's films that are likewise works of art yet also the best means yet achieved for recording other works of audio-visual art. But in the new millennium the status of film, especially art films like Im's, was suddenly jeopardized, globally but perhaps especially in Korea. By the turn of the millennium, the rise of digital imaging prompted widespread concern about the death of cinema, or at least the death of cinema created on celluloid film. At the same time, the importance of television and pop music in *Hallyu* stripped the art film

Figure 4. *Hanji*: making Thousand Year Paper at night in the mountains.

of the prestige it had attained during the period of the New Korean Cinema, while at the same time shifting attention to the digital culture that made Korea the most wired nation in the world.

All these developments are implicit in *Hanji*. While on the one hand, Chi-wŏn's *Hanji* resembles Im's *Hanji* in performing the same act of cultural renewal to which he is committed, on the other, it is made on digital video for broadcast television. In this it drastically falls short of Thousand Year Paper's durability; like all digital culture, even its short-term survival is in doubt, as is suggested when in her apartment Chi-wŏn draws P'ilyong's attention to her earlier work made on Beta videotapes that are now virtually obsolete. On the other hand, despite film's incomparably greater material durability, which ironically makes it the best medium for the long-term preservation of digital moving-image culture, film-making as a social practice is in danger of disappearing. The modern art to which Im had devoted his life is now on the edge of becoming a lost Korean cultural form. Im's film and Chi-wŏn's video inversely reflect each other: the materially less durable video appears to have a social future while the materially-durable celluloid film is on the edge of obsolescence.

Positioned across these historical contradictions, Im's film cannot of course resolve them, but an extended coda does. P'ilyong's sudden commitment to assist Chang Tŏk-sun to make the true Goryeo paper entails transporting the wooden frames and other equipment by foot to a Buddhist temple remote in the mountains. There, by a waterfall where "the angels come to bathe" and working only in the moonlight and only with pure Korean natural raw materials, Chang attempts to revive the lost art. As he does so, his paper becomes imbued with mystical significance and associated with the Buddhist scriptures that it has preserved. Touching the sensuous material, Chi-wŏn, who like Hyo-kyung has made the difficult and dangerous journey into the mountains, remarks, "It's more like a spirit than a material".

Here then *hanji* finally illuminates Im's artistic aspiration: not only to record the details of Korean culture, but to preserve its spirit. And in this case, the contradictions between the industrial collective nature of cinema and the folk qualities of the nativist culture are transcended. For *hanji* was itself commercially manufactured and distributed throughout East Asia, as indeed was the New Korean Cinema and now *Hallyu*. All such manufactured products can only be produced by the cooperation of many agents. And so the coda brings together instances of all these: P'ilyong, Chang Tŏk-sun, Chi-wŏn and Hyo-kyŏng. Each of them has a role in making the *hanji*, each is partially a figure for Im himself; but only in their collaboration can they represent the collective activity that *Hanji* entails. Like "art" paper, Im's "art" film is a commercial enterprise, yet one dedicated to preserving the spirit of Korean culture.

IV. *Han'gŭl*

The reflection of *hanji*'s cultural importance in *Hanji* brings into view another film that history requires Im to make, the film about *Han'gŭl*, the unique Korean alphabetical writing system. All essentialist arguments about nativist Korean culture flounder on the fundamental hybridity bequeathed by the Chinese origin of many of its most characteristic manifestations. In *Hanji*, this hybridity appears in the fact that all the ancient records that *hanji* has preserved were written in *hanmun*, Chinese characters. In the Fifteenth Century, the fourth king of the Chosŏn dynasty, Sejong the Great, recognized that *hanmun* was alien to the nature of the Korean language and ensured the illiteracy of the mass of the people; he therefore commanded that a script be created appropriate to the Korean language and accessible to all. *Han'gŭl* was completed in 1443 and described in a 1446 document, *Hunmin Jeongeum*, or "The Proper Sounds for the Education of the People".[5] If the Korean spirit exists in any cultural manifestation, it is surely in this beautiful and democratic visual language. We can only hope that Im Kwon-taek will turn his genius to its genesis.

Notes

1. The possibility of Im's critical cinema only emerged with the end of the military dictatorship. His nativist films began with *The Genealogy*, released the year before the assassination of Park Chung-hee and the end of the *Yusin* period. *Mandala*, the first film in which his new direction was widely recognized, and *Surrogate Mother* followed, separated by half a decade. The frequency of the new nativist films increased during the first years of the Sixth Republic, culminating in *Sopyonje* in 1993, the year after the election of the first civilian president. At the same time, the relaxation of censorship made possible the emergence of the Korean New Wave, including for the first time a radically contestatory political cinema, most importantly the work of Park Kwang-su; in the late 1980s and early 1990s his films were released virtually alternated year by year with Im's: *Chilsu and Mansu* (*Ch'ilsuwa Mansu*, 1988), *The Black Republic* (*Kŭdulto Urich'orom*, 1990), *To the Starry Island* (*Kŭ Some Kago Shipta*, 1993), and *A Single Spark* (*Arumdaun ch'ongnyon Chon T'ae-il*, 1995). But in this period, Im maintained his distance from the new political radicalism: in *Come Come Come Upward* (1989), for example, one of the main protagonists, a Buddhist nun struggling to find redemptive meaning in her life, explicitly rejects association with the student activists of the Democracy Movement and with "poor farmers and city laborers". And, even though his own parents had joined the partisans after the liberation, his lack of any discernable endorsement of the leftist guerillas of this period in *The Taebaek Mountains* (*T'aebaeksanmaek*, 1994) contrasted markedly with Park's sympathy for them in the previous year's *To The Starry Island*.

2. In theoretical writing on the Hollywood musical, this issue has been developed by Jane Feuer in respect to a genre she categorized as the "self-reflective musical". The interlaced references between the musical film itself and the show it depicts give the represented show the ideological responsibility of repressing the audience's self-consciousness of the commodity nature of the musical film itself and of the alienated social relations it sustains: "The musical … tries to compensate for its double whammy of alienation by creating humanistic 'folk' relations in the films; these folk relations in turn act to cancel out the economic values and relations associated with mass-produced art. Through such a rhetorical exchange, the creation of folk relations *in* the films cancels the mass entertainment substance *of* the films. The Hollywood musical becomes a mass art which aspires to the condition of folk art, produced and consumed by the same integrated community." "The Self-Reflective Musical and the Myth of Entertainment", *Quarterly Review of Film Studies* 2, no. 3 (August 1977): 313–326, and subsequently elaborated in *The Hollywood Musical*, 2nd ed. (Bloomington: Indiana University Press, 1993). Quote is from *The Hollywood Musical*, p. 3.

3. Beginning to work with Im on *Tears of the Idol* (*Usangŭi Nunmul*) in 1981, Chŏng Il-sŏng shot *Mandala, Adada, Fly High, Run Far: Kaebyok, Sopyonje, Ch'unhyang, Beyond the Years*, and many others of his greatest films of the 1980s and 1990s, including the blockbusters *The General's Son I, II*, and *III* (*Changgunŭi Adŭl*). Together with Im himself and his long-time producer at Taehung Pictures, Chong formed what was known as the "Troika of Korean Film"; see Chong Song-il, *Im Kwon-taek* (Seoul: Korean Film Council, 2006), p. 44.

4. The versions of these made in North Korea are especially interesting in quite differently inflecting an assertive class consciousness in Ch'unhyang herself. See Hyangjin Lee's chapter "Gender and cinematic adaptions of *Ch'unhyangjon*" in her *Contemporary Korean Cinema: Identity, Culture, and Politics* (Manchester; Manchester University Press, 2000), pp. 67–101.

5. The anniversary of the publication of the *Hunminjongŭm* is celebrated on 9 October, Han'gŭl Day.

Chapter Three The Name of a Desire: Recollections of Socialist Realism in East Asian Art Cinema

I.

In the late 1980s, a debate in a U.S cultural journal brought into sharp focus two antithetical visions of a progressive, anticapitalistic global culture that, though constructed with reference to literature, may easily be translated into cinematic terms. First, citing Lu Xun's story "Diary of a Madman" and Ousmane Sembène's novel *Xala*, Fredric Jameson argued that the separation of personal/libidinal life from the wider world of public politics that he believed characterized culture in the west had not yet occurred in what he called "third-world" literature. Consequently, accounts of interpersonal relations in such texts could – and in fact had to be – read as national allegories, specifically as allegories of the struggle for liberation and decolonization: *"the story of the private individual destiny is always an allegory of the embattled situation of the public third-world culture and society"*[1] (italics in original). In his reply, Aijaz Ahmad generously overlooked the anachronism of Jameson's use, as an example of third-world literature, "Diary of a Madman", a text that was first published in 1918 when China had suffered relatively slight colonial penetration and that predated the Soviet Revolution and hence predated the conceptual possibility of a second, let alone the third world. But Ahmad did dispute the inevitability of such allegorical structures and proposed as counterexamples writings in Urdu that he thought not to be nationalist in the way Jameson asserted. More fundamentally, he attacked Jameson's category of the third world itself, arguing that though it might have a function in polemics, it had "no theoretical status" because the third world could not "be constructed as an internally coherent object of theoretical knowledge".[2] Returning to the Marxian concept of the mode of production, he argued that the notion of three worlds should be replaced by a binary: one world formed by capitalism and the other by socialist resistance to it. And disputing Jameson's proposal that the only alternatives for third-world literature were "nationalisms" or "global American postmodernist culture", he rhetorically asked:

Is there no other choice? Could not one join the "second world", for example? There

47

used to be, in the Marxist discourse, a thing called socialist and/or communist culture which was neither nationalist or postmodernist. Has that vanished from our discourse altogether, even as a name of a desire?[3]

Allowing him to exploit Jameson's unnecessarily hyperbolic claim that third-world literature was *always* an allegory of national liberation, Ahmad's return to the theoretical model of the global struggle between the two contrary modes of production seemed to have won the debate. Yet only for a short time. Thirty years earlier, his axiom that socialism "is simply the name of a resistance that saturates the globe today"[4] may have been credible; but three years after his essay was published, it could only echo nostalgically through the ruins of the Communist states. The collapse of the Soviet bloc and the domestic turn of the People's Republic of China (PRC) to capitalism and class division and its entry into the system of global capital heralded a decade of which the best that can be said is that was not as vile and violent as the first of the new century that followed it: a massively renewed neo-liberalist imperialism under the banner of one form of religious fundamentalism and opposed to it another whose only redeeming feature was its opposition to "global American postmodernist culture". Socialist or Communist culture nowhere existed, "even as a name of a desire", its place preempted by a new name: "globalization" – itself, as Henry Kissinger proposed, "really another name for the dominant role of the United States".[5]

Since then, the "globalization of culture" has come to mean, if not the hegemony of "global American postmodernist culture", then certainly the international hegemony of the form of cultural production exemplified and largely directed by the integrated U.S. film, television, and music industries. Major components of the global culture industries are transnationally owned, that system includes productive centers outside the U.S., and, of course, it contains "differences and disjunctures".[6] The success of the South Korean film industry in competing domestically with Hollywood, developing a strong export record in East Asia, and even beginning to establish a reverse flow into the U.S. market is a dramatic example of the several recent challenges to U.S. domination of global cinema. But the achievements of Korean blockbuster filmmaking were enabled only by its rejection of previous attempts to build a national film style and a national cinema on the heritage of traditional culture (most notably, Im Kwon-taek's "national allegories") and its corresponding turn to the vocabularies and values of Schwarzenegger action films and MTV. Even where aggressive local industries with strong export markets have developed significant stylistic vocabularies of their own (as was the case with the Hong Kong industry in the 1990s), their innovations have simultaneously reaffirmed and renewed the mode of cultural production of the U.S. media industries, the system with which they compete:

3 – The Name of a Desire: Recollections of Socialist Realism in East Asian Art Cinema

to wit, cinema as the manufacture of commodities and films that mobilize styles and narrative structures that present no substantial challenge to the ideology of neo-liberalism and capitalism itself.

At the time of writing, the economic system this global culture sustains does face unprecedented national liberation struggles, many of them related to each other by the vision of a totalitarian Islamic internationalism. No less than the hegemony of Empire itself, this continues to obliterate the force, even the memory, of a cultural internationalism contrary to both of them; that is, the socialist culture that Ahmad invoked, especially the projects of the Communist Internationals before World War II and the linked forms of national resistance to U.S. neocolonialism in the Cold War period after it.

These and all the other socialist or protosocialist cultural initiatives, of course, possessed differences among themselves that reflected local geographical and historical conditions, so much so that the history of twentieth century Marxist aesthetics retrospectively appears as a minefield of contradictions. Nevertheless, this history can be seen to have revolved around two theoretical epicenters, one designating the content and/or style of a socialist work of art and the other a socialist mode of cultural activity or production: socialist film and socialist cinema respectively. Since for cinema the production process is so expensive, complex, distended, and technologically-dependent, the issue of mode of production was inescapable and recognized as impacting the form and content of the artwork much more fundamentally and forcefully than was the case for mediums such as poetry or even the novel, whose aesthetics were less integrally linked to their material instantiations. The early 1970s attempts of the *Groupe Dziga Vertov* to make *political* films but to make them *politically* is a summary instance of this interdependence between the work of art and its productive process, between filmic object and cinematic practice. Though conceptualized as a Maoist attempt to apply Marxist-Leninist ideas of self-criticism and cultural revolution to cinema, the group's priorities looked back to Vertov's own attack on the form and content of the acted fictional narrative film and to his notion of a popular participatory cinema; for example, to the "network of cameramen in the provinces" sending material to the "experimental film station" where the *Kinopravda*, the "periodical of events summarized into an agitational unit" was to be edited.[7] And, despite manifold categorical differences, their emphasis on collaboration both among multiple producers and between filmmakers and their audiences also aligned their work with the various "Third" and "Imperfect" Cinemas of Latin America and Viet Nam of the same period.[8]

More generally, however, arguments about socialist cinema have not thoroughly engaged issues of a participatory socialist form of production, and had Ahmad seriously thought what "a thing called socialist and/or communist culture which was neither nationalist or postmodernist" might be, he would have been obliged to confront the fact that the only candidate of any substantial historical credibility was socialist realism, an official art whose axioms were mandated from above by the party and in which popular participation and creative innovation at the point of production were often inhibited. In this respect, as a form of mass culture, socialist realism should be counterposed, not against the intellectual, agitational, and (in most cases) minority leftist cinemas, nor against its historic adversary, high modernism (which in its own period was an elite culture that neither sought nor attained mass appeal); rather, it should be counterposed against bourgeois industrial culture – "capitalist realism" – which is always and everywhere a commodity, similarly ideologically overdetermined, and whose social relations of production are even more integrally predicated on the masses remaining as consumers of culture rather its producers. Nevertheless, the political contradictions underlying the aesthetic contradictions of socialist realism remain as reflections of unresolved theoretical tensions between the roles of the party and of the proletariat itself in Communist theory and practice.

In Western, first-world cultural theory, not least in the various post-World War II existential, psychoanalytic, and deconstructive currents of Western Marxism, socialist realism has been almost universally ridiculed and despised, not on the grounds of its industrial production – for that recognition would entail the equivalent dismissal of capitalist culture *tout court* – but on a plethora of others: for its celebration of personality cults around party leaders such as Stalin, Mao, and Kim Il Sung; then more generally for its censoring function, its putatively monolithic didacticism, its specifically socialist didacticism, and for its disinterest in and indeed opposition to formal experimentation and the various crises of representation: in other words, its rejection of aesthetic modernism and its corresponding commitment to realism understood as combining specific formal protocols with a unique referential and cognitive potential, the knowledge of history. Until recently, variations in its principles and practice in different periods and especially in different locations – the USSR, other countries in the Soviet bloc, the People's Republic of China, North Korea, and Viet Nam – have been left as the province of academic specialists. In more general cultural discussion, they have not been acknowledged, let alone given substantial attention, but simply assumed to have been at all times the same and always bad. As Régine Robin noted a decade ago in her pioneering study, "socialist realism can only be mentioned with a disdainful smile. People already know everything worth knowing".[9] And though recently signs of more nuanced historical accounts have emerged,[10] especially of Soviet literature and Chinese painting, even on those – now admittedly rare – occasions when Western film studies endorse the various socialist modernisms, they persist in denigration or at best disregard of socialist realism.

As long as the global hegemony of capitalism and its cultures exists, it will be foolish to suppose that socialist realism will regain any mass cultural currency. But it would be equally wrong to suppose that, even in a present in which "the only starting-point for a realistic Left ... is a lucid registration of historical defeat",[11] the repressed memory of the utopian vision of a popularly accessible art premised on cognition of progressive social movements will not continue to return, if only as the "name of a desire". As long as that desire lives, attempts to imagine its implementation will have to come to terms with the fact that through the last two-thirds of the twentieth century, socialist realism's ability to adapt local peasant, proletarian, and bourgeois cultural traditions to create a mass popular culture expressive of socialist values leaves a unique legacy. It is, inevitably, a contested and contradictory legacy – but no more so than that of its adversarial other, modernism. For whatever their historical function might once have been, today and for many years now, collage, estrangement, reflexivity, the laying bare of formal devices, and all the other modernist shocks that were once supposed to inhibit primary identification with mimetic forms and hence the operation of their intrinsic ideological effects have been fully assimilated to capitalist mass culture. Stripped of their negativity and socially re-created as points of pleasurable and usually cynical recognition rather than critical reflection, the devices of modernism now compose the formal strategies of advertising, popular film and television, and indeed global corporate postmodernism generally.

In this context, both the ideal of socialist realism – "a truthful, historically concrete depiction of reality in its revolutionary development.... combined with the task of the ideological molding and education of workers in the spirit of socialism[12] – and its actual historical instantiations (however often they fell short of that ideal) may find new functions. These will not be reducible to a single attitude to past Communisms nor a single role within contemporary capitalism. At present satire predominates, for example, in Komar and Melamid's Sots Art combinations of socialist realism and Western styles and in similar strategies in recent Chinese painting, where the vocabulary of Maoist art and even the iconic images of Mao himself have been re-appropriated.[13] But the unstable semiosis of the Chinese case, in which an ironic distancing often morphs into an expressive nostalgia for at least some aspects of Communist society, opens up the possibility

Figure 1. *Two Stage Sisters*: Jian-bo introduces Chun-hua to Gu-Yuan's woodcut, "Xianglin's Wife", the protagonist of Lu Xun's story, "New Year's Sacrifice". Translated, the subtitle reads, "She was widowed twice and people shunned her as a bringer of misfortune".

of a nonironic narrativity. In a cultural environment where both its terms are anathema, invocations of socialist realism may themselves be the vehicle of the aesthetic shock by which perception is reignited and by which the historical memory of the social vision that originally justified them renewed.

So much at least is implicit in two important East Asian art films: Park Kwang-su's *A Single Spark* (*Arumdaŭn ch'ŏng'nyŏn Chŏn T'ae-il*, 1996) from South Korea and Hou Hsiao Hsien's *Good Men, Good Women* (*Hao nan hao nu*, 1995) from Taiwan. Both films use elements of the style and the ideological value system of socialist realism to reclaim memories of emancipatory political struggles that were simultaneously nationalist and linked to Communist internationalism. They do so only in extremely self-conscious forms, in collage structures that frame those principles, objectifying and estranging them and putting them in dialogue with contrary aesthetic modes and historical conditions; but the result is not an ironic disavowal of the socialist project so much as an affirmation of it and an attempt to reclaim it.

As a point of both comparison and contrast with these films, and to remind us of the cultural power and flexibility that socialist realism once mobilized, I will

3 – The Name of a Desire: Recollections of Socialist Realism in East Asian Art Cinema

begin with a crucial reflexive moment in the great Chinese film, Xie Jin's *Two Stage Sisters* (*Wutai Jiemei*, 1965).

II

Figure 2. *Two Stage Sisters*: Chun-hua sees herself and the peasant girl, Chun-hua in Gu Yuan's woodcut, "Xianglin's Wife"; Chun-hua in the opera, *New Year's Sacrifice*.

In a pivotal scene in *Two Stage Sisters*, Chun-hua, a performer in traditional opera with a strong but inchoate desire to link her art to the Liberation, is taken by Jiang-bo, a young cadre, to visit an art exhibition in Shanghai in 1946 on the tenth anniversary of the death of Lu Xun. There she sees a two-color woodcut by Gu Yuan, one of the most accomplished and influential Chinese woodcut artists of the twentieth century. Titled *Xianglin's Wife* (*Xianglin sao*), it depicts the poor, ostracized widow who is the protagonist of Lu Xun's short story, "New Year's Sacrifice", an indictment of the exploitation of women in feudal China.[14] Superimposed over the image of the widow in the woodcut, Chun-hua sees both herself as she had earlier been brutalized by Guomindang police and corrupt landlords, and also another Chun-hua, a peasant girl who brought her a drink of water when she was being pilloried by them. Identifying the common situation of the three abused women, this remarkable triple superimposition figures the history of repression and resistance that allows the actress to envision a radically modernized form of opera, one capable of dramatizing the feudal exploitation of the masses, especially of women, and so of participating in the Liberation struggle. The subsequent narrative depicts her creation of a revolutionary social realist opera based on Lu Xun's story, the resistance she encounters from reactionary theatrical and criminal elements in pre-Liberation Shanghai, and the eventual coincidence of her cultural project with the Communist victory. Broadly compatible with Mao's prescriptions in the "Talks at the Yan'an Forum on Literature and Art", her innovations are a model of the way in which traditional cultural forms and foreign forms, even those of Hollywood melodrama, may be adapted to produce a vernacular socialist culture.

This instance is particularly rich it that it depicts an itinerary by which the principles of correct revolutionary art are constructed across a series of four different mediums: Lu Xun's story provides the inspiration and model for Gu Yuan's woodcut, which in the film does the same for Chun-hua's new, revolutionary opera, *New Year's Sacrifice*; and this opera in turn provides the model for Xie Jin's film.[15] *Two Stage Sisters*, then, aspires to be the embodiment of politico-aesthetic principles previously manifested in the fiction, printmaking, and opera it intra-diegetically references or represents. Though the number of mediums involved makes this instance unusually complicated, in another respect it is quite simple; for despite variations reflecting the specific medium of each instantiation, socialist realism orders them all. Its informing principles combine aesthetic criteria – realism – and an ideological component – the confidence in the eventual political victory of the working class. But unlike modernism, whose principles are usually understood to be limitingly medium-specific, here these principles appear to be transmitted over time from one medium to the next directly and without contradiction.

The work of Lu Xun, Gu Yuan, Chun-hua, and Xie Jin all embody the correct principles of Communist art so that each of the four artists affirms and allegorizes the functions of the others. Together they produce a single politico-aesthetic system, one which moreover can migrate from the diegesis – the story of Chun-hua – to *Two Stage Sisters* itself, from the *énoncé* to the *énonciation*.[16] Because of this transposability, Xie Jin's socialist realist film can articulate its own principles via the interpolated mediums as well as itself manifesting them, both in those parts of it that follow this moment, for which it provides the model, and those preceding it, which it retroactively justifies.

The successful transmission of the qualities of the socialist realist art that is represented in *Two Stage Sisters* to the film in which it is represented – *Two Stage Sisters* itself – is a common form of reflexivity in East Asian cinema, especially in films about traditional opera. The first film made in China, for example, *Dingjun Mountain* (1905), was an adaptation of scenes from a Beijing opera, and since then countless Chinese films have been based on opera in which the aesthetics of the dramatic form more or less completely migrate to the new medium. Analogues can also be found in Asian films that use other art forms. Many of Im Kwon Taek's films including *Sopyonje* (1993) and *Chihwaseon* (2002), are based on traditional Korean arts and attempt to assimilate into their own style and structure the properties of the epic song or painting on which their narratives are based. All these works have much in common with Western films about filmmaking and films about their own production – the classic example is Fellini's *8 ½* (1963)

– reflexive works that are understood to possess a *mise en abyme* structure; that is to say, they contain an internal mirror by which the film that is represented reflects back on the film in which it is contained.[17]

The equivalence and continuity across these levels contrasts most categorically with exemplary modernist reflexive films such as *Contempt* (*Le mépris*, Jean-Luc Godard, 1963), for example, or *Beware of a Holy Whore* (*Warnung vor einer heiligen Nutte*, Rainer Werner Fassbinder, 1971), which typically pivot on the *difficulties* of making films or of translating into cinema a work from another medium. *Contempt* is on one level about the contradictions of making a film about a classic Western poem, which cannot be adequately translated into the form of the film and fails to provide a model for its style. Instead of being assimilated to the main film, the inset film style is objectified as alien; instead of reflecting similarity, it reflects disjunction and difference. I now turn to two films in which socialist realism has this role. In them, the characteristic modes of socialist realism occur fragmentarily, and they cannot unambiguously occupy the film as a whole as they do in *Two Stage Sisters*. Rather, the invocation of socialist realism as a combination of aesthetic and political ideals that are not completely attainable or feasible generates a self-conscious splitting that internally separates the film from itself, dramatizing both the utopian possibilities and the present impossibility of both socialism and realism.

III

Park Kwang-su was a major force in the Korean political cineclubs of the 1980s, in which students mobilized cultural and political opposition to the U.S.-supported military dictatorship. He was one of the founders of both the Yallasong Film Studies Group and the Seoul Film Group, the two most important film collectives that in the early 1980s pioneered small-format political filmmaking, and also translated several Third World cinema manifestoes. Park turned from small-gauge agitational documentaries to fiction features with *Chilsu and Mansu* (*Ch'ilsu wa Man-su*, 1988), the work that announced the emergence of what would soon be known as the New Korean Cinema. The film concerns a pair of contemporary commercial artists who eke out a meager living painting billboards in a Seoul colonized by video-games of car chases in Miami Beach, American pop music at Burger King, and *Rocky*, the most degraded form of Hollywood cinema.

Both artists come from broken families: Mansu is a solitary from the lower-middle class, but his economic opportunities at home and his freedom to work abroad are curtailed by the fact that his father is a political prisoner who has been jailed for the last thirty years. From a lumpen background with a dead mother and an alcoholic father, Chilsu, also wishes to leave Korea for the U.S., which he knows only through the images of cinema and video games. They are hired to paint across an entire side of high-rise building a huge advertisement for "Glamour Whiskey", featuring a bosomy white woman, complete with an English slogan, "Drinking less?". The intended effect of this ad, the consummate capitalist art form, is to increase narcotic consumption and pacify the masses, but it only exacerbates the social alienation of the cultural workers who produce it. Painting the advertisement against an urgent deadline, the two finally come to the end of their tethers. Seated atop the building and looking down over the endless traffic and high-rise apartments, they drink soju and scream their impotent anguish into the air. But ironically they are mistaken for suicidal labor agitators, and are soon surrounded by the police, army, and reporters. Mansu eventually jumps to his death and Chilsu is arrested.

Figure 3. *Chilsu and Mansu.*

Though neither painter is able fully to articulate the social implications of his individual situation, *Chilsu and Mansu*'s final scenes in which they are separated from the police by the huge breasts of the model on the whiskey advertisement is compelling figure for the negative political possibilities of art under the military dictatorship. Like other industries, advertising brings workers together, and is able to create an affiliation between a disenfranchised intellectual and a lumpen misfit; but that affiliation cannot produce an alternative, progressive culture. The film dramatizes the difficulties of progressive cultural activity in an environment dominated by capitalist culture. The qualities of the advertising art that is represented are exactly opposite to the progressive values to which the film itself aspires. As the intra-diegetically represented artwork reflects the film as a whole negatively, the two painters can figure the historical contradictions Park as a political artist faced, but not a successful resolution of them. Unlike Lu Xun's story or the woodcut illustrating it, the intra-diegetic art form does not provide a model for the filmmaker but allows him only to dramatize the restrictions that circumscribe his own practice. Almost a decade later, after the election of the first civilian president in Korea, Park returned to culture's role in bringing together artists and workers in another reflexive film in which his use of a modern political situation and a medium in certain ways closer to cinema allowed a more optimistic allegory. In *A Single Spark* made in 1996 in the period of the victory of minjung politics and the first democratically elected government since 1961, he again employed another art form as an allegorical intertext. This time it was not capitalist advertising art but a mode generally resembling socialist realism.

A Single Spark begins with a brief prologue of documentary footage of a demonstration in the streets of Seoul sometime in the early-1990s led by the Korean Democratic Union Congress against the suppression of labor activism. It then cuts to 1975 during the height of Park Chung Hee's [Pak Chŏng-hui] repressive regime. The main protagonist, Kim Yŏng-su, is an intellectual living underground and on the run from the paramilitary police while he researches and writes the biography of a celebrated labor activist, Chŏn T'ae-il, who immolated himself in 1970 to draw attention to the garment industry owners' criminal disregard of the labor laws in their exploitation of young workers in the clothing industry.[18] But the conceit of representing the biography on film allows Park to reproduce it, not as a book-within-a film but as a film-within-a-film. *A Single Spark* is, then, an alternating montage of two distinct diegeses: First, the story of Chŏn's labor activism in the late-1960s, shot mostly in black-and-white, which details his poor background, his attempts to educate himself, his identification with the other young workers who have tuberculosis caused by their working conditions, his mobilization of labor resistance, and his eventual death in which he immolates himself while burning the book of the *Labor Standard Law*, which was designed to protect workers from exploitation but which the owners ignore. Second, shot mostly in color, the story of Kim's researching and writing this biography in the mid-1970s. Symbolically bridging the two is a subplot concerning Kim's partner, Sin Chŏng-sun who, while pregnant with their child, is herself working as a union organizer. Chŏn, then, is an exemplary hero who gives his life in the struggle against class oppression, while Kim manifests a similar bravery and initiative in his own cultural work and revives the spark of Chŏn's heroism.

Park's attempt to imagine an alliance between intellectual/cultural work and direct political activism – the precise question faced by progressive minjung artists – is figured in the romantic relationship between Kim and Sin, but also in the implication that Kim's art work (his biography of Chŏn) is not merely a representation of Chŏn's political work and so subordinate to or contingent on it but also a continuation of it, its recreation in a different social sphere. Conversely, Kim's representation of Chŏn is not objectively independent of Kim's conscious-

POWER MISSES II: CINEMA, ASIAN AND MODERN

Figure 4. *A Single Spark*: Korean Democratic Union Congress leads demonstrations against the suppression of labor activism; Chŏn T'ae-il with the garment workers; Kim Yŏng-su researches Chŏn T'ae-il's biography; Chŏn T'ae-il's self-immolation.

ness, but rather an idea that he has to some extent created through his own commitment to liberation and his own imaginative, cultural work,[19] and he imagines it in the style of socialist realism. To figure the implication that in a modern, mass mediated society of the kind Park had decisively analyzed in *Chilsu and Mansu* both intellectual work and workplace organizing are necessary, at critical moments the boundaries between the two diegeses are blurred. As Chŏn's story increasingly inspires Kim, similar motifs in the two plots (buying an umbrella in a rainstorm, for example) echo each other, and the activist begins to enter the writer's diegesis; so, for example, looking into a contemporary factory, Kim appears to catch a glimpse of Chŏn. Kim's growing imaginary identification with Chŏn is completed in the film's climax when the photography of Chŏn's self-immolation turns into color, as if the prairie fire his single spark started is continued in the present film. And in the film's last scenes, which clothes and the fragment of an intra-diegetic pop song specify as taking place in the mid-1990s when the film was made, Chŏn re-appears, strolling by the sweatshop and carrying a copy of Kim's biography!

The spark that passes from Chŏn to Kim when he writes his biography has also passed to Park Kwang-su himself in his "biographies" of Kim and Chŏn. In using cinema to tell both their stories, he assumes the responsibility of continuing into the present their emancipatory struggle to create a proletarian public sphere. Chŏn's struggle, Kim's biography, and Park's film are all ideologically aligned and, as in the case of *Two Stage Sisters*, each stage inspires the next in the transmission. But there's also a difference: in the case of *Two Stage Sisters*, socialist realism is passed along the sequence of mediums in essentially the same form: the story, the print, the opera and the film all share essentially the same aesthetic. In *A Single Spark*, however, a formal difference separates Kim's realist narrative about Chŏn and Park's narrative about Kim and Chŏn. Despite Park's insistence that it is *not* realism, Kim's narrative invokes socialist realism in its dramatization of a relationship between the revolutionary hero and the masses, in its moral simplification that makes all sympathetic characters flawless and excludes mixed characters, and so on. But the narrative of the film as a whole is more modernist, fractured across its alternating montage of the two diegeses, Chŏn's and Kim's. Park, a modernist filmmaker but one deeply committed to democratic liberation, wants to tell stories of resistance; but he cannot tell the story of his revolutionary hero directly, in the idiom of socialist realism – but only indirectly, as it is imagined by the biographer, Kim. Combining elements of what in the West are thought of as the "Brechtian" and the "Lukácsian" traditions of political modernism, its success in transmitting some of socialist realism's ideological assurance via distancing reflexive narrative forms translates progressive social politics into the conventions of the commonly depoliticized art-film genre. And the narrative focus on exploited workers in the apparel industry speaks directly not only to present manufacturing conditions when China produces over half the world's clothing but also to emergent conditions in the East Asian periphery, especially Viet Nam and Indonesia, where labor is now even cheaper than in China and India, once the historically antagonistic centers of third world socialism.

A Single Spark is vulnerable to criticism from the left on the grounds that it privileges an individual rather than a mass hero; that Park failed to relate his own filmmaking to contemporary workers' struggles but instead displaced his immediate situation into the historical past; and that the male lineage of its protagonists slights the role of women workers in both the political and the cultural sphere. But against these must be counterposed not only the film's remarkable formal achievements and contemporary political relevance but also Park's radical transformation of the mode of feature-film production by involving the public as producers. While half the production cost of one-half-million dollars came from corporate capital (from Daewoo, which was then speculating in the movie business), the other half was financed by public subscription. That is to say, the contemporary working class was cinematically active, not simply in the idealist sense proposed in reception studies but in the materialist sense of enabling the film to be made. The film's conclusion of a scroll of the names of the "7,648 individuals who pledged financial support for this film and thereby made its production possible" brings them into the commonality created in their different ways by Chŏn, Kim, and Park himself; they become the "Prairie Fire" invoked in the English title that has been ignited by Chŏn's spark. Conversely the scroll aligns these three and the other workers with the labor activists whose demonstration introduces the film and with all the other Korean people who have successfully struggled for a popular democracy. The socialist narrative is reciprocated in the at-least partially socialist mode of film production. Overall, Park's combination of creating a sophisticated, widely celebrated film that affirms cinema's participation in working-class organizing and his cinematic success in including the public in its discourse and in so fundamentally involving them in its production is all but unique in recent cinema.

Framed though it may be, Park's endorsement of the political and aesthetic values of socialist realism reflects the film's specific historical moment, when the heritage of the radical film movements of the 1980s was fulfilled in the political and cinematic euphoria of the mid-1990s. Made in the period of the victory of minjung politics and the end of the U.S.-supported military dictatorship, *A Single Spark* mobilizes reflexive structures with an optimism and confidence that reflected a moment of expanding expectations about the possibility of progressive cultural work. Its overall structure and several of its motifs had, however, appeared in the year previously in another, even more complex, film about the present-day resonances of past heroic self-sacrifice, one made in a country undergoing a similar liberalization, Taiwan: Hou Hsiao Hsien's *Good Men, Good Women* (1995).

IV

Like *A Single Spark*, *Good Men, Good Women* is a doubled narrative with a *mise en abyme* structure that sets one film inside the other. But where in *A Single Spark* the interpolated narrative is intra-diegetically motivated and justified as the visualization of the biography that the protagonist is writing, here it is justified by being the representation of a play in which the main protagonist is acting. That protagonist, Liang Ching, is a generally dissolute and immoral young woman in contemporary Taiwan, while the play is set some fifty years earlier during the period of the Japanese colonial occupation and concerns a group of young Taiwanese patriots who go to Guangdong to help the Chinese Communist resistance and after the war return to continue Communist activity in Taiwan.[20] In the play, Liang Ching has the part of Jiang Bi-Yu, a leading figure in this group,

3 – The Name of a Desire: Recollections of Socialist Realism in East Asian Art Cinema

Figure 5. *Good Men, Good Women*: the young patriots leave for Guangdong; Liang Ching and Ah Wei; young patriots awaiting execution; Jiang Bi-Yu mourns over her husband's body.

so both characters are acted by the same woman, Annie Shizuka Inoh, a somewhat disreputable Taiwanese pop singer.

The film's first two shots, both quite long single takes (one-and-one-half minutes and four minutes, respectively) establish the distinction between the two main diegeses. The first, filmed in black-and-white with a stationary camera, shows a dozen or so young people wending their way across an agricultural landscape and singing a rousing but still plaintive song. When they have almost passed the camera, the scene ends and the film's title appears, but without any other details. The next scene, shot in color, opens in the broad daylight of the interior of an untidy urban apartment. The camera pans across the kitchen table and discovers Liang Ching, sleeping fully clothed on a heap of pillows. Wakened by the ringing phone, she gets a bottle of water from the refrigerator, and the camera pans down to a television set where a scene from Ozu's *Late Spring* is playing,[21] then up again to a fax machine. She tears out the just arrived sheet, which, it is later disclosed, is a faxed page from her own stolen diary. As her voice-over reads her earlier account – describing how on the third anniversary of Ah Wei's murder she had sex with "L" but that if she became pregnant it will be with Ah Wei's reincarnation – she goes into the bathroom.

Like *A Single Spark*, the film is an extended parallel montage constructed across the two contrasting diegeses initially introduced – one set in the distant past and one in the present and recent past – but in this case they are additionally complex in that each is internally divided into two periods. The result is an intricate pattern of cross-references across the four periods, especially as these revolve around Liang/Jiang, the only figure present in them all. The earlier period in Liang Ching's story reprises her involvement with Ah Wei, a gangster, several years earlier when she was a bar girl and singer; it reveals their tempestuous but passionate love for each other and desire to have a baby, as well as her drug addiction and his criminal involvement with corrupt politicians that leads to his being murdered. The scenes of her present life mostly show her in her apartment as she continues to receive the faxes from her stolen diary. In these she relives her involvement with Ah Wei, eventually admitting that she took blood money for his murder, and becoming increasingly frantic as she comes to believe that his ghost is addressing her via the faxes. This present also includes her relationship with her sister (who accuses her of having seduced her boyfriend and fights her) and refers to her participation in the play about the patriotic Communists.

That second diegesis grows out of the preparations and rehearsals for the play and modulates into the depiction of the history of the young patriots' involvement with Chinese communism. After Jiang Bi-Yu tells her father of her decision to marry Chung Hao-Tung, the group goes to Guangdong, but instead of being welcomed, they are accused of being Japanese spies and nearly executed. Finally freed, they work in a field hospital; Jiang and Chung have a baby but give it up for adoption in order to continue their struggle; and after the war they return to revolutionary organizing in Taiwan. As in Hou's earlier investigation of this period, *City of Sadness* (*Beiqing Chengshi*, 1989), there is no direct representation of the February 28 Incident in which an altercation between police and an old woman cigarette vendor in 1947 provoked a popular uprising against the Guomindang that led to the persecution of leftists and independent Taiwanese and resulted in the deaths of between 10,000 and 30,000 people – a period known as the "White Terror". But the group is seen to respond to the resistance against the Guomindang. They sell their homes to finance a journal, *The Enlightenment*, in which they plan to propagate their Marxist understanding of recent Chinese history, especially their interpretation of the February 28 Incident, not as a struggle between Mainlanders and Taiwanese but "as an issue of class conflict", that they agree to describe in "simple terms so people can understand". When the Korean War causes President Truman to make "Taiwan the frontline in the struggle against Communism", the Guomindang repression of leftists becomes acute, and the group's members are arrested and imprisoned. The film contains

3 – The Name of a Desire: Recollections of Socialist Realism in East Asian Art Cinema

extended scenes of them crowded in prison cells, waiting the court's verdict. In an ironically macabre reprise of their experiences in Guangdong, several of them are led out to execution. Posted lists of the dead reveal that Chung is among these. His family is told to retrieve his body, and the narrative concludes with Jiang, who has been released, weeping over her husband's body.

Though the long-takes, frequently stationary camera, and elliptical narration that had come to characterize Hou's idiosyncratic style are present in both diegeses,[22] nevertheless with all but one of its scenes shot in black-and-white, Jiang's story is distinct from Liang Ching's own. The idealistic revolutionary heroes' social commitment, their self-education, their subordination of their individual interests to those of the masses and the Revolution, and their final martyrdom inevitably recall the thematics of socialist realism, just as the story of incompetent gangsters, alienated bar girls, and the supernatural fax machine that links them recalls the contemporary urban melodramas that are ubiquitous in East Asian cinema. (As well as completing Hou's historical trilogy begun with *City of Sadness* and *The Puppetmaster* [*Hsimeng jensheng*, 1993], *Good Men, Good Women*, also incorporates the other main component of his oeuvre, the aesthetics of *Daughter of the Nile* [*Niluohe nuer*, 1987] and subsequent films about aimless and disaffected urban youth.) The contrasts between the two diegeses are further emphasized by a series of parallel narrative incidents: the scene where Liang Ching wonders if she may be carrying Ah Wei's baby cuts to the birth of Jiang Bi-Yu's baby; the scene where the patriots discuss and plan *The Enlightenment* follows the gangsters and politicians planning a big job and the murder of Ah Wei; and when Liang Ching regretfully admits she took blood money for Ah Wei's murder, the film cuts to Jiang Bi-Yu mourning over her husband's body.

Summarizing these differences are the words to songs prominent in each diegesis. As the young patriots march to Guangdong in the opening shot, their song manifests the socialist realism's revolutionary optimism: "When yesterday's sadness is about to die, when tomorrow's good cheer is marching towards us, then people say, Don't cry. So why don't we sing". But in the scene in the bar where Ah Wei conspires with the corrupt politicians just before he is murdered, Liang Ching takes the microphone and expresses her hopelessness: "All around I see gilded lives, but mine is tarnished. All around I hear words like jade, but mine are luckless". So the disparities are crystallized in the psychological and ethical contradictions that torment Liang Ching: the selfishness, narcissism, and amorality of her own life; its mediation and spectacularization in the ubiquitous cell phones, fax machines, television sets of "postmodern American culture"; and the visual confusion epitomized in the spinning disco lights of the nightclub where

63

Ah Wei is betrayed and killed. All these feel incommensurate with the ethical clarity and exemplary heroism of the Communist culture that inspires the Jiang Bi-Yu whom she enacts. To this extent, unlike *A Single Spark*'s continuities across the two diegeses that imply the present recreation of the earlier emancipatory struggle, Hou presents a more ambiguous relation, if not a categorical rupture, between the social possibilities of the two periods that may suggest the film is a satire on present-day Taiwan, as if "bad" or at least "mixed" contemporary characters were encountering the "good" characters of the past across the diegetic divide. The earlier era could sustain heroic and selfless commitment to working-class revolution, while the present is one of tawdry decadence and alienation. Such a disjuncture would insert an ironic nostalgia into the film's title: in the past, men and women were capable of being good, but not now.[23]

Because the montage structure can only juxtapose such key moments, leaving conclusions about their implications to the viewer, these parallels may signal similarities as easily as differences. Ah Wei's conspiracy, for example, may appear to resemble the Communists' plans and so, just as easily as being satirized by them, retroactively call them into question. As the film develops, such continuities begin to absorb the contrasts, and impossible nostalgia for Jiang's culture gradually turns into a more concrete possibility of its revival, even if only as the "name of a desire" felt by Liang Ching. Her plight subtends the film, and her voice often carries over from one diegesis to the other, as if she were discovering a truer self in her role in the play. As early as the second flashback to her life with Ah Wei, when they spend a joyful few days making love at a resort hotel, she says "I feel as if I am turning into Jiang Bi-Yu". And at the end, even as the faxes relentlessly remind her of her love for Ah Wei, it is not he but Jiang – also mourning her lost partner – who comes to life within her. In the closing scenes, when Chung's corpse is brought home, Jiang builds a small sacrificial fire. Her dead partner's voice-over reads his last letter to his parents and comrades, itself a parallel to the last letter from Ah Wei that comes to Liang Ching from her stolen dairy. As she sobs, the flames turn into color – exactly the motif and the filmic device that Park Kwang-Su independently and without knowledge of Hou's precedent would use the next year to indicate the porousness of time that allows the past to ignite the present.

As the film cuts to its final shot, a replay of the first in which the young revolutionaries walk towards the camera, Liang Ching's voice bemoans the fact that Jiang died just as they were leaving Taiwan to make a film version of their play about her. But this time the shot of the idealistic young people is in color like all the sequences in present-day Taipei, suggesting that though the utopian vision of Communist revolution and the aesthetics of socialist realism are not immediately available they may be passionately and productively imagined in the present. Just as Kim Yong-su reincarnates Chŏn Tae-il, so Liang Ching channels Jiang Bi-Yu, and the differences between the dieseges finally collapse: the play, *Good Men, Good Women*, that Liang Ching and her colleagues have been working on has now become their film, *Good Men, Good Women*; but that, of course, is subsumed into Hou's film, *Good Men, Good Women* – a migration of aesthetics and politics from one medium to another that, though it is not as diagrammatic, again resembles the migration of socialist realism across different mediums in *Two Stage Sisters*. As in the classic *en abyme* film *8 ½*, the dieseges converge: the film that is about to be made is the film we have been watching; the *énoncé* has swelled to occupy the *énonciation*; and perhaps all the personages are, in their different ways and according to the possibilities of their different historical moments, Good Men and Good Women.

Single Spark's optimistic use of socialist realism as the medium in which a heroic populist resistance could be rekindled in the present and *Good Men, Good Women*'s parallel but more complex and hesitant project reflect specific historical conjunctures. Both films were made in the capitalist sectors of countries that in the Cold War had been divided into capitalist and Communist zones, and so both reflected the spatial imminence of Communism and the Communist culture in the nations from which they had been divided – North Korea in the one case and the PRC in the other – which itself inevitably throws into sharp relief the tensions between the utopian promise of mid-century Communism and the forms it has subsequently taken. In both countries, control by U.S.-supported military dictatorships had only recently given way to an unprecedented social freedom, achieved by the combination of economic "miracles" and popular political engagement. Park's film reflected the success of minjung politics in Korea that led to the winning of democracy and the election of a civilian president in 1992. Hou's similarly reflected the liberalization that followed the lifting of martial law in Taiwan in 1987 (before which all discussion of the February 28 Incident had been prohibited): amnesty for political prisoners, the ending of the state of emergency, the other democratic reforms of Li Teng-hui's first administration, and the first presidential election in 1996 – a rapidly changing situation that allowed Hou to be categorically more explicit about Guomindang atrocities than he had been seven years earlier in *City of Sadness*. Both films were produced in places where the heritage of the dynamics of third world decolonization from Japan was unstably intertwined with both U.S. neocolonization and maneuverings against the second world and with the immediate possibility of reunification with, if not forced annexation by, their own second world neighbors.

Though the hopes and fears that surround these political developments in the last half of the twentieth century were not identical in South Korea and Taiwan, in both countries the sequence of political transformations within these macropolitical, world-historical terms were kaleidoscopically extreme: regimes of the right and the left, ideas of repression and liberation, and intimations of the first world and of the second replaced each other with a speed so dizzying as to create a political culture much more complicated than either Jameson's idea of allegories of national liberation or Ahmad's *grand récit* of a global oppositional second world culture would allow. The films' historical richness in reflecting this political intensity and the desires it sustains also makes them incomparably illuminating for those of us for whom socialism and socialist culture now seem so remote and unimaginable.

Notes

1. Fredric Jameson, "Third-World Literature in the Era of Multinational Capitalism", *Social Text* 15 (Fall 1986) 69; emphasis in original.

2. Aijaz Ahmad, "Jameson's Rhetoric of Otherness and the 'National Allegory'", *Social Text* 17 (Fall 1987): 4. The present essay does not assess the multiple terms of this debate as a whole.

3. Ahmad, "Jameson's Rhetoric", 8.

4. Ahamd, "Jameson's Rhetoric", 9. Perry Anderson has emphasized that in the early 1960s "a third of the planet had broken with capitalism" and that even in its Northern heartlands capitalism "was – and felt itself to be – under threat". Perry Anderson, "Renewals", *New Left Review* (Second Series) 1 (January–February 2000): 7.

5. Toby Miller, Nitin Govil, John McMurria, and Richard Maxwell, eds., *Global Hollywood* (London: British Film Institute, 2001), p. 17.

6. Published in 1990, Arjun Appadurai's "Disjuncture and Difference in the Global Cultural Economy" (*Public Culture* 2, no. 2 [Spring 1990)]: 1–11, 15–24, signally failed to recognize what since then has appeared to be the most radical form of disjuncture, Islamic fundamentalism.

7. *Kino-Eye: The Writings of Dziga Vertov* (Berkeley and Los Angeles: University of California Press, 1984), p. 22.

8. Those differences were figured in Glauber Rocha's appearance in *Vent d'Est* (1970) and the discussion of "the way towards a political cinema" it prompted. Though the formalist and semiotic elements in the Godardian critique of representation still faintly echo in academic film criticism, the *Groupe Dziga Vertov*'s political elaboration of it has been entirely lost. Perhaps the last time it was seriously bruited in anglophone writing was in Colin MacCabe, *Godard: Images, Sounds, Politics* (Bloomington: Indiana University Press, 1980), esp. pp. 49–78.

9. Régine Robin, *Socialist Realism: An Impossible Aesthetic*, trans. Catherine Porter (Stanford, Calif.: Stanford University Press, 1992), p. xviii.

10. A point of departure for a rethinking of socialist realism could well be Walter Benjamin's enthusiastic account of his observations of Soviet workers encountering Russian genre paintings like "The Poor Governess Arrives at the House of the Wealthy Merchant". Such art, he noted, "reaches out to the proletarian in a most familiar and assuring manner" and allows him "to recognize subjects from his own history ... [A]nd the fact that these scenes are rendered entirely in the spirit of bourgeois art does not in the least detract from them". Walter Benjamin, *Moscow Diary* (Cambridge, Mass.: Harvard University Press, 1986), pp. 77–78. It is important to remember that the critique of personality cults occurs *within* socialist realism itself, particularly in the USSR after 1956. See, for example, the argument that the "one-sided approach to many contemporary themes, the ostentatious pomposity, the nagging didactics and the insipid illustrativeness which [in the Stalinist period] plagued art served in the final analysis, to disguise the latent possibilities of socialist realism and engendered a narrow-minded, dogmatic application of the method". Oleg Sopotsinsky, "Soviet Art Is a Young Art", in *Art in the Soviet Union: Painting, Sculpture, Graphic Arts* (Leningrad: Aurora Art Publishers, 1978), pp. 12–13. For an account of the transformation of Soviet aesthetic theory since the death of Stalin and especially for the notion of socialist realism as a "Historically Open Aesthetic System", see Thomas Lahusen, "Socialist Realism in Search of Its Shores: Some Historical Remarks on the 'Historically Open Aesthetic System of the Truthful Representation of Life,'" in *Socialist Realism Without Shores*, ed. Thomas

Lahusen and Evgeny Dobrenko, special issue of *South Atlantic Quarterly* 94, no. 3 (Summer 1995): 661–686. The volume contains several other valuable essays, including, especially for the present purposes, Xudong Zhang, "The Power of Rewriting: Postrevolutionary Discourse on Chinese Socialist Realism", pp. 915–946. For overviews of Soviet socialist realism, see Thomas Lahusen, "Soviet Socialist Realism" in *The Encyclopedia of Literature and Politics*, ed. M. Keith Booker (Westport, Conn.: Greenwood, 2005) and Marek Bartelik, "Concerning Socialist Realism: Recent Publications of Russian Art", *Art Journal* 58, no. 4 (Winter 1999): 90–94. Julia F. Andrews's *Painters and Politics in the People's Republic of China, 1949–1979* (Berkeley and Los Angeles: University of California Press, 1994) is an extraordinarily accomplished history of Chinese art in the Maoist period. On North Korean art, see Jane Portal, *Art Under Control in North Korea* (London: Reaktion Books, 2005). On socialist realism in Vietnamese cinema, see John Tran, "Vietnamese Cultural Production during the American War", in *The Vietnam Era*, ed. Michael Klein (London: Pluto Press, 1990).

11. Anderson, "Renewals", p. 16.

12. Bylaws of the Union of Soviet Writers introduced at the First Soviet Writers' Congress in 1934, quoted in Herman Ermolaev, *Soviet Literary Theories 1917–1934: The Genesis of Socialist Realism* (Berkeley and Los Angeles: University of California Press, 1963), p. 197.

13. The work of Wang Guangyi manifests both strategies. See, for example, his "Great Castigation Series: Coca-Cola" (1993) and "Mao Zedong No. 1" (1988). Both are reproduced in Gao Minglu, ed., *Inside Out: New Chinese Art* (Berkeley and Los Angeles: University of California Press, 1998).

14. Lu Xun, "New Year's Sacrifice" in *Diary of a Madman and Other Stories*, trans. William A. Lyell (Honolulu: University of Hawaii Press, 1990), pp. 219–414. The woodcut by Gu Yuan (1919–1996) is now used throughout the country in middle-school Chinese textbooks. Though the scene in the film is set in 1948, the print in fact dates from the early to mid-1950s. (Thanks to Xiaobing Tang for this information.)

15. During the Communist period, *"New Year's Sacrifice"* was also reproduced as a large format comic book for both domestic and international distribution. See, for instance, *The New Year's Sacrifice*, illustrated by Yung Hsiang, Hung Jen, and Yao Chiao (Peking: Foreign Languages Press, 1978).

16. This is, of course, somewhat oversimplified for Lu Xun's status was subject to some re-evaluation in the various Chinese Communist Party ideological struggles. Nevertheless, even though his belief in the value of Western modernist literary models ran counter to Mao's preference for native peasant cultures expressed in his "Talks at the Yan'an Forum on Literature and Art", Lu Xun was virtually deified in the post-liberation period and reconstructed as an exemplar of socialist realism (a term that Mao himself introduced in the Yan'an talks). See Merle Goldman, "The Political Use of Lu Xun in the Cultural Revolution and After" in *Lu Xun and His Legacy*, ed. Leo Ou-fan Lee (Berkeley and Los Angeles: University of California Press, 1985), pp. 180–196. The film itself participates in this rewriting of Lu Xun in terms compatible with socialist realism: as Tang points out, "'New Year's Sacrifice' contains a first-person narrator who on going back to his hometown to visit his relatives encounters a miserable old woman, who in turn provokes a deep existential self-questioning on the part of the narrator, a modern-educated but indecisive and feeble-minded intellectual. In other words, in this text there is a very complex relationship between the narrator and the victim, between narration and reality. Written in the early 1920s, Lu Xun's story predated the articulation of a socialist realist aesthetic, even its predecessor in revolutionary literature or mass literature. Gu Yuan's print and real-life efforts to adapt the story into theater in the 1950s necessarily remove the first-person narrator and present Xianglin's Wife directly to the viewer/audience. This change reflects one central principle of socialist realism, i.e., removal of ambiguity or ambivalence, which are nonetheless fundamental values to modernism" (personal correspondence). The status of *Two Stage Sisters* was even more precarious. Personal and doctrinal conflicts within the party caused it to be attacked while it was still in production, and it was not publicly released until after the Cultural Revolution. See Gina Marchetti, "*Two Stage Sisters*: The Blossoming of a Revolutionary Aesthetic", in *Transnational Chinese Cinemas: Identity, Nationhood, Gender*, ed. Sheldon Hsiao-peng Lu (Honolulu: University of Hawai'i Press, 1997), pp. 75–78. The single indispensable anglophone history of post-Liberation Chinese cinema remains Paul Clark's *Chinese Cinema: Culture and Politics Since 1949* (Cambridge, U.K.: Cambridge University Press, 1987). For an exemplary analysis of the complications in a Chinese socialist realist film and in Chinese filmmaking during the 1940s and 1950s, see Esther C.M. Yau, "Compromised Liberation: The Politics of Class in Chinese Cinema of the early 1950s" in *The Hidden Foundation: Cinema and the Question of Class*, eds. David E. James and Rick Berg (Minnesota: University of Minnesota Press, 1996), pp. 138–172. Xudong Zhang cites Cia Shiyong, a Chinese critic, as arguing that Soviet films, especially Vasiliev's *Chapaev*, "set the standard for socialist realism" and that their influence improved "the quality of Chinese realism ... by providing more sophisticated film techniques and a dimension of socialist humanism". See *Chinese Modernism in the Era of Reforms* (Durham, N.C.: Duke University Press, 1997), p. 220.

17. For a consideration of recent reflexive East Asian political films, see my "Art / Film/Art Film: *Chihwaseon* and its Contexts", *Film Quarterly* 59, no. 2 (Winter 2005–2006): 4–17.

18. For background information on both the film itself and the politic developments it represents, see Seung Hyun Park, "The Memory of Labor Oppression in Korean Cinema: The Death of a Young Worker in *Single Spark* (1995)",

Asian Cinema 11, no. 2 (Fall–Winter 2000): 10–23. Park (21) affirms that the character Kim Yong-su was based on an actual antigovernment activist, Cho Young-Rae, who did write a book about Chŏn while on the run from the police.

19. As Park Kwang-su himself has argued, "The story of Chŏn Tae-il embodied in black and white is not that of a person who historically existed but that of a concept (not a memory) thought of by a man named Kim Young-su". See David E. James, "Opening the Channels of Communication: An Interview With Film Director Park Kwang-su", *Korean Culture* 23, no. 2 (Summer 2002): 17.

20. These events are all historically factual, but Hou derived the narrative from a short story published in 1988, "Song of the Covered Wagon" ("Huang mache zhi ge") by Lan Bozhou. Though historically accurate, the story is told by multiple narrators and is structured musically. I am indebted for this and other background information to Sylvia Li-chun's excellent essay, "Two Texts to a Story: Representing White Terror in Taiwan", *Modern Chinese Literature and Culture* 16, no. 1 (Spring 2004): 37–64. June Yip's "Constructing a Nation: Taiwanese History and the Films of Hou Hsiao-hsien" in *Transnational Chinese Cinemas*, ed. Lu, pp. 139–168, is also valuable. Of the relatively few anglophone reviews the film has received, David Walsh's "History and Sadness: Hou Hsiao-hsien's *Good Men, Good Women*", *World Socialist Web Site* www.wsws.org/articles/2000/aug2000/hou-a12.shtml is especially intelligent. Accessed 12 August 2000.

21. It is the scene where Noriko cycles with the young man we are led to believe is her suitor. Though it is probably simply an homage to Ozu's formal influence and to Shochiku, the Japanese studio that produced *Late Spring* and coproduced *Good Men, Good Women*, some of *Late Spring*'s concern with parent-child obligations do echo in Hou's film.

22. My argument would have been stronger had there been a socialist realist movement in progressive Taiwanese theater of this period that Hou might have been supposed to reference, but this theater was in fact avant-garde, nonlinear, and stylized. (Thanks to John Weinstein for this information.) The formal qualities of Hou's filmmaking have received more attention in anglophone commentary than the historical determinants on it, though one can provisionally point to the contradictory heritage of "health realism" (a Guomindang didactic cinema mandated to depict capitalist life in Taiwan in a positive way, and, so, inversely parallel to the PRC's socialist realism) during the "golden era" of Taiwanese cinema in the 1960s, as well as the emergence of nativist literary realism in the 1960s and 1970s associated with leftist politics and opposed to the literary modernism introduced by Guomindang writers after 1949. For this last, see Sung-Sheng Yvonne Chang, *Modernism and the Nativist Resistance: Contemporary Chinese Fiction from Taiwan* (Durham, N.C.: Duke University Press, 1993). David Bordwell's chapter, "Hou, or Constraints" in *Figures Traced in Light: On Cinematic Staging* (Berkeley and Los Angeles: University of California Press, 2005), is the most authoritative formalist account of Hou's work and its place in the Taiwanese New Cinema.

23. The closest to a statement by Hou himself relevant to this question that I have found is the following very oblique comment: "Of course, society is changing all the time ... . In the past we might have experienced the coming of a new epoch with its revolutions and suppressions, all the familiar things under an authoritarian regime. You would harbour a revolutionary sentiment or embrace socialism. But now it's completely changed. Now, in this age, which is absolutely modern and individualistic, there is this so-called 'unbearable lightness of being'. But essentially it's still very heavy. This lightness of an individual's love and feelings, however, has to deal with a world that's as hard as a rock". Hou Hsiao-hsien, "In Search of New Genres and Directions for Asian Cinema", trans. and ed. Lin Wenchi, *Rouge* 1 (2003), www.rouge.com.au/index.html.

Chapter Four   Tradition and the Movies: The Working-Class Asian American Avant-Garde in Los Angeles

"What is Chinese Tradition and what is the movies?"
Maxine Hong Kingston, *The Woman Warrior*

Chan is Missing
Wayne Wang

Charlie Chan Is Dead
Jessica Hagedorn

"And we were all the sons of Charlie Chan"
Frank Chin, *Gunga Din Highway*

I.

During her meditation on the relative importance of the nation and of family idiosyncrasies in the formation of Chinese American identity, Maxine Hong Kingston suddenly interjects an even more confounding uncertainty: "What is Chinese tradition and what is the movies?"[1] Each term in her antinomy has a spectrum of implications. Will identity be found in Asia – or in the U.S.; in a premodern, pre-industrial culture – or in a modern industrial culture; in culture that emerges in organic social processes – or in corporate commodity entertainment? Though in Kingston's formulation, these and other resonances are condensed, when unpacked they form a scaffold of competing images and vocabularies, of competing media systems and modes of cultural production, that all writers in the field must individually re-assemble. And if Kingston herself found her most important sources in Chinese tradition, other Asian Americans have turned to the movies. The works this essay considers in detail – *Sa-I-Gu*, a video made by Korean American women and *The Country of Dreams and Dust*, a collection of poems written by a Chinese American man – make their various selections from among the options Kingston's question implies. But both works were produced on the cultural margins in a way that can best be designated as avant-garde, and both encounter discriminations in ethnic and other forms of identity more complex than those Kingston envisaged. The present essay proposes a spatial and materialist reading of the two works and of the cultural situation they reflect.

Over the past decade, theoretical writing from several perspectives has recognized that the global restructuring of capital and changes in the U.S. immigration laws have produced population movements throughout the Pacific region, transforming both the commonalty designated by the term, "Asian American", and consequently the cultural activity associated with it. Coined in the late 1960s to reflect nationalistic political initiatives parallel to the black civil rights movement and the Chicano movement, Asian American initially referred to people of Chinese, Japanese, and Filipino ancestry who had lived in the United States for many generations (as many as seven in the case of Chinese), and whose recent engagement with the mother nation had been distended or sporadic at best. Since then, there has been a massive influx of new immigrants, coming from Korea, Viet Nam, Cambodia, and other East Asian countries that had previously been much less fully represented. These new immigrant communities are characterized by an unprecedented flexibility in movement between Asia and the U.S. and hence by newly complex territorial identifications.[2] As a result, the overall category, Asian American, has become de-stabilized, and fragmented into a plurality of subdivisions, producing vertiginous complications in the theorization of structural social division, and new obstacles to the building of social commonalties. These in turn have precipitated a crisis in the theorization of Asian American culture, more severe than those currently faced by the other ethnic groups in parallel to which it was initially formulated. Los Angeles has emerged as a privileged place for both the production and study of this new and newly complex Asian American culture. The concatenation of reasons for this extend and intensify the tension between the indigenous traditions of local communities and the entertainment industry that Kingston proposed, as well as concretizing them in the geography of the city.

If, as Walter Benjamin claimed, Paris was the capital of the nineteenth century, Los Angeles' situation as the capital of postmodernism and indeed late capital itself affords it an equivalent preeminence for the present time. Postmodern geographers have proposed the dispersed, polynucleated agglomeration of semi-autonomous communities in the basin proper and in the larger megalopolis that stretches almost unbroken from Santa Barbara to San Diego as the blueprint for the urban transformations of the twenty-first century. Their reconceptualizations of the city's significance are subtended by structural economic transformations: the de-industrialization of a heavy manufacturing sector based on armaments, aerospace, and automobiles, increased industrialization of craft economies (the entertainment industry and light manufacturing including textiles and furniture), and a hyper-expansion of the finance industries. Reflecting the city's pivotal role in the Pacific Rim economies, an influx of relatively wealthy immigrants have brought East Asian finance capital and multi-leveled exchanges of all kinds across the ocean. Concurrent with this immigration of wealth and the wealthy, there has been a massive immigration of poor and dispossessed people from Central America, but also of less privileged people from Asia.[3]

The figures for this are remarkable: before 1970, the majority of immigrants to the United States came from Europe, but since then most have been Latino or Asian. Currently half of all immigrants entering annually are from Asia, growing from 6 percent of the total in 1950–1960 to 36 percent in 1970–1980, and 48 percent in 1980–1990; these have recompositioned the population, decreasing the relative number of Chinese and especially Japanese, and introducing greatly enlarged proportions of Koreans and Asian Indians, as well as introducing Vietnamese, Laotians, Cambodians, Hmong and others. Most of them come to southern California: 88 percent of the inhabitants of Los Angeles Chinatown are foreign-born, and many of these and other Asian American immigrants speak little English.[4] In earlier periods, the arrival of previous immigrants in distinct waves, the lateral expansion of the city to accommodate them, and racist city administrative policies combined to make the city the most diversified, but also the most segregated in the country. Recent immigration has dramatically increased the long-standing social segmentation, leaving the central core surrounded by a virtual United Nations of "little" cities of different national heritages: along with the long-standing black and Latino communities and the old Chinatown and Little Tokyo, the city now includes a Koreatown, a Little Saigon, a Little India, and so on. Overall, then, the social structure of the city comprises two principle vectors: a strong centrifugal pull towards the decentered, relatively homogenous and segregated, local communities, where minority cultural initiatives develop, and an unusually powerful centripetal pull towards the integrated central economic, social, and cultural institutions, dominated by the entertainment industries.

The social and cultural tensions between assimilation and sustained ethnic identity are thus figured spatially in postmodern Los Angeles to a greater extent than in other cities. The powerful minority cultures that the city sustains are also confronted by the massive presence and gravitational pull of Hollywood and the corporate entertainment industry generally. Hollywood affects the city first as an all-pervading, all-colonizing system of spectacular representations, almost entirely inimical to minority and working-class self-consciousness. But it is also an economic system, an industry that holds out the promise of fame for some and employment for many. On both levels – as a textual system and as a mode of cultural production – it affects everything in the city, especially other forms of culture. Even if these are initially maverick or adversarial to it, they can only exist in dialogue with it; and even if their intention is to displace it, they often benefit from its resources in however small a way. Minority cultures in Los Angeles are then caught between "the tradition" and "the movies" in an extreme or paradigmatic fashion. And since there are so many of them, the city is a virtual laboratory for the examination of their relative development, and especially of the emergence of forms of Asian American cultural production that are marginal to the new mainstream Asian American culture; we may think of these as an Asian American avant-garde.

The literature associated with the previous long-standing, relatively homogenous and autonomous communities had reflected the transmission of indigenous traditions within them, and their conflicts with American society at large, especially as these were experienced differently by different generations of immigrants. The Asian American literary movement that began in the late 1960s proposed this writing as exemplary, and theorized it on the model of the cultural nationalism of the immediately prior black projects. The introduction to *Aiieeeee!*, the ground-breaking anthology of Asian American writing published in 1974, emphatically asserted the specificity of Chinese American and Japanese American identities, each of which was distinct from either Asian or (white) American forms – and especially from any notion of being split between the two, the "myth of being either/or and the equally goofy concept of the dual personality". Neither American nor Asian culture alone was capable of addressing that specificity, though the former had previously hindered its recognition: "American culture, equipped to deny us the legitimacy of our uniqueness as American minorities, did so".[5] To mobilize that uniqueness, the editors of *Aiieeeee!* turned to harshly realist novels like Louis Chu's *Eat a Bowl of Tea* (1961) and John Okada's *No-No Boy* (1957) that refused both the reassurance of a reliably passive immigrant community and the exotic stereotypes of mainstream versions of Asian American life, such as Earl Derr Biggers' Charlie Chan novels. And, again in parallel to contemporaneous black and Chicano nationalist writing, these were thought to document a unique historical experience and a similarly unique sensibility traced in local speech patterns: "Okada", the editors argued, "changes voices and characters inside his sentences, running off free form but shaping all the time … . The style itself is an expression of the multivoiced schizophrenia of the Japanese American compressed into an organic whole. It's crazy, but it's not madness".[6]

4 – Tradition and the Movies: The Working-Class Asian American Avant-Garde in Los Angeles

Titled "Fifty Years of Our Whole Voice", this essay proposed that the three stable Asian American communities were capable of expression in the fullness of an organic voice. Since that moment, the international best-selling novels of Maxine Hong Kingston and Amy Tan, and David Henry Hwang's Obie and Tony winning plays have transformed the horizon of Asian American literature in American culture overall – a mass cultural recognition that also precipitated vituperative polemics from the older school. In his introduction to *The Big Aiiieeeee!*, an update of *Aiiieeeee!*, and in a brilliant, coruscating satirical novel, *Gunga Din Highway*, Frank Chin attacked the historical distortions and fabrications of these writers, especially their denigration of Chinese manhood, which, he argued, parlayed their work into popularity with the white racist hegemony.[7] Reaffirming *Aiiieeeee!*'s earlier position, Chin invoked a heroic Chinese tradition, developed in the ancient literary classics and preserved into the present in the tongs, shop-signs, phrasebooks, and other popular aspects of Chinatown. But rather than being easily available, this tradition has been virtually swamped by mass culture, and especially its degraded representations of Asians, a degradation whose terms Kingston and Tan, he argued, reproduced. For Chin, Hollywood movies are the ether in which Chinese Americans have been forced to breathe, the language in which they have been constructed. *Gunga Din Highway* attempts to reassemble the unique but hybrid identity he had previously celebrated, and indeed to integrate "Chinese tradition" and "the movies" as together the context framing Chinese American identity. An audacious combination of the structure of Chinese myth with the fabric of American pop culture, it takes its point of departure from the "Oath of the Peach Garden" in the 14th Century Chinese historical novel, *Romance of the Three Kingdoms*, but uses it to tell the story of Ulysses, the son of the Cantonese opera heartthrob-turned-Hollywood-star who played Charlie Chan's number four son and other Asians in Hollywood. For Ulysses, reality is a palimpsest underwritten by movies and constantly shadowed by them; they are ubiquitous – seen, imagined, or recollected; in theaters, flickering in black and white on restaurant televisions, or subjectively projected on the surface of everyday life. His life is the "Movie about Me", and after a period as a movie critic, he ends up in Hollywood writing screenplays like the *Night of the Living Hollywood Dead* and the *Night of the Living Third World Dead*. But the only substantial female character in the novel is a caricature of Maxine Hong Kingston and Amy Tan.

Though *Gunga Din Highway* is an inspired recreation of the multi-voiced verbal virtuosity Chin found in John Okada, his polemic produces a reification parallel to the one he attributed to Kingston and Tan: his heroically-male Asian American nationalist essentialism confronts their feminist Asian American essentialism in a non-negotiable blankness. Recent theoretical work subsequent to his polemic has attempted to transcend this impasse, so as to accommodate the heterogeneous plurality now proposed as the dominant situation of Asian Americans and the new relations among them produced by new immigration patterns, and by the ease, speed, and relative cheapness of contemporary trans-Pacific travel. Modifying the finality of the break with the mother country, these conditions produce mobile identities not exclusively posited on either the culture of origin or a new, composite one. Developing in a context dominated by post-structural theories of subjectivity, theoretical response to the new forms of identity has emphasized the costs of the presumption of an organic uniformity and the repression of difference in Asian American communities. Elaine Kim, for example, whose *Asian American Literature: An Introduction to the Writings and Their Social Context*[8] was the breakthrough academic critical text of the earlier model, has historicized that period:

> Given the magnitude of general ignorance about Asian Americans, it was difficult to do anything but play a dead straight part. Dealing with subtleties, hybridities, paradoxes, and layers seemed almost out of the question when so much effort had to be expended simply justifying Asian Americans as discursive subjects in the first place ... . [but now] The lines between Asian and Asian American, so crucial to identity formations in the past, are increasingly blurred: transportation to and communication with Asia is no longer daunting, resulting in new crossovers and intersections and different kinds of material and cultural distances today.[9]

These "new crossovers and intersections" are reflected in Asian American cultures in Los Angeles; but also reflected is the most important issue determining the history of Asian American immigrants, a component that neither Kingston nor Chin – nor the poststructuralists – address in any detail, that is, the position of Asian immigrants in the movement of capital, and so the question of class. As the editor of a recent collection of essays on the new Asian American literatures recognizes, "Of the vectors in Asian American literary studies ... class issues have perhaps been the most neglected to date".[10]

Los Angeles was hardly mentioned in *Aiiieeeee!*, and of its fourteen writers only one – Hisaye Yamamoto – had any deep personal connection with the city. But, because of the demographic changes, especially the maturation of the children of post-1965 immigrants, and the flourishing of identity politics among the social movements that replaced the systemic social confrontations of the 1960s – all fueled by the endorsement of various state and educational subventions – a great expansion of Asian American cultural activity in the city was virtually inevitable. Some of this has been relatively mainstream. Though they have not had the cross-over, mass cultural success of *The Joy Luck Club*, the novels of Cynthia Kadohata have been well-received. In her first, *The Floating World*, a *bildungsro-*

4 – Tradition and the Movies: The Working-Class Asian American Avant-Garde in Los Angeles

man that echoes an actual biographical narrative translated from the Japanese,[11] the heroine's itinerary brings her to Los Angeles, where Kadohata herself continues to live and write, and where she set her next novel, *In the Heart of the Valley of Love*.[12] And Kim Ronyoung's novel, *Clay Walls* chronicles several generations of a Korean American immigrant family who come to Los Angeles in the 1920s, emphasizing the conflicts with the Anglos, but also the struggles against the Japanese annexation of Korea.[13]

Other innovations have sustained a greater independence from the culture industries, but even these have been shaped by an institutional urban structure pivoted on Hollywood. Independent filmmaking has inevitably been the most directly affected. The main source of the traditions of minority filmmaking in Los Angeles was the University of California, Los Angeles (UCLA) film school, whose dominant function is to train workers for the industry. In response to popular demands, in 1968 an affirmative action program, not in the film school proper but in an ethno-communications department associated with it, admitted black, Chicano, Asian American and Native American students. The two successful developments the program nurtured were quite different. While the black filmmakers, most notably Charles Burnett, focused on feature-length narratives capable of negotiating entry into the commercial industry, the Asian Americans created an institution committed to grass-roots documentaries about working-class communities, Visual Communications. Since the early-1970s, Visual Communications has nourished a very prolific Asian American working-class film and video culture.[14]

These Los Angeles-specific determinants of the overall transformation of the Asian American commonalty resonate fully in two recent works made in the city, respectively one of the first independent videos by Korean Americans focusing on working-class women; and the other, the first book of poems by a gay Chinese American man. In them, the unique, stable hybrid identity, defined against both the nation of origin and the white American hegemony and centered on the heterosexual males of Chin's bachelor communities or the defensive commonalty of Kingston's feminism, is reconstructed but in quite opposite ways. In the video, the Korean American identity appears as all but continuous with Korea itself, and it is defined, not against a white hegemony, but among and against competing ethnic groups, especially blacks. In the poetry, a series of shifting identifications disperses the specifically Chinese American lyric persona into a collective Chinese American subject, and then into a representativeness that includes the entire Pacific Basin and human kind as a whole. Both internationalize the general model of alternative cultural production in Los Angeles outlined above, and in both cases, the displacement of categorical ethnic and gender identities by hybrid, unstable identities begins to allow visibility to what has previously been repressed, that is, class. Class is a position in respect to ownership of the means of production and the extraction of surplus labor that is simultaneously objective yet nevertheless controlled by human agency. The implications of class positioning in the two works make it possible to raise the question of the role of capital in the production of minority cultures, and so to raise the possibility of social identities constructed across race and gender divisions, that is to say, class consciousness and solidarity.[15]

II.

Sa-I-Gu is an independent VHS videotape collaboratively produced by three Korean American women, Dai Sil Kim-Gibson, Christine Choy, and Elaine Kim.[16] It is dedicated to Edward Song Lee, an eighteen-year-old Korean American youth, shot and killed by mistake a month away from his nineteenth birthday by another Korean American during the 1992 rebellion that followed the not-guilty verdict returned on the police who brutalized Rodney King. Framed by footage of Lee's funeral, it consists of taped interviews with half-a-dozen first-generation immigrant women (beginning with his mother), all of whom had built-up business that were looted and burned.[17] The voice-over asserts that, though these Korean women "were caught in the L.A. crisis ... they speak for no one but themselves". They describe their efforts and sacrifices, reflect on the destruction of their lives' work, and explain their political movement to obtain reparations from the city. Since the narrative is one of the failure of immigration, the tropes of diaspora literature appear in oblique or inverted terms. Immigration has brought them a loss not a gain in wealth; their businesses were not created in America but funded with capital from the homeland, and now their survival depends on further homeland support, for as the currents of Pacific Rim economics change direction, the prosperous ones are those who stayed behind.[18] Most crucial of all, families are broken and sons are lost because the generations of families were catastrophically divided, not by the Pacific, but by newly complex class divisions within the United States.

While in fact more looting was done by Latinos than by blacks, the tape – like mass media accounts – revolves around black-Korean relations. The Koreans feel betrayed by the blacks, and are oblivious to the fact that their businesses, often financed by capital brought from Korea and bank-loans not available to blacks themselves, became a symbol of a domestic apartheid. They feel themselves to be the scapegoats for systemic white racism, which, they contend, also operated in

4 – Tradition and the Movies: The Working-Class Asian American Avant-Garde in Los Angeles

Figure 1. *Sa-I-Gu*: Korean American women speaking for themselves.

media accounts of the rebellion that concealed the underlying responsibility of the white establishment, especially the police who stood by watching the looting and burning. Local media encouraged understanding of it as a black-Korean conflict by showing primarily black looters and Korean snipers defending their stores.[19] All these misapprehensions and misrepresentations are, of course, fueled by class issues, and especially by the contradictory class-location of the store owners; as petty-bourgeois, they appear to themselves to be workers, while to the non-capitalized, under-employed African Americans they appear to be privileged exploiters, and in fact are presented as such in the black nationalist rhetoric promoted in the mass media. Because the tape's premise is to allow these owners the self-expression otherwise denied to them, some of their sense of their class advantages and disadvantages do occasionally come through, and indeed, accompanied by a cut-away to a family in Beverly Hills, one of the women recognizes the fundamental significance of pandemic wealth disparity in Los Angeles. But, in the absence of any speaker capable of elaborating the system of class-relations underpinning black-Korean relations or the rebellion generally, the only frames of analysis available to the video are those of the speakers themselves, that is, gender and especially race.

Figure 2. *Sa-I-Gu*: funeral of Edward Song Lee; the riots; Korean American self-defense; happy family in Beverly Hills.

Whatever the necessity of a class analysis of the underpinnings of the tragedy, it would be gratuitous to demand it of the beleaguered and traumatized women in *Sa-I-Gu*, whose self-construction exclusively in terms of race only reflects their interpellation in the same terms in all aspects of U.S. culture, especially the culture industries. But the process of that identity-construction and something of the repressions it entails may be glimpsed allegorically as it were in the interaction between the different media systems documented within the tape. Because the tape sees its own function as that of putting into circulation the images suppressed by the sensationalist mass media and so to enable the Korean women to gather support for their political organization and demand for reparations, it follows the traditions of American avant-garde film, marking its difference from corporate media with the signs of amateur, artisanal practices. It is an elaborated home-video that relies heavily on family snapshots and personal reminiscences to cement a sense of group solidarity on the most personal level. But despite this self-positioning in domestic, ethnically homogenous space, *Sa-I-Gu*'s political aspiration obliges it to confront the discourse of the hegemony, that is, the mass media.

4 – Tradition and the Movies: The Working-Class Asian American Avant-Garde in Los Angeles

All aspects of the Rodney King case were mediated through and to a large extent pre-scripted by the entertainment industries. Appropriated into corporate culture, George Holliday's home-video of the beating was repeatedly broadcast both before and during the trial, and the live televising of the rebellion itself was used by the rioters to direct their activities. Both before and after the King incident, the entertainment industry had exploited several highly inflammatory representations of Korean American storekeepers.[20] On the other hand, for the Koreans who speak in the tape, the initial desire to emigrate had been fueled by Hollywood: one of the women explains, "We dreamed about America like we saw in the movies [but] when we got here it's not like that, not white and blonde but like Mexico". Her unselfconscious racism epitomizes the immigrants' own internalization of racist media images – but also the obsolescence of the older white/non-white binary. In an era of multi-ethnic pluralism, the same forces that allow the dispersal of identity into new hybridities can, in the absence of the trans-ethnic class solidarity once supplied by socialism, also produce the opposite effect, new forms of defensive and offensive reification.

Such is the cacophony of media images in which *Sa-I-Gu* attempts to establish a stable voice. The women can speak their grief in their own video and Korean and/or U.S.-English verbal languages, but explanation of its causes in public events demands their confrontation with public communications industries. To tell their story fully, they have to tell the story of their relation to industrial culture. And so, along with the home-video footage, the tape re-presents stills of pages from newspapers, both dominant and Korean, and also news footage of the riots derived from the news-media. To express themselves, the women have to refer to the mendacious representations that have been so damaging, but try to change their meaning in their re-presentation of them; by superimposing their own voices and the Korean language over them, they try to make the mass media texts speak from Korean American perspectives.

A summary instance of these circulations across different media and languages, and of the shifting position of Koreans between other ethnic identities occurs in the account of Lee's death. He was killed, not by a black, but by a Korean who mistook him for a black or Latino looter; that is, because at a crucial moment in the rebellion his ethnic identity was unclear. In the most plangent section of the tape, Lee's mother recalls her search for her lost son, describing a quest that takes her, not through the streets, but through the conflicting meanings of images in different media apparatuses. After discovering that her son is missing, she sees a photograph of a dead Korean youth in the *Korea Times*, the daily, Korean-language newspaper. The youth appears to be wearing a *black* T-shirt, and since her

POWER MISSES II: CINEMA, ASIAN AND MODERN

Figure 3. *Sa-I-Gu*: news accounts of the death of Edward Song Lee.

son went out in a *white* T-shirt, the photograph gives her hope, even though it shows a dead Korean. But then in the (*white*-owned) *Los Angeles Times*, she finds a *colored* version of the same picture, and there the *black* T-shirt is revealed to be a *red* one: "What looked like black in the Korean paper", she explains, "was my son's blood".

This search among images in different media systems and its tragic conclusion offers itself as a rhetorical figure, a poetic illustration of the way ethnic identity is constructed. As Frank Chin so vividly demonstrated and as alternative media like *Sa-I-Gu* recognize, identity no longer has recourse to an origin outside the mass media. One-on-one encounters of the most personal kind – across the counter of a convenience store or through the scope of a rifle – are all textually overwritten. Minority identity is created in the textual struggle between different "movies", and so it is crucially determined by the struggle between those systems of cultural production and distribution controlled by the corporations and those with some degree of freedom, that is, between capitalist and popular cultures. Because poetry remains the medium most free from capital investment, it is where working people find their truest voice.

III.

Poets, the only artists that Hollywood cannot appropriate, were never recruited like artists in other mediums in the way that made the city such a glittering cultural mecca in the 1930s and 1940s. And so, without this institutional support, poetry had almost no presence in the city's bourgeois culture, nor did it have an energetic vernacular tradition equivalent to those in New York, Chicago, or San Francisco. Such a popular tradition did not develop until the beat era in the bohemian community of Venice, with the breakthrough coming later in the decade when Charles Bukowski, a German immigrant, resuscitated the colloquial working-class idiom of the 1940s Italian American novelist, John Fante. Bukowski's robust, often scatological vernacular verse was seized upon, first by Wanda Coleman and other working-class black women poets, and then a popular poetry was galvanized during the flowering of anti-corporate media around punk in the 1980s. This working-class poetry was sustained by individual editors and small, independently produced magazines, all but entirely outside corporate culture. Its summary anthology appeared in 1985 in Bill Mohr's *Poetry Loves Poetry*.[21] Asian American entry to this field was signaled four years later in *Invocation L.A.: Urban Multicultural Poetry*.[22] Correctly designated itself as "the first anthology that truly represents the multicultural character of the city",[23] this volume included four Asian American poets: Christine Choi Ahmed, Sesshu Foster, Russell Leong, and Amy Uyematsu. Since then, the last three of these have each published one or more single-author collections, all mobilizing visions of the place of Asian Americans in the city's multi-ethnic working-class communities.[24] Employing a medium with no capacity for capital valorization, these poets all exist on the extreme edges of commercial feasibility; unlike the cross-over Asian American novels which, as Frank Chin has pointed out, are all "published by big commercial houses", they are published by small independent presses.[25] Such are the historical, geographical, and social specificities in Russell Leong's collection, *The Country of Dreams and Dust* that, although its framing ideology is Buddhist, finally the best characterization of it can only be "socialist realism", even though it makes possible a wholly new meaning for that ideal.

Taking its title from an anonymous graffito, "As a traveler in wind and dust ... / I crossed to the end of the ocean", found on the walls of Angel Island Immigration Station, where Pacific country immigrants were processed into the United States, *The Country of Dreams and Dust* invokes an originary Chinese American literature and its crucial trope: exile. But a footnote to the title sequence reveals the source of the words, *meng* (dreams) and *chen* (dust) in Chinese Buddhism. From the beginning, then, historical experience of Chinese emigration is linked with a theory of the human condition as a whole. Buddhism supplies an appropriate vocabulary for the human story, not because – or not simply because – it is any longer purely Asian,[26] but because axiomatic in it is the delusion of belief in self-identity. It thus provides a fully articulate logic of perpetual dissemination, while still retaining the utopian, modernist socialist dream of universal liberation, lost in both identity micro-politics and the cynical ideologies of postmodernism. The voice of the book thus floats across a wide range of human (non)identities, and is informed by compassion for all of them.

The first of its three sections is mostly personal and autobiographical. In the second, different lyric personae narrate the collective subjectivity of the Chinese and eventually Vietnamese people through the history of many forms of Pacific diaspora: first, a collective "we" of the nineteenth century emigrants to San Francisco; then a girl, terrorized by the very missionaries who save her from prostitution; and then patriots who organize to send aid to China during the Japanese invasion. From these, a controlling dramatic voice emerges, revealed in quick sketches of 1950s Chinatown family life, the speaker's youth in the era of the U.S. invasion of Viet Nam, when he is molested by a Presbyterian minister, and his early-1970's travels in Asia. After his father's death severs the personal connection with China, this voice again dissolves into others: it speaks as a Vietnamese woman, rejected by both her family and the GI husband who brought her to Los Angeles; and then as Liu Xiang, the Tiananmen Square activist who disguises himself as a Hong Kong Chinese while trying to escape. Finally, the narrator returns to his own voice and his own specific experience: living in a tract home in Little Saigon, the Vietnamese section of Los Angeles where, between marauding police and street gangs on the one hand and the Buddhist monastic community on the other, he observes the death of his friends from AIDS.[27] And the third section deals with recent catastrophes from different places in the Pacific Basin, including the murder of six Thai Buddhist monks in Phoenix and the 1991 Bangladesh floods. The final sequence of seven poems, "Unfolding Flowers, Matchless Flames", concerns the Los Angeles rebellion, conceptualizing it in images drawn from the U.S. invasion of Viet Nam, but framing the whole in Buddhist terms of redemption.

These expanding areas of concern are reflected in a similar expansion of the frame of reference supplied by intertexts in each section; the first revolves around personal airmail letters from China; the poems in the second are prefixed by quotations from a nineteenth-century missionary phrase book, the vehicle of English and Christianity simultaneously; and the points of departure in the third are newspaper accounts of the different events. Some – though not all – of the

4 – Tradition and the Movies: The Working-Class Asian American Avant-Garde in Los Angeles

issues the book sets in play may be observed in the first section, in "Aerogrammes", which re-presents the letters from relatives the narrator meets on a trip back to his clan village in Sunwui County in Guangdong. The visit took place in 1984, after the collapse of Maoist isolationism that had kept previous generations of the family apart. In the letters and the responses to them, all the intricate and often conflicting emotions occasioned by the geographical reorientation and restoration of family relations are figured in images redolent of capitalist transformation. The guide drinks Coca Cola, and cartons of Marlboros are the expected visiting-gifts. Nevertheless, the umbilical connection remains; family members are discovered, and the villagers take him to a small house:

> I open the door.
> My father stares down
> from a wartime portrait on the wall.
> I cannot deny the relation
> When all the children
> in the room
> suddenly chime, "Uncle".[28]

This first poem, then, asserts a "relation" with China, whose obligations the clan members press after he returns to the United States. One wants money to open a dry goods shop and another wants five thousand dollars to buy a condominium. These letters from home eventually become almost comical as the transparency of the attempts at exploitation reverse the generic conventions of diaspora literature. In minority literature, vernacular writing from the homeland or from first-generation immigrants who had some unmediated experience of the homeland is often used as a sign of national authenticity; Olivia, the narrator of *The Floating World*, for example, is guided to a sense of her own identity by reading the Japanese-language diary kept by her deceased grandmother. But unlike this voice, or unlike the voice of China that, through her mother, tells Maxine Hong Kingston stories of warrior women, the voices from Leong's China (transmitted by the airletter itself stamped with the languages of modern Pacific communications: "par avion", "via airmail", "hung-kung") can tell only of the money-grubbing of market capitalism, itself an innovation introduced from the West. The ironies of the homeland's failure to produce an authentic self-image become especially complex in the fourth aerogram, when the family attempts to bring him back into the clan via marriage. They send news of "a young lass, / still single / and supple as a willow".[29]

As the text contains many suggestions that Leong is gay, such a re-insertion into the clan and transmission of the cultural heritage are not an option for him. In response, all he can do is "cruise" Hollywood Boulevard, the haunt of "Hookers

83

of both sexes". In the final poem of the sequence, the country girl writes to offer herself in marriage. The gesture recalls the "picture brides" of earlier emigrants, but instead of sending a photo of herself, she sends one "of a ten-story hotel / topped by a revolving restaurant".[30] The narrator's failure to reply halts the communication; its meaning is suspended for him until it is suddenly put into focus by a newspaper report about a Chinese businessman planning to export Chinese farmworkers to the U.S. as if they "were just concessions / for export – / like oil or silk slippers".[31] At this point, the whole net of personal transactions – the nostalgia of the return to the family home, the tracing of family lines and the testing of family ties – is revealed as his own recapitulation of a century-old social movement directed by capital.

The extraordinary range of inquiries Leong mobilizes in the book are finally coherent, then, not inside some narrowly defined ethnicity or the limited horizons of a closed ghetto community, but across the larger political reticulations of the Pacific century. His work is a triumph of the diasporic imagination in which the relations between the different contexts in which identity is formed – sexual, familial, linguistic, geographical, religious, political, and so on – are reconfigured across the macro-political transformations of the Pacific Rim and the migratory circulations they entail. Because of the world-historical significance of these transformations, Leong's work should not be thought of as minority, but rather as having the representatives of the great realisms of the past, as an equivalent of the historical novel. But it is nevertheless specifically lyric in its mode. The plurality of voices, capable of but not tied to narrative, and the synecdochical use of brief vignettes to imply extended historical scenes are essentially imagistic devices that, fortuitously (or not) are also, but in a different way, Asian American; their provenance is in the tradition of western modernism developed by Ezra Pound upon a theory of the pictorial basis of the Chinese ideogram, and more recently renewed by Gary Snyder. It is a very cinematic language, not the language of the industrial cinema, but that of Leong's other field of activity, the avant-garde cinema.

VI.

Both *Sa-I-Gu* and *The Country of Dreams and Dust* were crucially motivated by the April 1992 rebellion that followed the not-guilty verdict in the trial of the Los Angeles Police Department officers who beat Rodney King, a concatenation of events that stand as a decisive figuration of capitalist social relations in the city and of their penetration and manipulation by corporate media. As a coda to *Sa-I-Gu* and *Dreams and Dust*, we may recall that the chain of events leading to

4 – Tradition and the Movies: The Working-Class Asian American Avant-Garde in Los Angeles

the hyperbolic public re-enactment of the state violence initially perpetrated on Rodney King, this time performed by the dispossessed as the police stood idly by, was initiated by a home video of unprecedented political effect. George Holliday's tape appeared, however inadvertently, to fulfill all the dreams of the avant-garde cinemas of the 1960s. But it was distributed, not in the alternative cinemas pioneered in this tradition, but in the corporate media industries, within their contextualization. There it found a massive, indeed global circulation, but there its meaning was so thoroughly perverted that it fueled, not movements against police malfeasance, but increased racial polarization and civic decay. Hence, the postmodern form of "repressive tolerance": on the one hand new technologies from cheap xerography to public television and now the internet allow an unprecedented access to discursivity for previously excluded constituencies; and on the other, an all-enfolding corporate culture that allows the expression of any minority discourse, but represses any that opposes the system of capital as such. Opposition to capitalist culture can no longer be positioned fully outside it – for such a position no longer exists in any powerful form – but only on its margins, in its recesses, and across its contradictions. Poststructuralist literary theory has formulated this supplementarity idealistically, as a textual condition reflecting the literary dissemination of gender and ethnic identities; the parallel materialist project of cultural analysis in terms of differential and conflicting modes of production and the possibilities of class-based resistance within them awaits us.

The histories of California immigration that produce contemporary ethnic writing were generated almost entirely by the international requirements of capital; on occasions – as with the recent Vietnamese and El Salvadorans – by its political fallout, but primarily by immediate labor issues. From the Chinese who built the railroads to the Latinas and Thais who fill today's east Los Angeles sweatshops (and the Thais and Vietnamese who fill the sweatshops and work the construction sites of Taiwan) immigrants have rehearsed, albeit in not so horrendous a form, the special form of relocation that capital imposed on the ancestors of Rodney King. Both local minority cultures and transnational corporate media mostly obscure the function of immigration within labor history, and so its role in sustaining class relations. But, as the texts explored here reveal the global currents that run through local immigrant communities, they allow us to see the possibilities of the populist international cultures which must accompany the only form in which resistance to international capital can be conceived, that is an international labor movement. Such cultures will neither be global in the same way that consumption of the Spice Girls, *Titanic*, and Toyota truck commercials are, nor will they be contained within homogenous ethnic communities. But whatever form of internationally-articulated media a renewed labor movement can inspire, it can only begin in acts of spontaneous local creative activity, imaginatively identified with the world-wide commonalty of working people.

Notes

1. Maxine Hong Kingston, *The Woman Warrior: Memoirs of a Girlhood Among Ghosts* (New York: Alfred A. Knopf, 1976), p. 6.
2. These changes in territorial identification for overseas Chinese have been examined by Aihwa Ong in "On the Edge of Empires: Flexible Citizenship among Chinese in Diaspora", *positions* 1.3 (Winter 1993): 745–778. For their reverberation in Asian American literature, see especially Lisa Lowe, "Heterogeneity, Hybridity, Multiplicity: Asian American Differences", in *Immigrant Acts: On Asian American Cultural Politics* (Durham: Duke University Press, 1996); and Susan Koshy, "The Fiction of Asian American Literature", *Yale Journal of Criticism* 9.2 (1996): 315–346.
3. I take this analysis from Mike Davis's "*Chinatown*, Part Two? The 'Internationalization' of Downtown Los Angeles", *New Left Review* 164 (1988): 65–86.
4. These figures are from Ronald T. Takaki, *Strangers From A Different Shore: A History of Asian Americans* (New York: Penguin, 1989), pp. 4, 420–421, and 426; and Takaki, *A Different Mirror: A History of Multicultural America* (Boston: Little, Brown, 1993), p. 315. For a survey of recent Chinese immigrants to Los Angeles and the new Chinatown in Monterey Park, see "Chinese: Rapidly Changing Demographics in Southland", *Los Angeles Times*, 29 June 1997, pp. A1 and 32. Although recent increases in immigration are enormous, Chinese Americans have long lived in Los Angeles – and there have been racist attacks on them almost as long; in 1871, in the first of the city's many race riots, eighteen Chinese, a tenth of the population at that time, were lynched. This event has been recreated in an extraordinarily plangent novel for young adults, Angi Ma Wong's *Night of the Red Moon* (Palos Verdes: Pacific Heritage Books, 1995). In 1939, the *Writers' Project Guide to California* (New York: Pantheon, 1984) mentioned communities of 21,000 Japanese, 3,000 Chinese, and 3,000 Filipinos, though none of these had the history of cultural cohesion represented by the Chinatowns of New York and San Francisco or the Japanese communities in Hawai'i.
5. Frank Chin, Jeffery Chan, Lawson Inada, and Shawn Wong, "Fifty Years of Our Whole Voice: An Introduction to Chinese and Japanese American Literatures", in Chin et al., eds., *Aiiieeeee!: An Anthology of Asian American Writers* (New York: Mentor, 1991), p. xii.
6. Chin et al., "Fifty Years", p. 25.
7. Frank Chin, "Come All Ye Asian American Writers of the Real and the Fake", in Jeffery Chan et al., eds., *The Big Aiiieeeee!: An Anthology of Chinese American and Japanese American Literature* (New York: Meridian, 1991); and Frank Chin, *Gunga Din Highway* (Minneapolis: Coffee House Press, 1994).
8. Elaine Kim, *Asian American Literature: An Introduction to the Writings and Their Social Context* (Philadelphia: Temple University Press, 1982).
9. "Preface" in Jessica Hagedorn, ed., *Charlie Chan Is Dead* (New York: Penguin, 1993), pp. x–xi.
10. King-Kok Cheung, "Re-viewing Asian American Literary Studies", in Cheung, *An Interethnic Companion to Asian American Literature* (Cambridge, U.K.: Cambridge University Press, 1997), p. 13.
11. Akemi Kikumura, *Through Harsh Winters: The Life of a Japanese Immigrant Woman* (Novato, Calif.: Chandler and Sharp, 1981).
12. Cynthia Kadohata, *The Floating World* (New York: Viking, 1939) and Cynthia Kadohata, *In the Heart of the Valley of Love* (New York: Penguin, 1992).
13. Kim Ronyoung, *Clay Walls* (Sag Harbor, N.Y.: Permanent Press, 1986).
14. On independent Asian American filmmaking generally, see Russell Leong, ed., *Moving the Image: Independent Asian Pacific American Media Arts* (Los Angeles: UCLA Asian American Studies Center, 1991), especially Renee Tajima's essay, "Moving the Image: Asian American Independent Filmmaking 1970–1990". On Visual Communications, see David E. James, "Popular Cinema in Los Angeles: The Case of Visual Communications" in David E. James, ed., *The Sons and Daughters of Los: Culture and Community in L.A.* (Philadelphia: Temple University Press, 2003).
15. Kent Wong has described the formation of the Asian Pacific American Labor Alliance in Washington in 1992, giving its background in Asian American labor history, including the racism of the U.S. labor movement; see his "Building an Asian Pacific Labor Alliance" in Karin Aguilar-San Juan, ed., *The State of Asian America: Activism and Resistance in the 1990s* (Boston: South End Press, 1994).
16. The title is Korean for 29 April [1992], the day the rebellion first erupted. *Sa-I-Gu* was written and directed by Dai Sil Kim-Gibson, and produced by Kim-Gibson, Christine Choy (an American of mixed Korean and Chinese ethnicity, who for almost twenty years has been a leading figure in Third World Newsreel, the most important

4 – Tradition and the Movies: The Working-Class Asian American Avant-Garde in Los Angeles

minority film-producing organization in the United States), and Elaine Kim (a pioneer in Asian American literary scholarship). Some of the footage was shot by Charles Burnett.

17. Sucheta Mazumdar points out that "In Southern California today, between one-fourth and one-third of all Korean immigrant women operate small businesses". See her "General Introduction: A Woman-Centered Perspective on Asian American History", in Asian Women United of California, ed., *Making Waves: An Anthology of Writings By and About Asian American Women* (Boston: Beacon Press, 1989), p. 17. See Nancy Abelmann and John Lie, *Blue Dreams: Korean Americans and the Los Angeles Riots* (Cambridge, Mass.: Harvard University Press, 1995) for a marvelous history of Korean immigration into Los Angeles, including its transnational determination, and especially an analysis of Korean Americans' position in the class dynamics of Los Angeles generally.

18. See Abelman and Lie, *Blue Dreams*, for an account of Korean Americans caught in this economic contradiction. According to Takaki, as industrial plants move out of Los Angeles to Mexico and South Korea, unemployment in south-central Los Angeles is higher than the national rate during the Great Depression. See *A Different Mirror*, p. 423.

19. For an account of mass media misrepresentations, written by one of the women who made the tape, see Elaine Kim, "Home Is Where the Han Is: A Korean-American Perspective on the Los Angeles Upheavals", in Robert Gooding-Williams, ed., *Reading Rodney King: Reading Urban Uprising* (New York: Routledge, 1993), pp. 220–221.

20. Several events prior to the riots exacerbated African American hostility to Koreans. The most important was the case of a Korean shop owner who received a probationary sentence after murdering Latasha Harlins, a black teen, shooting her in the back of the head after wrongfully accusing her of stealing a carton of orange juice. Around the same time, an African American postman was jailed for four years for shooting a dog that had repeatedly attacked him while he was delivering mail. Both events received considerable publicity, and the store's security-tape showing the shooting of Harlins received considerable broadcast play. Other prejudicial entertainment industry images mediating the relationship quickly became common. In the neo-blaxploitation film, *Menace II Society* (Albert and Allen Hughes, 1993) black teenagers rob and in cold blood murder a Korean man and woman who operate a liquor store; they steal the surveillance-camera videotape of the murder, and play it on home television, reveling in the spectacle. In *Falling Down* (Joel Schumacher, 1993), the protagonist embarks on a killing spree when a Korean liquor store owner refuses to give him change for the telephone. After the Harlins case, Ice Cube, at the time the most respected rapper in Los Angeles, released a racist attack on Asians called "Black Korea" (on the album *Death Certificate*), that threatened violent reprisal: "Give respect to the black fist/ Or we'll burn your store down to a crisp". For a contextualization of "Black Korea" in previous representations of black-Korean relations, see Jeff Chang, "Race, Class, Conflict and Empowerment: On Ice Cube's 'Black Korea'", in Edward T. Chang and Russell C. Leong, eds., *Los Angeles – Struggles Toward Multiethnic Community* (Seattle: University of Washington Press, 1994).

21. Bill Mohr, *Poetry Loves Poetry* (Los Angeles: Momentum Press, 1985). Mohr's anthology featured several punk poets and African Americans, but no Asian Americans. For an analysis of the poetry publications on the margins of the punk scene in this period, see my "Poetry/ Punk/ Production: Some Postmodern Writing in L.A." in David E. James, *Power Misses: Essays Across (Un)Popular Culture* (London: Verso, 1996).

22. Edited by Michelle T. Clinton, Sesshu Foster, and Naomi Quiñonez, *Invocation L.A.: Urban Multicultural Poetry* (Albuquerque: West End Press, 1989).

23. Clinton, Foster, and Quiñonez, *Invocation L.A.*, p. ix.

24. Sesshu Foster, *Angry Days* (Los Angeles: West End Press, 1987); Sesshu Foster, *City Terrace Field Manual* (New York: Kaya Productions, 1996); Russell Leong, *The Country of Dreams and Dust* (Albuquerque: West End Press, 1993); and Amy Uyematsu, *30 Miles from J-Town* (Brownsville, Oregon: Story Line Press, 1992).

25. The Chin quote is from "Come All Ye Asian American Writers", p. 49. The West End Press books, including *Invocation L.A.*, were all published by an independent, John Crawford, a native Angelino, who has dedicated himself to publishing radical and minority writers. He also published two other books by minority Los Angeles' writers, Naomi Quiñonez's *Hummingbird Dreams* (1985) and Julie Stein's *Under the Ladder to Heaven* (1984).

26. Lately repressed in China and Viet Nam, the eastern branch of the Mayahana Buddhism that Leong espouses has migrated to the United States. For an account of how Asian teachers of Buddhism "are giving Caucasians authority to hand on the tradition", see Peter Harvey, *An Introduction to Buddhism: Teachings, History and Practices* (New York: Cambridge University Press, 1990), p. 310.

27. This general milieu is also explored in Leong's short stories; see, for example, his "Geography One" in Hagedorn, *Charlie Chan*, pp. 215–229.

28. Leong, *The Country of Dreams and Dust*, p. 7.

29. Leong, *The Country of Dreams and Dust*, p. 12.

30. Leong, *The Country of Dreams and Dust*, p. 13.

31. Leong, *The Country of Dreams and Dust*, p. 14.

Chapter Five The Sons and Daughters of Los: Culture and Community in Los Angeles

In the initial stages of the project whose results are collected in the present volume, we approached popular culture in Los Angeles using as a heuristic the idea of "grassroots cultural organizations".[1] By this, we had in mind the more or less *ad hoc* instances where people who were marginal to the city's established cultural institutions came together to share their poetry, painting, dance, and other forms of art, and in so doing created communities that then developed lives and momentums of their own. Conceived in dissatisfaction with both capitalist-industrial and other publicly sanctioned forms of culture, these communities generally produced themselves as demotic alternatives to establishments that they perceived to be alienated and compromised. Within the framework of this orientation, the associations we explored were diverse in respect to both their internal organization and their eventual relations with the dominant cultural institutions. Growing from the initial efforts of very small groups, in some cases only one or two people, they were originally independent and autonomous, at least to the degree to which these concepts can presently be meaningful. But as they developed wider constituencies, they inevitably became affiliated in various ways with the kind of organizations with which they had before been in conflict, both public – such as city, state and federal agencies – and private – such as foundations and corporations. Despite these affiliations, their creativity remained to some degree of refractory, still honed on a stone of critical alterity.[2]

The associations we examined were formed in the tide of populist social contestations mobilized in the 1960s; and mostly they were shaped by the ideas in which social and political identity were conceptualized and lived in this period, that is, through struggles for civil rights by ethnic and sexual minorities. The local emergence and self-assertion of these political identity-groups were of course part of national movements, and indeed the remarkable ethnic diversity and other demographic features of Los Angeles ensured that they were also often affected by global issues, especially by population shifts and changing patterns of migration. On the other hand, the more immediate motive in their creation was usually an interest in a particular cultural form, often a medium with a distinctive and integral relationship to the development of the specific social group. For example, though African Americans in the city have made public art in the form of murals for many years, the combination of indigenous and European elements in the traditions of mural painting developed in post-revolutionary Mexico became a primary reference-point in the assertion of a Mexican American identity in Los Angeles. Even if they were locally forged and if they were not quite so thoroughly constitutive, similar relations have obtained between other groups and specific mediums. Performance art, for example, has proven particularly valuable for women, gays, and lesbians, and so the current flier distributed by a performance collective that is the subject of the one of the essays below announces: "This workshop is for gay men to gather together and create community through performance".[3] Sometimes a given medium and the institution that developed around it proved valuable for different groups at different times; thus, when the poetry center, Beyond Baroque became a focus for minority poets, part of its constituency changed from what it had been in preceding periods when it revolved around beat and punk subcultures. And though most of the associations studied here based themselves on mediums with less rather than more concurrent commercial viability, sometimes these and certainly parallel communities have flourished by employing the art forms of the culture industry itself – film, television and recorded music. Visual Communications (V.C.), an Asian American community cinema considered below is such an instance. Like all attempts to create popular practices of commercial cultural forms, these last have to construct themselves both within and against the immense social authority and economic resources of the industrial usage of the mediums in question, and so V.C. and similar popular cinemas have been especially precarious, though by the same token their achievements remain of special interest.

But whatever the relative importance of their immediate aesthetic or social motivations, the organizations examined all have in common a foundation in integral human usefulness, the non-instrumental exercise of the creative faculties. All were created by people, some of them feeling themselves oppressed or otherwise marginalized and disenfranchised, who found cultural activity to be a means of self- and communal discovery and realization. All were sustained as popular activities in which people developed forms of symbolic self-expression and joined with others of similar interests. Within the communities they formed, art was not engaged as primarily the production of commodities, and so its role in increasing the value of invested capital or in preserving the system of capitalism as such was negligible. Even though their existence has been besieged and importuned by a rampant market economy, they have known from the beginning

5 – The Sons and Daughters of Los: Culture and Community in Los Angeles

Figure 1. William Blake, *Jerusalem*, plate 100: two images of Los with his emanation, Enitharmon.

what William Blake, as he lived through the emergence of the commodification and industrialization of culture in the late eighteenth century, came at last to understand: "Where any view of Money exists Art cannot be carried on, but War only".[4] Nor were their practices initially supported by the institutions of the established museum and conservatory cultures, for since their interests were no more purely aesthetic than they were purely social, they could not be coerced into the defensive, putatively extra-social reservations premised on aesthetic autonomy. Initially they were opposed to both to the sublation of popular participatory culture into *haut bourgeois*, fetishized real estate and to the entertainment industries' commercialization of it into standardized, marketable commodities. Their point of origin and their ongoing aspiration was thus popular activity prior to both poles of the contemporary "high/low" bifurcation of cultural possibilities, prior to both forms of reification by which social creativity is assimilated into complementary fractions of capital.

Sailing without regard to the Scylla and the Charybdis of the high/low binary, popular cultural activity finds itself and its constituencies outside both arms of capitalist culture – the industry and the museum – and as a consequence has hardly developed a theoretical armature of any general social leverage or persuasiveness. A full theoretical elaboration of such a contrary model of contemporary popular culture cannot be attempted here, and any assessment of the implications of the communities (anti-capitalist? proto-socialist?) it might subtend must remain provisional. On the one hand, the complexities of both crucial terms – "culture" and "community" – bespeak the huge social transformations of the period of advanced capital.[5] A comprehensive encounter between the two terms would have to include the way they have been constructed in the fields of sociology, social and cultural anthropology, urban geography, and the various minority studies areas, as well as in the specific disciplines of poetry, art history, performance art, video, and the other artistic mediums. On the other hand, the available data about actual community cultural projects is extremely limited, and indeed the present project should be understood as a contribution to the collection of primary material upon which more generalized hypotheses about new forms of progressive popular culture could be elaborated. So though specific theoretical presuppositions are implicit and sometimes explicit in each of the essays below, the alternative theories of popular cultural production they project are subordinate to the historical details, the aesthetic achievements, and the varying social possibilities of the individual case-studies. Any attempt to deduce or synthesize a general theory of a genuinely popular culture from them would necessarily involve a critique of the institutions and the theoretical apparatus that presently legitimize and naturalize capitalist culture as a whole. In lieu of such a general theory and propaedeutic to it, here we will only sketch the environment in which the sodalities studied below came into being, the cultural conditions in the city in which they were created, and hence give some concrete grounding for their various innovations and interventions.

Such a geographical focus on Los Angeles may well initially appear to be quixotic, if not misguided; for the city is famous for being the center of industrial culture – the capital of the culture of capital – and, at least until recent developments in museums and art schools reversed this, hostile to autonomous art. But what has appeared to be the city's categorical anomalousness is in fact a compounded prototypicality that gives the present project a more than regional significance. For if the specific urban and spatial structures developed in Los Angeles are, as many claim, the model for future cities, and if the culture industries located in it have a global hegemony, then the conditions that variously shape, inhibit, but also nurture the emergence of truly popular cultural communities in Los Angeles may reasonably be considered to exemplify a general situation; the specific institutions and histories examined below have implications about alternatives to capitalist culture more generally. Here, then, we will be concerned with a pattern of homologies and other relations between social space and culture in a city whose drastic reconfiguration of both appears to be historically prototypical.

5 – The Sons and Daughters of Los: Culture and Community in Los Angeles

Whether despising Los Angeles or celebrating it, whether understanding it (as they used to) as an exception or (as they now do) as a paradigm for future conurbations all over the world, geographers have recognized it as a distinctly new kind of metropolis. The great nineteenth century cities, they argue, were each comprised of a vertically expanding core surrounded by dependent rings, but Los Angeles developed as an agglomeration of separate communities, dispersed across the desert plains between the San Gabriel Mountains and the Pacific Ocean. There, successive waves of immigration – Spanish invaders in the colonial period, then Anglos and other Europeans from the mid-west and south, blacks and Mexicans, and most recently, Asians – created distinct enclaves, many of them internally homogenous and largely segregated from each other. Together these formed, not the radial melting-pot of the modern city, but a polynucleated postmodern megalopolis. In the phrase of Robert M. Fogelson, one of its pioneering historians, the Los Angeles that became a great city, did so as "a fragmented metropolis".[6] Its fragmentation only intensified over the last third of the twentieth century when it became ethnically and culturally one of the most diverse cities in the nation. Changes in the U.S. immigration laws in the mid-1960s combined with the city's expanded role as a center for Pacific Rim capital and with the Reagan administration's neo-imperialist ventures in Meso-America that made it the premier port of entry for immigrants simultaneously transformed the city's demographic structure. But fragmentation had characterized its development from the beginnings, and awareness that phased immigration, voracious peripheral growth, and horizontal rather than vertical development was producing an unprecedented galaxy of unintegrated satellites is itself anything but new. Postmodern geography now proposes a "Sixty-Mile Circle" of "at least 132 incorporated cities" or "the most differentiated of all cities", "a combination of enclaves with high identity, and multiclaves with mixed identity ... perhaps the most heterogeneous city in the world".[7] But before World War II, well before Los Angeles became so conspicuously a microcosm of global diaspora, the 1939 WPA guide to California described it as "nineteen suburbs in search of a city" – already a tripling of the "six suburbs in search of a city" noted in 1920s' witticisms.[8] And, summarizing in the midst of the urban expansion, for the rubric to his 1946 chapter on the "Los Angeles Archipelago" of "social and ethnic islands, economically interrelated but culturally disparate" – still the best analysis of the historical evolution of the city – Carey McWilliams quoted one Charles A. Stoddard who in 1894 had noticed that "Southern California is made up of groups who often live in isolated communities, continuing their own customs, language, and religious habits and associations".[9]

Reinforced by the long history of anti-labor politics that hindered trans-ethnic working-class consciousness and solidarity, the social dispersal that allowed immigrant groups to settle in relatively homogeneous, relatively autonomous clusters produced a distinctive segregation. Though historically, these communities all too commonly become visible to the hegemony at moments of racial or cultural strife – the anti-Chinese riots of the 1870s, for example, or the military's terrorization of zoot-suiters in the 1940s, and the uprisings of blacks in the 1960s and Latinos in the 1990s – all the while, within themselves they have nurtured and sustained local traditions of enormous and distinctive vitality. The barrios of East Los Angeles, for example, or the neighborhoods of South Central where African Americans have preserved the customs of the rural south and even echoes of Africa, and more recently the "little" Asian cities of Tokyo, Manila, Taipei, Saigon, and so on have all lived as vibrant and substantially self-sustained cultural milieus. Re-establishing some of the elements that formed the land- and cityscapes of other spatialities – the family structures, the customs and the festivals, but also the creative rhythms of street behavior and social living – these communities have fashioned themselves between the cultural patterns of their originals and those of their new environment, forging a new local life for often globally-distant identities.[10]

Spatiality in Los Angeles is then structured between two primary vectors: a centripetal pull towards its Hollywood/downtown core, which has always been and remains the focus of the civic, economic, and transport networks of the basin, and the centrifugal pull generated by the semi-autonomous industrial and residential enclaves. If the segregated peripherality of these enclaves precluded their full integration and representation in the city and full participation in its rewards, it also compensated by allowing a spontaneous culture to flourish and to mediate in some measure the social traumas that pervade the postmodern city – for which again Los Angeles is recognized as the prototype.

For the global movement of capital that impelled many of the population flows that created the city has also devastated its social fabric. In the past quarter-century, massive if selective de-industrialization and the growth of precarious, low-income jobs especially in the service and tourist industries, have been compounded by white-collar crime, virulent police corruption and brutality, and the exploitation and destruction of the land, water and air. Trickling down to the lives of working-class people, these socio-economic developments manifest themselves in un- and underemployment, poverty, homelessness, and alienation, in crises in public health, housing, and education, and in suspicion and conflict among sexualities and ethnicities. With the world-historical victory of neo-liberalism, similar and in some case much worse forms of intertwined social destabilization, atomization, and massification have become globally pandemic; but the paucity of attempts to address them in Los Angeles have been no less extreme than the economic developments that produced them. Paralyzed by what has been called "a collective or civic aversion to dealing with social, economic and political problems", local governance has not begun adequately to address the erosion of the older forms of urban community, and instead "governments and populace have colluded in a decline of the commonwealth ... the collapse of community".[11]

In this, again, the city is a paradigm of the widespread lived experience of loneliness, alienation and social impotence, of the cultural attenuation and anomie that are now more intense and inescapable than even during the upheavals and dislocations of high modernity. Then at least, however corrupted its actual instantiations may have been, socialism as a political philosophy sustained the ideal of a non-exploitative human commonality, whether projected as popular participatory control over local life or as a future classless society. But now it is the market, abetted wherever possible by military power, that administers the world, and free market fundamentalism appears locally, not in communal social projects, but as *privatization*. In the telling image of one popular analyst, we now go "bowling alone" for, as a more abstract one reminds us, the "gravest and most painful testimony of the modern world, the one that possibly involves all other testimonies to which this epoch must answer is the testimony of the dissolution, the dislocation, or the conflagration of community".[12]

Though this crisis in community is a cultural crisis in all senses, it has been enacted especially dramatically in the industrialization of older forms of culture, and in their transformation into the business of entertainment during their assimilation by and integration into first finance and then corporate capital. Summarily designated as "Hollywood", the corporate entertainment industry now comprises virtually all forms of film, television, and recorded music, and all their various satellites, spin-offs, franchises, and surrogates, their pimps and proxies. These industries have now extended to the spheres of politics, sport, religion, and other distinct areas of public life, reconstructing them within its own values and priorities, commodifying what once were popular activities and turning them too into entertainment. The traditions that inform the culture of popular participation may be implicitly or residually present in industrial culture, but only as they too are also reduced to entertainment. The resulting divided culture, the culture of separated monopolized industrial production and of popular consumption, is the culture with which Los Angeles has become globally synonymous, and locally it is so overwhelmingly powerful that the forms of popular cultural practices in the city that are the present concern have become virtually invisible. For Hollywood's ubiquitous and all-pervasive presence in Los Angeles makes its attractions and rewards the context for all popular cultural activity. So great is the gravitational pull of the industry's stars and its star-system, that all other arts are forced to revolve around it. The structural core-periphery tensions that shape the city geographically and economically thus generate parallel determinations within its culture: the minority arts of the local communities in Los Angeles are created in the tension between the centrifugal pull of independent and indigenous aspirations and the centripetal pull of corporate capitalist culture. In Los Angeles culture and geography are reciprocal: the social tensions of cultural marginality are isomorphic with the city's spatiality.

Until the 1950s "Hollywood" designated simply the companies that manufactured films and recouped their expenses and profit in theatrical ticket sales. But since then their production has simultaneously diversified and also consolidated what before were several separate industries while, especially with television, distribution sites have metastasized throughout the range of once-public places running from homes and schools to prisons and hospitals. The limits of the film text itself have eroded and fused into all its marketing extensions; sequels, t-shirts, theme-parks, lunch pails, toys, comic books, video games, the miasma of hype that makes it hard to imagine, let alone glimpse any space outside the business.

This apotheosized culture-as-capital is identified with Los Angeles more completely than an art form was ever before associated with a single place. Infants together in the first decade of the century when the movies were little more than a cottage-industry, the city and the industry fostered each other's growth to maturity. Late in 1907, the Selig company built a stage on Olive Street for the shooting of *The Count of Monte Cristo*, and two years later, the company established a permanent base in the city. Other companies followed, including a troupe of Biograph players to shoot the local epic *Ramona*, and the Keystone Comedy Company, and by 1912, over seventy production companies in Los Angeles employed three thousand people. During the teens the manifest advantages of the region's year-round sunshine and topographical variety persuaded even more companies to relocate to the region, and eventually some of them merged into larger combines that joined film production and distribution – the vertical integration of the industry. By mid-decade the industry's annual payroll had reached $20 million, and the identification of Hollywood the medium and Hollywood the city was established, with sixty percent of U.S. films being produced there.[13] In the post-war years the studios surpassed the French, Italian, and British film industries to become the single most important source of production, and by the 1930s the U.S. film industry was dominant throughout the world. Even Carey McWilliams's unusual rhetorical excess does not seem an inappropriate summary of the city's debt to the medium: "If ever an industry played the Fairy Prince to an impoverished Cinderella, it has been the motion-picture industry in relation to Los Angeles".[14]

After World War II and Hollywood's second major global expansion, the other branches of the entertainment industries were assimilated to it. Though the rise of television coincided with a series of crises in the 1950s that forced the industry to restructure, in the early 1970s it again re-invented itself. Generating subsidiary industries as well as accelerating the development of other labor-intensive craft industries in the area, Hollywood attracted all the other components of the broadcasting industry. Since then, the television industry has itself expanded enormously and the two industries are now completely integrated, not only with each other, but also with the popular music industry, whose move west became conclusive in the 1980s. The strength of the industry's infrastructure and the abundance of creative and technical workers in the area supported the economic explosion of the 1990s, lifting Southern California out of the slump caused by cutbacks in the defense industries. With the expanded need for product to fill the new multi-channeled global television systems of the decade, by the turn of the century the annual business of the entertainment industries based in Los Angeles had grown to $40 billion, with more people in Los Angeles working in Hollywood than in electronics and aerospace combined. The concentration of control over these media industries by a small number of corporations increased rapidly during the 1990s, representing the centralization of control over the industry's production parallel to the longer-standing globalization of the market. Japanese corporations began to invest heavily in the industry in the late 1980s, with Sony buying Columbia Pictures in 1989 for $3.4 billion, and Matsushita buying MCA (Universal) in 1990 for nearly $7 billion.[15] Though film production had been controlled by a handful of major studios since the 1930s, by the late 1990s the six largest of them accounted for 90% of theatrical revenue, and all but sixteen of the 148 features Hollywood released in 1997 were produced by only six firms. By that time, six firms also effectively monopolized more than 80% of the country's cable television, and only four companies controlled one-third of all radio station income.[16]

Especially after the deregulation of the communications industries in the 1996 Telecommunications Act, the elimination of restrictions on corporations moving across different branches of the communications industries led to enormous increases in conglomeratization. Just to take one, locally important example, the Walt Disney Company, with annual revenues of *only* $25.4 billion (by comparison, General Electric, owner of NBC grossed $129.9 billion in 2001): among Disney's movie holdings are Walt Disney Pictures, Touchstone Pictures, Hollywood Pictures, and Miramax Film Corporation; it owns the ABC television network, together with the Disney Channel, Soap Net, all divisions of ESPN, and 80% of A&E and the History and Biography Channels; in addition to Disneyland itself, its theme park holdings include Disney World, Disney Cruise Line, and Disneylands in Paris, Tokyo and Hong Kong; and as well as extensive holdings in book publishing, it owns half of the magazines, *U.S. Weekly*, *Discover*, and *ESPN*, fifty radio stations, 741 Disney stores, and extensive theatrical interest.[17] This list is just a selection, and diversification of an equivalent or greater extensiveness has been documented for AT&T, Sony, AOL/Time Warner, Vivendi Universal, Viacom, and one or two more of the integrated communications and entertainment cartels. Some indication of the momentum of this consolidated corporate ownership of American culture is revealed in the periodic summaries by one of its most important analysts, Ben Bagdikian. When he published the first edition of his book *The Media Monopoly* in 1983, fifty corporations dominated mass media in the United States; by the second edition in 1987, the fifty companies had shrunk to twenty-nine; by 1997 that number had been further reduced to ten and by 2000 he found that only six dominant firms controlled more of the industry than the combined fifty-seventeen years earlier.[18]

Manufacturing the culture that is marketed and consumed all over the world, the Los Angeles entertainment industry has become the vehicle, not so much of a U.S. imperialism as the imperialism of capital itself, inflating into a global omnipotence the implications of the Supreme Court's 1915 diagnosis that "The exhibition of moving pictures is a business, pure and simple, originated and conducted for profit, like any other spectacles".[19] Just one instance of this voraciousness may suffice, the case of *Jurassic Park* (Steven Spielberg, 1993). The film *Jurassic Park* was not only "accompanied by over 1,000 products identified as official Jurassic Park merchandise, distributed by 100 official Jurassic Park manufacturers around the world", but the Jurassic Park logo from the merchandising was displayed *in the film itself* in the park's gift shop; thus, the "film itself was a tie-in", intradiegetically displaying its combined merchandising, product placement and other forms of economic proliferation.[20]

Though cultural activity has always been subject to economic transactions, only in the recent past have the culture industries themselves become so thoroughly integrated with each other, with all other forms of material production, and with the state. Training the world in consumerism, entertainment becomes capital's mode of operation. As Theodor Adorno (writing in Los Angeles half a century ago) noted, corporate culture has amalgamated with advertising.[21] Or, as a Coca-Cola marketing chief more recently remarked, it is the medium in which capital operates: "The culture that comes out of L.A. – films, television, recorded music, concerts – is the popular culture of the world and it is through that culture that we communicate with the consumers of Coke".[22]

Guy Debord and others among the Situationists, the French philosophers who provided the most profound analysis of the assimilation of human life into this cultural-economic system, designated it as the *Spectacle*. In the "Society of the Spectacle", the immediate relationships among people appear to have been replaced by relations between people and images, an imaginary relationship that also has the effect of concealing the actual social relations created by the capitalist system's production of material wealth. The symbol and fulcrum of this condition, Los Angeles is thus the Capital of the Spectacle, and the comprehensive form of the city's economic, spatial, social and cultural alienations is ontological: "The spectator feels at home nowhere, for the spectacle is everywhere".[23] Though the ruin of community, the alienation of the imagination and authentic social relations that constitutes the Spectacle, now affects almost everyone in the world, it affects people in Los Angeles especially powerfully and comprehensively. At once a cynosure and an *ignis fatuus*, and alternately enriching and depleting all other arts in the city, Hollywood attempts to frame all cultural practice in Los Angeles in its own economic imperatives and entrepreneurial ambitions; life there is enthralled by it.

To designate as "popular culture", not Hollywood itself but practices outside and opposed to it contravenes what has become the term's dominant usage, its reference to the consumer culture produced by capitalist industries. This recent transformation and narrowing of the concept of popular culture is not accidental, but rather has accompanied parallel transformations and narrowings in the cultural field as a whole. Commodity culture's colonization of all areas of life – the individual psyche, the public realm, the political process, and indeed all forms of art – now appears to be so complete that, it is often argued, any popular practice outside it is impossible, if not inconceivable. And responding to the preoccupation of the cultural field by capital, many journalists and academics have made corresponding investments. Whereas early attempts to legitimate the study of what was then called "mass culture" approached it as sociological or ethnographical data, more recent methodologies employ aesthetic criteria that allow for newly positive understandings of its social role. So though the fact of the structural integration of the dominant forms of contemporary culture in the general operations of capital is indisputable, its implications are widely disputed. More or less determinist positions like those of Adorno and the Situationists mentioned above, for example, that are rooted in Hegelian analyses of capitalism's intrinsic alienation and so propose that cultural domination and exploitation follow necessarily from the economic structure of the entertainment industries, have become key points of reference, usually negative ones, in contemporary debates over the social implications of the mass consumption of culture produced by corporate interests.

On the one hand, it is argued that capitalist culture, especially broadcast television, has been pivotal in the disintegration of the democratic process, the collapse of community, the rise of the New Right, and the emergence of a universal cynicism.[24] But as with all other forms of capitalist production, the culture industries' constant need to reconstruct themselves produces disjunctions and contradictions that render the overall system unstable and vulnerable to intervention by the people involved in its various stages. So on the other hand, other commentators emphasize the possibilities that the industrial production of entertainment does not preclude authorial self-expression during the process of its manufacture, nor does mass consumption of it preclude the audiences' parallel assertion of their own identity and creativity, specifically their ability to mobilize their own critical, against-the-grain reception of its intended messages. When such creative responses to entertainment become socially extensive, they produce fan cultures that may elaborate the imaginary identifications we all make with others who share our tastes into virtual or even real communities that become to various degrees independent of the original mass media sources; the Grateful Dead and *Star Trek* fan cultures are among those most often cited as sustaining such communities. Indeed an entire academic discipline now exists, premised on the moments of autonomy and alterity that the system as a whole allows, and so on the supposition that resistance to capitalist culture is marshaled within its own processes: cultural studies.

Though the cultural studies literature is now so immense that every position on the question of the relation between culture and political economy in these industries can somewhere be found in it, its main tradition derived from the work of the Birmingham Center for Contemporary Cultural Studies in the 1970s and 1980s. The Birmingham group formulated itself initially around the investigation of the more or less delinquent activity of specifically working-class subcultures: dress, hairstyles, dance styles, and so on – the traditional field of anthropology or sociology rather than the aesthetic per se. It proposed that these subcultures reflected the transformed class tensions of advanced capitalist society and were, at least partially, ritually symbolic continuations of earlier and more overtly political working-class social contestations. In this formulation, popular culture was understood to comprise "Resistance Through Rituals;[25] that is specifically working-class opposition to the dominant culture, which in Britain at that time was still the culture of the bourgeois and the aristocratic establishment, not yet melted into air by the entertainment industries.

The primacy of this working-class resistance to the dominant culture was largely lost in the Americanization and "postmodernization" of the Birmingham project that produced contemporary cultural studies. Occurring during the Reagan/Thatcher era's assaults on trade unions and all other forms of working-class self-organization, the transformation of the discipline entailed parallel offensives; the term, "popular culture" was decisively relocated from working-class oppositional subcultures to the entertainment industries, which in the U.S. (and increasingly so in Britain and the rest of the world) had itself become the dominant culture. Its exclusive reference became the consumer culture manufactured by corporate industries rather than street-level attempts to resist or transform it, let alone to sustain alternatives to it. Popular culture was now produced by corporate capital, not by the people. As the term acquired the market definition of popular, its specific associations with the working class and hence the possibility that culture could focus structural social resistance were dumped. In a period where the significant crises in capitalism were explained as crises in over-production, to be assuaged by increasing the consumption of commodities of all and every kind, the academic study of culture followed suit by deploying itself primarily around the consumption of commodity culture.[26] The academy became yet another stage where capitalist culture as a whole was legitimated and naturalized; affirming rather than interrogating the status quo, cultural studies amalgamated with advertising.

Though the present work does not assume that any autonomous sphere of popular culture, whether specified as the activity of an ethnic or sexual minority or as some fraction of the working-class understood more generally, may now exist outside the gravitational field of the culture industries, it is oriented to those popular practices that attempt to produce themselves outside the priorities and process of the culture of capital, and so outside the field that cultural studies now demarks. Though they are surrounded by and inevitably linked to Hollywood, the initiatives considered in this book are displaced from it in multiple ways, but especially in being pursued as essentially amateur practices, and almost all in mediums that the entertainment industry has not occupied. Hollywood and Los Angeles, the industry and the city, culture and geography form the context, comprise the cloth on the edges of which participatory popular cultures weave new forms of community.

In this they mark the continuation of the cultural resistance that began when the arts were first industrialized in the print business of eighteenth-century England. William Blake earned a meager living for himself and his wife on the edges of this industry, but he devoted himself to the composition of epic poems that he illustrated and engraved himself, the two of them coloring the printed sheets by hand. In these poems, Blake detailed a mythology describing the emergence of the modern world system – the specters of science, imperialism, the industrial revolution, and commodity culture – but also envisioning revolutionary republican attempts to humanize it. He coined the name Los for his central figure, an anagram for "Sol", the sun, that also punned on the *loss* that surrounded him; and Blake imagined Los as a poet, but also as a blacksmith, hammering out a vision of a fully-human, fully-emancipated commonality. In the furnaces of his imagination, Los labored to build Jerusalem, or Liberty, by producing a genuinely popular culture, a Republican Art, such as could be made at home like Blake's own, or one owned and exhibited by the general public, like early Renaissance frescoes – or modern murals. Some two hundred years later, the word Los became current among working-class Latinos, many of them displaced from their homelands by the global forces of capital and empire, as the name for the city to which they had fled, a city where they hoped to find liberty and fellowship and which they sometimes illuminated with exquisite, spontaneous frescoes.[27] From one of the first to one of the most recent instances of crucial cultural resistance, the Sons and Daughters of Los continue to contend in their furnaces.

Notes

1. This was written in 2001 as the introduction to a collection of essays I edited, *The Sons and Daughters of Los: Culture and Community in L.A.* (Philadelphia: Temple University Press, 2003); some minor traces of its role as an introduction are omitted here. Its title derived from William Blake's poem, *Jerusalem*, in which he figured Los, the embodiment of imaginative cultural creation, as a blacksmith:

    and Los drew them forth, compelling the harsh Spectre
    Into the Furnaces & into the Valleys of the Anvils Death
    And into the mountains of the Anvils & of the heavy Hammers
    Till he should bring the Sons & Daughters of Jerusalem to be
    The Sons and Daughters of Los

    (David V. Erdman, ed., *The Complete Poetry and Prose of William Blake* [Garden City: Doubleday Anchor Books, 1982], p. 152). The essays primarily concerned collective community-based cultural initiatives in the city deployed around, for example, poetry, woman's art making, gay performance, Mexican American printmaking, Asian American filmmaking, and African American video. My role in the project was an extrapolation from a history of avant-garde, amateur, working-class, and other minority cinemas in Los Angeles on which I was then at work: *The Most Typical Avant-Garde: History and Geography of Minor Cinemas in Los Angeles* (Berkeley: University of California Press, 2005). In this, I attempted to demonstrate that, despite the identification of the city with the capitalist film industry that supplies commodity culture for the world's consumption, Los Angeles had an unrivalled history of grassroots popular film practices. Even though their mode of production was constructed in alterity to the industry, thematically, formally and in other ways, they were often engaged in various kinds of critical dialogue with industrial culture and even direct contestation of it. That emphasis on popular cultural production rather than on the entertainment

5 – The Sons and Daughters of Los: Culture and Community in Los Angeles

industries placed my project in opposition to the dominant orientation of U.S. cultural studies, then in its moment of ascendency. Soon after the inception of U.K. cultural studies, Stuart Hall had insisted that social transformations between the 1880s and the 1920s eradicated the possibility of any "separate, autonomous, 'authentic layer' of working-class culture" ("Notes on Deconstructing the 'Popular'", in Raphael Samuel, ed., *People's History and Socialist Theory* [London: Routledge and Kegan Paul, 1981], p. 229); nevertheless, initially in the U.K. cultural studies focused on post-war ritual and other symbolic forms of working-class opposition to the power of the dominant capitalist (if also vestigially feudal) authoritarian state. But as cultural studies developed in the U.K. and especially as it was adopted in the U.S., the notion of the popular was relocated from oppositional practices to commodity consumption, and the discipline transmogrified into affirmative arguments for the forms of empowerment that capitalist culture were supposed to allow. Following many of its signal soundbites, "intellectuals" were rebuked for having "no respect" for what was speciously proposed as "popular culture". While not wishing to deny that popular consumption of commodity culture could indeed profitably fasten on its contradictions, the essays in *The Sons and Daughters of Los* identified vernacular practices in Los Angeles that were to a substantial degree – though never totally – outside the culture industries. These, I supposed, would be all the more important since they had been created in the heart of Hollywood, yet in communities that it had not yet totally colonized. In this they would be akin to the radical cultural practices sympathetic to the French and American revolutions that Blake designated as "Republican Art".

2. The survey is by no means exhaustive in its account of either cultural communities that have existed in the recent past, or are presently coming into being. Prominent among the omissions are the Woman's Building, the Wallenboyd and the Boyd Street Theaters, the Los Angeles Center for Photographic Studies, various public television initiatives, and Pasadena NewTown; of new organizations, the many forms of community that are growing around the internet (the Los Angeles Alternative Media Network, for example) are beyond the scope of the present volume, as are organizations specifically responsive to very recent immigration, such as the Mayan organization, IXIM, and the Salvadoran American National Association; on these last see Nora Hamilton and Norma Stoltz Chinchilla, *Seeking Community in a Global City: Guatemalans and Salvadorans in Los Angeles* (Philadelphia: Temple University Press, 2001), pp. 66–67. Attention was given only to those grassroots community movements that developed specifically around cultural activities; for the role of parks, neighborhood and homeowners associations, community newspapers, public libraries, and the like in creating communities in Los Angeles, see *Metamorphosis Project White Paper Series: White Paper 1, Number One, The Challenge of Belonging in the 21st Century: The Case of Los Angeles* (The Annenberg School for Communication, 2001, http://www.metamorph.org/vault). Another major omission here is attention to the many communities that have formed around music. These include classical music, ranging from the "Evenings on the Roof" of the 1940s and the "Monday Evening Concerts" (for which see Dorothy Crawford, *Evenings On and Off the Roof: Pioneering Concerts in Los Angeles, 1939–1971* [Berkeley: University of California Press, 1995]), to the music and sound events organized by Cindy Bernard, initially in the late 1990s at the Sacred Grounds coffeehouse in San Pedro and then at the MAK Center for Art and Architecture at the Schindler House in West Hollywood. And they include more popular practices of music, of which the Los Angeles punk movement in the 1980s and the South Central rap movement in the 1990s are the most important recent examples. These latter were not examined here because mostly (though not entirely) they developed in nightclubs, record labels or informal tape distribution mechanism that grew on the edges of or within the music industry itself.

3. "Highways Spring 2002 Schedule", notice for "Gay Men's Performance Workshop."

4. "The Laocoön", in *The Complete Poetry and Prose of William Blake*, p. 272.

5. For user-friendly introductions to these concepts, see especially Anthony P. Cohen, *The Symbolic Construction of Community* (New York: Tavistock Publications, 1985) and Raymond Williams, *Culture* (London: Fontana, 1989).

6. See Robert M. Fogelson, *The Fragmented Metropolis: Los Angeles, 1850–1930* (Berkeley: University of California Press, 1993).

7. Edward W. Soja, *Postmodern Geographies: The Reassertion of Space in Critical Social Theory* (London and New York: Verso, 1989), p. 224; and Charles Jenks, *Heteropolis* (London: Academy Editions, 1993), pp. 17 and 32.

8. Kevin Starr, *Material Dreams: Southern California Through the 1920s* (New York: Oxford University Press, 1990), p. 84; and the *WPA Guide to California* (New York: Pantheon Books, [1939] 1984), p. 208.

9. Carey McWilliams, *Southern California: An Island on the Land* (Salt Lake City: Peregrine Smith, [1946] 1973), p. 314.

10. The notion of "cultural bifocality" or pluralism is now more germane than older assimilationist models of acculturation; see Hamilton and Chinchilla, *Seeking Community in a Global City*, p. 9.

11. Greg Hise, Michael J. Dear, and H. Eric Schockman, "Rethinking Los Angeles", Greg Hise, Michael J. Dear, and H. Eric Schockman, eds., *Rethinking Los Angeles* (Thousand Oaks, Calif.: Sage Publications, 1996), p. 11.

12. Respectively Robert D. Putnam, *Bowling Alone: The Collapse and Revival of American Community* (New York: Simon & Schuster, 2000), and Jean-Luc Nancy, *The Inoperative Community* (Minneapolis: University of Minnesota Press, 1991), p. 1.

13. David Bordwell, et al., *The Classical Hollywood Cinema: Film Style and Mode of Production to 1960* (New York; Columbia University Press, 1985). p. 123. By 1922, 84 percent of U.S. films were made there.
14. McWilliams, *Southern California*, p. 341.
15. Five years later, Matsushita sold 80 percent of MCA to Seagrams for $5.7 million. These figures are taken from Colin Hoskins, Stuart McFadyn, and Adam Finn, *Global Television and Film: An Introduction to the Economics of the Business* (Oxford: Clarendon Press, 1997), p. 23. For a complete analysis of the effect of the corporatization of the media system, see Robert W. McChesney, *Rich Media, Poor Democracy: Communication Politics in Dubious Times* (Chicago: University of Illinois Press, 1999).
16. Figures in this paragraph are from McChesney, *Rich Media, Poor Democracy*, pp. 17–18.
17. Selected from listings in "The Big Ten", *The Nation* 274, no. 1 (7 January 2002): pp. 27–32.
18. Ben H. Bagdikian, *The Media Monopoly*, 6th ed. (Boston: Beacon Press, 2000), p. xxi.
19. Mutual Film Corporation v. Ohio Industrial Commission. See Richard Koszarski, *An Evening's Entertainment: The Age of the Silent Feature Picture, 1915–1928* (Berkeley: University of Californian Press, 1994), p. 199.
20. Janet Wasko, *Hollywood in the Information Age* (Austin: University of Texas Press, 1994), p. 205.
21. See Max Horkheimer and Theodor W. Adorno, *Dialectic of Enlightenment*, trans. John Cumming (New York: Herder and Herder, 1972), p. 161: "So completely is [culture] subject to the law of exchange that is no longer exchanged; it is so blindly consumed in use that it can no longer be used. Therefore it amalgamates with advertising".
22. Quoted in Andrew Jaffe, "The Hollywood Threat to Madison Avenue", *Los Angeles Times*, 11 September 1991, B7. The article reported that Coca-Cola Co. had retained Michael Ovitz and his Creative Artists Agency to "put it in touch with 'global pop culture'."
23. Guy Debord, *The Society of the Spectacle*, trans. Donald Nicholson-Smith (New York: Zone Books, 1995), p. 23.
24. Some recent examples of such wholesale critiques include Pierre Bourdieu, *On Television*, trans. Priscilla Ferguson (New York: New Press, 1998), and Jeffrey Scheuer, *The Sound Bite Society: Television and the American Mind* (New York: Four Walls Eight Windows, 1999). Robert D. Putnam has argued that television watching is negatively correlated with civic participation and social involvement: "Television ... is bad for both individualized and collective civic engagement, but it is particularly toxic for activities that we do together... . just as television privatizes our leisure time, it also privatizes our civic activity, dampening our interactions with one another even more than it dampens individual political activities" (*Bowling Alone*, p. 229). On the other hand, some recent empirical evidence from Los Angeles is equivocal about the negative effects of television, finding that whereas it had a direct negative effect on the relatively privileged Westside of the city, it had "indirect positive effects" among the largely immigrant populations of East Los Angeles; see *Metamorphosis Project White Paper Series: White Paper 1*, p. 34.
25. See Stuart Hall and Tony Jefferson, eds., *Resistance Through Rituals: Youth Subcultures in Post-War Britain* (London: Hutchinson, 1976).
26. As Nicholas Garnham has noted, the emphasis in affirmative cultural studies on cultural consumption rather than production "played politically into the hands of a right whose ideological assault has been structured in large part around an effort to persuade people to construct themselves as consumers in opposition to producers"; see Garnham, "Political Economy and Cultural studies: Reconciliation or Divorce", *Critical Studies in Mass Communication* 12, no. 1 (1995): 65.
27. On the urban writing of working-class Latinos in Los Angeles, see Susan A. Phillips, *Wallbangin': Graffiti and Gangs in L.A.* (Chicago: University of Chicago Press, 1999). The city is designated as "Los" on a map on page 151. As part of his *California Trilogy*, James Benning made a wonderful film in 2001 about Los Angeles that prominently featured its Latino citizens; he titled it *Los*.

Chapter Six Toward a Geo-Cinematic Hermeneutics / The City as Means of Production: Representations of Los Angeles in *Killer of Sheep* and *Water and Power*

> The cultural landscape is fashioned from a natural landscape by a culture group. Culture is the agent, the natural area is the medium, the cultural landscape is the result.
> Carl Ortwin Sauer

I. Working-class Places

In 1986 in preparation for the 1988 Olympic Games, the South Korean government began redevelopment projects that displaced and destroyed several poor neighborhoods of Seoul, one of them being Sanggye-dong, home to some 200 people. Kim Dong-won, an aspiring young filmmaking, was at that time trying to find a place for himself in the New Korean Cinema, already an essential component of the popular democracy or *minjung* movement that in 1992 successfully elected a civilian president and so ended the U.S. supported military dictatorship. He was asked at first simply to document the demolition at Sanggye-dong in order to preserve evidence of the dispossession of the people and the demolition of their homes. But Kim became so outraged by the government brutality that he joined the community, eventually living with them and, instead of simply making a film about them, cooperated with them in collectively producing a film about their struggle, *Sanggye-dong Olympics* (*Sanggye-dong olrimpic*, 1988). The experience so transformed him that he gave up his plans to work in the feature industry and instead founded a documentary film collective, P.U.R.N. Production. Kim is only the most prominent of a generation of Korean filmmakers who, in a period of radical social transformation, in various ways identified themselves with their subjects, rather than making films about them from outside. Others in the movement not only made films about working-class struggles from within them, but taught working-class people how to make their own films and videos.[1]

105

There had, of course, been earlier examples of the use of image-making as a means of working-class self-production. The classic precedent is the Weimar still photography of the *Arbeiterphotographen*, the Worker Photography Movement, and its magazine AIZ (*Arbeiter-Illustrierte-Zeitung*).[2] Its commitments to the Soviet revolution and to amateur rather than professional production inspired filmmakers across Europe in the 1930s. In the U.S., branches of the Workers Film and Photo Leagues were organized in New York, Detroit, Los Angeles and several other cities to participate the radical social movements of the time. As well as distributing films from other cities, the Los Angeles branch of the WFPL made a dozen films detailing local strikes and demonstrations, as well as the police riots around them. One, for example, a documentary on the effects of the depression called *Conditions in Los Angeles* (1934), was constructed as a parallel montage of the different cities available to the rich and the poor.

A title reading "Thousands seek work" shows masses of unemployed workers; then "While the rich enjoy leisure" reveals Rolls Royces bringing golfers to a palatial resort hotel. In another section, "Poverty and starvation for those who have built" introduces long lines at soup kitchens, followed by "Food in abundance" showing crates of fresh produce at wholesalers, guarded by corpulent police. The communist party newspaper, the *Western Worker*, greeted the WFPL films, noting that while Hollywood created capitalist propaganda film, League was producing "that sort of film which Hollywood has so long deliberately repressed – pictures showing aspects of the class struggle".[3] In both cases, a vision of the city contesting the officially sanctioned ideal – of the propagandizing South Korean government in the one case and the capitalist movie industry in the other – was made possible only by the innovation of alternative means of production. Alternative, oppositional films require alternative, oppositional cinemas.

The more recent equivalents to this *prise de la parole* by the otherwise cinematically disenfranchised have been based not in working-class struggles but in minority communities self-identified in terms of sexuality or ethnicity. The identity-political cinemas that have dominated the U.S. avant-garde since the last quarter of the Twentieth Century were made by women and gays or African-Asian- and Mexican American people contesting exploitative and prejudicial mass-media representations of them in varieties of self-ethnography: telling their own stories themselves and portraying the communities in which they lived. In the U.S., the major center for the production of all of these minority cinemas has been Los Angeles, and so Los Angeles has been the place where the tension between capitalist cinema and popular opposition to it has been most comprehensive and profound. In them the representation of minority neighborhoods of

Los Angles has been most crucial and revelatory; so also have they been enabled by the resources of the same places.

II. Hollywood in and as Los Angeles

So rich and dense has been the mutual imbrication of Los Angeles and the movies that considerations of the city easily collapse it into media spectacle. Revisionist modernists may still affirm the ontological priority of the city; David Harvey, for example, insists that film is "in the final analysis, a spectacle projected within an enclosed space on a depthless screen".[4] But a more common point of departure – as here in the introduction to a collection of geographical considerations of cinema – is Baudrillard's conflation of the city and the cinema, a conflation that understands the cityscape as itself a screenscape: "Where is the cinema? It is all around you outside, all over the city, that marvelous, continuous performance of films and scenarios".[5] When the city "seems to have stepped right out of the movies", then its material and social reality may be subordinated to its representation: "To grasp its secret, you should not, then, begin with the city and move outwards towards the screen, you should begin with the screen and move outwards to the city".[6] Approaching reality as textuality, such readings of contemporary urban space as intrinsically cinematic are especially enticing in Los Angeles where, for the century of its existence as a major city, cinema has been central to its economic, social, and cultural developments. All have been shaped in the magnetic field of cinema, which has imitated urban growth in metastasizing at points increasingly remote from the original downtown center: Hollywood, Culver City, the San Fernando Valley, and (as the mutual imbrication of the electronics and the entertainment industries bridges the north/south division of the state) now in Silicon Valley. As Reyner Banham observed, "Hollywood ... the movies found Los Angeles a diffuse fruit-growing super-village of some eight hundred thousand souls, and handed it over to the infant television industry in 1950 a world metropolis of over four million".[7] More scrupulous historians have recognized the formative role of other industries, though from real-estate through aerospace to crack cocaine, they have been imaginary signifiers, exhibiting a Hollywood-like combination of reality and fiction, of spectacle and speculation. And so wherever the industry's actual manufacturing centers, "Hollywood" has been nationally and internationally recognized as the tertium quid between Los Angeles and the movies, simultaneously the proper synecdoche for each.

Unmatched in the history of the arts, Los Angeles' unique appropriation of an entire medium is reciprocated by that medium's similarly unique influence on a city, on its industrial base, its architecture, and its overall cultural tenor. The "Hollywood" sign remains the city's trademark and stamps its influence on other arts in the city, enriching them or depleting them, financing their experimentation or drawing them into its own aesthetic and entrepreneurial orbits. From the urban facades satirized by 1930s' novelists to the more extravagant forms of hyperspace epitomized initially by Disneyland and more recently by the fabricated entertainment, dining, and shopping urban environment of Universal's City Walk, the continually-reconstructed identification has been architecturally embodied, if not in concrete then at least in stucco, with a renewed cross-fertilization evident in the work of Frank Israel and other contemporary architects. In other cultural forms, the incorporation has been no less integral. Until relatively recent innovations by minority writers, the Hollywood novel was taken as the Los Angeles novel, while the city's other significant literature has been the screenplay.

The supposed attenuation of any real outside the media in Los Angeles has been reciprocated by a parallel tautological reflexivity in the way the city has been assimilated into Hollywood films. Even in those that depend on local topography, its features are essentially mobile and non-specific, with the demand that they be internationally legible prohibiting any comprehensive or accurate mapping of the city's social structure and spatiality.[8] The topographical variety, abundant light, availability of space, and other local conditions that sustained the industry have been deracinated, displaced from the actual geography of the region to the non-restrictive, diegetic geography of "the movies". Two main processes may be distinguished.

First, in eras when location shooting has been common and the city has provided the environment for narratives set in other places, its own specificity has been occluded. Even films that mobilize a thematic polarization of Los Angeles against some geographical alternative often use the city as the site – and sight – of both itself and its other. Most of the "Berkeley" scenes in the classic Los Angeles comedy, *The Graduate* (Mike Nichols, 1967), for example, purportedly more real than the regnant plastic of Beverly Hills, were represented by the library at the University of Southern California (USC), while *NYPD Blue*, *Seinfeld*, and similar television shows trading on the authenticity of their take on New York life are filmed in L.A. The syndrome is long-standing. As early as 1911, it was recognized that the growth of the film industry in the region was substantially attributable to the topographical and architectural diversity that facilitated location shooting able to simulate virtually anywhere in the world.[9] A map of Southern California produced at Paramount Studio in the 1920s shows the entire region over-written as other places; the area north of Malibu is designated Coast of Spain; the Palos Verdes peninsula is Wales, Catalina is South Sea Islands; the channel between it and Long Beach is both Malay Coast and Long Island Sound; the Salton Sea is the Red Sea, and south of it lies the Sahara Desert.[10] The Los Angeles area is then effectively what Foucault envisaged as a heterotopia, a site "capable of juxtaposing in a single real place several spaces, several sites that are in themselves incompatible".[11]

Figure 1. Paramount Studio Location Map, 1925.

So for Hollywood, Los Angeles was always inherently not-itself. The growth of the industry and the plentitude of its representations of the city were always premised on nonidentity; it became the capital of capitalist cinema because it could play anywhere.

Second, in feature films set in Los Angeles where local topography is used to supply narratives supposedly taking place there, the specific spatial conditions are similarly elided. Even celebrated apparent exceptions like *Chinatown* (Roman Polanski, 1974) that reference actual events and so have been able to trade on their putative historical and geographical specificity are largely myth and fiction.[12] More generally, the city is replaced by a handful of metonymic images: the beaches, Beverly Hills streets lined with high palm trees, aerial shots of layered freeway intersections, and the Hollywood sign itself have a greater resonance than other, nondescript images of the city because their implication of Los Angeles has already been coded in previous media incarnations. Or, when taken as a whole rather than as parts, the city is made the site of utopian or dystopian spectacles that may be justified by invoking real Los Angeles events – earthquakes, immigration, race-riots, life in Hollywood and Beverly Hills, and so on are among the most prominent – these are transformed according to the needs of the genre,

109

ideology, or the entertainment function itself.¹³ In such cases, heterotopia is replaced by utopia; again, Foucault: "Utopias are sites with no real place. They are sites that have a general relation of direct or inverted analogy with the real space of Society. They present society itself in a perfected form, or else society turned upside down, but in any case these utopias are fundamentally unreal spaces.¹⁴

In both usages, then, representations of Los Angeles in mainstream film and television have overlapped with and been overdetermined by the requirements of the media itself. Whether the actual heterotopic diversity of the region that facilities the media industry is repressed in each film's selection of the particular aspect its diegesis requires, or whether the city is presented in an idealized or inverted perfect form, Los Angeles has been envisaged by Hollywood as an everywhere or a nowhere, but never itself. Media images of Los Angeles refer essentially to the media; in them the city's spatiality becomes the space of the cinema industry. The industry's inability to map the space of its own operation in any but the broadest and most sensationalized forms has concealed the other extraordinary, if not unique, property of the city that supplies its postmodern prototypicality – the urban structure itself.

While to the entertainment industry Los Angeles was "fundamentally unreal", the city became an all-too real prototype of the postmodern conurbations now developing in many parts of the world. Reflecting the human development of the topography, climate, and biota of the land and water masses, for the past century spatiality in Los Angeles has been most determined by hydrology, the automobile, and immigration. The first supplied the successive booms of suburban real estate development and the second consolidated the rail and road-car networks into the most extensive freeway system in the world that simultaneously linked and segregated the local communities. Through immigration, these turned into "the most differentiated of all cities", "a combination of enclaves with high identity, and multiclaves with mixed identity ... perhaps the most heterogeneous city in the world".¹⁵ For the successive waves of immigration – Anglos from the mid-west and south, blacks and Mexicans, and most recently East Asians and refugees from US imperial adventures in Meso-America – precipitated, not the radial, homogenous modern city, but a cosmopolitan megalopolis, inhabited by people from all over the world – a microcosm of global diaspora. The unreal places of the Paramount Studio map have been occupied, and now a corner at a mini mall, with shop signs in Chinese and Tagalog as well as English, leads from Mexico to Korea.

Together with the long history of anti-labor politics that inhibited any trans-ethnic working-class consciousness, this social dispersal precluded melting-pot urban integration. But it also had the advantage of allowing minority social groups, especially those that arrived in distinct waves of immigration, to settle in relatively homogenous, relatively autonomous clusters. There, as well as infiltrating into Los Angeles aspects of distant spatialities, they have better sustained their original identity. The structural tensions that shape the city geographically have generated parallel tensions that shape its arts. Minority cultures in Los Angeles are created in the tension between the centrifugal pull of the local communities and their indigenous practices and the centripetal pull of the entertainment industry. As over time and at different rates for different groups the balance between these pulls has shifted, the mediums they have used to sustain themselves culturally have similarly matured and declined. But, reflecting the extent to which film has been the city's medium in dominance, independent filmmaking in Los Angeles has been a crucial site of alternative cultural activity. Either unrepresented or misrepresented by the film industry, the city's local communities have had to develop modes of film production alternative to and counter to the studios' capitalist mode of production. And in the alternative cinemas they have pioneered, both the discursive structures of their films and their visions of the city and their own relation to it have all been antithetical to Hollywood's.

III A Geo-cinematic Hermeneutic: Modes of Production and Means of Production

The dispersed, polynucleated but nevertheless ultimately centered structure of the Los Angeles megalopolis and the broadly homologous conditions determining both industrial studio production and minority cinemas alternative to it frame the question of the geographical relation of any film to the city, whether made in the studios or in some alternative cinema. Considerations of the adequacy or inadequacy of representation – the adjudication of the accuracy of a film's depiction of the city's social and architectural components – may be contextualized in the specific forces and conditions determining the production of films.

In capitalist social formations, the manufacture of narrative feature films has in many ways structurally paralleled the manufacture of other commodities. This continuity between material and cultural commodity production was especially distinct in Hollywood's classic period between the 1920s and 1960s when the major studios were consolidated monopolistic industries controlling both the production and the distribution of films, the latter leading to the point of consumption where the productive process was completed, allowing new cycles to begin. In this system, the *mode of production* involved the controlled activity of labor upon the means of *means of production*, itself comprised of the *instruments of labor* and the *subjects of labor*. The former includes tools and equipment used in shooting, developing, editing, and distributing film (cameras, lights, soundstages; labs, editing rooms, printing facilities, etc.) the productive units, and the overall infrastructure. The latter consists of the natural resources and raw materials used in the manufacture. The raw material includes the external world that is photographed and the light that allows it to be transferred to film. Initially the topography and cityscapes were essentially free raw materials for the industry; indeed its move from New York to Los Angeles was occasioned by the dependable availability of these: simulacra of global environments (as illustrated by the Paramount map) on the one hand, and on the other, light, sunshine, and predictable weather. After the introduction of sound caused the shift to in-studio shooting, the relative importance of these raw materials declined. But only temporarily, and after World War II the industry again returned to using the virtually free raw materials of the California landscapes and urban cityscapes. For the postwar noir and other films set in Los Angeles in the 1940s and 1950s and the comedies and neo-noirs that followed, the relation of Hollywood to the city was then doubled. The movie and later the television studios were themselves intrinsic to the economy, architecture, and culture of Los Angeles, substantially responsible for shaping them all; but as the objects of representation, the economy, architecture, and culture of Los Angeles also figured importantly among the means of production, specifically the subjects of labor.

At its historical apogee, this industrial mode of production – professional filmmaking – generated a new importance for its dialectical opposite: amateur filmmaking. Varieties of non-commodity production had existed from the beginnings of the medium: as home movies, for example, and as the domestic production of art film in the early 1930s, like that of James Sibley Watson and Melville Webber. But it was not until Maya Deren proposed the idea of a cinema based on "the love of the thing rather than for economic reasons or necessity" that it achieved significant cultural leverage. Though not published until 1959, her essay, "Amateur Versus Professional",[16] theorized the radical potential of the mode of film production that she and Alexander Hammid inaugurated in *Meshes of the Afternoon*, made in Los Angeles in 1943. Like Man Ray's *Juliet*, made close-by the same year and also by a pair of newly-weds, it reconstructed the stylistics of European avant-garde of the 1920s and established the ideal form of the mode of production that evolved into the postwar U.S. avant-gardes and minority cinemas.

Meshes contained echoes of the Parisian avant-garde, especially of Luis Buñuel and Salvador Dalí's *Un chien Andalou* (1929), as well as of surrealist interludes in Buster Keaton's *Sherlock, Jr.* (1924) and other classic Hollywood films. But it pioneered an art of cinema as a process of psycho-sexual self-interrogation and actualization in which filmmakers were "realizing the themes of their films through making and acting them".[17] This psychodramatic "trance film" provided the strongest generic model, first for Kenneth Anger, Curtis Harrington, and Gregory Markopoulos and other young filmmakers in Los Angeles and thence generally in the U.S. through the mid-1960s. Also made in personal domestic space – at Man Ray's apartment at 1245 Vine Street in Hollywood (three miles from Deren's house at 1466 North King's Road) – *Juliet* was a short 8 mm home movie for which he and his new wife filmed each other as they informally hammed for the camera. It both recapitulated the interactive surrealist cinema that he and Dudley Murphy had pioneered in Paris in the photography of their respective lovers for the avant-garde classic *Ballet mécanique* (1924) and anticipated the use of the same trope in Underground film, in Stan Brakhage's *Wedlock House: An Intercourse* (1959), for instance. The modes of production instanced in Man Ray's *jeu d'esprit*, made sheerly for pleasure and with recourse to only the most minimal domestic form of the cinematic apparatus, and Deren's own aesthetically-ambitious but self-financed project, using her body to wield her camera and herself, family, and friends as actors liberated U.S. cinema for counter-cultural formation.

Deren's essay diametrically contrasted the professional means of production against the amateur. The former had "the trained actors, the elaborate staffs and sets, the enormous production budgets… . their many-ton monsters, cables and crews", but the amateur had "freedom – both artistic and physical" and her versatile human body was superior in every way for the manipulation of small, light-weight equipment.[18] But while these very inexpensive if not entirely free personal resources supplied the means of production that enabled films to be shot, their distribution and the amalgamation of the enterprises of like-minded artists in the creation of the avant-gardes of the 1950s and 1960s and the minority cinemas since the 1970s required more extensive apparatuses. In the evolution of these alternative cinemas from Deren and Man Ray's different forms of amateur production, two developments coincided, both with fundamentally spatial components; one involved filmic representation and the other cinematic production.

The erotic interactions between newly-weds expanded into the wider social contexts of the New American Cinema and Underground film, eventually to dramatize the evolution of the beats and other subcultures, counter-cultural groups, political groups working on behalf of civil rights, for example, and attempts to end the invasion of Viet Nam, and minority groups as a whole, all of which took place in social rather than domestic environments: the pad, the streets, the community, eventually the nation. As this wider socialization expanded, and both the people and the institutions in which they organized themselves were seen to occupy public spaces, bringing the neighborhood and the city into the films, so they were obliged to create and engage new means of production, new apparatuses and new cinemas that could mediate between the groups' aspirations and their realization. Allowing marginal communities to develop autonomous or quasi-autonomous cinemas, these *mediating apparatuses* fall into three broad groups: First, the means of production proper, including actors, equipment sales and rental houses, and laboratories that make equipment available to filmmakers and arts centers, and community workshops that organize production. Second, the means of distribution and consumption or exhibition, including theaters, distribution organizations, and promotional mechanisms. And, third, suffusing these, ideological apparatuses, including journals, magazines, museums, archives, libraries, schools and academic conferences and publications.

These mediating apparatuses typically grow on its edges of the industry proper or within its interstices, with degrees of autonomy reflecting the overall political tenor of the period. In Los Angeles, for example, the distribution agencies and specialty theaters that comprised the means of distribution included Curtis Harrington and Kenneth Anger's cooperative Creative Film Associates and Bob Pike's more commercially oriented Creative Film Society on the one hand, and on the other, art galleries (American Contemporary Gallery on Hollywood Boulevard), then again commercial enterprises (the Cinema Theatre), and later publicly funded screening groups (the Pasadena Filmforum). Since Los Angeles has historically been rich in cinematic resources that supply Hollywood, the tools of production outside the studio have been readily available for production on its margins. This presence of the industry and its permeability ironically also allowed Los Angeles, over the twentieth century as a whole, to become the most important center of many non-industrial modes of film production in the U.S. In them, the mode of filmic production mediates between the reality of the city and the production of its appearance in film.

This doubled inscription of geography provides the basis for a *geo-cinematic hermeneutic:* the properly materialist and spatial analysis of the way a representation of a specific region of the city and the people who inhabit it is determined by the productive resources available in its social and spatial position in the city: the social, cultural, and material means of production. That is, *the way the city is figured in a film reflects the way the city figured in the filmmaking.*

To illustrate this reciprocity, the issue of Los Angeles's multiple spatialities may be simplified by Reyner Banham's topographical solution to the question of whether Los Angeles was one city or 132. Banham argued that its architectural originality and multiplicity could be schematized into four "ecologies": the beaches (surfurbia), the foothills, the central flatlands, and the freeways. Combining Sauer's term, "cultural landscape" with Banham's ecologies, we can then think of the spatialities in which independent film is produced – including the different mediating cinematic apparatuses to which they permit access – as "cultural ecologies", and so propose a geo-hermeneutic allegory; in silently telling the story of the social relations and the material functions it serves, so every film tells the story of the cultural ecology in which it was produced.[19]

The possibilities of such a *geo-cinematic hermeneutic* may be sketched by a comparison of two films produced in different, though geographically adjacent spatialities: Charles Burnett's *Killer of Sheep* (1977) and Pat O'Neill's *Water and Power* (1988). In these, the relation between each film's crucially original representation of one Los Angeles cultural ecology and the mediating apparatuses that allowed its production it is especially pointed. Both films follow traditional avant-gardes in being intensely personal, for though both involved extensive collaboration, they were each conceived, photographed, and edited essentially by one person; and both were undertaken as self-justifying projects with comparatively little attention to the possibilities of financial return, certainly not to the valorization of invested capital. But both are more specifically prototypical of the Los Angeles avant-garde in being independent and implicitly critical of Hollywood and yet in clear negotiation with it. Despite stunning formal originality, both approach industrial norms in that one is a feature-length narrative, while the other is close to feature-length, and shot and distributed in 35 mm. Though in these respects they are similar, their styles are so diametrically different as to constitute a virtual case-study in what introductory film aesthetics terms the "Bazin-Eisenstein debate", a textbook contrast between "faith in reality" and "faith in the image". And while one is overtly "political", the other is overtly "aesthetic". Their two film languages and their envisioning of Los Angeles reflect equally different spatialities in terms of both representation and production. And each involves one of the two specific deployments of mediating apparatuses that facilitate non-industrial production: the first being academic institutions and the second, small individually-owned workshops that sustain themselves financially on projects outsourced tasks by major studios.

IV. The Academic Mode Of Film Production: *Killer of Sheep*

Since the 1960s, college film programs have facilitated independent production while also sustaining a communication between industrial and non-industrial cinemas. The University of Southern California (USC) film school has been especially integrated with the industry since its founding in the late 1920s as a result of meetings between the USC president and Douglas Fairbanks, then president of the Academy of Motion Picture Arts and Sciences, in anticipation of an increased need for technical workers with the advent of sound. In the 1960s George Lucas and the "movie brats" elevated the relationship into the upper-echelon of production as USC-trained directors, producers, writers, and camera crew entered the industry. Other colleges are less thoroughly imbricated in the industry. California Institute of the Arts, for example, though founded by Walt Disney to educate industry workers, has also employed and trained avant-garde and experimental filmmakers. The other major university, UCLA, is also primarily tributary to the industry, but in the late 1960s it became the crucible for minority cinemas.

Los Angeles was without question the single most important place for the emergence of minority ethnic cinemas in the US in the 1970s and 1980s. Some early independent Asian American films were made in San Francisco, and New York saw some early African American filmmaking. But in the period of minority mobilization the most important African-, Asian- and Mexican American minority cinemas all emerged together in Los Angeles. The city's singular importance reflects the proximity of the industry, but also a unique combination of ethnic demographics and urban structure. Since World War II, Los Angeles became home to very substantial numbers of each of the three main minority groups. In 1970, 60% of the city was white, 11% was black, 15% Chicano, and 4% Asian. But by 2000, whites had halved from 60 to 30%, blacks were down slightly to 10%, Asians were up from 4 to 15%, and Latinos had tripled from 15 to 44%. That is to say, the ethnic composition of the city was inverted: in 30 years LA went from 60% white to 70% minority, and now together minorities are the majority. The city's geographical structure both enabled and reflected these population shifts. The lateral rather than vertical expansion of the city created polycentric conglomerations of urban villages, spatially segregated, quasi-autonomous, and substantially ethnically homogenous enclaves: the largely Latino East Los Angeles, the largely black South Central Los Angeles and a scattering of Asian "little Cities": Chinatown, Little Tokyo, Korea Town, Little Manila, and so on. The absence of the urban melting pot of multi-ethnic working-class communalities allowed distinct ethnic identity to be consolidated to some degree across class lines. By the same token, these ethnically homogenous communities provided a backdrop and a context for persuasive ethnically-specific narratives.

Killer of Sheep takes place almost entirely in the African American working-class neighborhoods of South Central. Architecturally, the ghetto differs from its counterparts in other cities in the predominance of single-family dwellings and small apartment buildings. The cityscape is flat, dilapidated, of limited image-ability, and without conspicuous internal differentiation; yet the angular forms and shifting greys in Burnett's studied takes of the dusty streets and alleyways, the clapboard houses and stucco apartments are all enlivened by the children's endlessly inventive play. There are no signs of commerce except a liquor store, or of industry except the slaughterhouse where the protagonist works; this is generally seen only from the inside, so that its articulation with the community is not visible. And there are no signs of connections with other parts of the city except the Southern Pacific railroad that appears to share the area's defunct lethargy; its railcars are immobile and its tracks the children's playgrounds. No trace of any other Los Angeles may be seen; no business districts, no supermarkets, no luxurious high-rise apartment, no technicolor sunsets, no homes of the stars – not even the Watts Towers. Most remarkable of all, there are no freeways. Indeed, there are almost no cars; those few that are not so permanently disabled that they have been re-invented as street-furniture are at best unreliable. Life here is entirely constrained within one of Banham's ecologies, the central flatlands. The only substantial narrative event is the protagonist's attempt to piece together a car to take his family for a day trip to the races. But hardly is a country outside the city glimpsed than the car breaks down, forcing a return to a stultifying carceral stasis. As photographed by Burnett, the lack of spatial mobility in this geography figures above all the lack of social mobility, and in presenting poverty as simultaneously an economic and a spatial condition, the film foregrounds the racial and class apartheid that constitutes the Los Angeles of South Central: that lack of access to work, to communications networks, to self-governance, or to any of the other resources of the city proper, commonly proposed as the immediate cause of the 1965 uprising, and which has only deteriorated since.

The unprecedented representation of African-American family life and the quasi-documentary verisimilitude both categorically differ, not only from mainstream Hollywood (for which the area is essentially unrepresentable and known only as a lair from which emerge the predators who prey on bourgeois society), but also from the two eras of para-studio African American filmmaking that frame it, the early 1970s blaxploitation that followed *Sweet Sweetback's Baadasss Song* (Melvin Van Peebles, 1971) and the neo-exploitation of *Boyz N the Hood* (John Singleton, 1991), *South Central* (Steve Anderson, 1992), *Menace II Society* (Albert and Allen Hughes, 1993), and so on. In contrast to the exploitative sexuality and other generic conventions of both eras, in *Killer of Sheep* the family is whole. Its foundation is Stan, the father, who is present, regularly employed, and proudly independent; and, however precariously, he supports his wife, son, and daughter.

Figure 2. *Killer of Sheep*

He disdains petty crime and the petty criminals of the community; alongside fellow workers in the slaughterhouse, both black and white, he continues in back-breaking labor; coffee is his drug of choice, and the grind of his life's labor doesn't provoke promiscuity but rather destroys sexual desire. Mostly alone and imprisoned in their house and desperate for a love that he cannot give, his wife nevertheless sustains him and their children. Though the boundaries of the family appear fluid, with the energetic activity of the children enlivening the community as a whole, Stan's principle commitment remains to his family. So while the film counterposes the melodrama of domestic space to the poverty of exterior public space, still the children's vitality in the streets sustains a humanist optimism all through that is consummated in the last scene when a crippled young woman announces her pregnancy to family friends. The film's portrayal of the African

American working-class stands as a heroic rebuke to the capitalist media's combination of neglect and exploitation, not only of black but of all working-class life, and an exemplary premonition of a community-inspired alternative cinema.

But its production was not a case of spontaneous community self-expression, so much as a historically and geographically specific negotiation between the community in which Burnett had lived since coming to Los Angeles from Mississippi as a child and the equally specific apparatuses mediating between that community and the film industry. The principle agency was UCLA, where Burnett was the leading figure in a generation of young black filmmakers. Along with parallel groups of Asian and Mexican American filmmakers, the blacks were nurtured, not in the film school itself but in an Ethno-Communications Program in the Anthropology department, founded in 1968 in the wake of the 1965 Watts rebellion and the civil rights movements and in immediate response to student complaints about the racial exclusivity of the film school itself. Eventually the Program was incorporated into the film school where in the early 1970s Burnett was joined by Billy Woodberry, Haile Gerima, and Ben Caldwell; in the same period, Julie Dash was at the American Film Institute, an organization even more thoroughly aligned with Hollywood than UCLA. Unlike the Asian Americans at UCLA, who focused on educational community documentaries, most of the Blacks students aspired to produce feature films, neo-realistic narratives for popular audiences made with a view toward initial dissemination via the festival circuit and liberal public institutions: that is, the art film, and specifically neo-realism, "a revolutionary cinema in a non-revolutionary society".[20] To this end, they all collaborated on each other's projects. Burnett, for example, wrote and photographed Woodberry's *Bless Their Little Hearts* (1983), and photographed Dash's *Illusions* (1982), Gerima's *Bush Mama* (1976), and parts of Larry Clark's *Passing Through* (1977). For these filmmakers, the UCLA provided a combination of three resources: production equipment and a semi-professional filmmaking community; a degree of access to the industry; and models of alternative film languages compatible with low-budget feature production.

The determining effect of these specific community and institutional resources is everywhere apparent in *Killer of Sheep*. They produce its thematics, its liberal humanist appeal for sympathy and understanding from mainstream society, rather than a historical analysis of racism or a militant call to contestation. As a result, the film has been primarily distributed, not in the black spatiality it depicts, but in the white institutions of liberal humanism, in festivals, schools, and museums.[21] And they produced its form: the combination of narrative strategies and economic imperatives that prompt the use of deep-focus, long-takes; the non-professional actors playing roles close to themselves; the documentary feel of grainy black and white; and especially the attenuation of narrative, its replacement as a site of meaning by studied takes of human faces permitting the observation of what Rossellini called "the movements of the soul". In these respects, the film is an audaciously ambitious accommodation of impoverishment in resources and an accommodation to the politics of the liberal institutions which, in the absence of a militant black cinema, allowed it to be made. But in one other respect the film is wealthy. Immediately available to it was the most bountiful resource of African American culture, music, and Burnett uses it to enrich and extend the visual track of *Killer of Sheep*.

Used intra-diegetically, recorded songs affirm music's special role as a means of spiritual sustenance and imaginative expression for African American people. But Burnett's use of non-diegetic music in elaboration of that role allows him metonymically to expand early-1970s South Central into the whole history of African American resistance. His visual mapping of the environment may be constrained by the empiricism of realist photography, as well as by the poverty of the community and by the poverty of the resources for which he, in his position as a UCLA student was only partially able to compensate; but in the soundtrack he loosened the realism and used music to access other times and spaces, and so introduce a historical dimension and a sense of continuity, whose destruction he regarded as primarily responsible for the degradation of black community.[22]

Indeed, if the visuals alone resemble the verisimilitude of neo-realism, the image-music relations create a variety of highly artificial montage effects, in which classical black music from the thirties and forties adds resonance and counterpoint to themes which the attenuated narrative itself holds suspended: Paul Robeson's singing "Ballad for Americans"[23] as youngsters play on ruined lots, for example, and Dinah Washington singing "This Bitter Earth" as Stan and his wife embrace each other in their misery and slowly dance.

In some instances, the play of song lyrics across the visuals is very complex. The scene where for the first time it becomes clear that Stan's anomie is destroying his relationship with his wife, for example, is accompanied by Earth, Wind and Fire's mid-1970s mega-hit, "Reasons". The tension between the timbre of Philip Bailey's ecstatic falsetto that affirms erotic passion and the lyrics that broach the inevitability of its fading over time perfectly encompasses the tensions in the woman's life. But since the sequence begins with their baby daughter singing along to the record, the questioning of love is initially redirected from husband/wife to daughter/mother, with the child placed as simultaneously the objective correlative of the erotic passion which once existed but has now been drained away by the grind of poverty, and herself already in process of being constituted as a subject by the mass media. "I don't want to feel", the child sings, groping to follow the record, "I'm in the wrong place to be real". Contextualized in this specific narrative, these lyrics suddenly transcend their banality, and the moment becomes a summary index of the history of a people, allowing *Killer of Sheep*, even as it references the systematic mass media exploitation that has framed the history of African American people, also to transcend it.

Workshop Craft Production: *Water and Power*

If Burnett's Los Angeles appears as an oppressive enclosure that thwarts all attempts to escape, O'Neill's is a shimmering vision through which disembodied figures are transported by magic. No prison this; rather a plethora of radically dissimilar spatialities that, linked by the restless trajectories of camera-movement, all incessantly dissolve or transform one into another. Their multiple-superimposition and constant interpenetration create a composite space, for implicit in any one topography is an unlimited number of others. For Burnett, the ontology of the neighborhood and its boundaries are undeniable; for O'Neill any one place is only a pocket in another, not even a momentary rest in the ceaseless twining of heterotopias. None of these ever stabilizes sufficiently to become normative, but instead a relation among them emerges as a kind of deep structure to most of the film's sequences and its overall theme. This consists of a dissolve from one or more shots of desert scenes into one or more shots of the city with the transition bridged by an interior showing traces of human creativity and craft, a workshop, or an abandoned industrial space turned into an artist's loft.

Fundamentally then the film is an extended parallel montage that marks a radical development for O'Neill. His earliest works had been each mobilized around a single formal and thematic principle, but his immediately previous films, such as *Saugus Series* (1974) and *Sidewinder's Delta* (1976) had rather been dossier-like compilations of discrete sections, each mobilizing a different formal procedure in optical printing, and linked to the others by only the loosest thematic continuity – they were generally scenes of everyday events and wilderness landscapes all transformed by art.[24] These were essentially late Underground films, even though the theoretical and institutional infrastructure supporting such short films had collapsed by the late 1970s under the combined assaults of structural film, the politicization of the avant-garde by feminism and other identity groups, and the catastrophic increase in film costs. The avant-garde's consequent turn to feature-length works designed for commercial distribution was not inimical to

O'Neill, except that the compositional principle of his entire oeuvre to date had been montage. *Water and Power* marked a tentative engagement with narrative.

In published notes, O'Neill sketched a narrative underlay to the film.[25] Its main character is Aaron Haskell, who commits suicide by plunging from the bridge in the movie's opening shot, just before the title. (Perhaps the film is what he sees in the moment of his death, parallel to the expanded moment of consciousness of the man in *Incident at Owl Creek* [*La Rivière du hibou*, Robert Enrico, 1962], who also falls from a bridge as he is hanged – or of Stan Brakhage, whose suicide by hanging frames his visionary *Anticipation of the Night* [1958]). At any rate, according to the notes, Jack, a detective investigating Haskell's death visits his wife, who lives in a trailer in the desert near their mine, and her lover, Rudy, who tells stories about corruption in the Russian army. Scenes from various Westerns follow, which in turn lead the story back to The Studio, where shooting is underway on the crowd scenes for "The Biggest Picture of All"; the movie is sponsored by four multinational corporations, led by Seoul businessman, Kim Chong, who is actually Haskell, "very much alive and ... deeply involved in the picture business".[26] Many of these incidents do appear in the film – the corruption in the Russian army, for example, is illustrated by scenes from *The Lost Command* that are floated in over time-lapse photography of a desert lake bed – and others are spoken or presented as text accompanied by black leader, with the visual equivalents appearing elsewhere. But such a narrative substrate is certainly not recoverable from the film, nor does the film imply narrative as a compositional principle, except in so far that subtitles satirize it by generating contradictory continuities in the manner of the intertitles of *Un chien Andalou*. As remote as the motive of a dream, narrative is dispelled by the immediacy and intricacy of the optical printing, and by the insistence of the montage.

Knitting together a skein of Los Angeles associations, O'Neill's deconstruction of the opposition between city and desert recalls the metaphors of local lore: "Los Angeles is a cultural desert" and so on. And the visual trope may be read literally in several ways: human industry has turned the desert into a city, or the artist's vision is capable of seeing through the urban fabric to the landform below. It also has a very specific historical basis in the Owens Valley Project that brought the water allowing the city's expansion, even while it turned the previously fertile valley into a desert. This was in fact the beginning of the city's Department of Water and Power, and the pipelines bringing the water through the desert to the city are a leitmotif in the film. But O'Neill's historical retrospection is intertwined with a more contemporary attention to the rhetoric that matured in the period of the film's production, proposing the city's historical representativeness. Over-

6 – Toward a Geo-Cinematic Hermeneutics/The City as Means of Production

Figure 3. *Water and Power*.

night and from several different directions simultaneously, it was transformed from a more or less hideous anomaly, a kind of late-capitalist Philadelphia, into "a *protopos*, a paradigmatic place ... a *mesocosm*, an ordered world in which the micro and the macro, the idiographic and the nomothetic, the concrete and the abstract, can be seen simultaneously in an articulated and interactive combination" – the representative postmodern city invoked above.[27]

Within the many different agendas at stake in such promotions, two are especially important: first, the post-Fordist economics of the Pacific Rim, and second, a putatively new mode of subjectivity, usually correlated with the post-structural theory promoted in Orange County by the "Parisian fakirs"[28] who flocked to the University of California at Irvine in the 1970s. Traces of the city's role in Pacific Rim finance capital and the massive importation of both third world workers and third world labor relations are glimpsed in *Water and Power*: in the juxtapositions of the different downtown skylines, for example, and in the fragments of a history of capital restructuring stretching from Sir Francis Drake to Kim Chong, the Korean businessman involved in shady corporate transactions in the picture business. But implications of this kind are subordinate to those of second area, postmodern subjectivity, specifically to a formal structure which disassembles the filmic vocabularies of the classic narrative and the humanist subject.

In *Water and Power*, stable narrative subjects are replaced by fragmentary and evanescent protagonists, what Paul Arthur has called "a set of vagabond voices and images connected briefly by theme or proximity" and narrative continuity itself is replaced by the "intricate semicoherence" of the montage.[29] Consequently the medium's unique capacity to redeem reality by simulating unified, continuous space and time is abandoned in the film's two most fundamental strategies, collage superimpositions of multiple registers of the former and time-lapse photography condensations of the latter. These technical effects are persuasive as allegorical figurations of the conditions of postmodernity, of its putative time-space compression and the continued dissolution of one place into another that constitutes the Foucauldian heterotopic space, "capable of juxtaposing in a single real place several sites that are in themselves incompatible".[30] Such resonances may be pushed even further since, in so forcefully making material space and subject to the medium itself, these filmic techniques lead all but inevitably to the superimposition of found footage over the landscapes, and so to the discovery that – as the Paramount Studio map revealed – the topographies of Southern California are all already inhabited by old Hollywood movies.[31] The difference between natural and filmic space is confounded, and diegeses photographed elsewhere and often long-ago for other films are discovered within O'Neill's own photography of the local landscapes – an inverse recapitulation of the process that historically allowed Hollywood to find all other places in its backyard.

In respect to these multiple figurations of media-dependent hyperreality, O'Neill's chief industrial intertext is then the essential Hollywood film, not of the 1970s, but of the 1980s: not *Chinatown* (which is usually cited as the correlative to his investigation of the Owens Valley Project), but *Blade Runner*. But rather than choosing between the nostalgic modernist film and the dystopian postmodernist vision that has replaced it as the key representation of Los Angeles, it is probably more fruitful to see *Water and Power* as superimposing these too. For its take on hyperreality and the trappings of postmodernism is deeply ambivalent. Explaining this and so explaining the film's unique visual appearance again involves a geographical detour, for though like *Killer of Sheep*, *Water and Power* occupies an interzone between the industry proper and the disaffiliated avant-garde, its liminality is one of quite different contexts.

6 – Toward a Geo-Cinematic Hermeneutics/The City as Means of Production

In Banham's terms, O'Neill's ecology is that of the foothills, the space where several modes of cultural production intersect and nurture each other. Predominantly it is the social space of Hollywood and para-Hollywood workers; Hollywood Boulevard is its "main street",[32] and its main activity is the manufacture of commodity entertainment. This Hollywood also sustains the host of para-industrial enterprises of the kind that, from the mid-sixties until computer-imaging became the industry norm, allowed O'Neill to make a living and subsidized his independent projects; his special effects work on commercials and features, such as *Return of the Jedi* (Richard Marquand, 1983) and *Poltergeist* (Tobe Hooper, 1982) continues then the tradition of avant-garde interpolations in Hollywood films that began with Slavko Vorkapich's experimental montage interludes in 1930s features.

But the foothills also sustain art that is not so oriented to or completely dependent on the interests of capital. For O'Neill himself, its significant institutions were UCLA, where he was formally educated (not in the film school, whose industry-orientation was so fruitful for Burnett, but in art and design), and two of Los Angeles's long-standing art theaters, the Coronet and the Cinema Theater, where in the 1960s he informally educated himself in the classic European and contemporary U.S. avant-gardes.[33] And they sustain the other institutions of the avant-garde: art galleries, cafés and bars, bookstores, and screening organizations, most notably the Los Angeles Independent Film Oasis. For a number of years in the late-1970s, Oasis was one of two independent screening organizations in the city. Collectively organized by avant-garde filmmakers, it became the focus of a distinct era in avant-garde production; O'Neill was a founding member, and he premiered the most consummate of his fourteen shorts there.

Located in the middle of this mixed cultural ecology is Lookout Mountain Films, the most recent of the several independent production companies O'Neill has headed. From this aerie on Lookout Mountain Avenue, high in the Hollywood Hills off the Cahuenga pass, O'Neill does indeed look out over some of the chief geographical and historical divides of the city and the industry, all of which structure *Water and Power*. He is midway between Los Angeles proper to the south, and to the north the San Fernando Valley, the area added to the city to meet the terms of the Owens River bond issue. He is also midway between the pre-and post-war locations of the industry, between Hollywood itself and Studio and Universal Cities. Further to the north lies the Owens Valley itself (where most of the desert footage was shot), while closer is the town of Saugus and California Institute of the Arts, where he taught for the first half of the 70s, with several of his ex-students returning to him to work on *Water and Power* in a team that also included three animators, along with specialists in audio design, mechanical design and construction, and optical printing.

These geographies and the schizophrenic combination of industrial and artisanal potentials in this cultural ecology ubiquitously inform *Water and Power*'s production. A home-made film, only partially funded by the National Endowment for the Humanities, it nevertheless cost $90,000 of his own money; it uses a very sophisticated motion-controlled time-lapse camera, but the images were shot spontaneously; though the image processing is beyond the industrial standards, it was ordered intuitively; it contains fragments from O'Neill's commercial jobs and also from his dreams. This interpenetration of avant-garde and industrial proclivities and the combination of imaginative and arcane manual skills are also historically specific, the former instancing the switch from shorts to feature-length projects that a generation of avant-garde filmmakers made in the 1980s, and the latter a not-unconnected tension between technological nostalgia and prolepsis. Occurring on the threshold of a totalized electronic environment and electronic image processing, the implications of the film's elaborate fabrication nevertheless shy away from the aesthetics of postmodernism to reclaim a thick, modernist materiality, and invoke a homespun pride in hands-on craftsmanship and authenticity figured in the images of artisanal environments that bridge the city and the desert in the film.

These tensions trace an individual and a general crisis for avant-garde film. The pull between a modern past and a postmodern future, both of which (though in quite different ways) were in the mid-80s *not really here*, was a specific historical and geographical moment. For the filmic effects of which O'Neill is a virtuoso master were all becoming routinely possible, but as computer-generated using digital technology. At this point the yearnings of avant-garde film to be autonomous practice, independent of the now-international industrial culture, give up the ghost. Antipathy to rationalized, corporate electronic media will be expressed as a radical conservatism that privileges earlier phases of Hollywood itself – a response that has been endemic in the avant-garde at least since Kenneth Anger. To work as O'Neill did, photochemically and in film bespeaks a longing for a world of mechanical reproduction, of simple apparatuses like optical printers that can be domestically assembled from WWII cameras (as O'Neill himself did), and so it is a nostalgia for visual precision, for full visual sensuousness, for vision itself. As we are absorbed by television, a medium which makes vision redundant, *Water and Power* appears as an attempt to reclaim Los Angeles for film and to reclaim the medium in which Los Angeles lived. One of the last machine's last master-craftsmen, O'Neill made one of the last Los Angeles *films*.

6 – Toward a Geo-Cinematic Hermeneutics/The City as Means of Production

Notes

1. The longest standing of these groups is Labor News Production, founded in 1989, which as well as making its own documentaries on behalf of the working-class, also taught militant workers how to make their own documentaries. For a history of radical Korean documentaries and their relation to the minjung movement, see, Nam In-young, "Fifteen Years of Committed Documentaries in Korea: From *Sangge-dong Olympic* to *Repatriation*", https://www.yidff.jp/docbox/25/box25-3-e.html. Accessed 29 January 2020. Giving examples of each, Nam identifies four forms of filmmaker-community involvement: i. "films where the filmmaker or production team collaborates with the community in the entire process including planning, production (filming and editing) and distribution"; ii. "films produced by social groups or local communities themselves after they learn production skills and techniques from independent documentary filmmakers"; iii. cases "where the filmmaker is commissioned by a social movement group or civic group and plans and produces a work together with that group"; and iv. cases "where the filmmaker becomes a member of the community and makes the film while living with the community".

2. The Workers International Relief (*Internationale Arbeiter-Hilfe*: IAH) was based in Berlin and led by William (Willi) Münzenberg. *Arbeiter-Illustrierte-Zeitung* or *AIZ* (*The Workers Pictorial Newspaper*) was a German illustrated magazine published between 1924 and March 1933 in Berlin.

3. "Winter 1931–32 and Newsreels 1, 2, and 3", *The Western Worker*, 1 August 1932, p. 6.

4. David Harvey, *The Condition of Postmodernity: An Enquiry into the Origins of Cultural Change* (Oxford: Blackwell, 1989), p. 308.

5. David B. Clarke, "Introduction: Previewing the Cinematic City", in Clarke and Colin McArthur, eds., *The Cinematic City* (Hove, U.K.: Psychology Press, 1997), p. 3. The Baudrillard quotation is from *America* (London: Verso, 1988), p. 56.

6. *America*, p. 56.

7. Reyner Banham, *Los Angeles: The Architecture of Four Ecologies* (London: Penguin, 1971), p. 35.

8. "Spatiality" is Edward Soja's summary term for the "created space of social organization and production", mediating between space as a topographical given and the social relations constructed in it. "The structure of organized space is not a separate structure with its own autonomous laws of construction and transformation, nor is it simply an expression of the class structure emerging from social (and thus aspatial?) relations of production. It represents, instead, a dialectically defined component of the general relations of production which are simultaneously social and spatial." *Postmodern Geographies: The Reassertion of Space in Critical Social Theory* (Verso: London and New York, 1989), pp. 78–79.

9. Richard V. Spencer, "Los Angeles as a Producing Center", *Moving Picture World*, 8 April 1911. Excerpts from the article are reprinted in Eileen Bowser, *The Transformation of Cinema, 1907–1915* (Berkeley: University of California Press, 1990), pp. 160–161.

10. The map was reprinted in a prospectus produced by Halsey, Stuart and Co., "The Motion Picture Industry as a Basis for Bond Financing", dated 27 May 1927. The prospectus including the map was published in Tino Balio, ed., *The American Film Industry*, Revised Ed. (Wisconsin: University of Wisconsin Press, 1985), pp. 195–217.

11. Michel Foucault, "Of Other Spaces", *Diacritics* 16 (Spring 1986), p. 25.

12. Partial exceptions to this are often the industry's most transparently ideological projects. In his walk from one side of the city to the other, the protagonist of *Falling Down* (Joel Schumacher, 1993), for example, passes through a cross-section of the city's ethnic and class divisions, mostly fairly accurate in their geographical placing.

13. See Mike Davis's summary conclusion: "No city, in fiction or film, has been more likely to figure as the icon of a really bad future (or present, for that matter). Post-apocalyptic Los Angeles, overrun by terminators, androids, and gangs, has become as much a cliché as Marlowe's means streets or Gidget's beach party. The decay of the city's old glamor has been inverted by the entertainment industry into a new glamor of decay." *Ecology of Fear: Los Angeles and the Imagination of Disaster* (New York: Henry Holt, 1998), p. 278.

14. Foucault, "Of Other Spaces", p. 24.

15. These are drawn respectively from Kevin Starr, *Material Dreams*, p. 84; the *WPA Guide to California* (New York: Pantheon Books, 1984), p. 208; Soja, *Postmodern Geographies*, p. 224; and Charles Jenks, *Heteropolis* (London: Academy Editions, 1993), pp. 17 and 32.

16. Maya Deren's "Amateur vs. Professional" was first published in *Movie Makers Annual*, 1959, reprinted in *Film Culture* 39 (Winter 1965): 45–46.

17. P. Adams Sitney, *Visionary Film: The American Avant-Garde in the 20th Century*, 3rd ed. (New York: Oxford University Press, 2002), p. 14.

18. Deren, "Amateur vs. Professional", 45–46.

19. A lapidary instance of a Los Angeles community cinema created in a community mode of production is the Echo

Park Film Center, a non-profit media arts organization founded in 2002 in what was historically a working-class and bohemian neighborhood in Los Angeles, so radical that it earned the name Red Hill. It provides community access to film/video resources for members of marginalized and underserved communities to enable them to become active, empowered participants in the creation and dissemination of experimental, documentary and narrative film. Its projects include a neighborhood micro-cinema space in a converted storefront; free education programs for youth and seniors; and a film equipment and service retail department. It receives some city, county, and state funding, but most work is done by unpaid volunteers. At present it claims to have taught basic filmmaking to more than 10,000 young people. Its classes are 12 weeks long and each devoted to a topic of local interest and / or social justice: the Los Angeles River, for example, or graffiti, or the intimidation of immigrants. In Spring 2009 it took as its topic the history of Red Hill, its own community where most of the students resided. Along with structured classes in sound and image recording and editing at the storefront, the kids were expected to go out into the community to explore its history, especially by interviewing social activists. The material they gathered was initially screened as rushes and eventually edited into a 1 ¾ hour documentary that was shown to the community in screenings at the center and later at other community groups and schools, and also disseminated widely, even internationally on DVD.

20. Penelope Houston, *The Contemporary Cinema* (London: Penguin, 1963), p. 29. There were attempts in the same period by more radical Los Angeles Newsreel filmmakers to affiliate with the Black Panther Party in their resistance to the extreme brutality of the Los Angeles Police Department (LAPD), but the projected film, *Resistance*, was not completed. Burnett described his own disapproval of the Los Angeles Panthers in an interview with Monona Wali, "Life Drawings: Charles Burnett's Realism", *The Independent* (October 1988), p. 19. Despite this, he did tape L.A. Panther, Geronimo Pratt in San Quentin (when he was incarcerated after being framed by the LAPD for murder), but the project never came to fruition; see, Lynell George, *No Crystal Stair: African-Americans in the City of Angels* (New York: Anchor Books, 1994), p. 140.

21. *Killer of Sheep* won First Prize at the United States Film Festival and the Critics' Prize at the Berlin International Film Festival in 1981; in 1990, it was selected by the Library of Congress as one of twenty-five films chosen for preservation. Burnett has received a Rockefeller Grant, a Guggenheim Fellowship, and in 1988 he was awarded a MacArthur Foundation Fellowship.

22. In terms that directly address the narrative of *Killer of Sheep*, Burnett has linked the loss of this historical sense to attacks on African American social structures: "There has always been the attempt to destroy our consciousness of who we were, to deny the past, and destroy the family structure; and, since for us each day has not a yesterday or a tomorrow, to make the use of experience a lost art"; see his "Inner City Blues" in Jim Pines and Paul Willemen, ed., *Questions of Third Cinema* (London: British Film Institute, 1989), p. 225.

23. Written by Earl Robinson of the Workers Laboratory Theatre, "Ballad for Americans", has, as Michael Denning pointed out, "come to stand for the aesthetic forms and ideologies of the Popular Front", with Robeson's recording of it the "unofficial anthem of the movement." (*The Cultural Front: The Laboring of American Culture in the Twentieth Century* [New York: Verso, 1996], p. 115).

24. P. Adams Sitney observed, "One strains in vain to find a unity to the 'series' aside from the obvious invention of the imagery", and proposed that the systematic disjuncture to Los Angeles, "which is so overwhelmed by fragmentation and gerrybuilt perspectives". See *"Saugus Series"*, *Millennium Film Journal* 16–17–18 (Fall/Winter 1986), pp. 158 and 160.

25. See O'Neill's own, *"Water and Power, A Fragmentary Synopsis"*, *Motion Picture* 3.1–2 (Winter 1989): 19–20. A selection of his working notes for the film, "Notes for *Water and Power*", was published in *Millennium Film Journal* 25 (1991): 42–49.

26. "A Fragmentary Synopsis", p. 20.

27. Soja, *Postmodern Geographies*, p. 191.

28. The phrase is Mike Davis's; see his *City of Quartz: Excavating the Future in Los Angeles* (London: Verso, 1990), p. 70.

29. "In Two Dimensions: Lewis Klahr's *In the Month of Crickets*, Pat O'Neill's *Water and Power*", *Motion Picture* 3.1–2 (1989), p. 23. I take the phrase, "intricate semicoherence" from Peter Plagens' account of San Francisco collagist, Jess in his *Sunshine Muse: Contemporary Art on the West Coast* (New York: Praeger, 1974), p. 94.

30. Foucault, "Of Other Spaces", p. 25.

31. Arthur lists these interpolations: *Detour*, *The Last Command*, *The Docks of New York*, and *The Ten Commandments*, as well as references to Kenneth Anger's *Fireworks* ("In Two Dimensions", p. 21).

32. Banham, *Four Ecologies*, p. 101.

33. See Pat O"Neill, "Transcript of a Discussion" *Cantrill's Filmnotes* 59/60 (1989): 24–28, for his account of his youth "in the shadow of the Paramount water tower" and for production details for *Water and Power*.

Chapter Seven Expanded Cinema in Los Angeles: The Single Wing Turquoise Bird

During the last years of the 1960s and the first of the 1970s – the heyday of the psychedelic era – the premier light show in Los Angeles and one of the best in the world was the Single Wing Turquoise Bird.[1]

Long before this period, the city had seen several projects involving the projection of abstract light, "color organs" and similar apparatuses, versions of which date back at least to the 1720s when Louis-Bertrand Castel proposed that color transparencies could be linked to the keys of a harpsichord. In the early 1920s, Stanton MacDonald-Wright, a painter and self-styled "Color Motion Picturist", began to research abstract color projection and eventually made several kinetic light projectors, one of which was used in several theatrical productions in Santa Monica in 1927. Probably the most sophisticated of such light machines was Thomas Wilfred's Clavilux, built in the early 1920s; it consisted of a cabinet in which revolving discs and mirrors could be "played" so as to rear-project light onto a two-foot square screen. Wilfred wrote compositions for it that he called *lumia* and performed them publicly. Seeing a performance when he was recovering from a syphilitic eye-infection, Los Angeles avant-garde filmmaker Dudley Murphy found it "one of the most ecstatic experiences of [his] life", and when artist, Sara Kathryn Arledge saw Wilfred perform in Pasadena in 1928, she was inspired to become involved in time-based visual art and eventually to make important avant-garde films.[2] Oskar Fischinger, who shared Wilfred's mystical bent, worked in a similar vein. In 1950 he built his "lumigraph", an upright wooden frame about five feet high containing light sources that project inwards onto an open area three to four feet square holding an elastic white screen just behind the light sources. In a darkened room, the screen is invisible, but any area of it lightly pushed forward by the player catches the light, so that the player may spontaneously shape light in space.

Inspired by both the technological and the socio-cultural possibilities of its own time, the Single Wing Turquoise Bird expanded and elaborated such intersections between avant-garde film and visual music. First formed in the spring of 1968 to accompany rock concerts at the Shrine Auditorium and Exposition Hall in Los

Angeles, the light show several times reconfigured its membership and its performance modes, freeing itself from supplementarity to the rock events. Developing many different technologies and sources of both imagery and abstract light, it evolved into an autonomous multi-media unit that innovated the collectively-improvised, real-time composition of projected light. The group was able to maintain itself for over five years, but eventually several of its members became involved with cinematic projects of a more traditional kind and, though they still did occasional performances for several years after, the Single Wing effectively dissolved into a theatrical film exhibition company in 1973.

In fall 1967, John Van Hamersveld, an artist who had trained at Chouinard Art Institute and who had designed the iconic poster for Bruce Brown's surfing epic, *The Endless Summer* (1966) and, very recently, the cover for the Beatles' *Magical Mystery Tour* album (1967), received a grant to organize a happening. With a business and a journalism student from the University of Southern California (USC), he formed Pinnacle Productions, and on 10 and 15 November they staged the "Electric Wonder", a rock concert at the Shrine, featuring the Grateful Dead, Buffalo Springfield, and Blue Cheer, accompanied by various lighting effects. The event was so successful that they decided to sponsor more concerts, and for them they hired a local light show, the Thomas Edison Lighting Company, who projected on several screens at different points in the Shrine's cavernous interior, a space large enough to accommodate some five thousand spectators. Dissatisfied with the light show, Pinnacle invited several young filmmakers, most of whom were either enrolled in or had recently graduated from University of California at Los Angeles (UCLA), to form a new one.

This group included Burton Gershfield, Jon Greene,[3] Bruce Lane, David Lebrun, Peter Mays, and Jeff Perkins.[4] Motivated by developments in the New York and San Francisco undergrounds and by the Los Angeles heritage of abstract animation, especially the work of Fischinger and John and James Whitney, these were trying to expand the visual language of cinema with effects inspired by psychedelic drugs. Gershfield's ecstatic film, *Now That the Buffalo's Gone* (1965, edited by Lebrun), in which ethnographic imagery of the Plains Indians is transformed into solarized red or amber monochrome and re-animated by interruptive blank and negative frames, was in many ways the exemplary production of the group, with Pat O'Neill's *7362* (1967) also influential (and in fact several of the group were experimenting with a contact printer that O'Neill, then a UCLA photography instructor, had set up in the basement of the art department). Several of them were living at a house on Cresthill Road just above the Sunset Strip, then the focal point for the city's hippie subcultures, of which the Doors (of whom Ray

Manzarek and Jim Morrison were both former UCLA film students) were one of the leading bands. Mays had in fact first met Perkins in 1966 when the latter was the projectionist at the Cinematheque 16 on the Strip, the first theater in Los Angeles to specialize in underground films; Perkins had appeared in Mays's experimental films, one of which had been booked into the theater. Since then, they had been experimenting with light shows at UCLA and also sometimes at USC, using eight small projectors and outtakes from *Buffalo*, and working with others, including Scott Hardy, a liquid projectionist from San Francisco, whom they had met through an advertisement in the *Los Angeles Free Press*. As was common in San Francisco, Hardy worked with liquid projection: two overhead projectors, each with a clear dish (typically a large clock glass) in which he manipulated mixtures of oil and water with different colored dyes, dimmers on each allowing him to dissolve from one to the other. He had also experimented with spraying Crystal Craze on the water surface.[5]

Lebrun was a bridge between this UCLA group and another whose home was the Hog Farm, a commune in Sunland, a township just north of Los Angeles.[6] Formed around Christmas 1966, the commune also included Helena Hartshorn, who had met Lebrun in Mexico, where he had been shooting his film, *Sanctus* (1967). She had been traveling, performing liquid projection light shows in bars and schools, and they married soon after. Hartshorn had learned liquid projection in San Francisco from Bill Ham and Elias Romero, who had pioneered its use in countercultural events and who had projected for Ken Kesey's San Francisco Trips Festival in January 1966 and other Acid Tests.[7] Hartshorn taught the dye chemistries and technical procedures she had learned in San Francisco to Lebrun and others at the commune, including Jon Greene, a friend of Gershfield's who had lived at the Cresthill house, and Michael Scroggins, a surfer who had been living on a commune in Topanga Canyon that joined with the Hog Farm. Apart from high school classes and a brief period working as an apprentice in the studio of sculptor Miguel Miramontes, Scroggins had no formal art background; but he had been fascinated with light shows since childhood and, inspired by the planetarium sequence in *Rebel Without a Cause* (Nicholas Ray, 1955) and by seeing the films of Len Lye, Fischinger, Jordan Belson and others at the "Movies 'Round Midnight" series at the Cinema Theatre in Hollywood, he had maintained his interest in abstract animation.

The Single Wing Turquoise Bird came together as a group of the Hog Farm liquid projectionists, including Hartshorn, Scroggins, Evan Engber, Bonnie Z., and Rick and Erin Sullivan, began working with the filmmakers, primarily Gershfield (who soon dropped out of the group), Lebrun, Mays, and Perkins from UCLA and Charles Lippincott from USC. Other friends occasionally participated, working the projectors, washing the liquid plates, or doing other odd jobs. As well as projecting films, Lebrun acted as the group's business manager while Lippincott became the general manager. Alan Keesling, who specialized in hand painted slides and owned a set of six projectors with dimmers and strobe wheels, and Rol Murrow also became associated with the group. The name was supposedly found by Perkins by stabbing his finger blindly into a book of Vedic hymns,[8] while he and Lebrun were driving to meet with John Van Hamersveld at the "White House" near Hoover and Third Street (where the members of Pinnacle) lived to discuss their first show at the Shrine.

The first Single Wing Shrine performance on 15 and 16 March accompanied Cream, James Cotton, and Mint Tattoo. For the next few months they performed approximately every second weekend on Friday and Saturday nights for all the big groups of the period that Pinnacle booked, including Traffic, Quicksilver Messenger Service, Big Brother and the Holding Company with Janis Joplin, Pink Floyd, the Grateful Dead and the Velvet Underground.[9] Pinnacle paid them $1,200 for each weekend, half of which was split evenly among the dozen regulars with the other half invested in new material and equipment and the occasional guest artist.

Their first innovation was to replace the half-dozen small screens on the perimeter of the Shrine space used by Thomas Edison Lighting Company with a single large translucent screen behind the band, a move that typified what emerged as the group's characteristic emphasis on densely complex but tightly organized and bounded visual compositions rather than a dispersed all-over environment. For the first two shows, they rear-projected on this screen, but then for the third moved in front of a now slightly V-shaped, 20' x 70' screen placed behind the band on which the liquids and slides were projected diagonally from balconies while the high intensity film projectors worked head-on from a twelve-foot high platform specially constructed in the dance-floor of the auditorium. The group used six parabolic-mirror overhead projectors whose very strong lights overlapped to cover the entire screen, several slide projectors, and two rheostat-based high-intensity 16 mm film projectors obtained by Lippincott from USC, whose anamorphic lenses could also cover the entire screen. The liquid projectionists worked simultaneously on two machines, each with a separate "Variac" variable transformer coil dimmer; Scroggins who along with Mays became a core member around this time, altered these by installing a rod extension on the dimmer that could be pushed by the knee, allowing the projectionist to have both hands free to tilt the liquid plates while fading in and out.

7 – Expanded Cinema in Los Angeles: The Single Wing Turquoise Bird

Figure 1. Poster by John Van Hamersveld for Pinnacle Productions concert, Shrine Exposition Hall, Los Angeles, 1968.

The filmmakers used both their own and their friends' footage, especially clips and out-takes from *Now that the Buffalo's Gone* (Burton Gershfield, 1967), 7362, and John Stehura's early computer animation, *Cybernetik 5.3* (1965). They also used the UCLA contact printer to copy films borrowed from the Los Angeles and Santa Monica public libraries, seeking out kinetic images photographed against a black field to allow them to be superimposed over the abstract forms created by the liquid projectors. Films by Jordan Belson, Scott Bartlett, and John and James Whitney, especially the latter's *Yantra* (1957) and *Lapis (1966)*, and Francis Thompson's *N.Y., N.Y.* (1957), Bruce Conner's *Cosmic Ray* (1961) and *A Movie (1958)*, *Wonders in Miniature* (an underwater nature film), and Denys Colomb Daunant's short, *Dream of Wild Horses* (*Le Songe des chevaux sauvages*, 1960) all became favorites, as did very early black-and-white animated cartoons, sometimes printed in negative. Various educational films were also used (including a training film on American sign language that Lebrun projected over Albert King performing "Born Under A Bad Sign"). Frequently the film projectionists threaded a film first through one of the high intensity projectors then, leaving a slight loop, through the second projector, so as to produce two versions of the same film about ten seconds out of phase, either projected side by side or, with Cinemascope lenses, both covering the entirety of the 70' x 20' screen. Lebrun also contributed what became known as the "Lebrun loops", high-contrast black-and-white flickering animations of alchemical symbols, pottery designs, snowflakes, and abstract forms. The group gradually assembled a library of these and other films and also of slides, which for easy retrieval were organized by subject: op art, architectural faces, planets, eyes, and so on. Sometimes material was prepared in advance for specific bands; for example, the Velvet Underground show was entirely in black-and-white, and the imagery much harsher than usual.

The library of materials the group collected became the equivalent of a painter's palette, with which they wove multi-leveled and kinetic, fleeting and ephemeral compositions in light, mingling both imagery and abstract shapes. Their various projectors were instruments that they played with a specifically somatic engagement; Mays and Lebrun, for example, used their hands to shape or mask off sections of the film images so as to insert them in the context created by the others, while the manipulation of the dishes of colored oil and water was a manual as well as a visual skill. Though the films and slides used pre-prepared imagery, still the projection overall was spontaneous and improvisatory, growing equally from random as from premeditated progressions. This liberation into the present was possible, not only for each member individually, but most crucially in relation to the compositions of the others and of the group as a whole, which – all members report – often took on an energy and coherence of its own and into which individual egos were subsumed. The most commonly invoked analogy to this group improvisation is the combined composition and performance situation of modern jazz, or indeed that of the Grateful Dead and others of the bands whom they accompanied who had abandoned the regular repetitive structures of early rock'n'roll for extended jams. The interaction among the projectionists themselves mirrored their responsiveness to the music, for rhythms, textures, and even graphic images were conjured out of their sensitivity to the bands' performances; sometimes the bands themselves would turn and face the screen and play to the images they saw, and indeed on several occasions the light show continued after the band had finished.[10] At these points, rather than the light show taking its direction from the music and being subordinated to it, the whole ensemble was a fully reciprocal collective audio-visual organism. Liberated by other kinds of chemicals, the audience members themselves became participants, engaging the music aurally and physically (in their dance) as well as engaging the optical environment in their sight. Within light show's overall dissolution of the boundaries between perception and hallucination, the rhythm of the strobes sculpted

7 – Expanded Cinema in Los Angeles: The Single Wing Turquoise Bird

Figure 2. Poster for Single Wing Turquoise Bird performance, Santa Barbara, 1969.

new spaces, shattering the audience's self-visualization into slivers of recognition and revelation.

The Single Wing Turquoise Bird performed in this way through the spring of 1968 until June, when the Hog Farm went on the road,[11] taking half the members and some of the equipment with them (though Lebrun left copies of his loops). The remainder stabilized around the reduced core of Mays, Perkins, Murrow, and Lippincott on films and slides; Greene, Hardy, and Scroggins on overhead projection of liquids and transparencies; Keesling on slides and rheostats, with Lippincott still as manager. Their core equipment now consisted of two xenon

16 mm film projectors, eight slide projectors and four overhead projectors. In this reduced form the group continued to perform at the Shrine; now all of them worked together on the platform in front of the stage which allowed them to communicate more directly with each other. But in early fall 1968, after an extremely ambitious all-day "American Music Show" at the Pasadena Rose Bowl on 15 September featuring a dozen major groups drew only a small audience, Pinnacle failed financially, and the Shrine concerts ended. By this point, however, the Single Wing had already begun to shift their aesthetic orientation and ambitions.

They found a rehearsal space at Joe Funk's litho shop (which had been featured in Murrow's 1967 UCLA student film, *The Tin Shack*), adjacent to the Pot Shop ceramic studio at 334 Sunset Avenue in Venice. The painter, Sam Francis, who had been introduced to the group's Shrine performances by Greene,[12] was then making lithographs there. Well known for his support for younger artists, Francis became the group's patron, providing more equipment and eventually allowing them to use his studio on Ashland Street in the Ocean Park distinct of Santa Monica. There they both rehearsed, projecting onto his canvasses which were at that time very large, and performed publicly on two or three occasions, though for smaller audiences of thirty to forty people. At this time, Single Wing had consolidated itself around six members, Keesling, Lippincot, Mays, Perkins, Scroggins, and Greene, and in their ongoing rehearsals, this group augmented and then transformed the on-the-spot improvisation of their initial period and created a wholly unique artistic identity.

Where previously their projection had been supplementary to the rock concerts, now they became an autonomous performing entity. The performances were still collaborative and fundamentally spontaneous, but the discipline of the practice sessions and the discoveries they produced allowed their work new refinement, control, and complexity. They still composed in real-time in coordination to music, but since it was chosen from records and tapes (sometimes spliced and extended into hypnotic lengths), they were able to practice repeatedly to the same piece. The Velvet Underground's "Sister Ray" was a favorite among the rock songs, but they also used works by Steve Reich and other contemporary composers, especially Terry Riley's then recent, "In C". Artists including James Turrell, Wallace Berman, Ed Moses, and Dewaine Valentine visited, Francis introduced the group to his patrons, and these entrées reoriented the group toward more formal institutions, especially those of the art world. As well as performing in Francis's Ashland Street studio, the group appeared at Occidental College (where William Moritz was then teaching), UCLA, the Santa Barbara Museum of Art

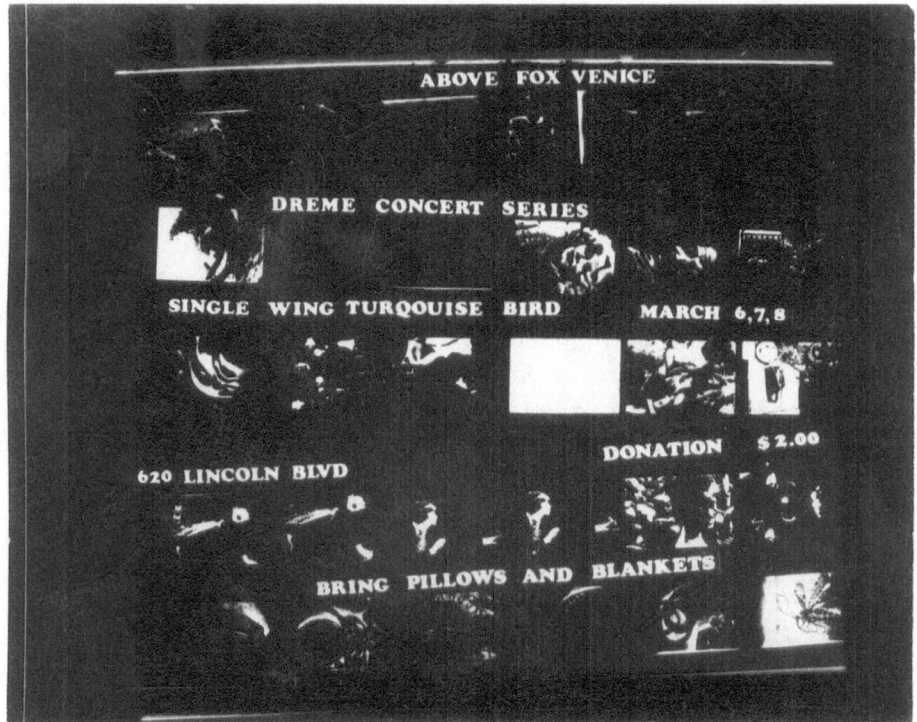

Figure 3. Single Wing Turquoise Bird performance announcement, 1970.

(where on the same occasion Judy Chicago did a piece using colored smoke), the Venice public library, Hollywood High School (for a celebration of Huey Newton's birthday), Loyola Marymount University, and the Cinematheque 16. Many members regard the approximately six months from late-1968 to mid-1969 as the period of their best and most distinctive work. We are fortunate in having several first-person accounts of it.

One evening in late summer 1968 Anaïs Nin attended one of the litho shop performances, along with Henry Miller, P. Adams Sitney, and Gene Youngblood. In her diary, Nin noted: "Like a thousand modern paintings flowing and sparkling, alive and dynamic, of incredible richness, a death blow to painting in frames, stills".[13] Youngblood, at that time film critic for the *Los Angeles Free Press*, also described the performance in his "Expanded Cinema" column:

> It's a combination of Jackson Pollock and *2001*. Of Hieronymus Bosch and Victor Vasarely. Of Dali and Buckminster Fuller. Time-lapse clouds run across magenta bull's-eyes. Horses charge in slow motion through solar fires. The hands of a clock run backward. The moon revolves around the earth in a galaxy of Op Art polka dots. Flashing trapezoids and rhomboids whirl out of Buddha's eye. Pristine polygraphic forms are

suspended in a phosphate void. Exploding isometrics give birth to insects. A praying mantis dances across an Oriental garden. Spiraling cellular cubes crash into electric-green fossil molds. The organic symbiosis of universal man. A huge magnified centipede creeps across a glowing sun. Sound: Tod Dockstader's Quatermass Cascading phosphorescent sparks. Waffle grid-patterns strobe-flash over Roy Lichtenstein's 1930 Ultramoderne architecture. A butterfly emerges from its cocoon. New dimensions of space and time. Bodies become plants. Acid-Oracle visions of universal unity. White translucent squids wrestle with geometric clusters.[14]

Where both Nin and Youngblood referenced painting in their descriptions, in William Moritz's account of the Cinémathèque 16 performance, published in January 1969 in a local underground paper and the fullest verbal record of a Single Wing performance we have, he emphasized the film component, though also invoking the sense of a continuous present he associated with Gertrude Stein's writing:

> Friday and Saturday, January 17 and 18, at midnight in the Cinematheque 16 on Sunset Strip, Single Wing Turquoise Bird presented a two-and-a-half hour light show, EIDOLA, as an artwork in its own right separate from the context of a rock dance or a happening, proving that a "living" art work of organic complexity was (in addition to commercially feasible) considerably more interesting, challenging, and satisfying than any of the flat, static art styles of the past, including painting and the traditional fictional cinema.
>
> EIDOLA demonstrated in five half-hour segments five different styles or formats that the Single Wing Turquoise Bird have mastered ... .
>
> First the 180-degree screens light up with scenes of the street outside, across from the door of the theater, and the noises of traffic and pedestrian cackles seem to be leaking in as well. Vertical shadow bars whiz by to the sound of passing cars faster and faster until the street is a flickering strobe and the neon signs leap out and flash a hundred times too large or maybe that's the way they always were DON'T WALK DON'T WALK Don't Walk don't walk don't don't. The voices of the idle passerby become mixed with the voices of the idle newscaster straight muffled electronically altered fragmented but telling us just by inflections that they're saying these same things again just like WALK WALK WALK WALK and MUNTZ MUNTZ MUNTZ and the smooth electronic music gliding beautifully in between the noise-music of the city pulsing. And then suddenly, as if all that could be erased, as it can, the revolving neon becomes also revolving wings of a mandala, a garuda, a bodhisattva choir, faces now of people instead of faces then of media and once it's started the other lost faces come too – the bleeding twisted Christ of a Reformation nightmare and the phosphorescent faces of an Indian tribe in the dancing and smoking rituals seen by Bert Gershfield's *Now That the Buffalo's Gone* with its sounds of chanting drumming inside the other sounds and the other Indians appear again in the piercing gaze of the Lord Shiva which the more it flashes the more you know the face is really made up of people like that rishi whose lotused legs are lips and mustache and his folded hands nostrils and so on until flames begin erasing everything except the electronic sounds and the sun blazes up and then fades out as the tones of the music cool, metallic, pale and paler ... .
>
> One measure of the genius of this first movement is perhaps that we have no language to describe it – no way of telling simultaneity, no precise words for the electronic-musical

sounds and modulations, no terms for so many of those hues and tones and motions that the light show had revealed to us as an essential part of our daily lives ... .

The first movement performed the continually nowness of the present. The second movement took as its point of departure a short film of considerable artistic integrity and force, *Dream of Wild Horses*, which was subtly altered, expanded with additional material, extended with flumes of its color and echoes of its shapes, the nuances looped in mirror cadences bathing a space and time much grander than the little square of the original. The sound as well extrapolated the lush organ-like tones of Jacques Lasry's sounding sculptures from the film's soundtrack into a more symphonic development.

The third movement similarly presented a fantasia on the theme of Pat O'Neill's film *7362*, which offered a mood and subject-matter radically different from the slow-motion romance of fleeing stallions. *7362* juxtaposes hard, fast imagery of naked women and escalating oil-pumping machinery, rendered abstract by close-ups and layering, solarized textures and iridescent colors. Once more the light show filled out the complex universe where those images could live, letting cadences echo, taking a flickering abstraction to its limits and back again, mirroring O'Neill's images with considerable new film footage shot especially for this piece by Peter Mays (an old school pal of O'Neill's).

The fourth movement, using Pink Floyd's "Interstellar Overdrive" as a soundtrack, evoked sensations of travel in time and space using only non-objective, non-representational abstractions: boiling corduroy bubbles, enamel soapsuds breaking like surf, fluorescent crystals branching out, pulsating circles, pure geometrical shapes greased slipping away from you, spurts of chalky white exploding and re-exploding out of itself like a cauliflower periscope or high-rise mushroom clouds.

The final movement, almost entirely black-and-white, generated a wide spectrum of forms and iridescent colors that were not directly projected by the light machines but rather induced either by the Grateful Dead's "Alligator" or as carefully calculated after-images of the projections with your mind's eye as the ultimate screen this time ... .

These words are not telling it all because it is a 1960s thing and most English words are a 14th or 16th century thing and if Single Wing Turquoise Bird could be writing it they would be writing it, but they are showing it and always only once because Friday January 17, 1969 was not like Saturday January 18, 1969, even though many things about them seemed to be being the same and if you did not see Friday January 17, 1969 when it happened you will not have a chance now because it was living not writing and this is just writing you are doing now ... .[15]

Ever ambitious for the group, in summer 1969 Francis rented the ballroom of the Santa Monica Hotel, where they gessoed seven of his huge canvasses for use as screens. But though they held numerous rehearsals in the large space, the hotel management expelled them at the end of September 1969 because of their hippie appearance and the fact that several of them were living in the ballroom. After a short period without a regular rehearsal space, the group entered into its third major phase when they found a home from the end of 1969 until 1975 in a studio and business space in a large loft above the Fox Venice Theatre at 620 Lincoln Boulevard in Venice, which Murrow had leased to house the Cumberland Mountain Film Company, his production group.[16] They continued to allow guest

POWER MISSES II: CINEMA, ASIAN AND MODERN

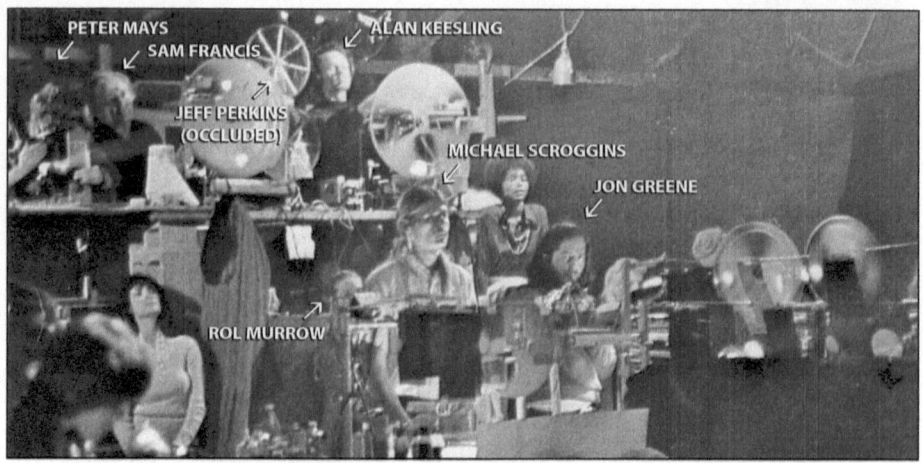

Figure 4. Frame enlargement, Single Wing Turquoise Bird performing in *The Baby Maker*, annotations by Michael Scroggins.

artists to perform with them, and Larry Janss, who had worked with them occasionally at Sam Francis's studio, joined to perform slides. In this period the regular group consisted of Greene, Janss, Keesling, Mays, Murrow, Perkins, and Scroggins. As during their previous phase, their projection platform was multi-level, with film and slide projectors on risers at the rear, and overhead projectors at the front, with an additional high-powered film projector located high up in the rafters effectively adding a third tier. They rehearsed regularly in Murrow's space, and also performed there for small public groups as they had in Francis's studio, and made innovations in their use of sound, sometimes drawing in the sound of the traffic outside and people talking on the sidewalk by means of outside microphones fixed to the theater marquee.[17] And here the rapprochement with Hollywood, virtually inevitable for any countercultural art practice in Los Angeles not specifically identified with the working class, occurred.

Francis had introduced the group to his friend, Jim Bridges, as he was planning to direct his first feature, *The Baby Maker* (1970). Bridges persuaded his production company to give the group $10,000 to produce a 35 mm film to be used to simulate a light show performance in a rock'n'roll nightclub scene in his movie. Since the light levels and film sensitivity made it impossible to photograph an actual performance adequately for theatrical film projection, coordinated sequences of the various components – the liquids, the movies, and the slides – were made separately on 35 mm, and then these were edited together by Peter Mays with Butler-Glowner, an optical house, providing dissolves and superimpositions. In *The Baby Maker*, the Single Wing material is featured in a four-minute sequence in which a hippie couple visit a rock'n'roll night club; the girl is

7 – Expanded Cinema in Los Angeles: The Single Wing Turquoise Bird

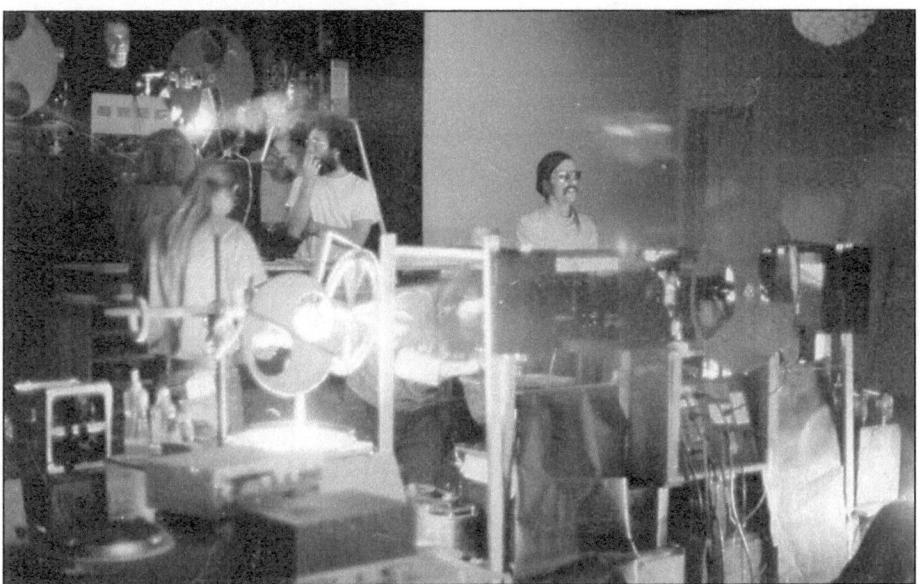

Figure 5. Single Wing Turquoise Bird performing in *The Baby Maker*.

pregnant as a surrogate mother for a bourgeois family, and they quarrel just before a police raid ends the performance. Composed from the superimposition of three separately edited films, the light show is somewhat denser than a typical Single Wing performance, but on the other hand the 24 frames per second of film photography and projection fails to capture the much faster effects of the strobes. Since the sequence may be seen in the video of *The Baby Maker*, only a simplified description of it will be given here. It begins with swirling nebulous organic forms in red and blue made by liquid projection over which a movie of a solar eclipse enters in the center with rapidly strobed slides from Gustave Doré's illustrations for Dante's *Inferno* in the bottom half of the frame. Two alternating but slightly offset slides, one with a blue and the other with a red filter and featuring a close-up of Jim Morrison's face, enter in the black center of the eclipse. As the liquids fade out, a different movie of galaxies of stars seen through alternating green and blue color wheels covers the transition from Morrison's face to several rapidly alternating anthropological high-contrast slides of the face of an Amazonian man. This is strobically intercut with a home-movie of a man emerging from the sea seen though a yellow and red color wheel, while several slides of Egyptian figures come to dominate the center. By this point Morrison's face has been thrown out of focus and disappears under Lebrun loops of the thin white lines of multiple geometric drawings, but then Morrison reappears again strobically alternating with the Egyptian figures. An effect made by projecting out-of-focus a black slide

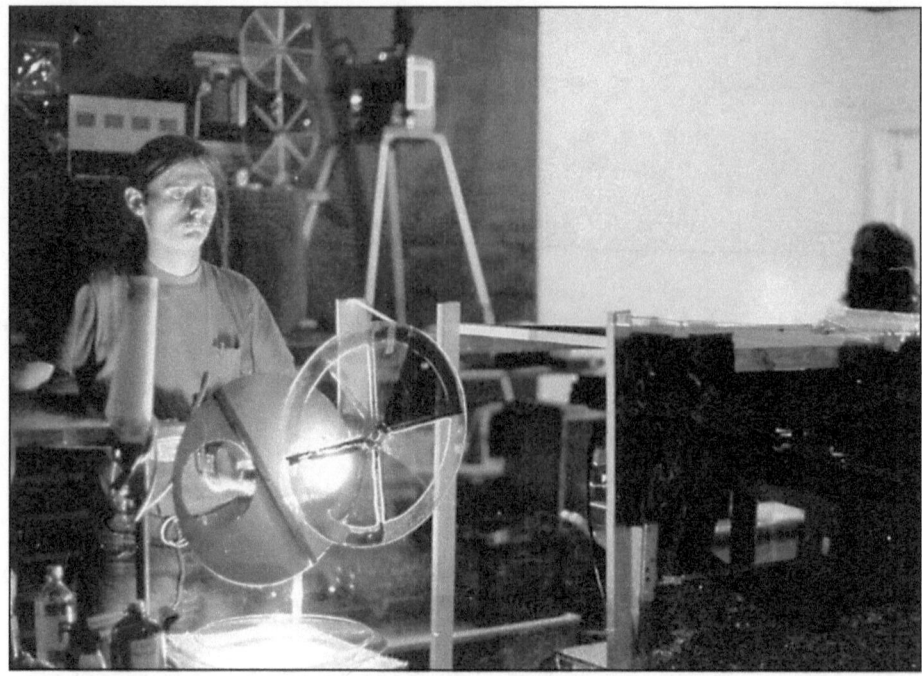

Figure 6. Single Wing Turquoise Bird performing in *The Baby Maker*. Michael Scroggins at liquid overhead projector with strobe and color wheels.

with a hole in the center creates a fuzzy sphere in the center for a few seconds, alternating with a slide of a yogi, before the Lebrun loops change first to outlines of mythical animals and then of mystical symbols. These occupy the center, as the bipacked images of outtakes from Pat O'Neill's movie, *7362* appear behind them, until the bubble-like forms of a silvery clear oil slowly churn behind them. A red liquid projection takes over the foreground and the two plates intermingle as the golden-green lines of outtakes from John Stehura's *Cybernetik 5.3* make their appearance and, as yet another liquid projection enters, the sequence ends.

The group continued to work in the studio space above the Fox Venice for several years. Every spring they held a series of five to ten public shows, accompanying either records (still typically the Grateful Dead's "Dark Star", The Velvet Underground's "Sister Ray", Henri Posseur's "Trois Visages à Liège", and Steve Reich's "Come Out") or live music, to audiences of around forty to sixty people drawn by mailings or word of mouth. But by 1973 the public culture that had sustained them was in decline, and the financial support obtained through admission charges was insufficient. Though he occasionally returned for special events, Scroggins left the group to attend the recently opened California Institute of the

7 – Expanded Cinema in Los Angeles: The Single Wing Turquoise Bird

Figure 7. Frame enlargement, Single Wing Turquoise Bird light-show in *The Baby Maker*: film of solar eclipse (Mays) with slide of photograph of Jim Morrison (Perkins) and overhead of Gustave Doré's illustrations for Dante's *Inferno* (Greene or Scroggins).

Arts, where he worked in real-time videographic animation and eventually in interactive computer virtual reality animation. At the same time Murrow (who had meanwhile worked on the editing of Dennis Hopper's epic, *The Last Movie* [1971]), Janss, Maestri, and theater-manager, Kim Jorgensen, formed Cumberland Mountain Theaters. The company took over the Fox's cinema space and turned it into the premier repertory revival theater in Los Angeles, with a new double bill every night. With several Single Wing Turquoise Bird members working for them – Perkins as a graphic designer, Scroggins as a calendar distributor, and Mays as projectionist – the Fox Venice prospered, its screenings including *Night of the Living Dead* (George A. Romero, 1968), *Performance* (Donald Cammell and Nicolas Roeg, 1970), *Walkabout* (Nicolas Roeg, 1971), *The Last Movie*, *Underground*, John Waters' films, and similar countercultural classics, as well as Mays's own underground feature, *Sister Midnight* (1975). *The Rocky Horror Picture Show* (Jim Sharman, 1975) had its first public screening there, at a sneak preview at midnight just before it officially opened, foreshadowing decades of Friday night midnight screenings held for it since.

As the group members threw their energies into operating the theatre, interest in the light show waned, but they still did occasional performances. As late as 1976, at the Fox they staged a "Freak Night", a 60's revival show when the group projected its signature imagery from both the theatre projection booth and a large platform constructed on top of the seats at the rear of the theater. The event included a snake dance led by Hugh Romney (aka "Wavy Gravy"), and Alejandro Jodorowsky danced around the projection platform in excited delight. This was the Single Wing Turquoise Bird's final performance, but Perkins and Mays regrouped for a handful of revival concerts in a different cultural era. On New Year's Eve 1980, briefly assisted by Lebrun, they projected films and slides for a concert featuring X, DOA, and other Los Angeles punk bands at the Stardust Ballroom that concluded with Exene Cervenka, lead singer of X, tearing down a paper screen on which was being projected a fragment of *Un chien Andalou* (Luis Buñuel and Salvador Dalí, 1928).

* * *

As a collaboration among its members and their audiences, the art of the Single Wing Turquoise Bird was, as William Moritz emphasized, fundamentally a new medium, the cultural creation and self-articulation of a social group in a historical moment that are both gone forever: "always only once", as Moritz's Steinian syntax had it. Such a *past*, as Thoreau remarked, cannot be *presented*, and no one who didn't participate in it then will ever experience the light show. Nor has history been attentive. Few traces of the group remain, and their memory has not been preserved in either the scholarly records or television commercials where other shades of the sixties linger. But we are fortunate in that Moritz and Youngblood, two of the most perceptive commentators both described it in the accounts already quoted and made summary evaluations. Moritz, the foremost American scholar of visual music who saw many of the most prominent light shows of the late twentieth century in the U.S. and Europe, testified that the Single Wing Turquoise Bird "stood head-and-shoulders above all the rest".[18] And Youngblood concluded, some two years after he first saw them: "In almost total obscurity the group perfected an art of light manipulation virtually unequalled by any mixed-media organization with the possible exception of USCO".[19] As for other twentieth century vanguard cultural movements in Los Angeles, and especially all forms of experimental cinema, that combination of achievement and obscurity is part of the Single Wing's social meaning, specifically in marking a historical possibility in the ongoing struggle for liberation from the capitalist media industry that exists there in an overwhelmingly proximate form.

Youngblood's celebration of the group as the apotheosis of multiple-projection

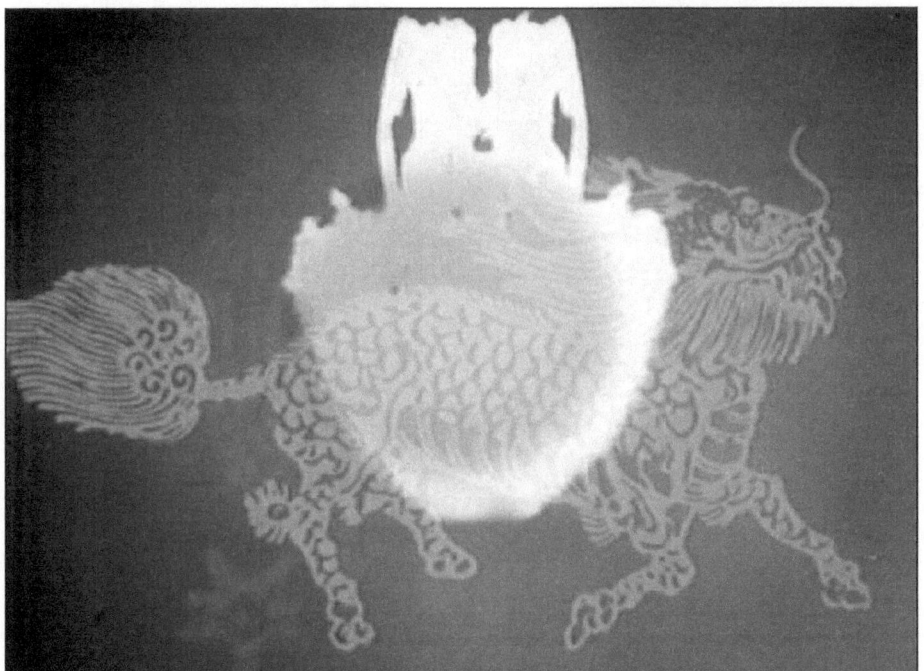

Figure 8. Frame enlargement, Single Wing Turquoise Bird light-show in *The Baby Maker:* "Lebrun loop" film (Mays) with outtakes from *7362* (16 mm film by Pat O'Neill) and burred spheres slide (Perkins).

environments reflected his reiteration of Jonas Mekas's expectations for Expanded Cinema generally in the mid-1960s. Mekas envisaged that, on the one hand, the narrative syntax associated with Underground film and the expansion of film's visual languages beyond the restrictions of the commercial cinema's illusionism and, on the other, the expansion of the projection situation out from the flat theatrical screen into three-dimensional environments associated with developments in the art world prefigured the eventual transcendence of the materiality of cinema *tout court* into the actualization of the dreams and visions of the human mind: "we give up all movies and become movies".[20] Mekas was writing in a context in which Expanded Cinema was only one, though certainly a privileged one, of cognate "Expanded Arts", all of which were supposed to be similarly auspicious. Their cultural impetus was such that in 1966 *Film Culture* published a special edition on that very topic – one in a special expanded format[21] – that prominently featured Stan Vanderbeek's experiments in multi-media environments at his Movie Drome in Stony Point, New York. Earlier that year, *Film Culture* had already published Vanderbeek's "Culture: Intercom and Expanded Cinema: A Proposal and Manifesto"[22] that, as well as glossing his own work,

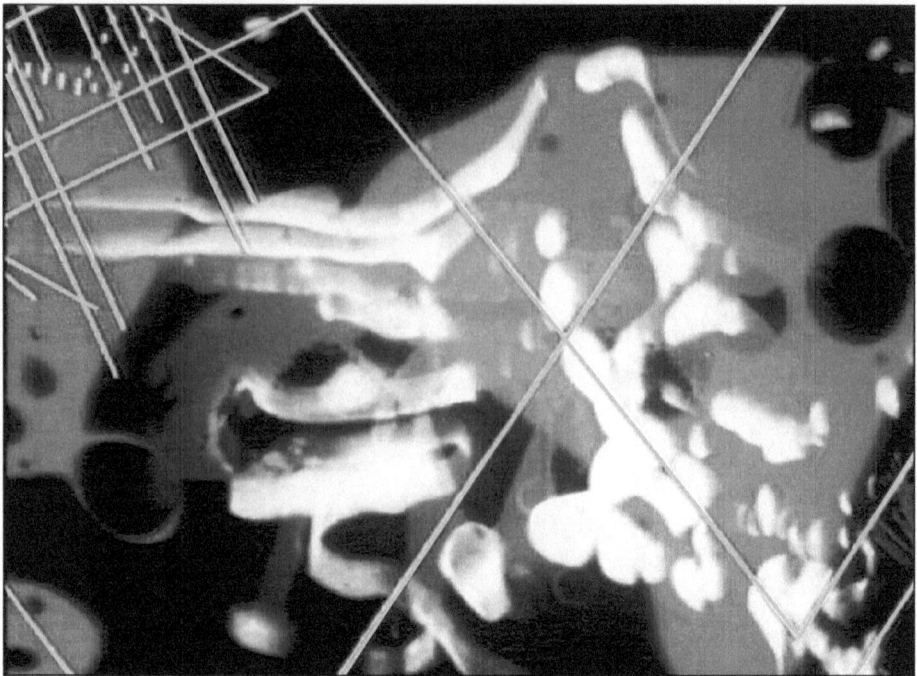

Figure 9. Frame enlargement, Single Wing Turquoise Bird light-show in *The Baby Maker*: overhead liquid projections, Greene and Scroggins with outtakes from *Cybernetik 5.3* (16 mm film by John Stehura).

summarized the urgent need for massively enlarged modes of cognition, the centrality in them of new forms in cinema, and the utopian expectations associated with them:

> ... a rapid panoply of graphics and light calling upon thousands of images, both still and in motion [... .] if an individual is exposed to an overwhelming information experience ... [i]t might be possible to re-order the levels of awareness of any person ... it certainly will re-order the structure of motion pictures as we know them ... Cinema will become a "performing" art ... and image-library.[23]

Made both more concrete and apocalyptic by his assiduous attention to contemporary developments in cybernetics, Youngblood's parallel projections for Expanded Cinema inflated it into a universal metaphor within which developments in the inner world of the human spirit were reciprocated in the spirit's actualization in the outer world of scientific advancement: "When we say expanded cinema we actually mean expanded consciousness. Expanded cinema does not mean computer films, video phosphors, atomic light, or spherical projections. Expanded cinema isn't a movie at all: like life, it's a process of becoming, man's ongoing historical drive to manifest his consciousness outside his mind, in front of his eyes".²⁴ Even though, in Youngblood's 1968 *Free Press* account, the Single Wing performance depended on movies and other forms of projected light, in fact its greatest achievement was the artists' success in subordinating their individual egos to the group that enabled them to combine the diverse constituent projection elements so integrally that the result appeared to have the organic coherence of a movie – this was for him only the form of appearance of a more radical achievement. Dismissive about the group's initial activities in the Shrine, when he thought it merely a light show for rock'n'roll bands, Youngblood believed that it had subsequently developed as a performance unit of revolutionary promise, albeit, "more occult than psychedelic; mystic rather than Maoist". A new consciousness was being born, he argued, internationally but initially and most dramatically in California, and "in an artists' cooperative in Venice, a group of six visionaries are defining the first words of an entirely different kind of vocabulary, a tribal language which expresses not ideas but states of consciousness – not of individuals but of groups". And the possibilities for this kind of "social interaction on a global scale are limitless: one imagines entire nations cooperating through computers and satellites to produce an intercultural 'light show' which would never end".²⁵

We now know that the global cultural revolution of which Youngblood, Vanderbeek, and other visionaries of the time dreamed in fact produced, not utopia, but the imperial expanded cinemas of electronic advertising, Fox News, CNN, and so on – the consciousness industries that frame the invasion of Iraq, the manufacture global misery, and the rape of the Earth. Sublated into this dystopian actualization of spirit, the historical moment of the Single Wing and other Expanded Arts is not yet sufficiently far from us that a definitive reckoning of its function can be expected. Beginnings in the reconstruction of the lost connections between the cultural possibilities engendered in that moment and other forms of resistance to the corporate state are being made by, for example, reconsiderations of the cognitive and psychic implications of the perceptual re-organizations that events like light shows entailed.²⁶ But in cases of expanded cinema in Los Angeles, the imminence of Hollywood – their socially and psychically "contracted" other – that historically overshadowed them also ensured that the fault-lines between them and corporate culture are especially revelatory. The connections and disconnections among different forms of expanded cinema in Los Angeles, and the connections and disconnections between them and the film industry itself illustrate the way local developments in the city anticipate cultural movements in the U.S. generally.

During the period of the Single Wing, Los Angeles was home to an unequalled efflorescence of attempts to extend the boundaries of cinema. The late-sixties Ethno-Communications Program at UCLA, for example, introduced African, Asian and Mexican American students into the film school and so inaugurated the minority filmmaking of the 1970s that allowed large sectors of the working class to contest their previous objectification and to become producers rather than merely consumers of cinema. Another venture, one that was precisely "Maoist rather than mystic", was the Los Angeles Newsreel. Founded also in Venice, and also by a group of, mainly UCLA, film students (some of whom were also involved in the Single Wing) and also in October 1968 (when Single Wing were beginning their unique self-creation in the rehearsals during their second phase at Joe Funk's Litho Shop), the Los Angeles Newsreel dedicated itself to a global working class revolution.[27] Believing the Black Panther party to be the domestic arm of a political avant-garde led globally by the Vietnamese struggle against neocolonial U.S. imperialism, they screened films made by other Newsreel branches and by Third World revolutionaries in factories, union halls and colleges, meanwhile working on their own film about the Los Angeles Panthers. Their project, called *Repression*, was interrupted when the Los Angeles Police Department collaborated with the FBI and destroyed the Los Angeles Panther headquarters on 8 December 1969, two days after the Illinois police murdered Black Panther Party Deputy Chairman, Fred Hampton, and a month or so before the Single Wing moved to the Fox Venice to begin their third phase. The Newsreel reconstructed their film, adding footage of the police occupying the black community and the burnt-out building, and completed the editing of both sound and visual tracks. But then, unable to raise funds to finish it, they abandoned it.

The repression of Newsreel was, of course, more crucial than the gradual depletion of the Single Wing, but neither this nor their different value systems – Maoist or mystic – should obscure the fact that they lived in immediate proximity to their common adversary, corporate culture, which was already mobilizing a counter-offensive. In summer 1969, Columbia Pictures released Dennis Hopper's *Easy Rider*, the studios' first successful attempt to exploit and assimilate the counter-culture of which, in their different ways both Single Wing and Newsreel were the dialectically complementary halves. In other films, Hollywood continued to ridicule or neutralize oppositional cultural movements, before reasserting industrial control by appropriating expanded visuality itself in *Star Wars* (George Lucas, 1977) and the subsequent renewed blockbuster production. Light shows from other parts of the country are preserved in independent films where they unironically occupy the entire diegesis – USCO in Jud Yaklut's *Diffraction Film* (1965) and *Us* (1966), the Trips Festival in Ben Van Meter's film, and the Exploding Plastic Inevitable in Ronald Nameth's eponymous film of 1966; but it is symptomatic of the capitalist entertainment industry's framing of all countercultural activity in Los Angeles that the only visual record of the Single Wing – who *never* used fragments of Hollywood films in their otherwise limitless image library – should be a brief, thematically overdetermined, interlude in a commercial film. Its position there limns the contradictory threat it posed to the cultural establishment.

The Baby Maker's plot revolves around an affluent upper middle-class couple, Suzanne and Jay Wilcox, who live in Brentwood, and a working-class bohemian couple, Tish and her boyfriend Tad, who live in a shack in Venice (where most the Single Wing members lived). Since Suzanne cannot bear children, the Wilcoxes make a financial arrangement with clearly stipulated rules for Tish to be a surrogate mother for Jay's child. But as the pregnancy proceeds, all become personally involved. Suzanne begins to resemble her husband, an "efficiency expert" or "management engineer", and insist on monitoring and regulating Tish's pregnancy; Tish and Jay become emotionally entangled; and Tad grows frustrated and angry at being sexually deprived of Tish. The crisis comes when Tad takes Tish, by this time well into her pregnancy, to a rock'n'roll nightclub up the Pacific Coast Highway towards Malibu, where the Single Wing are performing. Dominated by the light show, the sequence in the club places the dramatic action against a background of the screen on which the group is projecting; scenes of the performers creating the light show, including wide-angle shots of them and their equipment, close-ups on Scroggins' manipulation of the liquids; and extended footage of the show itself, including several minutes where it occupies full screen. Angry at Tish, Tad openly flirts with an African American woman, sharing his joint with her, and causing Tish, who has previously boasted of their "open" relationship, to demand to be taken home. But before they can leave, the club (like the Panther headquarters in *Repression*) is invaded by the police and in the ensuing fracas, Tad is arrested for disturbing the peace. Tish goes to live with the Wilcoxes where she becomes deeply attached to Jay as his surrogate wife, but the film ends with her sadly watching the Wilcoxes drive away with her new-born baby. Though *The Baby Maker*'s overall insubstantiality resists it being taken too seriously, it also allows its political unconsciousness relatively uncensored expression. Based on the common fantasy of a relationship between a bourgeois man and a working-class girl that dates back the earliest days of bourgeois society, the film is a clear allegory of class society, however sugared over with humanist pathos. Class relations are dramatized in generational and lifestyle terms, and general relations of production are recast in terms of sexual reproduction. Itself non-productive, the bourgeoisie hires the working-class to produce for it (in this case, Jay actually *fucks* Trish), imposes its own standards of efficiency on it, and temporarily draws its productive members into its own ideological and social orbit before abandoning them when their productivity is exhausted, while excluding recalcitrant, non-productive lumpen elements. The Single Wing sequence occurs at a pivotal moment in this process. Resentful of the bourgeoisie's appropriation of his partner's sexuality, her (re)productive power, Tad follows the various sixties radicals who understood the civil rights struggles in class rather than nationalist terms and attempted to affiliate with the black working class – like, most notably, the Los Angeles Newsreel. He is interrupted from doing so by Tish, the faction of the working class who has sold her labor power to the bourgeoisie and become effectively co-opted, and by the police, the Repressive State Apparatus in the period's idiom.

The Baby Maker, then, schematically envisions the Single Wing as organizing a Dionysian cultural space where unruly energies are released and subversive inter-racial class affiliations explored, and also a catalytic space where social realignments are organized. Occupying the habitat and habitus of the Single Wing members themselves, Tish and Tad are both a resource to be plundered and a threat to be contained, a counterculture that must be divided and its separate factions appropriately assigned. As the filmic form of this counterculture, the Single Wing is similarly a productive resource: hired like Tish for a few thousand dollars, it increases the Hollywood film's value by supplying youth appeal that will expand the capital invested in it and participate in the renewal of the industry and the production of the "New Hollywood". But as an expanded visual language and as an expanded mode of film production, it is a cultural threat that must be denigrated and policed, for if – as Vanderbeek and the underground anticipated – cinema were to become a performing art and the masses became performers rather than merely consumers, then "the structure of motion pictures as we know them" would be reconstructed, their commodity function and their economic and ideological roles in late capital would be jeopardized. Hence the sequence is terminated by the police, and the group disappears entirely from the film, remaining only as a brief glimpse, a framed memory of a cultural form that can be exploited, but not endorsed.

The Baby Maker's use of the Single Wing Turquoise Bird does not provide a definitive analysis of the light show's historical meaning, only of what the dominant culture desired and feared in it. In fact, para-Hollywood modes of production had begun to appropriate parallel countercultural initiatives, even before they had been fully formed and, as these proved profitable, commercial media's exploitation of the counterculture rapidly escalated.[28] But in this case, what remains outside the attempted industrial assimilation is the promise of a form of film practice in which expanded visual and sensual experience was reciprocated in the liberation of similarly expanded social energies, the cynosure of a cultural revolution.

Notes

1. This account was constructed from interviews with Peter Mays (30 July 2004), Michael Scroggins (2 August 2004) and David Lebrun (10 August 2004), with other information from John Van Hamersveld, Rol Murrow, and Jeff Perkins. See also Rol Murrow's Single Wing Turquoise Bird website: www.swtb.info. In response to a recent strong renewal of interest in the Single Wing Turquoise Bird, the group has re-formed. Its current configuration includes five original members: Peter Mays and David Lebrun on film (now using digital video switchers and projectors), Jeff Perkins and Larry Janss on slides, and Michael Scroggins on overhead projectors. They have been joined by Amy Halpern and Shayne Hood on overheads. Since 2009 this group has been rehearsing together, preparing the ground for future live performances.

2. For information on color organs, see William Moritz, "Abstract Film and Color Music" in *The Spiritual In Art: Abstract Painting 1890–1985*, ed. Maurice Tuchman (Los Angeles: Los Angeles County Museum of Art, 1986); on MacDonald-Wright, see Will South, *Color Myth and Music: Stanton MacDonald-Wright and Synchromism* (Raleigh, N.C.: North Carolina Museum of Art, 2001), pp. 81–83; for Murphy's revelations, see his unpublished autobiography, *Murphy by Murphy*, written in 1966, a photo-copy of which is held at the iotaCenter in Los Angeles, p. 30; on Fischinger's lumigraph, see William Moritz, *Optical Poetry: The Life and Work of Oskar Fischinger* (Bloomington: Indiana University Press, 2004), pp. 137–138.

3. Greene's liquid projection was distinguished by a strong senses of the overall structure of a show, perhaps reflecting his training in classical music. After Single Wing disbanded, he continued to stage multimedia performances incorporating props, dancers and actors; around 1974 he moved to San Francisco, where he produced his unique form of theater for twenty years. He died in 2002.

4. After serving in the Air Force in Tokyo in the early 60s, Perkins had become acquainted with Yoko Ono when she was a performance artist and associated with Fluxus, elements of whose overall aesthetic he introduced into the Single Wing.

5. Usually the liquid projectionists combined dibutyl phthalate with dyed water, mineral oil, glycerin, alcohol, and occasionally liquid watercolors such as Dr. Martin's. They would also in certain instances use detergents that caused the surface emulsion of the oil to break down. Scroggins recalled that Hardy and Greene used to pour Crystal Craze onto the surface of water held in a two-inch-deep cylindrical dish and perturb the surface by blowing through thin flexible plastic tubing to direct the motion of the swirling mixture. The colors remained in somewhat discreet bands similar those of "marbleized" endpapers of books.

6. Others of the thirty to fifty core members of the Hog Farm included Hugh Romney and his wife Bonnie Jean, Evan Engber and his wife Bonnie Zee (who, as Dr. West's Medicine Show and Jug Band had made the hit record, "The Eggplant that Ate Chicago"), Rick Sullivan, and Paul Foster (a former member of Ken Kesey's Merry Pranksters). Under the name "Wavy Gravy", Romney wrote a somewhat fanciful account of the commune, *The Hog Farm and Friends, As Told to Hugh Romney and Vice Versa* (New York: Links Books, 1974).

7. In San Francisco, the traditions of the real time projection of colored light had been renewed by the Vortex concerts at the Morrison Planetarium arranged by the poet and electronic music composer, Henry Jacobs, and by filmmaker, Jordan Belson, from 1957 to 1960. Though Belson and artists such as Paul Beattie and Warner Jepson had continued experiments along similar lines, what became the dominant mode was developed by Ham and Romero in the early 1960s. The item that made San Francisco light shows unique was their use of techniques of liquid projection that had been invented in the early 1950s by Seymour Locks, a San Francisco State College professor, which Ham had learned from one of Locks' students, Elias Romero; see Charles Perry, *The Haight-Ashbury: A History* (New York: Random House, 1984), pp. 66–70. On light shows and San Francisco psychedelic art generally, see also Thomas Albright, *Art in the San Francisco Bay Area, 1945–1980: An Illustrated History* (Berkeley and Los Angeles: University of California Press, 1985) and Gene Sculatti and Davin Seay, *San Francisco Nights: The Psychedelic Music Trip, 1965–1968* (New York: St. Martin's Press, 1985). The Trips Festival was filmed by Ban Van Meter (himself a light show artist) for his *S.F. Trips Festival, An Opening* (1966). Hartshorn's letters about the San Francisco counterculture so interested her father-in-law, Tom Wolfe, that he visited the city and eventually wrote *The Electric Kool-Aid Acid Test*. After Ken Kesey fled to Mexico, the Pranksters came to Los Angeles and made contact with Hugh Romney who collaborated with them in local Acid Tests, including one in Watts (12 February 1966) that included an extended light show; see Tom Wolfe, *The Electric Kool-Aid Acid Test* (New York: Farrar, Straus, and Giroux, 1968), pp. 241–253.

8. Though exhaustive research failed to turn up any such source.

9. Pinnacle Productions (later Pinnacle Rock Concerts) events at the Shrine accompanied by The Single Wing Turquoise Bird light show include the following, all in 1968 (all concerts included additional supporting acts): 15 and 16 March: Cream, James Cotton, Mint Tattoo; 29 and 30 March: Traffic, Quicksilver Messenger Company; 3 and 4 May: Big Brother and the Holding Company, Albert King; 17 and 18 May: Grateful Dead, Steve Miller Band, Taj Mahal; 24 and 25 May: Velvet Underground, Chambers Brothers, Dr. John the Night Tripper; 31 May and 1 June: Yardbirds, B.B. King, Sons of Champlain; 28 and 29 June: The Who, Fleetwood Mac, Crazy World of Arthur Brown; 26 and 27 July: Jeff Beck, Pink Floyd, Blue Cheer; 2 August: Jeff Beck, Charles Lloyd, Steve Miller Band; 3 August: Jeff Beck, Charles Lloyd, Steve Miller Band, Blue Cheer; 4 August: Electric Flag, Paul Butterfield Blues Band, Steve Miller Band, Ike and Tina Turner; 23 and 24 August: Grateful Dead, Taj Mahal; 6 and 7 September: John Mayall, Junior Wells, Taj Mahal. On 15 September Pinnacle and the Los Angeles Free Clinic together sponsored "The American Music Show" at the Rose Bowl from noon to midnight. Though featuring Joan Baez, the Everly Brothers, the Byrds, Janis Joplin and Big Brother and the Holding Company, Country Joe and the Fish, Junior Wells, Buddy Guy, Mothers of Invention, Buffy Sainte-Marie, and Wilson Pickett, the event drew only a small audience. The posters for almost all these concerts were designed by John Van Hamersveld, though on two or three of them he included collaborative work done by San Francisco artists, Rick Griffin and Victor Moscoso; Neon Park, a local artist, designed the poster for the Paul Butterfield Blues Band concert.

10. Lebrun, for example, recalls "a night at the Shrine when the drummer stayed on stage playing for an hour after the audience filed out, and we kept projecting with him…. When the hall was virtually empty, Helena, whose liquids were set up on a table in the auditorium, put on a beautiful plate that was all large, slowly drifting white and pale blue bubbles … . I discovered that we had been given a reel of George Méliès shorts that we had neglected to use during the main show. I put that on, and dozens of tiny black and white Méliès Victorian fairies began to cavort in the blue bubbles – sheer magic, and my last memory of a Single Wing show" (email to David E. James, 4 October 2004).

11. The Hog Farm planned to deliver one of their hogs, Pigasus, to be a presidential candidate at the Chicago Democratic convention, where they were also to be in charge of keeping the peace at the hippie assemblies. On their way across country with half a dozen busses and two geodesic domes, this "wing" of the Bird performed rock concerts with light shows at several small towns. Unfortunately the commune became stricken with infectious hepatitis in New Mexico and did not get to Chicago. Some of the members returned to Los Angeles the following year and did smaller light shows of their own and occasionally collaborated with the Single Wing Turquoise Bird. David Lebrun's *The Hog Farm Movie* (1970) depicts the commune's everyday life in Los Angeles and the traveling rock'n'roll multi-media show.

12. Francis himself independently made designs for large-scale light events; for example, in 1966 he made a plan for five helicopters to stream colored lights above the bay of Tokyo, and in 1971 he proposed that the opening of the "Art and Technology Exhibition" at the Los Angeles County Museum of Art be accompanied by salvos of rockets that would create light patterns in the sky. See Peter Selz, *Sam Francis* (New York: Harry N. Abrams, 1975), pp. 95–97.

13. Anaïs Nin, *The Diary of Anaïs Nin, 1966–1974* (New York: Harcourt Brace Jovanovich, 1980), p. 74

14. "Single Wing Turquoise Bird: New Cosmic Consciousness", *Los Angeles Free Press*, 22 November 1968, pp. 40–41. The article also included interviews with Mays, Perkins, Keesling, Scroggins, Greene, and Lippincott. Youngblood's overall account was much abbreviated and the quoted passage slightly revised in its inclusion in his collection of his *Free Press* pieces, *Expanded Cinema* (New York: Dutton, 1970), pp. 392–396. Youngblood also took black-and-white photographs of the show, three of which were published with his account, together with a collage of three of the group members.

15. "A Weekend in L.A.", *Weekly Planet* (Los Angeles), 24 January 1969, pp. 4–5. The formatting has been slightly altered and four quotations from Stein herself (at the points of the ellipses) eliminated; Stein's phrasing and syntax are imitated in the last paragraph. Moritz mistakenly called the show, "Eidols", which I have corrected.

16. Murrow also purchased a huge Norelco 16 mm xenon arc projector built for a World's Fair and added speed controls and strobe and color wheels. Its Geneva intermittent movement allowed him to sandwich two films together in the gate, permitting the vignetting of imagery within imagery to fit spaces created within the images created on other projectors used by the group.

17. Though, as Moritz's account illustrates, they had at least occasionally already been utilizing ambient street sounds.

18. From an undated letter (probably 1998), photo-copy in the possession of Peter Mays.

19. Youngblood, *Expanded Cinema*, p. 394.

20. This trajectory was sketched at least as early 25 June 1964 in the *Village Voice* article "Spiritualization of the Image", reprinted in *Movie Journal: The Rise of the New American Cinema, 1959–1971* (New York: Collier Books, 1972), pp. 144–146.

21. "Film Culture – Expanded Arts", *Film Culture* 43 (Winter 1966).

22. Stan Vanderbeek, "Culture: Intercom and Expanded Cinema: A Proposal and Manifesto", *Film Culture* 40 (Spring 1966): 15–18.
23. Vanderbeek, "Culture: Intercom", 17–18, all ellipses in original except those in square brackets.
24. Youngblood, *Expanded Cinema*, p. 41.
25. Youngblood, "Single Wing Turquoise Bird", *Los Angeles Free Press*, p. 40. Vanderbeek's manifesto had emphasized the need for precisely such a global cooperation.
26. See especially Branden W. Joseph's demonstration that Warhol's Exploding Plastic Inevitable should be distinguished from multi-media installations such as those of Charles and Ray Eames that naturalized the multidirectional, synesthetic environment created by contemporary commercial electronic media. Joseph argues that the EPI "emerged to contest ideological naturalizations of the type proposed by McLuhan and the Eameses" by producing "a dislocating, environmental montage where different media interfered and competed with each other, accelerating their distracting, shock-like effects". "'My Mind Split Open': Andy Warhol's *Exploding Plastic Inevitable*" in *X-Screen: Film Installations and Actions in the 1960s and 1970s*, ed. Matthias Michalka (Vienna: Museum Moderner Kunst Stiftung Ludwig, 2003), p. 24.
27. For a full account of the Los Angeles Newsreel and ethnic filmmaking in Los Angeles, see David E. James, *The Most Typical Avant-Garde: History and Geography of Minor Cinemas in Los Angeles* (Berkeley: University of California Press, 2005). The Newsreel also had meetings and screenings in Rol Murrow's studio above the Fox Venice theater.
28. Roger Corman's *The Trip* (1967), for example, had included numerous episodes imitating psychedelic underground film, including a scene in nightclub in which both band and audience are illuminated by a light-show. The visual effects for this scene were created by Bob Beck, himself a light show artist, who had previously created similar scenes for television and a film about Timothy Leary. He gave an account of them in "Creating the 'Psychedelic' Visual Effects for *The Trip*", in *American Cinematographer* 49, no. 3 (March 1968): 176–179, 196–197. Beck had previously researched Thomas Wilfed and other earlier forms of visual music and written a manual for producing light-shows.

Chapter Eight L.A.'s Hipster Cinema

I. An Evening at the Movies

On a balmy Thursday evening late in May 2008, I went to the Los Angeles' Museum of Contemporary Art (MOCA), Arata Isozaki's bunker across the road from Frank Gehry's celebrated Walt Disney Concert Hall, the Music Center, and the other downtown culture citadels on the edge of the corporate monoliths on which they so integrally depend. Although admission was free that day, the museum was all but deserted, especially the brutalist stainless steel and concrete theater where not more than half a dozen of us had gathered for one of the seven screenings of films and videos by conceptual artist Lawrence Weiner that accompanied the retrospective of his work at MOCA's other branch. A couple of people left after few minutes, while the rest of us fixed our attention on these abstruse works in a painfully eloquent silence. Though others of Weiner's moving-image works range from what you would expect (films built around texts) to what you would not (hardcore pornography), featured that evening was a film that at least invoked narrative. *Nothing to Lose* (*Niets Ann Verloren*, 1984) begins with a close-up of a beautiful, perhaps too beautiful, young man in a sailor's suit and cap. He cruises an industrial building in Amsterdam, in a window of which a skimpily dressed blonde proffers herself. Overlaid by an aural veneer of indecipherable chatter, their hesitant seduction is played out before another couple (dressed in period Dutch costume with lace bonnets) in another doorway to the same building. One is a man in drag, sulkily whittling on a cucumber, while the other, who is in fact a woman, scrubs her sheets on a washboard, looking up from time to time to cry out "Good Manners Spoil Good Food" and encourage the sailor on. As the camera moves freely among the four characters, the ritualized tableau is interrupted when from off-screen an apple is tossed into the scene, soon after which the sailor musters his courage – but only to kiss the lady quickly on the lips, then exit the frame to end the film.

I was intrigued but puzzled: how was I to understand the relation between the narrative and the washerwoman's cry, reminiscent as it was of the terse, often enigmatic, phrases that are Weiner's idiosyncratic form of sculpture? Was it a reflexive comment on the sailor's desultory shopping, or was the narrative a

Figure 1. Echo Park Film Center audience, 22 May 2008.

dramatization of the phrase, parallel to, if visually much richer than, the realization of Weiner's other aphorisms on the museum's walls? Both routes between words and images seemed to presuppose, not just that an appropriate hermeneutics would involve reading back from the artwork's material manifestation to the concept that generated it (Sol Lewitt's the "machine that makes the art"), but also that a complete explication was possible and indeed the point of the exercise.

After the screening, I drove ten minutes up the bad end of Sunset Boulevard from MOCA to Echo Park, a working-class, largely Latino and bohemian, community just up the road from the Echo, the hippest alternative music club in the city. The area used to be known as Red Hill, and some of its radical past and present is documented in Erika Suderburg's documentary video, *Somatography* (2000). The bustling intersection with Alvarado Street is marked by gas stations, bus stops, and taco stands, and next to a coffee shop festooned with fliers and Machine Project, a store-front exhibition space, I found the Echo Park Film Center (EPFC). In a decrepit storefront lined with rental videos, among shelves of ancient projectors and editing equipment, rows of old theater and kitchen chairs had been set up. People milled around greeting each other, drinking coffee or beer in paper bags, while a woman kept chasing in after her dog, who preferred the scene here to next door at Machine Project (that night featuring a show about an endurance race for cars valued at $500 or less). Twenty minutes late, Lisa Marr introduced the evening's program of vintage Scopitones, music shorts that in the 1960s played on specially designed juke boxes. Featuring all kinds of pop songs, these precursors of music videos were mostly so bad that Susan Sontag thought them exemplary of camp. The crowd at EPFC would have agreed, hooting and cheering as various lounge singers mouthed along, mostly out of sync, accompanied by visuals featuring bevies of female dancers, stripped to the briefest of bikinis then permissible, who frugged, hitch-hiked, or swam for the maximum jiggle. The crowd's enjoyment and applause rose to a dizzying crescendo with Joi Lansing's "The Web of Love", the Scopitone summa in which the buxom blonde is boiled by cannibals, enfolded by a human snake and enmeshed in a rope web, all in lurid 1960s colors preserved in dye-transfer Technicolor.

For me, the evening was on its way to being epiphanic: the two events in two of L.A.'s adjacent but disjunct urban spatialities appeared to span the possibilities of contemporary non-industrial film culture in general. Hadn't I inadvertently traveled between the two surviving but diametrically opposed forms of the modernist avant-garde film traditions: on the one hand, Weiner's arcane, reflexive hermeticism whose determined resistance to mass culture leaves it impenetrable to all but cognoscenti (and maybe even to them, for none of the poststructuralist

Figure 2. Sonny King, "I Cried For You". Scopitone, c. 1959.

Figure 3. Lawrence Weiner screening, Museum of Contemporary Art, Los Angeles, 14 June 2008.

art scribes who consecrated him in the catalogue undertook to demystify his films) and, on the other, a demotic populism, bringing art back to the practice of everyday life by repurposing the detritus of industrial culture in an informal social ritual, one where hermeneutics was hardly an issue? My hypothesis held until the second set when, after more beer or coffee, the Scopitone of Sonny King's "I Cried For You" was screened. As the lewd para-Ratpacker croons victoriously, the girls he now rejects strip to reveal the song's lyrics stenciled first on their underclothes and then, when these are removed, on their bodies. Here – suddenly and in the wrong place – were Weiner's materializations of language and, if not his porn, then something not far from it.

My musings on the contradictions in this instance of the reciprocal imbrication rather than the mutual exclusion of high and low were brought full circle a couple of weeks later, when MOCA hosted a Saturday night outdoor free screening of Weiner's films. Buoyed by beers, well-drinks, and DJ beats, the crowd appeared to be enjoying both the films and the starry evening, and even if they were as baffled as intrigued, they clearly relished the evening's creation of a cultural community, young people equally at home in an art museum as at the Echo. Here was L.A.'s Hipster Cinema.

II. Hipster Cinema: Polemics

In its original use in Thomas Kent Alexander's brief essay "San Francisco's Hipster Cinema"[1] written in June 1966, the term invoked recent work by Bruce Baillie, Robert Nelson, Kenneth Anger, Bruce Conner, and other Bay Area "Underground" filmmakers that was understood in terms of its categorical alterity to, if not the realism, then certainly the formal language of the Hollywood feature. Alexander's moment was caught in transition between, on the one hand, Beat generation politics of detachment and disaffiliation, and Jonas Mekas's idea of the oppositional, fundamentally ethical and existential (rather than aesthetic) nature of the New American Cinema and, on the other, the more ecstatic countercultural politics mobilized by the hippies. Between these, the hipster was supposed to affirm a cool humanism constructed in "detachment from the mechanized, depersonalized computer society", a rat race characterized, according to Alexander, by superficiality, vapidity, dullness, and violence.

Though the precise meaning of "hipster" is presently in flux, since its revival in the late 1990s in Los Angeles it has usually referred to the cultural formations based around indie music and film, many of whom are casual workers on the edges of the city's multiple culture and infotainment industries. Sometimes the term carries a derogatory implication of the fashionista's appropriation of the accoutrements of various post-punk and hip-hop cultures combined with the refusal or avoidance of whatever real social contestation these might have initially entailed. The simultaneous revival and reconstruction of the term imply then both a desire for some authentically real politics combined with the present difficulty of actually engaging them. Occupying the space between this desire and its impossibility is the Spectacle, the contemporary media system in which life as it might be lived is reflected back in the mirror of the signs of commodities and signs as commodities. Any cultural activity that engages this media system will find its search for authenticity inhabited by irony and ambivalence.

Of the myriad of other social and cultural developments that separate the hipster of summer 1966 from the hipster of fall 2008, none is more important than the reconfiguration of the imaginary role of the computer. Then it was associated with social control and so opposed to humane life, but now it is integral to everything; whereas the earlier hipster looked to avant-garde film as a "vital, alive and moving" defense against it, today the computer has become the essential vehicle of culture. Despite the ancestry of new media's formal properties in the innovations of experimental film, whatever avant-garde moving-image culture might mean or accomplish in the future, it will not be filmic but computerized and hence digital.

That such combined technological and social developments have inevitably already redirected the aspirations and practices of the filmic avant-garde is evidenced in the recent activity of the two senior Los Angeles practitioners, Pat O'Neill and Morgan Fisher. Both came to maturity with definitive bodies of work in the 1970s, the last time when the concept of the avant-garde in any of its modernist senses had any stability; both *oeuvres* were crucially film-specific, and by that token now superceded. O'Neill's sublime image manipulations, conducted within the very skin of the film, whose precision obliged him to move from 16 mm to 35 mm, can now be approximated with home-computer software, while Fisher's reflexive meditations on the specificity of 35 mm technology are perforce archeological. Perhaps as a consequence, neither has made a film in the past five years. Both, however, have found at least a temporary haven in the art world with recent shows in important galleries, respectively of sculpture and digital installations and of painting.

Such reorientations don't necessarily mean the end of advanced filmmaking; as long as the technology is available, people will make films, just as they still occasionally unhook their iPods and sing folksongs. But they do indicate that its historical project is being reconstructed in a new technological and social environment, one that is – ironically and contradictorily – characterized by the realization of many of the ambitions of the historical avant-garde in intertwined utopian and dystopian forms.

On the one hand, first on the level of form: the modernist formal innovations that San Francisco Underground film and the mid-century avant-garde used to assault the linear narrative of the illusionist feature film (and the repressive bourgeois culture it generally sustained) are now ubiquitous in corporate media. Collage, reflexivity, denatured imagery, multiple fractured diegeses, interpenetrating windows, shifting combinations of image, text, and sound – all these form the vehicular language that presently operates across all cultural levels. Second, on the level of practice: where avant-garde film struggled heroically but usually unsuccessfully against capital's need to segregate cultural producers and consumers, digital technologies have facilitated a pro-am media democratization. A previously unimaginable production and distribution of user-generated content on YouTube, blogs, viral videos, and a range of other platforms can now give a homemade YouTube clip more hits than the most successful blockbuster film. Beneath its advent under the guise of "empowerment", this form of labor is, of course, as functional within the present stage of capital as was physical labor in the period where material production was primary and industrial cultural activity restricted to consumption.

So, on the other hand, the cultural field is now entirely permeated by capital and its multiple molecular estrangements to the point where advertising has become the summary and all-pervasive mode of culture. As recently as thirty years ago in the twilight of modernism, the *production* of films that mobilized alternatives to a reified bourgeois order had a felt utility; but now – in an era of saturated over-production of all kinds – emancipation is thought to revolve around the politics of *consumption*. Driving consumption, advertising subtends, not just economic transactions, but also cultural production. While it's now a commonplace that avant-garde stylistics have been appropriated and defused by advertising, more fundamental and important are the processes that began well before the Internet and digital technology made them ubiquitous: advertising's communication codes that work in fragments across multiple media and are received piecemeal in distraction and subconsciously reassembled now provide the dominant procedures of all contemporary aesthetic reception.

As we find ourselves amidst the multiple screens of corporate kitsch that endlessly insist on consumption, the Situationist utopian injunction, "Never Work" can now only mean "Never Watch, Never Listen". This impossibility will ride with us and the vanguard hipsters in our automotive *flânerie* across the fragmented metropolis to make a more or less distracted sampling of the Spectacle and its alternatives. What follows is a synchronic slice through the alternative media systems encountered in the summer and fall of 2008. This period, the run up to the election of the forty-fourth U.S. president, was one of unusually significant cultural contestation that, it should be noted, will be remembered most of all by the image of Barack Obama made by Shepard Fairey, the quintessential hipster artist. If that and the other sights in the hipster cinema do not comprise a modernist critical avant-garde, they may nevertheless suggest ways of consuming what the age does provide, at least somewhat, *avant-gardedly*.

III. The Los Angeles Filmforum

Founded in 1975 as the Pasadena Filmforum, in a bright period where three or four other similar screening organizations flourished in the city, the Los Angeles Filmforum outlived them all, surviving cutbacks in public funding, the academicization and then the corporatization of identity-politics, the shift from 16 mm film to video and then to digital production, and tough times generally to become what itself it describes as "the longest-running showcase for independent, experimental and progressive moving-image art in Southern California".[2] Often only by the skill of its hot-splices, it survived cutbacks in public funding, the academicization and then the corporatization of identity-politics, the shift from 16 mm film to video and then to digital production. By the mid-1990s it was the only ongoing alternative screening organization in the city, sustained more by the sheer will of its nucleus of members than by any manifest civic or indeed social recognition. But revitalized by Adam Hyman, who became Executive Director and Programmer in 2003, it has sustained the main traditions of the avant-garde by mounting around thirty-five shows a year. Programming in 2008, for example, included evenings devoted to Carolee Schneemann, Heinz Emigholz, Bruce and Norman Yonemoto, Robert Breer, Coleen Fitzgibbon, Walter Ungerer, as well as several younger filmmakers. The year was completed with a sold-out return engagement for Susan Mogul with her new feature-length, *Driving Men*. An autobiographical excavation of the intertwined genealogies of her sexual and artistic identities, it deftly interweaves fragments of her earlier work as one of L.A.'s pioneer video artists and video diarists with both still and moving images drawn from her forty-year self-documentation projects and interviews with family members, former lovers, and her present partner. Mogul's turn from short, often confrontational, video art to feature-length works that at least hold the possibility of wider distribution is, of course, one of several historically determined responses to the decline of the autonomous avant-garde.

For most of its history Filmforum moved among various venues across the city, but since 2002 it has settled at one of the most famous of movie palaces, Sid Grauman's Egyptian Theatre on Hollywood Boulevard, opened in 1922 and recently restored. Located now in the "Belly of the Beast" (the title of an extensive 1994 Filmforum retrospective of the L.A. avant-garde), the new home figures the integrated and reciprocal relations between the avant-garde and the industry that has given Los Angeles filmmaking its prototypicality. Reflecting this both this reciprocity and Hyman's communitarian vision, the Filmforum website links to other non-commercial cinemas that have sprung up since the millennium and now reticulate the city. Hyman also sends out regular email listings of other alternative film screenings, supplementing Film Radar, a website that tracks all kinds of local non-mainstream cinema events, news and reviews, and Flicker, which provides the same service nationally.

The more recently established venues form a spectrum that ranges from amateur screenings, through various kinds of indie production, to the projections of the industry itself. The other avant-garde screening organizations are typically either associated with educational institutions or museums – like MOCA – or based in community projects of one kind or another – like the EPFC. The former group also includes REDCAT, the Roy and Edna Disney/Cal Arts Theater, housed downtown in the bottom of the Disney Concert Hall; the Bijou Theater at

Figure 4. REDCAT Theater.

California Institute of the Arts (Cal Arts) itself that regularly screens the best in global art and avant-garde film; Cinematheque 108, an irregular series of public screenings at the University of Southern California (USC) and the Film and Television Archives at the University of California at Los Angeles (UCLA). Grassroots establishments, sustained as they are by a greater – or more usually lesser – degree of public funding, include LA Freewaves, self-described as a "grassroots yet global arts organization connecting innovative, relevant, independent new media from around the world", best known for an enormously innovative annual video festival; NewTown Pasadena, a curatorial collective, self-described as a "Persistent Weed in the Garden of Art" that among many pioneering undertakings has screened avant-garde films in a variety of unconventional venues; KAOS Network, a community arts center that since 1984 has provided training in video production and other media arts for mostly African American youth; Visual Communications, inarguably the premier Asian Pacific media arts center in the U. S. that since 1970 has promoted Asian American film and video production; Cinefamily, a community cinematheque, and 7 Dudley Cinema, a storefront by the beach, known especially for radically confrontational documentaries. All these either screen or sponsor screenings of non-corporate and often anti-corporate time-based media, and of them, REDCAT and an anomalous organization, Cinefamily, have made the strongest impact.

An annex added during the protracted construction period of the Walt Disney Concert Hall for the Los Angeles Philharmonic, REDCAT was designed to be the downtown experimental satellite for Cal Arts, founded by Walt Disney in

1961 and the most renowned of the city's many major art schools whose presence is fundamental to its overall cultural vitality – and its hipster culture. REDCAT comprises a gallery and an especially flexible and technologically advanced presentation space that accommodates dance, music, theater, film, video, as well as intermedia combinations of these. With a remarkably precise and bright 16 mm projection (one of the best in the world on the testimony of Peter Kubelka, no less) and a bar and bookshop, in the five years it has been open it has become a popular screening space, usually featuring audiences of between forty and two hundred people many Monday evenings.

The screenings are curated by Steve Anker, Dean of the Cal Arts film school, and Bérénice Reynaud, one of the school's most distinguished professors. Though both have a wide knowledge of non-commercial cinema, Anker's primary commitment is, broadly speaking, to the U.S. avant-garde, with Reynaud's to global art cinema; her interest in post-Fifth Generation film, for example, has meant that the Chinese avant-garde has often been more widely accessible in Los Angeles than in Beijing. Aiming for overall programming of one third each of local, U.S., and globally produced works, and backed by the publicity and other resources of REDCAT, their fall 2007 season was first-rate, the equal of any comparable venue in the world. In November alone, they presented evenings devoted to Robert Breer, Kenneth Anger, Paul McCarthy, Sandra Gibson and Luis Recoder, Martin Arnold, and Joan Jonas, all with the filmmakers present. Perhaps more oriented to the U.S. avant-garde than is usual, the schedule included world premieres of new films by Anger and the first theatrical presentation of McCarthy's *Caribbean Pirates* (2001–2005), previously seen only in Germany and as an installation.

Though McCarthy's work was vacuous and bombastic and Anger's new films slight in comparison to his classics, the reputations of both artists are so high that even these limitations did not detract from the social significance of their presentation. Anger is one of the few surviving avatars of Underground film and McCarthy, a doyen of transgressive performance art turned filmmaker, has an art world cachet as powerful as the socially sanctioned theater and classical music of the Bunker Hill elites. Despite this, neither was powerful enough to puncture the ignorance of, and disdain for, any form of non-Hollywood cinema that is widespread in the city's established institutions; and so in a special feature on REDCAT on its fifth anniversary in November 2008, the *Los Angeles Times* sent its ace theater, music, and art critics to evaluate the record – but completely omitted any reference to the film and video programming.

If, despite the *Times*, REDCAT elevates the generally marginalized filmic avant-garde to parity with high bourgeois culture, Cinefamily does the opposite, taking the avant-garde back below the salt, and reasserting its populist, demotic roots. Located on Fairfax Avenue not far from Melrose Avenue, L.A. hipsterdom's central shopping district, Cinefamily is housed in what until a few years ago was the last operating venue dedicated to silent films, and which – despite the recent installation of sound equipment – is still called the Silent Movie Theater. The theater had been closed since 1997, when the owner was shot three times in the face with a .357 magnum by a hit man hired by the projectionist, his lover. It was then bought and run by Charlie Lustman for several years with middling success and programming as a silent movie venue. The Harkham family, who own many properties on Fairfax Avenue, bought it from Lustman in 2007. Cinefamily took over the dead space, banished its ghosts, and turned it into a carnival. Founded by Hadrian Belove (former co-owner of Cinefile Video) and Dan Harkham, and now maintained by them along with Amalia Levari, Tom Fitzgerald, and occasional volunteers, its declared aspiration to create "unusual programs of exceptional, distinctive, weird and wonderful films" welcomes the avant-garde. The fall screenings included George Kuchar; experimental animator Don Hertzfeldt; former punk filmmaker Jem Cohen; Bill Morrison; a series of forgotten films selected from the catalogues of Canyon Cinema, Electronic Arts Intermix and The Filmmaker's Co-op; and *Berlin: Symphony of a Great City* (1927) with live musical accompaniment. All these could have appeared at REDCAT or Filmforum, and indeed several were co-presented by the latter. But Cinefamily intermixed them with, on the one hand, classic art films from both Hollywood and abroad (Aleksandr Medvedkin's *Happiness*, Hou Hsiao-Hsien's *Café Lumière*, Rudolph Valentino in *The Eagle*, and an Ozu series) and, on the other, with para-cinematic oddments and rarities (*Decampment*, a silent experimental horror short by Midwestern musical grindmeisters, Adult; protest films from the 1960s; a series of homemade horror films; early hip-hop films; a series of films about evil children co-presented by Meltdown Comics & Pimpadelic Wonderland; Christploitation; and "Fucked-Up Kids' Movies" – "the most demented batch of made-for-kiddie goodies").

Heretically interrupting and contextualizing the purity of the avant-garde, these innovations in scheduling, in the structure of the *filmic*, are accompanied by similarly radical innovations in the *cinematic*, in the social functions the films sustain. The Cinefamily's publicly stated goal is "to foster a spirit of community and a sense of discovery, while reinvigorating the movie-going experience. Like campfires, sporting events and church services, we believe that movies work best as social experiences". The emphasis on the community of film lovers is sustained by several innovations: instead of charging for separate admissions, Cinefamily encourages people to pay $25 a month, "the cost of two tickets and a bucket of popcorn", in return for which they receive unlimited entry; though the theater itself is relatively conventional, it is supplemented by a backyard patio where between shows people drink the coffee that is for sale, along whatever else they may have smuggled in; and many screenings are coordinated with musical events (early in the new year, Tom Verlaine and Jimmy Rip played live to accompany shorts by Man Ray, Fernand Léger, and Hans Richter in two – needless to say – sold-out shows). But the Labor Day event was an awesome cinematic reimagining of the traditional backyard barbeque.

It began with "The 5 Minutes Game", in which the first five minutes of twenty rare films, not available on DVD, were screened, with the audience choosing the one to be projected in it entirety after the meal. As the program read:

6:00pm–8:00pm: The 5 Minutes Game

8:00pm–9:00pm: BBQ time!

9:00pm–11:00pm: we watch the winning film!

An irreverent escapade, it nevertheless possessed a flawless avant-garde lineage: the first part was a filmic *"exquisite corpse"* recalling the Surrealists' *dérive* from theater to theater in order to create a discontinuous dream narrative; the second part interrupted the autonomy of the filmic with a celebratory communal ritual; and the final screening, which turned out to be the low-budget classic, *Death Promise* (1977), reflected the spectators' immediate communal desires as well perhaps their problems with obnoxious landlords. A panoply of radical gestures, all mobilized together on the one day a year we celebrate the working class!

In creating a local community in a city where all commentators agree that civic governance is the tool of corporate development, Cinefamily has in the one year of its existence been magnificently successful, not only in creating its own loyal audience (with regular attendance between 100 and a sell-out 175 five nights a week), but also in contributing to the revitalization of its immediate environment. Neighboring storefronts that recently were dark and empty are now bookshops, including the Harkham's own Family Bookstore a couple of blocks away (which via Sammy Harkham's work as a graphic novelist, links Cinefamily to another semi-underground community), record, designer-sneaker, and skate stores, and soon another café.

Surrounding or subtending these flagship developments are complementary cultural initiatives. One is formed by the several important preservation and historical recovery projects including the Center for Visual Music (CVM), a nonprofit archive directed by Cindy Keefer that restores and distributes the work of Oscar Fischinger, Jordan Belson and other abstract animators; the iotaCenter, a self-described "arts organization devoted to Abstract Cinema and Visual Music";

Figure 5. Mark Toscano working on restoration at AMPAS.

the UCLA Film and Television Archive, where Ross Lipman specializes in avant-garde and independent cinema; and the Academy of Motion Picture Arts and Sciences (AMPAS) that for several years has been preserving avant-garde films, by both local and often otherwise inadequately recognized artists and the titans of the medium. Under the guidance of Mark Toscano, AMPAS's present projects include restoring Stan Brakhage's entire *oeuvre*. And, modeled on a writers' workshop, the Los Angeles Abstract Movie Workshop meets monthly at the Museum of Jurassic Technology (created by one-time avant-garde filmmaker, David Wilson) for members to show and critique new works and works-in-progress. Around these well-established institutions lies a host of more or less ephemeral, more or less virtual, and more or less reclusive micro-cinemas that emanate primarily from three ancillary cultural spheres: the art world, the music world, and the film industry itself, which indeed substantially shapes the other two.

Since at least the early 1920s, fine artists in Los Angeles have both found professional occupation in the film industry and worked independently outside it, the latter generating a strong, if uneven and idiosyncratic, tradition of artists' films that runs from Boris Deutsch through Ed Ruscha and John Baldessari to, at present, Sharon Lockhart, Charlie White and Jennifer West (all three of whom teach in the art – not film – school at USC). Drawing on the strong local tradition of visual music epitomized by the career of Oskar Fischinger (who on several occasions himself sold his skills to advertisers, the last being a commercial he made in Los Angeles for televisions manufactured by "Madman" Muntz), an adjacent tradition of fine-art video and now high-tech digital projection has developed over the past two decades and produced several bona fide stars who make what a couple of decades ago would have been thought of as expanded cinema. Most notable are Diana Thater, who makes large site-specific installations, often featuring natural imagery, and Jennifer Steinkamp, who works with both natural imagery and quasi-psychedelic abstractions. For "Left Humerus", a summer show at the Acme gallery, for example, Steinkamp projected swirling clouds of mostly primary colors surging into and out of the elbow formed by two adjacent gallery walls.

The stature of digital projection of this kind is currently so high that every third gallery shows some form of time-based imagery; the appropriately named Lightbox at the Kim Light gallery is one of the most interesting of them. And screens, windows, and projections are similarly ubiquitous on the monthly downtown art walk through the hippest new galleries and even, in a sumptuously ironic return, in a converted Main Street movie palace. Other, more peripheral or non-commercial art-world micro-cinemas include "The abc of cinema: Gilles Deleuze's 'From A to Z'", curated by Marie Jager and Hedi El Kholti under the auspices of the publishing enterprise *Semiotext(e)*, that since 2006 has been occasionally screening avant-garde films at a fashionable – if noisy – bar, the Mandrake; and a new online exhibition project called "Moving Index" hosted by the Art Office for Film + Video that each two months features digital work by three different artists.

As assimilated into the art world, digital projections have become the most prominent form of visual music, but in a more ephemeral way they have also become integral to musical performance, especially rock and dance music. The local practice of this kind of film was inaugurated by the Single Wing Turquoise Bird, the most important of L.A.'s 1960s psychedelic rock'n'roll light-shows. Its descendants are integral to raves, but they also appear in the funkiest little clubs. The last I saw, for example, was a performance at the Echo, close to the EPFC, by Black Dice, a band that generates its own music and lightshow simultaneously. Several local organizations systematically sustain this connection between indie music and film, the most prominent being Dublab, a decade-old nonprofit group that maintains an Internet radio station primarily concerned with electronic,

Figure 6. Black Dice in performance at the Echo.

post-punk, and ambient music, but that also sponsors videos and films, and produces an email newsletter publicizing their own and other audio-visual events.

An unbroken spectrum links corporate pop to the most determinedly anti-corporate music, and every point on that spectrum produces film and video correlatives whose languages mostly derive from avant-garde film; consequently, the circumambient presence of music in urban life is ever more rapidly being reciprocated in the increased environmental presence of the avant-garde. Similarly ranging from the amateur to the most commercial, these create a visual architecture that is coming to be as inescapable as the aural environment of music. One of the specificities that continues to make Los Angeles the prototype of the postmodern conurbation is the pervasive presence of cinematic, para-cinematic, and now virtual screens in the urban fabric. Twenty years ago, Baudrillard asked "Where is the cinema? It is all around you outside, all over the city, that marvelous, continuous performance of films and scenarios".[3] His question may have prematurely collapsed the ontological difference between film and reality, but the conception of the cityscape as itself a screenscape is now phenomenologically indisputable. No account of cinema in L.A. can avoid the injunctions of postmodern geographers (including the schools at UCLA and USC) that we must think spatially, one aspect of which entails recognition that contemporary moving-image culture is realized architecturally. Urban hipsters find avant-garde film, not simply by visiting the institutions surveyed above, but ambiently in the visuality of the city itself where, whether tiny or huge, screens are so ubiquitous that together they become almost as seamless as sound. Everywhere, the avant-garde takes place.

V. Between City Lights and Cell Phones

A logical if not chronological point of origin for the spatial surround of visuals that derive from avant-garde film is the tradition of outdoor screenings (like Weiner's at MOCA) that began in Los Angeles with Louis Hock's early 1970s projections of his wry travelogue, *Southern California* (1979) on the walls of city buildings or on the sides of trucks. This tradition has recently been revived and institutionally sustained. Perhaps the most dramatic instance in the period covered was a late-summer, three-week series of science-fiction-inspired films and artists' videos on an outside wall of the downtown postmodern citadel, the Bonaventure Hotel, hosted by Afterall, a publishing project affiliated with both Cal Arts and Central Saint Martins College of Art in London. The evening I attended, August 21, was a Kuchar double bill: George's *Ascension of the Demonoids* (1985) and Mike's *Sins of the Fleshapoids* (1965). Seeing *Fleshapoids*' fake spaceships framed by the hotel's mirrored towers and space-shuttle elevators while police and corporate helicopters hovered above and the squad-car sirens screamed in the streets below eerily reminded me of Fredric Jameson's designation of the Bonaventure as the paradigmatic postmodern building; but it slipped into another dimension when I realized that *Fleshapoids*' plot of two robots falling in love in the far distant future was the same as *Blade Runner*'s and that it was now being projected in *Blade Runner*'s own hyper-hallucinogenic architectural environment.

Other instances of these outdoor and often peripatetic screenings range from the Engine Theater to the Hollywood MobMov and the Cinespia Cemetery Screenings. Inspired by the putative capacity of so-called prosumer moving-image technology to threaten "the corporate media empire as never before", the former rolls out its portable projection system featuring a 1000-pound light-and-steel sculpture that kinetically supports a seventeen-foot screen to show "underground films" at various outdoor locations. Fall offerings range from "Experimental Eros" (erotic-themed work by George Kuchar, Lewis Klahr and Peggy Ahwesh) to "Experiments in Terror" that combined recreations of 1960s psychedelic nightmares and 70s drive-in horror. Both were curated by Noel Lawrence, formerly associated with Craig Baldwin's Other Cinema in San Francisco. Like a filmic rave, MobMov (MOBile MOVie) is a "Guerilla Drive-in" that surreptitiously shows movies in unused city spaces. And Cinespia screens in the Hollywood Forever Cemetery, resting place of Rudolph Valentino, Douglas Fairbanks, Jayne

Figure 7. Mike Kuchar, *Sins of the Fleshapoids*. Afterall screening, Westin Bonaventure Hotel, 21 August 2008.

Mansfield, and many more Hollywood greats, immediately adjacent to the Paramount Pictures studio, built in 1912. Audiences as large as 2,500 bring blankets, cushions, and gourmet dinners along with wine and candles to spend summer weekend evenings on a half-acre lawn between the tombs to watch films projected on the white marble mausoleum. Their fare tends to be cult classics, but if the recontextualization of the films, the creation of a community around them, the DJs spinning dance music before the show – and the possibility that what remains of Peter Lorre is silently turning in the ground under you as you relish his virtual image in *The Maltese Falcon* (1941) – don't make them avant-garde then nothing will. These instances are institutionally framed, and for cinema's spontaneous occupation of the city proper we have to go to the streets themselves, where real struggles are occurring.

The general context involves the ongoing Billboard Wars, currently being fought by neighborhood activists against the billboard industry and the city's craven planning commission over "sign districts", where massive (up to seventy-six-feet-high) digital billboards would be permitted. In this battle, avant-garde film's history of formal innovation and especially the utopian dreams of "expanded cinema" now find themselves confronted by the negative, inverted forms of the emancipatory politics that once inspired them.

For some time artists have been contesting the commercialization of public space by "*detourning*" billboards. Such interventions range from the use of graffiti in poorer areas (a practice that in L.A. goes back at least forty years, when Harry Gamboa Jr. began spraying "Chicano Cinema" on East L.A. hoardings) to a project in the spring by one Mike Mills.[4] As well as being a maker of music videos, commercials, documentaries, and the well-received feature *Thumbsucker* (2005), Mills is a graphic designer and artist. Wearing the last of these hats, early in 2008 he appropriated a billboard on La Brea Avenue, painted it pink, and then printed on it, "The cops are inside us" in white Helvetica. Shortly afterward, underneath his sententiously vacuous proclamation, an unknown tagger scrawled a reply, "They Ain't Inside Me". As such layered contestations are mobilized more grandly and in moving images, cycles of corporate initiatives and art-world or populist contestations of them, of protest and counter-protest, sustain each other.

A demotic, progressive instance is Phantom Galleries L.A. Modeled on a San Jose precedent, the organization arranges for local arts groups, independent curators, and artists to exhibits video and other work in vacant storefront windows, transforming them into 24/7 public art. As well giving visibility to the art, Phantom Galleries also contributes to urban renewal, encouraging foot traffic, public use of social space, and community involvement. One I saw earlier in the spring, "The Long Weekend", organized by Nancy Buchanan and Joseph Santarromana in a Pasadena shopping district, had taken over a failed furniture store with half a dozen street-level windows. In each had been placed an installation, performance, sculpture, or video projection, all engaging some aspect of the relationship between art and commerce. Buchanan's own, for example, *3 Fates*, presented myth reduced to marketing in filmed images of a fashion model successively draped in three gowns whose various colors – siren-red, prison-jumpsuit orange, and camouflage – hinted at their destiny. The panorama as a whole appeared as a series of adjacent movie-screens, in which – appropriately enough – were reflected the marquee lights of Laemmle's first-run arthouse theater on the opposite side of Colorado Boulevard.

The other pole of both urban development and corporate cultural investment is exemplified by the new downtown Nokia Theatre L.A. LIVE that opened in October 2007. Inside is devoted to pricey pop music, but outside is a visual spectacle of multicolored pulsating screens that recalls nothing so much as Stan VanDerBeek's Movie Drome projection system or John Cage and Ronald Nameth's 1967–69 performance work, *HPSCHD* – reconstructed in Hell.

That the site/sight should have been developed by a cell-phone company is precisely appropriate since phones at present are the cutting-edge of movie technologies; they have already redirected the structure of music videos away from earlier aspirations to cinematic scale towards simpler images that lose nothing by

8 – L.A.'s Hipster Cinema

Figure 8. Nancy Buchanan, *3 Fates*. at Phantom Galleries.

reduction to phone size. Since, along with other forms of advertising, music videos are the nexus where the avant-garde's formal innovations have been commercially appropriated, a comparison between, for example, Jake Nava's video for Beyoncé's "Single Ladies (Put A Ring On It)", released in October and

Figure 9. Nokia Plaza.

ranked as the best 2008 single by *Rolling Stone*, and the Michael Jackson or Madonna videos of twenty years ago gives some indication of where the avant-garde itself is headed. The cell-phone industry's current obsession with mapping which suggests that – just as we now drive using various satellite-navigation systems – we will before long be finding our way on foot through real space by referring to virtual images on our phones. So, if you do go to L.A. LIVE, you may still expect to be jostled by Nokia customers traversing the visual cacophony of the real-space of Nokia Plaza by looking at their phones – unless, that is, they are interrupted by their "Single Ladies" ringtone.

Existing midway between Phantom Galleries and L.A. Live and the contradictions they respectively embody was "Women in the City", curated by Emi Fontana," a "viral public art exhibition" of work by Barbara Kruger, Louise Lawler, and Jenny Holzer on view at more than fifty locations including billboards, video screens, storefronts, and a movie theater. Kruger's new video *Plenty*, that according the website "appropriates advertisements and stereotypes commenting on consumerism", was presented on video billboards at the flagship Los Angeles Museum of Contemporary Art, and also at the ultra-hip Key Club on the Sunset Strip, where it was "screened daily and fragmented between advertisements".[5]

Aren't we all?

Notes

1. *Film Culture* 44 (Spring 1967), 70–74.
2. In the interests of total disclosure, I note that I have been a Filmforum board member since 1981.
3. *America* (London: Verso, 1988), 56.
4. See www.mikemillsweb.com/
5. Kruger's video may be seen at www.youtube.com/watch?v=w0HHOIpUddI&feature=PlayList&p=ED13B213DA577ECA&index=1

Chapter Nine Film as an Instrument of Thought, Cinema as an Augury of Redemption: Ken Jacobs' *The Sky Socialist*

> The only philosophy that can be responsibly practiced in the face of despair is the attempt to contemplate all things as they would present themselves from the standpoint of redemption… . Perspectives must be fashioned that displace and estrange the world, reveal it to be, with its rifts and crevices, as indigent and distorted as it will appear one day in the messianic light. To gain such perspectives without velleity or violence, entirely from felt contact with its objects – this alone is the task of thought.
> Theodore Adorno, *Minima Moralia: Reflections from a Damaged Life*

> Undoubtedly, this man will some day be a great – failure.
> Isadore Lhevinne, *Ariadne*

> You necessary film, continue to envelope the soul.
> Walt Whitman, "Crossing Brooklyn Ferry"

> a aquel muchacho que llora porque no sabe la invención del Puente
> Federico García Lorca, "Ciudad sin sueño (Nocturno del Brooklyn Bridge)"

I.

In his announcement for "Essential Filmmaking", a class he taught in 1978, Ken Jacobs proposed a distinction between two forms of cinema: one as "a device of power" and the other as "an instrument of thought". The former, presumably the dominant capitalist industrial use of film, was, he argued, essentially a form of poster art that directs people, not "by informing, which would prompt thought, hesitation, unpredictable individual response", but by stupefying them; in the latter, on the other hand, "certain thoughts or kinds of thinking for the first time became possible, realizable, and certain experiences unique to the capacity of cinema, available".[1] As the declamations in *Star Spangled to Death* (2004) and other instances reveal, Jacobs' political frustrations have on more than one occasion provoked him to the *plumpes Denken* of poster art and even to dalliance with "subliminal, subaudible stimuli pitched to the unconscious".[2] But his oeuvre as a whole has comprised a quite different attempt to turn film into an instrument of thought for both himself and those who experience his work, and by that to turn cinema, if not into a means of social redemption, then perhaps an augury of it.

In this last respect his own filmmaking has always involved parallel work in cinema, in creating social organizations that promote a popular, participatory use for the medium rather than a capitalist, propagandistic one: his family life at the hub of a community of filmmakers, in which his camera became a " Community camera";[3] his work as a teacher of film history and filmmaking that inspired several generations of students, many of whom became important artists; and his role as one of the chief founders of the Millennium Film Workshop in New York, a nonprofit filmmaker's co-operative – "a little space of Socialism"[4] – that made equipment, workspace, screenings, and classes available to the general public. Taking place in a context of ongoing personal poverty and in the absence of a domestic Socialist political program or even any substantial social grounding outside the bohemian enclaves of New York, these efforts accompanied Jacobs' own filmmaking, an especially diverse and innovative spectrum of alternatives to the controlling forms of the medium. In a world where film is all but entirely reified as "a device of power" and where attempts to use it as an agent of emancipation find it already alienated, Jacobs' own films have been mostly contributions to what has been proposed as a "critical cinema", an avant-garde constructed, not as the innovation of technical or stylistic features eventually adapted by the industry, but as analytic explorations of "the nature and impact of the commercial cinema".[5]

The thought in the works for which Jacobs has been most celebrated – *Tom, Tom, The Piper's Son* (1969), *The Doctor's Dream* (1968), *Star Spangled to Death*, and of course the various incarnations of the Nervous System – has, then, primarily involved investigation of the unseen or overlooked techniques and material elements within commercial film that sustain its exploitative and propagandistic functions. Much less common have been films made by himself independent of previous commercial works. Most of these – synthetic positives as distinct from the analytic negations – have been either documentations of Dadaist street theater or instances of highly-formal, medium-specific *vues* of domestic scenes, whose critical significance has not always been readily apparent. One of the finest of the latter, *Airshaft* (1964), for example, is a fixed-camera single-take of the light in a window opening onto the space between buildings. It was booed at a screening of films opposed to the U.S. invasion of Viet Nam, but Jonas Mekas proposed that, in fact, it did entail an emancipatory dimension: "It gets to us and makes us more radiant. All things that are clear make us more radiant".[6]

But only once has Jacobs made a feature-length, character-driven narrative that could instantiate what thinking in film could be beyond immanent visual apprehension and within the possibilities of a Hollywood genre. *The Sky Socialist*

(1965), a romantic melodrama in which an ingénue couple overcome all obstacles to achieve their love, thus presents itself as a redeemed example of what, in the debased, thoughtless form of capitalist entertainment, has dominated the medium's history. But this geste was freighted with dramatically enlarged conceptual issues. The generic narrative was designed to resonate with a utopian metaphysical vision: "In keeping with the fantasy character of the film, the title is intended to evoke a just God".[7] And so the project was to be the vehicle by which the modern history of the Jews and indeed "all things" could be reimagined "from the standpoint of redemption". As such, according to all received definitions of cinema, *The Sky Socialist* must appear a failure; indeed, according to its own dialectical logic, in order to succeed it had to be one. Shot in Kodachrome II on the amateur regular 8 gauge rather than on professional 35 mm, the film was transferred to 16 mm for editing, but lack of funds ensured that even in this format it was not released into public distribution until 1988; until then it lived, not in theatrical exhibition and public recognition, but in a neglect and invisibility that testify to its extraordinary ambition.

The Sky Socialist attempts to think, simultaneously and the one by means of the other, two absent and impossible oxymorons: a redeemed history and a redeemed cinema. In this attempt, Socialism becomes the pivot, the tertium quid, standing with – and against – God in history, and with – and against – modernism in art. In the former case, divine love is invoked in the secular form of a just social order, and in the latter, a film language is constructed across the century's aesthetic aporiae: renouncing both socialist realism and its formal model, Capitalist Realism, *The Sky Socialist* makes a narrative of love and history by creating an (un)populist, modernist film language. In consequence, as Jacobs proposed, "certain thoughts or kinds of thinking for the first time" become possible and "certain experiences unique to the capacity of cinema, available". A reinvention of cognitive processes that existed prior to the positivistic mental flattening of the scientific era, this new kind of thinking in film is allegorical, and it is immanent in the sensory experience the film offers, mobilized in its multi-dimensional discursivity and manifest in the mode of its production.

II.

The Sky Socialist is divided roughly equally between a portrait of a place and a loosely improvised narrative that takes place there.[8] The place is the roof of the loft in a previously industrial building where Jacobs then lived at 25 Ferry Street in New York, close to its intersection with Jacob Street, and the two blocks around it on each side of the Brooklyn Bridge's Manhattan landing. The narrative is comprised of a series of sequences introduced by titles that portray the courtship and marriage of a young couple, "the obscure thirties author, Isadore Lhevinne" and "a miraculously spared Anne Frank", played respectively by Dave Leveson and Florence Karpf, then Jacobs' girlfriend and subsequently his wife. Other characters are "Maurice, the dragging force of Despair ever reminding Isadore of rotten history and the fragility of things" played by Bob Cowan; "Love's Labor" played by Joyce Wieland; "The Muse of Cinema" played by Julie Motz; and "Nazi Mentality" played by Mel Garfinkel.[9] The film also includes two interpolated short extracts from what is thought to be the first Yiddish talkie, *His Wife's Lover* (Sidney M. Goldin, 1931). Apart from several interludes where passages of Soviet jazz, Schoenberg's *Opus 24*, and other music accompany the action, sync dialogue during the second extract from *His Wife's Lover*, and a fragment of dialogue from Edgar G. Ulmer's low-budget horror film, *The Black Cat* (1934), the film is silent.

After a brief prologue introducing the main personages, Isadore courts Anne on the roof of the building and, despite Maurice's dogged discouragement of her, eventually surrounds her with shopping bags and boxes of clothes and fabric in a "Bestowal of the Material Goods". Though Anne receives this promise of marriage joyously, she is warned by the first extract from *His Wife's Lover*, which shows a distracted young woman who was promised a young and handsome husband, but has been tricked into marriage with a nebbish. Love's Labor is seen in the act of repairing the Bridge with scotch tape – a kind of film – and Maurice reminds Isadore of the fate of the American couple in *The Black Cat*, "honey-mooning in a Europe mined with explosives". Her indecision is marked by an especially abstract interlude of night-time lights on the bridge followed by several minutes of black leader, but the Muse of Cinema flies to the rescue and is greeted by the inter-title, "You are our collective projection. Invent Hope". Anne dances and begins to make a rudimentary form of cinema with a small hand-mirror, and the two resume their courtship. Appearing with a grotesque African American doll and other racist insignias, Nazi Mentality attempts to disrupt them, stabbing at microbes in the air, at a ribbon made of U.S. flags, and even at Anne herself. But, having more fully embraced cinema in the forms of a mirror fixed to her forehead, Anne now has hope and, wearing a hat adorned with small dolls of a married couple, she accepts Isadore.

In a "Divine Retribution Sequence" fear returns in the form of Nazi Mentality wearing swastikas and a skeleton vest. But he strikes his head on an axe held by Anne, and his death prompts an extended ecstatic celebratory review of the Brooklyn Bridge and the environment around it. As the film and the courtship enter their final phase, the Muse reappears with reel of film flapping in the wind,

9 – Film as an Instrument of Thought, Cinema as an Augury of Redemption

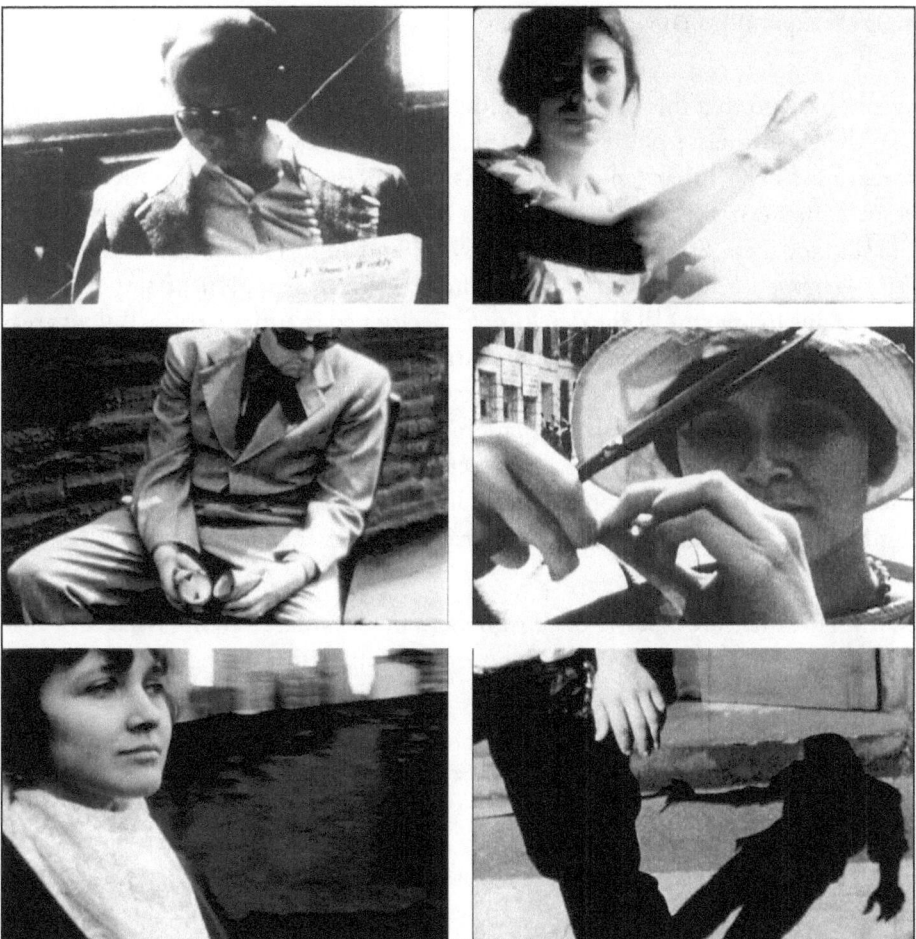

Figure 1. *The Sky Socialist*, main characters: Isadore Lhevinne; Anne Frank; Maurice, "the dragging force of Despair"; Love's Labor; the Muse of Cinema; Nazi Mentality.

snips it, and edits on a "Substitution for the Logical Ending". The second extract from *His Wife's Lover* reveals the nebbish to be in fact a handsome young man in disguise, and the couple happily sing a duet before going to bed. Anne brings food and a glass of water for Isadore and, with a line of clothing forming a makeshift *chuppah*, the marriage is "Witnessed by Bleeding Humanity". As a result, the film is able to depict "Isadore's Transmogrification" in which he, the bridge, the rooftops, and the streets below are transformed and abstracted by photography, first though a rotating anamorphic lens and then the water glass. Maurice reappears, but now in light rather than gloomy clothes with a pillow that he treats as his baby, and the film rewards him with a "Myth of His Own" and finally the title "Brooklyn Connects with Manhattan" introduces a brief coda, a series of superimposed views of the city, some shot through the hands of a dancing woman.

Jacobs has said that this "setting is at least of as much concern as the story",[10] and like the signal masterpieces of literary and filmic modernism, *The Sky Socialist* foregrounds the urban environment as a participant in the narrative. In this respect, its most significant antecedents in the U.S. avant-garde include Charles Sheeler and Paul Strand's *Manhatta* (1921) and John Flory's depression classic *Mr. Motorboat's Last Stand* (1933), whose satirical depiction of impoverished bohemians living amidst the detritus of the city's edge anticipates it. But whereas these are, if not realistic, still fundamentally descriptive, Jacob's narrative and its environment are realized abstractly. They are filmed in perspectives that "displace and estrange the world" in order to mobilize and foreground a thematic, conceptual matrix. In his own words, "The acting is not intended to be 'convincing,' the approach is not illusionistic but allusionistic. It is a way to objectify the conflict for me of moving towards marriage. My friends lent faces to aspects of the conflict".[11]

Within the intricate tapestry of allusions and intertextual references that comprise *The Sky Socialist*'s narrative, three interrelated but distinct allegorical levels may be isolated:

> 1. the relations between Ken Jacobs and his lover and future bride, Florence; on this level, the Brooklyn Bridge and the buildings beneath it comprise the material world in which they meet.
>
> 2. the relation between the "miraculously spared Anne Frank" and Isadore Lhevinne; on this level, the Bridge is a figure for the emancipatory possibilities of art and love.
>
> 3. the nature of cinema, specifically a redeemed cinema as way of living: on this level, the Bridge is a figure for the film itself.

III. Ken and Florence

Shooting in 1965–66 coincided with the courtship of Ken Jacobs, then in his early thirties, and Florence Karpf,[12] and the realization of their commitment to each other and to cinema. As "an instrument of thought", *The Sky Socialist* provided a symbolic language in which Ken could, as he claimed, consider marriage. Its making was an aestheticized courtship ritual by which he wooed Florence, and as such it invokes the traditions of Hebrew erotic poetry and also of U.S. avant-garde filmmakers who have used their medium, not simply to represent their lives, but to engage and negotiate them. A personalization and depoliticization of the utopian use of film in the mid-twenties Soviet avant-garde and the U.S. Film Photo Leagues' of the 1930s, such an integration of film and private life had been inaugurated in Maya Deren and Alexander Hamid's *Meshes of the Afternoon* (1943), where, as P. Adams Sitney saw, film was used, not merely as a depiction of a relationship, but as itself "a process of self-realization".[13] Continued by Kenneth Anger, Curtis Harrington, and others, this function for cinema had been made fully comprehensive and articulate by Stan Brakhage only a few years previously. But unlike in the major works of this pyschodramatic tradition, the maker of *The Sky Socialist* does not appear as the protagonist: rather he objectifies himself and narrates his erotic quest via a surrogate. In this, the film recalls especially Boris Deutsch's *Lullaby* (1929), the story of a young servant girl, played by Deutsch's wife, Riva, who is abused by her brutish Christian masters until she falls in love with a musician and escapes. Also an expressionistic treatment of Jewish themes, *Lullaby* anticipates the hyper-intense, distorted subjectivity of Jacobs' protagonist and its projection in the form of a denaturalized landscape, and, also like Deutsch before him, Jacobs is a filmmaker who takes as his surrogate an artist in a different medium.[14]

Despite this displacement, for Jacobs, as for Brakhage, marriage coincided with the resolution of debilitating psychological torment and the discovery of the mode of film practice that would henceforth constitute his life-work, and that would in both cases be defined as the production of the marriage. Ken's constant invocation of Flo's integral role in their joint work marks the same recognition as his colleague's assertion that, "'By Brakhage' should be understood to mean 'by way of Stan and Jane Brakhage'".[15] In both cases, the beloved is also a muse, wife, and co-worker in a creative unit.

In these respects then, *The Sky Socialist*, both depicts and performs the realization of love and art in the domestic microcosm of Ken and Florence Jacobs; but film elaborates this enactment as the "collective projection" of a public, political metaphor.

IV: Isadore and Anne

The personal relationship between Ken and Flo is dramatized as the courtship of two historical figures, both Jewish writers: "the obscure thirties author, Isadore Lhevinne, who emigrated from Russia to write grotesque novels, clear-eyed yet on the side of the revolution, and who died young, a suicide I suspect, at the onset of W.W. II" and a "miraculously spared Anne Frank".[16] Surrounded and elaborated by other allegorical figures, the drama of the courtship and marriage of the two writers mobilizes themes of love, death, and art as they are variously interwoven in their respective life and work. The narrative thus resonates denotatively with their specific biographies, but also connotatively with the history of Jews in general, and of other estranged people who share in "the Jewish predicament",[17] in the period between the Soviet Revolution and the end of World War II.

Anne Frank has, of course, become a summary figure for the victims of the *Shoah* and by extension for Jews generally and all other victims of fascism. She was one of two daughters of Otto Frank, a prosperous German Jewish manufacturer, and his wife, Edith, who had moved the family to Amsterdam in 1933, just after Hitler seized power. When the deportation of Dutch Jews to the death camps began two years after the Nazis invaded Holland, the family went into hiding in an attic annex with four others. Sustained by Dutch sympathizers, they survived there until they were betrayed and sent on the last transport to Auschwitz. Of the eight, only Otto himself survived, while his two daughters perished in Bergen-Belsen two weeks before British troops liberated it. Anne's diary covers the period when they were in hiding between June 1942 and August 1944, and its last entry was made three days before Nazis captured them, and strewed its pages on the attic floor. Dutch sympathizers retrieved them and after the war returned them to Otto. First published in Dutch in 1947, the diary was eventually translated into sixty languages, and became an international sensation. In the U.S., it was made into a Pulitzer Prize winning play in 1955, and in 1959 into a Hollywood film, *The Diary of Anne Frank*. Directed by George Stevens (who, as an army filmmaker, had been present at the liberation of Dachau), it was nominated for eight Academy Awards. Though Anne's *Diary* contains no account of the *Shoah*, it has become the single most important record of the experience of Nazi brutality. And, by privileging the testament she made two weeks before capture – "I still believe, in spite of everything, that people are truly good at heart" – rather than her final words – " ... if only there were no other people in the world" – Anne has herself been apotheosized as the epitome of humanist compassion.[18]

Anne Frank's literary and political stature and the recent success of Stevens' film made her an obvious choice for a female protagonist in an allegory of Jewish self-consciousness in the early 1960s. Young Jews anywhere could hardly have escaped feeling interpellated by her story, but within her record of her family's everyday routines and terrors, two aspects resonate especially within *The Sky Socialist*'s imaginary transcendence of her historical destruction that allows her to live, love Isadore, and star in a biographical film: her literary self-consciousness and her sexual awakening.

The other family confined along with the Franks was the van Daans, whose son Peter was three years older than Anne. Something of a flirt in school before the confinement, Anne is initially dismissive of Peter, seeing him as "a shy, awkward boy whose company won't amount to much",[19] but as she grows into puberty she

9 – Film as an Instrument of Thought, Cinema as an Augury of Redemption

Figure 2. *The Diary of Anne Frank* (George Stevens, 1959).

increasingly finds refuge from her own family and solace in his company and, despite the objections of both families, eventually she falls in love with him. Though their love is never consummated, its power allows Anne to rise above her incarceration, and her accounts of the maturation of her feelings towards Peter and their first kisses in the spring of 1944 are some of her most soaring passages of emotional and literary redemption. On 23 February, for example, she begins by noting, "My writing, the best thing I have, is coming along well", then continues to describe how she and Peter go up to the attic window to greet the wonderful weather. "The two of us looked out at the blue sky, the bare chestnut tree glistening with dew, the seagulls and other birds glinting with silver as they swooped through the air, and we were so moved and entranced that we couldn't speak". Peter eventually leaves to chop wood, convincing her that "he was a good, decent boy", and she continues: "'As long as this exists,' I thought, 'this sunshine and this cloudless sky, and as long as I can enjoy it, how can I be sad?'".[20] Anne's

183

Figure 3. Isadore Lhevinne: "The author with a Jibaro chief" (detail) from *The Enchanted Jungle*.

ability to transcend the genocidal hatred that imprisons her is founded on her love for the world and another human being, but also on her writing, which both sustains her in her torment and allows for the dissemination of her vision after her death.

Like Anne Frank, Isadore Lhevinne simultaneously embodies and narrates the peculiar contradictoriness of a Jew writing in the imminence of destruction, but he does so in antithetical terms. Both Anne and he are witnesses to cataclysmic historical events. But her drama is lived as eros in the cramped domestic mundanity of the attic only to be terminated by thanatos outside it, while in his work, eros and thanatos – and melos – are coiled together across the horrific landscape of the U.S.S.R. in the Civil War. We have corroborating evidence for Anne Frank's account of herself and indeed we know more about her than she does, specifically the fate that, waiting for her outside the diary, supplies its enormous power. But we know virtually nothing of Lhevinne; apart from his name on the title page of several books, themselves forgotten, there is only oblivion, sealed, so Jacobs believes, by suicide. Whereas Anne's *Diary* transcends her death to live in the mutually-sustaining relation between her renown and her writing, the significance of Lhevinne's art resides in the irony of his historical obscurity as it echoes negatively in the apocalyptic events he describes and in the hallucinatory delirium of his prose. Two of his novels are especially pertinent to *The Sky Socialist*: *Ariadne* and *Napoleons All*.[21]

Both take place amid the indiscriminate slaughter and chaos of the White counter-revolution, where "nightmare upon nightmare wove into the night",[22] and love, death, and art are phantasmagorically intertwined. The famine, carnage, and confusion of war are shot through with violent polymorphous sexuality manifesting itself in insatiable obsession, orgies, and despair. In both books, the main protagonist is again a Jewish artist, who is sympathetic to the humanist ideals of Communism, even though the corruption and depravity of the actual forms in which it exists in the war years renders those ideals chimerical, especially for Jews who, as Isaac Babel (whose account of the same milieu resembles Lhevinne's) noted, "were waiting for Soviet power to arrive as liberators, and all of a sudden it's there, yelling and whipping, 'You dirty Kikes'".[23] Both artists are consumed by desire for a beautiful *femme fatale*, who partially gives herself to him, but who herself is obsessively in love with a reactionary White leader; and even though both rivals are killed in spectacularly brutal fashions, neither protagonist realizes his desires. They too are eventually killed, but just before dying, each – like Anne – experiences a visionary transcendence of the horror of his actual life.

The earlier novel begins in New York, where the sublimity of Ariadne's Madonna-like beauty inspires Vladi Corngold,[24] an émigré Russian musician, to compose a *Prelude Symphonique* in her honor. It is acknowledged as a work of genius, and Ariadne receives him nude in her apartment; but soon she follows her lover, a count, back to Russia, where he is torn to pieces by Red peasants. Corngold pursues Adriane across the northern steppes, and the novel dissolves into a delirious surrealist miasma. He joins forces with "a huge U.S. negro", the "image of Naaman, the hangman in Wilde's Salome",[25] who had come to join the revolution in the name of the millions enslaved by capitalism and had become

185

the chief executioner, first for the Cheka but then for the Whites. They become trapped in a village of vicious hermaphroditic dwarves, where Corngold falls in love with Lidda, mistaking her in his delirium for Ariadne. The two escape from the village, but are captured by the Reds, along with a beautiful, Ganymede-like boy who turns out to be the escaped Tsarevich, Alexy. Alexy is murdered but Corngold escapes, only to be captured by a tribe of centaurs, one of whom is another incarnation of Ariadne. Dream dissolves into dream, and eventually Corngold resumes his life as a composer in New York. Both Ariadne and Lidda re-appear, Corngold merges with them, and they all dissolve in to the dream of a time when "There would be no artists and no listeners, for the whole world would be one huge cathedral where day and night divine chorals would re-sound".[26]

The parallel and very similar protagonist of *Napoleons All* is Tayirov, a destitute actor and poet befriended by a wealthy merchant in Yalta, for whom he organizes weekly orgies for the elite and beautiful, including a woman, Aglaya. Tayirov reads to her from his own translation of the French symbolist poet, Aloysius Bertrand's *Gaspard de la nuit*, "about moonlight and dangling corpses in the night and the sound of wind running through their stirring hair".[27] But Aglaya loves a man whom she believes to be a White general, Baron von Holstein, who has committed barbarous cruelties upon the people of the Crimea, but who is in fact Albert Goldshtein, an extremely beautiful Jew who found Holstein's corpse after he was killed by the Reds on the surrender of Odessa and assumed his identity. Tayirov joins a cell of utopian communists who, despite all the depravity around them, believe in the eventual victory of justice; and where before he had seen himself as "a parasite, a poet, a nobody, a nothing",[28] he becomes a committed revolutionary. He arranges for Holstein to be strangled before Aglaya's eyes, and ferments revolution during the White retreat to Sebastopol. Shot by a fifteen-year-old boy who had seen his father killed by the Reds, he falls into a delirium and, in his last moments of clarity surrounded by masses of mutilated corpses on the icy battlefield, he sees himself as "a Napoleon and not a louse" and "on the threshold of a new life, a life based on justice and candor".[29]

In their mirrored and complementary responses to the history of the Jews within the intertwined utopian and dystopian components in the world-historical emergence of Communism and Fascism, Lhevinne and Frank – their protagonists and their oeuvres – provide a vocabulary through which a Jewish artist could think his own historical situation and envisage the political possibilities of his work. Within them, the impossibility of personal love refracts the century's larger political contradictions. But by symbolically and ritually bringing the two writers

Figure 4. *The Sky Socialist*: Isadore and Anne.

back to life and to marriage with each other – "as they would present themselves from the standpoint of redemption" – Jacobs fashions a narrative transcendence of their various failures and defeats. In doing so he projects a vision for the possibilities of his own life in art. Though this may not be as historically representative as Anne's or Isadore's, nor remotely as traumatic, still it can exist only within post-war U.S. capitalism, whose history of imperialist atrocities stretching from Viet Nam to Iraq will resonate within its possibilities and responsibilities.

As well as dramatizing the themes of twentieth-century history, the two writers' styles provide stylistic models for other artists. Reflecting his vision of their union, Jacobs marries filmic equivalents of the florid rhetoric of Lhevinne's Symbolist prose poetry and Frank's empirical dailiness to create an idiolect of the (un)popular modernism common in early sixties Underground film. For this movement, Abstract Expressionist painting was the stylistic touchstone; but whereas links between Abstract Expressionism and, for example, Stan Brakhage typically reference his denaturalising of the film image by scratching and otherwise defacing the emulsion, in Jacobs' case they inhere in the gestural dynamism of his photography and the refusal of centeredness in his framing. Rather than invisibly suturing the viewer into the characters and the diegesis, the photography and the editing disorient and estrange; they aspire, not to stable, transparent revelation, but to complex, multileveled, artificial visual compositions with places and shapes in dynamic altercation.

Another instance of the aesthetic binaries Jacobs sublates, this (un)popular modernism is further amplified in the interplay between the aesthetic and social implications of the spectrum of modernist practices of the two artists Lhevinne imagined, Corngold and Tayirov. As the extract from Tayirov's translation from Bertrand "about moonlight and dangling corpses in the night and the sound of wind running through their stirring hair" indicates, Tayirov's writing is the model for Lhevinne's own; its use for erotic seduction is only a hyperbolic form of the erotic function of avant-garde film in the period, which was manifestly at play in Jacobs' cinematic romance of Flo. Otherwise Tayirov's art exists as an anomaly in what is otherwise an entirely political sphere, wholly de-aestheticised apart from ritual forms of cruelty and murder. But Corngold's cultural milieu, New York in the early 1920s at the intersection of immigrant bohemian musicians and their haute bourgeois patrons, resembles Jacobs' own, a few blocks further south-east and forty years later. It sustains a variety of other forms of modernism that clearly anticipate the post-war musical and filmic avant-gardes. While making a living playing kettle-drums in a Philharmonic orchestra, Corngold aspires to reincarnate "the world's chaos in a profoundly stirring melody, the thematic development of which would purify mankind and relieve its tension", but in fact he has begun to write only a symphony for "two drums and a mouse-trap".[30] Though usually self-effacing, he is at one soirée so enraptured by the sight of Ariadne that he gives an inspired performance of "Mendelsohn's Concerto on the violin".[31] Ariadne brings him "ecstatic dreams of greatness",[32] and he devotes himself to writing a "Symphony of Life" in her honor. And in one of his dreams, he and Ariadne see "a male quartette, four negroes, in high hats, devilishly slim, in tight black trousers, swinging their canes and singing *Down in Dixie*" that prompts him to explain "the wonders of Negro music" to her.[33] His friends are similarly progressive: Yasha Yashu, for example, descendent of horse-thieves who brought to music "the unappeased yearnings of his ancestors" is powerless to "utilize the noises of blood pulsations musically.... [but] he made good use of broomsticks and coins" (shades of John Cage), and invented "an entirely new musical instrument that would embody the elements of all known instruments – the glorious violaxophiano, a combination of violin-flute-piano-saxophone" that augurs Harry Partch, the one-man fairground band, and the digital synthesizer. All these utopian vernacular aspirations are realized in Corngold's final visionary merging into the various forms of Ariadne:

> In the dim twilight thousands of faces beckoned them. They wanted no light. The visions glistened in their gorgeous coloring with all the tangibility of delightful dreams. Ariadne swept by like a panting dryad on the back of a mad centaur ... .
>
> In the adjoining room Yashu played on his violaxophiano. The day was near when people would draw music out of the air simply by raising their hands and regulating the position of their knuckles. There would be no artists and no listeners, for the whole world would be one huge cathedral where day and night divine chorals would resound. With stirring candor the gipsy played ...
>
> Do not blame me, my beloved,
>
> For my hopeless love of you ...[34]

The aesthetic parallel to Tayirov's ethical dying glimpse "of new life, a life based on justice and candor", this vision is a blueprint for the ecstatic cultural happenings staged by Jacobs, Jack Smith and their co-conspirators in the Theater of Embarrassment (for which, in fact, Smith learned passages of *Ariadne* by heart).[35]

Such dissolutions of the formal stylistics of an art into the joyful spontaneity of its practice occur relatively easily in music and other performative arts. In the period when *The Sky Socialist* was made, the referential ideal of the spontaneous collective composition of modern jazz led to its internalization in other arts, in "spontaneous" prose, "action" painting, and so on.[36] But some art forms, including filmmaking (and bridge-building) that involve the manufacture of objects and hence entail multiple diverse operations extended over time present special challenges to such aesthetic priorities, and oblige artists to reconstruct the mode of their practice specifically in contradistinction to the procedures of the commodity industrial arts, especially cinema. Other aspects of Frank and Lhevinne's writings, then, especially their respective modes of literary production, as well their marriage in *The Sky Socialist* and the architectural environment in which it occurs, suggest the means by which a redeemed cinema could and should be practiced. If the making of the film was a way for Jacobs "to objectify the conflict... of moving towards marriage", it was similarly a way for him to objectify the conflict of moving from street theater to filmmaking, and a meditation on the possible nature of his own filmmaking. On this third allegorical level, *The Sky Socialist* narrates the issues that precipitate and subtend the mode of its own production; in becoming an allegory of itself, it becomes an allegory of cinema seen "from the standpoint of redemption".

V. Cinema in the Messianic Light

Anne Frank's domestic diary, subsequently elevated to world-historical significance, and Isadore Lhevinne's ecstatic but unknown glimpses of a Socialist utopia variously embody success in a world of failure and failure in a world of success; in this they frame the utopian possibilities of art, both its form and its mode of production, respectively film and cinema. And though their writings may not be directly translated into the other medium, nevertheless they limn what it might one day be.

Considered as literary production, Anne's writing moves though several functions. In her first entry, she greets her diary: "I hope I will be able to confide everything to you, as I have never been able to confide in anyone, and I hope you will be a great source of comfort and support".[37] Even though she has "never written anything before" and though she suspects "that neither I nor anyone else will be interested in the musings of a thirteen-year-old schoolgirl", she writes because "I feel like writing and have an even greater need to get things off my chest". Already, then, rather than being simply a record of her constrained existence, her writing and her diary are constructed as a human interlocutor and companion: "I want the diary to be my friend, and I'm going to call this friend, *Kitty*".[38]

Though Kitty plays a part in the social microcosm of the eight prisoners, the diary is fundamentally a personal activity, a pure use value. But Anne also begins to write short stories independent of it and to recognize that her personal practice of writing might be propaedeutic to a professional career as a writer: she realizes that she must do her schoolwork so as "to become a journalist, because that's what I want!" and though she can always write for herself, she wants more, "to write books or newspaper articles".[39] Her speculation that her writing might be transformed into the professional production of commodities with exchange value escalates when a few months before her capture she hears a broadcast from London in which a Dutch Cabinet Minister declares that "after the war a collection would be made of diaries and letters dealing with the war".[40] The announcement transforms Anne's practice, and from this point on her artisinal, private text is implicitly subtended by her expectation of publication and a public readership beyond the reflexive Kitty, an expectation that causes her to rewrite the previous entries, improving some and omitting others so as to make a publicly viable book.[41]

Corresponding to the distinction between a film diary and a diary film, the tensions between a purely private practice of an art and the production of a work for public distribution and consumption were fundamental aesthetic issues in avant-garde filmmaking in *The Sky Socialist*'s period. Though the question was hardly theorized, "the Product Film" was specifically indicted in "First Statement of the New American Cinema Group" in 1961,[42] and it was fundamental in the work of Jacobs' close friend, Jonas Mekas, the most important diary filmmaker of the 1960s and 1970s.[43] The issues are especially complex for an art that is practiced in the context of capitalist commodity culture, and especially for one that understands itself as in some sense Socialist and hence is obliged to resist the process of its own commodification and the consequent reproduction of capitalist social relations – or at least to internalize these tensions as a specific thematic concern.

In Jacobs' oeuvre as a whole, the address to these issues and the commitment to a practice that will conclusively resist reification or commodification produce an oscillation between the analytic destruction of previous films and the production of original films that, according to receive criteria, were deliberate and decisive failures. The constitutive necessity of failure so defined – *Blonde Cobra* (1963) is prototypical – is the pivot of his investigation of what, in a capitalist culture, a Socialist film and a Socialist cinema might be, the meta-thematic of his entire career. As Jack Smith especially learned from Jacobs, to be a success within the alienation of capitalist culture would be to fail categorically in all other terms. And whatever its source in Jacobs' libidinal economy, his commitment to failure – his refusal of mastery, perfection, and control, and his insistence on rejectamenta, breakdown, and ephemerality – reflects an objective political condition, obsessive recurrence to which makes him as one of the most important artists of the period of late capitalism.

In this respect, *The Sky Socialist* has an ironically double relation to Anne's diary. In reproducing her rewriting by editing his raw footage and adding a sound-track and the interpolated film extracts, Jacobs displaced filming as sheer practice towards its reified, "product" form as a completed work. But, while Anne's book was a global success, *The Sky Socialist* failed to find a place in a distribution system that would have allowed its proper commodification and its existence as a "Product Film" among other commodities. Neither Jacobs himself nor the community that sustained him was able to raise money to make a release print until 1988, more than twenty years after it was complete. The failure also extended to the film's lead actress, Florence who, however much she was loved in her immediate community, never became a film star outside it: not the film star that Anne herself aspired to be nor the one she became in the surrogate form of Millie Perkins in George Stevens' film. But in failing so radically, *The Sky Socialist* attained the visionary oblivion apotheosized by Lhevinne's writing.

In the union of Frank and Lhevinne, the meditation on the theoretical possibilities of a Socialist cinema comes to rest on the ideal of an essentially amateur practice in which a domestic private diary filmmaking is married to the stylistics of the modernist, especially painterly, avant-garde. Such a cinema existed in New York for a few years in the early 1960s on the narrow berm that the temporary, provisional, and unstable institutions and communities of the underground were able to sustain between the varieties of home movie making developed by Brakhage, Mekas, and many others and the desire to become part of the commercial cinema exemplified by Warhol. The other actors and participants in the film were denizens of this underground cinema, and as individuals and as an ensemble they embody various positions between, or amalgamations of, populist filmmaking and high modernism, most notably the Kuchar brothers' conspicuously amateur remakes of Hollywood melodramas, and the formalist experimentation subsequently designated as structural film.[44]

The various salients of this cinema are elaborated in *The Sky Socialist*'s narrative where they are amplified and enriched by "Love's Labor", the "Muse of Cinema", and other allegorical figures, but also and especially by the urban environment: the "setting is at least of as much concern as the story". Conceptualized and organized by the palette of Jacobs' filming techniques, the depiction of this environment and its denizens generates the work's sensuous visual presence. Here the Bridge's concrete and steel monumentality is displaced and estranged: it becomes film and light.

VI: The Bridge

> Isn't it surprising ... that one of the names of God in Hebrew should be PLACE.
> Edmond Jabès

Above the rooftops and the streets where Anne and Isadore find love rises the Brooklyn Bridge, the summary architectural figuration, rather than narrative articulation, of Jacobs' aesthetic.[45] Its imposing presence, soaring gothic arches, and harp-like suspension wires hover above the mundane levels of the allegory enacted below, lending them intimations of transcendence to justify the filmmaker's intentions: "In keeping with the fantasy character of the film, the title is intended to evoke a just God. Less mordantly it refers to the man who made the Brooklyn Bridge, John Roebling, émigré student of Hegel".[46] A human re-enactment of the divine creations of a "just God" – a Sky Socialist – the Bridge is a prototype for Jacob's own creation: "Roebling is the Sky Socialist and so am I as the maker of the film".⁴⁷ But Jacobs' invocation of Roebling's bridge as a work of Socialist art and hence a figure for *The Sky Socialist* entailed an intervention in the history of its contradictory meanings more polemical even than his use of Frank and Lhevinne.

A European immigrant born in Germany in 1806, Roebling had indeed attended Hegel's lectures at the University of Berlin, absorbing the evolutionary historicism expressed in the *Philosophy of History* that the U.S. was the land of the future, where "the burden of the World's History shall reveal itself". Buoyed by Jacksonian expansionism, his belief in human progress persuaded him to quit farming and return to his profession as a civil engineer. He built notable suspension bridges in Pittsburg, Cincinnati, and elsewhere using a steel cable that he had himself invented, and as both builder and a metaphysician, he followed Hegel in understanding historical evolution as the manifestation of *geist*. Injured in a ferry accident a few days after construction of his Brooklyn Bridge began in 1869, he died of tetanus within the month, leaving the construction to be completed by his son, Washington, and the latter's wife, Emily. Half as long again as any other suspension bridge in the world, it opened in May 1883. Though anguished by profiteering, slavery, and his realization that human history is comprised of "a long series of individual and national crimes of all sorts, of enmity, cruelty, oppression, massacres, persecution, wars without end",⁴⁸ (with which Frank, Lhevinne, and Jacobs would have concurred), he remained confident in the eventual triumph of reason and harmony. These principles, he believed, were instantiated in his designs: fusing architecture and history, his bridge would manifest the Hegelian *Wirklichkeit*.⁴⁹

Along with its Whitmanian nimbus (which in fact derives entirely from his celebration of Brooklyn and the ferry, for he wrote no poem that even mentioned it), the bridge became one of the two or three most renowned triumphalist icons for U.S. technological achievements, made to figure progress, liberty, and democracy. A supreme instance of the Technological Sublime, its associated meanings have sometimes revealed but more often concealed the nature of its social use that would be at stake in any reading of it as a figure for Socialism. Even if it had been possible to overlook the twenty workers killed in its building and the corruption in the company supplying the steel cables that made the bridge only four times as strong as Roebling thought necessary rather than the six he had planned, these contradictions were endemic in the construction, in the opening, and ever since. Orchestrated as a public celebration, the opening was scheduled for 24 May, Queen Victoria's birthday; but the possibility that the incensed Irish and other workers would boycot it was pre-empted by a civic decision that excluded all trade-union and other working-class social organizations from the festivities.[50] In the event, the general public was not allowed on the bridge until after midnight, then only by paying a toll, and a frightening mêlée ensued. Subsequently, as Richard Haw has shown in his "Cultural History" of the Bridge, understandings of its significance have ranged between "assent", in which it is transformed into "a depopulated, aestheticized showcase for American technological and economic progress" that often involves "a studied avoidance of physical, social, and economic context", and dissenting voices that "have sought to contextualize the bridge as a profoundly public, communal place … a 'vernacular' image … that is essentially anthropocentric".[51]

Reflecting the tensions between these contradictory interpretations, visual representations of the bridge have been diverse. The first turns away from the early emphases on its heroic monumentality and the perspectives offered by its walkways came with the onset of the depression, when a phylum of New Deal painters and printmakers focused attention on the lives of the working and not-working poor beneath the bridge. For most of these artists the bridge itself did not figure prominently, and the only one for whom it did, Louis Lozowick, a Ukrainian immigrant and *New Masses* board-member, saw it as "an icon of a Socialist future".[52] Henri Cartier-Bresson, Eric Hartmann, and other post-war documentary photographers continued to focus on street life beneath the bridge.[53] But with the improved economic situation of the next decade, attention shifted back to its superstructural architecture as symbolic of American achievement, especially in the work of Andreas Feininger, who took more photos of the bridge than of any other sight in New York, and then in mythic abstract paintings such as Ellsworth Kelly's *Brooklyn Bridge IV* (1956–1958) and Robert Indiana's *Silver Bridge* (1964–1968).

Filmic representations, however, have been more continuously celebratory, and usually emphasized its monumentality as symbolic of U.S. technological and political power.[54] The earliest were in experimental shorts: Edwin S. Porter's dramatization of Windsor McCay's comic strip, *Dream of a Rarebit Fiend* (1906), for example, used special effects to portray a bed flying past the stabile bridge. In its two appearances in *Manhatta*, it is first silhouetted against the Manhattan skyline and then, towards the end in the only street-level shot in the film, it resembles a cathedral, as if consecrating the heroic constructions and heavy industry the film as a whole exalts. In the 1930s, glimpses of it were mostly fabricated in Hollywood, but the renewal of location shooting in New York after WWII gave it a unprecedented visibility, most notably in two Sinatra vehicles, *It*

9 – Film as an Instrument of Thought, Cinema as an Augury of Redemption

Figure 5. Milford Zornes, "Master Bridge", linoleum block print after a 1936 painting.

Happened in Brooklyn (Richard Whorf, 1947) and *On the Town* (Stanley Donen and Gene Kelly, 1949) where, stable and typically centered, its physical beauty frames love songs to New York.[55] But subsequently its link with the popular affection of the working-class Brooklyn community was severed as it became the symbol of escape to a yuppified Manhattan, as in *Saturday Night Fever* (John Badham, 1977) – or in the Spice Girls video, "2 Become 1" (1997).

This tradition of mythic iconicity in service of manifest destiny rather than Socialism was challenged in two crucial avant-garde films, Rudy Burkhardt's *Under the Brooklyn Bridge* (1953) and Shirley Clarke's *Bridges-Go-Round* (1958). *Under the Brooklyn Bridge* is a black and white portrait of the area around the Brooklyn landing, in which close-ups of architectural details and shots of the bridge itself quickly give way to a focus on popular activity around it: workmen hammering walls as they demolish a building and then crowding a hash house at lunch; a group of naked young boys diving and swimming in the river; and groups of women leaving work in the afternoon and walking to the subway; these are presented in studied, stationary-camera compositions displaying the exquisite tonal range and other qualities of Burkhardt's still photographs of the same environment. *Bridges-Go-Round*, on the other hand, is a short visual dance

POWER MISSES II: CINEMA, ASIAN AND MODERN

Figure 6. *Manhatta*; *It Happened in Brooklyn*; *Under the Brooklyn Bridge*; *Bridges-Go-Round*.

composed of moving-camera shots of New York bridges, flattened into contrasting monochromes, superimposed and woven together. *The Sky Socialist*'s unique formal achievement is to have synthesized the emphases of both of these: Jacobs retains Burkhardt's (and the Depression artists') humanist focus on the communities under the bridge; but he replaces his style – what is essentially a sequence of animated still-photographs that organize their formal contrasts around the illusion of deep-focus space – with a hyperbolically-elaborated form of Clarke's kinetic abstraction – a film style that justifies his claim that "My approach to film is that of a painter (abstract-expressionist) rather than dramatist".[56]

Jacobs' visualization of the Bridge is, then, radically contrary to previous filmic representations. Relatively rarely do its iconic arches rise out above the landing, and after a couple of brief early shots that sketch its overall architectural form, it never again appears stable and whole. Instead Jacobs' lyric, subjective camera is constantly questing, refiguring the dense cacophony of brick, concrete, wood and other differently textured and colored materials, and the disjunctive layered shapes of the doors, walls, loft-roofs, and so on that the defunct industrial buildings and the neighborhood streets have generated over their long history.

Figure 7. *The Sky Socialist*, Place.

Rather than finding the kind of symmetry or frontality that would sustain a stable two-dimensional film frame, the camera seeks splintered, skewed, kinetic compositions in which faces, bodies, and architectural elements are fragmented, de-centered and displaced to the frame's edges, "privileging oblique angles, transverse perspectives, and asymmetric frames".[57] On the rare moments when his mercurial, swooping camera comes to rest, it is on a canted composition in which bodies are fragmented, displaced to the edges of the frame and oriented to scenes outside it. Augmented especially by the simultaneous combination of rapid panning and zooming the camera-work mobilizes a filmic version of the Hofmannian "push and pull" between the flat screen surface and often dizzying illusions of depth. That is to say, both the environment of Jacobs' allegorical narrative and the figures within it are realized in an abstract expressionist film language, one that is made possible by the fluidity and cheapness of 8 mm photography, the amateur, populist gauge.

Jacobs' cinematic achievement of a populist cinematic modernism that envisions the Bridge as reflexively equivalent to the film itself was anticipated in at least one major literary instance in the history of Socialist modernism. During his visit to North America in the summer of 1925, Vladimir Mayakovsky wrote a diaristic cycle of "Poems About America". In the New York compositions, criticisms of capitalism are interlaced with wonder at its achievements, and the best of them is an ecstatic lyric celebration, "Brooklyn Bridge". Though it appears that objections by some Brooklyn Socialists to whom he recited it persuaded him to add an observation that some "men without work" had committed suicide from it, otherwise he celebrates the bridge as an engineering achievement that makes his own art possible.[58]

> I pride
> > in the stride
> > > of this steel-wrought mile.
> Embodied in it
> > my visions come real –

The grounds upon which Mayakovsky could claim the bridge as a reciprocal figure for his own poem reflect a Constructivist interchangeability of artistic craft and industry more objective and rational than Jacobs' aesthetic premises. But his claim that in his poem about Roebling's Bridge he realized his own aesthetic parallels Jacobs' claims for its role in his own work, and hence for his parity with its designer and with the original Sky Socialist. Recreating his corner of the city and his life's love in this modernist and populist, Socialist and ecstatic, film, Jacobs displaced and estranged his world, and in doing so he presented it "from the standpoint of redemption".

Notes

1. The announcement for the class, taught at the University of Colorado at Boulder, was reprinted in David Schwartz, ed., *Films That Tell Time: A Ken Jacobs Retrospective* (New York: American Museum of the Moving Image, 1989), p. 82. Another formulation of thinking in cinema whose terms are specifically germane to the following essay is Jacobs' description of a further course: "The idea was to create opportunities for heuristic learning in opposition to indoctrination, creating cine-constellations within which the live mind could actively relate this to that, that to this, more often than not a no-message tasting of moods". See "Painted Air: The Joys and Sorrows of Evanescent Cinema", *Millennium Film Journal* 43/44 (Summer 2005): 51.

2. *Films That Tell Time*, p. 82.

3. Both Ernie Gehr and Michael Snow used Jacobs' camera, the latter to shoot *Wavelength (1967)*. In the mid-1960s the community around the Jacobs' Chambers Street loft also included Joyce Wieland, Hollis Frampton, and George and Mike Kuchar; for details see Tom Gunning and David Schwartz, "Interview with Ken Jacobs: August 10 and 11, 1989", in *Films That Tell Time*, p. 48.

4. Ken Jacobs in Lindley Hanlon and Tony Pipolo, "Interview With Ken and Flo Jacobs", *Millennium Film Journal* 16/17/18 (Fall–Winter, 1986–1987): 32.
5. Scott MacDonald, *A Critical Cinema: Interviews with Independent Filmmakers* (Berkeley: University of California Press, 1988), p. 1.
6. *Movie Journal: The Rise of the New American Cinema, 1959–1971* (New York: Collier Books, 1972), p. 351. Jacobs' film *Soft Rain* (1968) involves similar perceptual issues.
7. Jacobs' "Program Notes" for *The Sky Socialist*, rpt. in Schwartz, ed., *Films That Tell Time*, p. 19.
8. The version of *The Sky Socialist* considered here consists of three sections that, perhaps referencing pre-Renaissance religious painting, Jacobs calls "panels": *The Sky Socialist: Prelude* (1965; 14 minutes); *The Sky Socialist* (1965/66; 111.5 minutes): and *The Sky Socialist: Flight* (1968; 14.5 minutes), for a total of 2 hours, 20 minutes. These times are those of the current dvd version, with dates as given on titles. Despite important developments in the third panel, the present essay refers only to the full form of the second.
9. "Program Notes", p. 19.
10. "Program Notes", p. 19.
11. "Program Notes", p. 19.
12. Florence Karpf was born 15 June 1941 in Brooklyn. She and Ken met in 1961 in Provincetown and were formally married in 1965, soon after shooting was complete.
13. P. Adams Sitney, *Visionary Film: The American Avant-Garde, 1924–2000* (New York: Oxford University Press, 2000), p. 14.
14. For *Lullaby*, see David E. James, *The Most Typical Avant-Garde: History and Geography of Minor Cinemas in Los Angeles* (Berkeley: University of California Press, 2005), pp. 36–38.
15. Stan Brakhage, *Metaphors on Vision* (New York: Film Culture, 1963), n.p.
16. "Program Notes", p. 19.
17. "Jews are not so much a religion as people sharing a predicament; the Jewish predicament, "Ken Jacobs" (transcript of a slide-lecture, Collective For Living Cinema, 11 March 1979), *The Cinemanews* 79, nos. 2, 3, & 4 (triple issue, n.d.): 12. In this talk, Jacobs traced the history of Christian anti-Semitism, limning a continuity from Martin Luther's "The Jew is our misfortune" to Nazi atrocities.
18. Anne Frank, *The Diary of a Young Girl* (New York: Doubleday, 1991); respectively, p. 332, entry for 15 July 1944; and p. 336, entry for 1 August 1944. For a consideration of the diary's political and literary implications, see Hyman Enzer and Sandra Solotaroff-Enzer, eds., *Anne Frank: Reflections on Her Life and Legacy* (Urbana, University of Illinois Press, 2000).
19. Frank, *Diary*, p. 30.
20. Frank, *Diary*, pp. 195–196.
21. *Ariadne* (New York: Globus Press, 1928) and *Napoleons All* (New York: Mohawk Press, 1931); both are illustrated by small line-drawings by the author. Lhevinne also wrote *The Leper Ship* (New York: The Halcyon Press, 1929), *Tsantsa* (New York: Brentano's, 1932), and *The Enchanted Jungle* (New York: Coward-McCann, 1933). *Napoleons All* contains an announcement of a further novel in preparation, *Four Hundred Phantoms*, but I have found no other trace of it. He obtained a Ph.D. in Romance Philology from the University of Pennsylvania with a dissertation, *The Language of the Glossary Sangallensis 912 and Its Relationship To the Language of Other Latin Glossaries* (Philadelphia Publications of the University of Pennsylvania, Series in Romanic Languages and Literatures, 1924). Strikingly anticipating the harrowing but ecstatic themes and style of the two major novels, *The Leper Ship* is comprised of three stories that appear to have some autobiographical basis: the first is set on a ship that sails from Vladivostok towards America; the second concerns a Latin teacher in New York who becomes infatuated with one of his students and, though rejected by her, finds a home with her family; and the third is an account of a university lecturer in philology who is cursed by his father from beyond the graver for concealing his Jewish heritage. It was very favorably reviewed as "Three Tales of Wide-Flung Jewry" in the *New York Times Book Review*, 27 June 1926, pp. 15 and 36. *The Enchanted Jungle* appears to be a lightly fictionalized account of Lhevinne's own 1931 expedition to the jungles of Ecuador, where he spent the summer living with the Jíbaro, head-shrinking, Indians, and among its photographs is one of him with a Jíbaro chief; his fictional alter-ego protagonist goes there specifically to collect their music. *Tsantsa* is a novel set in the same environment: the protagonist is a white American working for a gold-mining firm who becomes infatuated with a fifteen-year old Jíbaro girl; he steals her away from her husband, kills him in a duel, and takes her back to civilization. In its fervid eroticism, lurid details about head-shrinking, drug-enhanced rituals, and idealization of noble, independent Indians, it recalls the two European novels, but overall is less hallucinatory and complex. *The Enchanted Jungle* holds little literary interest.

Biographical information on Lhevinne is scant. He is ignored by present-day scholarship, and almost all our knowledge is from his own testimony. He dedicated his dissertation to his "beloved parents, Elaiakim and Rehoma", and later wrote: "I was born in Bobruisk, Russia, December 15, 1896. Expelled from Warsaw high school after quarrel with anti-semitic teacher. Graduated with highest honors from Pultusk (Poland) high school. Entered Medical School of Rostov (Cossack Region) University in 1915, then switched to Law. Before graduation left for Odessa, then for Constantinople, thence for America in 1920. Entered University of Pittsburgh, graduated in 1921 (A.B., and A.M.). Two years later received Ph.D. at the University of Pennsylvania, studying comparative Romance philology [As had Ezra Pound had fifteen years earlier.] Thesis on Vulgar Latin Glossaries, published in 1924. In 1922 taught at Delaware University, in 1923 at Temple University, half of 1925 was spent in hunger. Now teaching French and Spanish in Seward High School New York. First stories published in Russian, at the age of eighteen. First articles in English appeared in the *Forum, Evening Post*, and *New York Call*, in 1923. Stories now frequently appear in the *Jewish Tribune*, and *American Hebrew*. Author of 'The Leper Ship', 1926. Lives in New York City". ("The Biographical Roll of Honor of American Short Stories, October 1925–August 1926", in *The Best Short Stories of 1926 and the Yearbook of the American Short Story*, Edward J. O'Brien, ed. [New York: Dodd, Mead and Company, 1926], pp. 330–31). He was listed in *American Jewish Year Book* for 1934–1935 (vol. 36) under the names of notable achievements that year for having been "decorated by the Government of Ecuador, South America, with medal of the Order of Almarita (first Jew), December 1933" (257), probably for the anthropological investigations recorded in *The Enchanted Jungle*; see http://ajcarchives.us/AJC_DATA/Files/1934_1935_5_YRAppendices.pdf. Accessed 28 January 2009.

Lhevinne later became embroiled in a crusade led by the New York Society for the Suppression of Vice, and was specifically targeted by censorship zealot, John Sumner, and his enforcer, Charles Bamberger. Bamberger entrapped Lhevinne into selling him a copy of *Ariadne* and then prosecuted him on the grounds that it was "indecent", but the case was dismissed. See Paul S. Boyer, *Purity in Print; The Vice-Society Movement and Book Censorship in America* (New York: Scribners, 1968), p. 137, and Jay A. Gertzman, *Bookleggers and Smuthounds: The Trade in Erotica, 1920–1940* (Philadelphia: University of Pennsylvania Press, 1999), p. 147. The prosecution eerily anticipates the arrest of Ken and Flo and their subsequent trial over the screening of *Flaming Creatures*.

22. *Napoleons All*, p. 35.
23. Quoted from Babel's *1920 Diary* in Chris Marker's film biography of Medvedkin, *The Last Bolshevik* (*Le Tombeau d'Alexandre*, 1992). The text of the English translation of the diaries is slightly different: "The population is waiting for liberators, the Jews for freedom – but who arrives? The Kuban Cossacks ... "; see, Nathalie Babel, ed., *The Complete Works of Isaac Babel* (New York, Norton, 2001), p. 403. Babel was born in Odessa, where much of *Napoleons All* is set and saw action in the area during the civil war; his stories of the Civil War are hardly less phantasmagoric than Lhevinne's novels.
24. The contrasts between Lhevinne's Corngold and the career of the émigré Jewish composer Erich Wolfgang Korngold, born one year later than Lhevinne in 1897 and who became famous for his non-modernist chromatic film scores for Hollywood films, inevitably resonate ironically through Ariadne; but they cannot have been intentional, Korngold not coming to the U.S. till 1934.
25. *Ariadne*, p. 98.
26. *Ariadne*, p. 248.
27. *Napoleons All*, p. 26.
28. *Napoleons All*, p. 101.
29. *Napoleons All*, pp. 365–366.
30. *Ariadne*, p. 6.
31. Presumably, Mendelssohn's *Violin Concerto in E Minor*.
32. *Ariadne*, p. 21.
33. *Ariadne*, p. 206.
34. *Ariadne*, p. 248.
35. According to Jacobs, in the scene toward the end of *Star Spangled to Death*, when Smith is seen making a toast, he is silently reciting one of the memorized passages (personal correspondence, 14 March 2009).
36. See David E. James, *Allegories of Cinema: American Film in the Sixties* (Princeton, New Jersey: Princeton University Press, 1989), pp. 120–140.
37. Frank, *Diary*, p. 1.
38. 20 June 1942, ibid, pp. 6–7. See also, for example, the entry for 24 December 1943, where an account of her misery concludes "My writing has raised me some what from 'the depths of despair'" (p. 155).
39. Frank, *Diary*, p. 249.
40. 29 March 1944, Frank, *Diary*, p. 243.
41. Published texts are combinations of Anne's first, unedited diary, referred to as "version a" and the edited, "version

9 – Film as an Instrument of Thought, Cinema as an Augury of Redemption

b"; see, "Foreword", Frank, *Diary*, v–vi. In the revisions, Anne consolidated the several initial addressees of her early entries drawn from Cissy van Marxveldt's *Joop ter Heul* novels into the single, "Kitty". For the first published version, *Het Achterhuis*, published in Dutch in the Netherlands, Otto Frank's editing of Anne's manuscript removed a good deal of her comments about her mother and, especially, about her own sexuality.

42. "First Statement of the New American Cinema Group", *Film Culture* 22–23 (Summer 1961): 131.

43. See David E. James, "Film Diary/ Diary Film: Practice and Product in Jonas Mekas's *Walden*", in *Power Misses: Essays Across (Un)Popular Culture* (New York: Verso, 1996), pp. 122–152.

44. Bob Cowan (Maurice) moved to New York from Toronto and – like Jacobs – studied painting with Hans Hofmann before becoming more interested in cinema. He attended Maya Deren's lectures, experimented with 8 mm films, and eventually made twenty-two 16 mm films, a dozen of which are presently in distribution from the Film-Makers' Co-op. He featured prominently in *Sins of the Fleshapoids* (Mike Kuchar, 1965), *Color Me Shameless* (George Kuchar, 1967), *The Craven Sluck* (Mike Kuchar, 1967), and others of the Kuchars' films. One the underground's main projectionists, he later served on the Film-Makers' Co-op Board of Directors and worked at the Millennium film workshop. Dave Leveson (Lhevinne) also appeared in *Color Me Shameless*. A Ferry Street neighbor, Mel Garfinkel (Nazi Mentality) was the projectionist the night when Jacobs and Mekas were arrested for screening *Flaming Creatures*; he later worked as an assistant cameraman to Ed Emshwiller and was marginally involved with other independent features. Also a Canadian, Joyce Wieland (Love's Labor) was herself an artists and filmmaker, and soon became a very important one with *Rat Life and Diet in North America* (1968), *Dripping Water* (1969), *Reason Over Passion* (*La Raison avant la passion*, 1969), *The Far Shore* (*L'Autre rive*, 1976), and other works that were associated with the structural film movement; she was also featured in her husband, Michael Snow's *Wavelength* (1967), *Standard Time* (1967), and other works, and in George Kuchar's *Lust for Ecstasy* (1964) and *The Mammal Palace* (1969). Information on Cowan is from Jack Stevenson, "Robert Cowan: Superstar of the Underground", On Wieland's position in this subculture, see Iris Nowell, *Joyce Wieland: A Life in Art* (Toronto, Canada: ECW Press, 2001), pp. 241–44. Wieland's contribution to the film also includes one of her own art works, *Josephine's Box*: she is seen holding on her lap a small cigar box appliquéd with a red cloth heart in side which are nested several small quilted penises. Thinking of it as an "authentic dream" and associating it with Wieland's fear that she would not be able to conceive a child, Jacobs has said, "I wanted that box and all the longing it implied or embodied" to be in the film (Nowell, *Joyce Wieland*, p. 243).

45. On the bridge and its architect John Roebling, see Alan Trachtenberg, *Brooklyn Bridge: Fact and Symbol*, 2nd ed. (Chicago: University of Chicago Press, 1979); Richard Haw, *The Brooklyn Bridge: A Cultural History* (New Brunswick, N.J.: Rutgers University Press, 2005); and Richard Haw, *Art of the Brooklyn Bridge: A Visual History* (New York: Routledge, 2008).

46. "Program Notes", p. 19.

47. Sitney, *Visionary Film*, p. 341. While recognizing that Jacobs "had not seriously read" Hart Crane, P Adams Sitney cites Crane's poem, "To Brooklyn Bridge", in which the bridge is invoked to "lend a myth to God", and proposes that "the sheer magnificence of the bridge and the aspiration of the Roeblings, its builders [are posited as] an eccentric form which weaves through history and invokes a sense of the divine in a world bereft (as far as Jacobs sees it) of divinity". Sitney, *Visionary Film*, pp. 340–341.

48. See Roebling's essay, "A Few Truths for the Consideration of American Citizens", Trachtenberg, *Brooklyn Bridge*, p. 62.

49. Trachtenberg, *Brooklyn Bridge*, pp. 67–68.

50. Richard Haw, the foremost historian of the bridge's cultural ramifications, has attributed this and similar exclusions of workers in civic parades in the late nineteenth century to "the growing antagonisms between capital and labor" that three years later, almost to the day, culminated in the Haymarket Massacre. Haw, *The Brooklyn Bridge*, p. 25.

51. Haw, *The Brooklyn Bridge*, pp. 13–14.

52. The printmakers included Harry Taskey, Charles Ernest Pont, Howard Simon, Milford Zornes, and Lozowick, while the photographers included Berenice Abbott and James Suydam; see Haw, *Art of the Brooklyn Bridge*, pp. 164–170; Lozowick citation is on p. 170. Walker Evans' photographs emphasizing the bridge's mass and design, some of which were used as illustrations to the first edition of Crane's *The Bridge*, were made just before the Depression. The history sketched here is indebted to Haw, *Art of the Brooklyn Bridge* and its copious illustrations.

53. See especially Henri Cartier-Bresson's "Below the Brooklyn Bridge" (1946), which shows a worker sitting atop bales of rags, and Eric Hartmann's "Man in Street Under the Brooklyn Bridge" (1955) (Haw, *Art of the Brooklyn Bridge*, pp. 195 and 197 respectively), both of which anticipate visual motifs in *The Sky Socialist*.

54. See, Haw, *Art of the Brooklyn Bridge*, pp. 220–227, and John B. Manbeck and Robert Singer, eds., *The Brooklyn Film* (Jefferson, N.C.: McFarland & Company, 2003).

55. In *It Happened in Brooklyn*, Sinatra plays a World War II GI whose pin-up girl is the bridge; immediately on returning from Europe, he takes a cab there and celebrates his love for her in the song, "The Brooklyn Bridge":

"Isn't she a beauty, isn't she a queen, nicest bridge that I have seen". Citing Rita Hayworth in *Cover Girl* and Betty Grable in *Coney Island*, Pete Hamill notes how in Hollywood film, crossing the bridge "characterizes upward and outward mobility .... [to] the capital of success, the mecca of mercantilism: Manhattan": see his "Introduction" in Manbeck and Singer, eds., *The Brooklyn Film*, p. 11.

56. "Program Notes", p. 19.
57. Umberto Eco, "De Interpretatione, or the Difficulty of Being Marco Polo (On the Occasion of Antonioni's China Film)", *Film Quarterly* 30, no. 4 (Summer 1977), pp. 8–12. Eco is describing the photography in Michelangelo Antonioni's documentary, *Chung Kuo – Cina* (*China*, 1972), a remarkable analogue to *The Sky Socialist* in being another film about a bridge caught in a disastrous but instructive encounter between modernist aesthetics and Socialist politics. A committed Communist, welcomed to China by the government when he was at the height of his fame, Antonioni made what he thought to be a sympathetic human documentary of the PRC's accomplishments, including a universal health-care system, a refinery built from discarded materials, and the Nanjing [Nanking] Yangtze River Bridge. Completed in 1968 and engineered by the Chinese themselves without outside assistance after the Sino-Soviet Split, the bridge demonstrated the new nation's unexpected technological progress and its *Wirklichkeit* had made it as much an item of national pride as the Brooklyn Bridge in its day. But rather than accepting Antonioni's film as a celebration of a similar Hegelian vision of progress, the Chinese saw it as an attempt to "smear the Socialist new China, slander China's Great Proletarian Cultural Revolution and insult the Chinese People". (*A Vicious Motive, Despicable Tricks – A Criticism of M. Antonioni's Anti-China Film "China"* [Beijing: Foreign Languages Press, 1974], p. 2. The pamphlet is an English translation of an unsigned article in *Renmin Ribao* of 30 November 1970.) The photography of the bridge was specifically attacked: "the camera was intentionally turned on this magnificent bridge from very bad angles in order to make it appear crooked and tottering. A shot of trousers hanging on a line to dry below the bridge is inserted as a mockery of the scene" (*A Vicious Motive, Despicable Tricks*, p. 11), both features that resemble many moments in *The Sky Socialist*. *China*'s other stylistic features similarly matched in Jacobs' film include varying shot lengths and a mobile camera (in the Tien An Men Square scenes, "there are sometimes long-shots, sometimes close-ups, sometimes from the front and sometimes from behind"); loose editing ("the film seems to a jumble of desultory shots pieced together at random"); lack of clear primary colors ("The use of light and color in the film likewise gives a malicious slant. It is shot mainly in grey, dim light and chilling tones ... . Many scenes give the audience a forlorn, gloomy, melancholy and sombre impression"); and contrapuntal sound ("The aria 'Raise your head' ... is used ... to accompany the scene of a pig shaking its head") (ibid, pp. 12–13). Susan Sontag also commented on the controversy in *On Photography* (New York: Delta, 1978), pp. 169–175.
58. Vladimir Mayakovsky, *Poems*, trans. Dorian Rottenberg (Moscow: Progress Publishers, 1972), p. 61. For a full account of "Poems About America", see Edward J. Brown, *Mayakovsky: A Poet in the Revolution* (Princeton, N.J.; Princeton University Press, 1973), pp. 272–285. Brown argues that, in their original Russian, the quoted lines "are the best, quite possibly the only, poetic realization of the theories about art and literature developed in the *Lef* milieu" (p. 283).

Chapter Ten "Apotheosis Into Tragedy": Catoptrics of Self in Andy Warhol's Lupe

"to hold, as 'twere, the mirror up to nature"
Hamlet

I.

Avant-garde films have historically manifested a wide spectrum of relations with the commercial cinema, and the great post-World War II U.S. tradition of practices that evolved entirely outside and opposed to Hollywood's institutions and styles, exemplified by Maya Deren, Stan Brakhage, and Jonas Mekas, was paralleled by another involving various kinds of dialogue and other productive relations with the industry. Andy Warhol career is the exemplary instance of the latter project. Though *Sleep* (1963), his first film, posed an alterity to commercial norms as severe and uncompromising as any of Brakhage's work, over the next decade he increasingly turned toward Hollywood in subject matter, genre and style, and mode of production. At last, with *Heat* (Paul Morrissey, 1972), *Flesh for Frankenstein* (Paul Morrissey, 1973), and others, he became a producer of narrative features designed to compete with the industry on its own terms.

Made at the end of 1965, *Lupe* found him midway through this transition. Using a script by a well-known playwright about a Hollywood star, photographed in color and boasting sound recorded with a level of competence greater than in his previous work, the film was, at least compared with his earlier work, relatively entertaining and accessible to a general public. On the other hand, his readiness to allow it to be projected as either a quasi-theatrical linear movie or as a twin-screen installation marked the emergence of a new phase of his art-world innovations. The coexistence in *Lupe* of elements from both the avant-garde and the industrial feature and their uneven interaction generate a thematic and formal richness absent from the more extreme poles of his cinema as a whole.

From his childhood to his final pronouncements (that included a wish to be reborn as a ring on Elizabeth Taylor's finger), Warhol's obsessive fascination with Hollywood and the culture industries generally was the single most generative influence on his art. Focusing on Lupe Vélez (1908–1944), the first Mexican actress to achieve great success in Hollywood, *Lupe* is one of three films he made about famous movie actresses, the others being *More Milk, Yvette* (1965), his immediately previous melodrama about Lana Turner and her gangster lover Johnny Stompanato, and the following year's *Hedy* (1966), about Hedy Lamarr's trial for shoplifting. Both starred Mario Montez, who also appeared in Warhol's first sound film, *Harlot* (1964) that putatively invoked Jean Harlow. Vélez, Turner, and Lamarr were all renowned for their on-screen personae as highly sexualized and aggressively desiring women that matched their tempestuous and often scandalous personal lives. And the three films about them are spiteful and vindictive, focusing on the most public scandals associated with their respective protagonists, their weakness and failings, and in the case of *Lupe*, on a wholly spurious and degrading misrepresentation of her death.

Beginning in the silent era and continuing into the 1930s, Vélez worked in B-movies, mostly screwball comedies, for William Wyler, Cecil B. DeMille, Gregory La Cava, and other important directors, as well as in Broadway musicals. Her popularity declined somewhat after the Production Code limited her vibrant if sometimes salacious repartee, but the box-office success of *The Girl from Mexico* (Leslie Goodwins, 1939) crystallized her comedic talents into what became a popular icon: the *"Mexican Spitfire"*. She deployed this character again in 1940 as the star of a film taking that epithet as its title, and then in six more (*Mexican Spitfire Out West, The Mexican Spitfire's Baby*, etc.), all directed by Goodwins.[1] Although her fiery "Tabasco" Latin temperament, assertive sexuality, broken English, and overall exoticism might be seen as promoting racist stereotypes, Latina/o, feminist, and queer artists and critics have proposed that in her historical moment she was in various ways empowering for minorities.

Vélez's personal life included highly public affairs with John Gilbert, Clark Gable, Charlie Chaplin, Gary Cooper, and other famous actors, and a five-year marriage to Johnny "Tarzan" Weissmuller in the mid-1930s. In 1944 she met a young Austrian actor, Harald Ramond, and became pregnant by him. Their subsequent relationship was volatile, with Vélez apparently uncertain what to do, but in the early hours of 14 December she took an overdose of barbiturates, and later that morning her secretary, Beulah Kinder, found her lying peacefully in bed, as if in a deep sleep. Ensconced within her satin pillowcase were two handwritten notes, one of them reading, "To Harald: May God forgive you, and forgive me too but I prefer to take my life away and our babys before I bring him with shame or killing him".[2]

But by the time of Warhol's film a very different account of her last hours had been spread by Kenneth Anger. In *Hollywood Babylon*, his salacious book about

10 – "Apotheosis Into Tragedy": Catoptrics of Self in Andy Warhol's *Lupe*

Hollywood scandals first published in the US in 1965, he claimed that, overwhelmed by financial and other troubles, Vélez had decided to kill herself, and determined to turn her suicide "into one of the most beautiful moments of her life; to turn tragedy into *apotheosis*". She filled her house with flowers, called in her makeup man and hairdresser, dressed herself in a lamé gown, ate a last meal, and went to bed to take the barbiturates:

> Half an hour later, the meticulous staging suddenly took an unforeseen turn which would have been worthy of Buñuel. All the effects planned by the fiery Mexican had been ordered; the flowers paid her a final homage, the glistening chandeliers shone on the lamé of her dress. Lupe died in *beauty*.
>
> The harmony was complete, with the sole exception of the *Seconal* and the spicy food, when the solemn lights around her body were abruptly bespattered. Lupe obeyed an instinct even stronger than death and ran, teetering on her high heels, toward the bathroom. But she slipped on the marble lies as she ran up to the toilet bowl – which turned out to be her last mirror! – and head first, she fell in and broke her neck. Thus she was found, stuck and half-submerged in this *bowl*, strange and macabre. And thus was extinguished one of Hollywood's glories![3]

No justification for Anger's scurrilous fabrication existed, but it became part of Hollywood folklore and Warhol himself savored it. Looking back a decade and a half after *Lupe*, he described his film's origin in his circle's obsession "with the mystique of Hollywood, the camp of it all". He went on to say that they all knew the stories about Lupe Vélez, how she "decided to commit the most beautiful Bird of Paradise suicide ever, complete with an altar and burning candles", but "at the last minute she started to vomit and died with her head wrapped round the toilet bowl." The altar and the candles may have been a projection of his own Catholicism, but the suicide gone awry and the crucial toilet bowl derive from Anger, whose sadistic glee Warhol's conclusion echoes: "We thought it was wonderful".[4]

Most of Warhol's films in this period, including *More Milk, Yvette* and *Hedy*, were scripted by Ronald Tavel.[5] But for *Lupe* he solicited Robert Heide, of whose play *The Bed* he had made a film version.[6] According to Heide, Warhol was fascinated by the idea of snuff films and, when informed that Freddy Herko, a dancer and actor in several of his films, had staged a performance for friends that culminated in his committing suicide by leaping out of a window five stories high, he had expressed a wish that Herko had given him advance notice so he could have filmed it.[7] Earlier that year he had commissioned Tavel to write a scenario called *Suicide* and suicide was also the focus of Heide's script.

At the time, Warhol was deeply involved with a new superstar, Edie Sedgwick.

A daughter of a scion of an extremely wealthy New England family through which ran an unfortunate seam of mental illness, Sedgwick herself had been hospitalized twice in her teens. Hoping for a career in modeling, she moved to New York in 1964 and met Warhol at a dinner party the following March. Entranced with her, Warhol invited her to the Factory and immediately began to feature her in his filmmaking, to which he had turned almost completely full time the previous year. Sedgwick's friend Sandy Kirkland recalled, "When Edie met Warhol, it was this immediate thing. They were going to make movies. Andy started escorting her, and drew her into the fold really fast. She became this extraordinary camera object … . Any time the camera was turned on, she would gravitate toward it like Gloria Swanson at the end of *Sunset Boulevard*. She had this real romance with it. She could be a totally bedraggled, wiped out wreck, and then the camera would go on and she would just be this magical star. It was crazy, but it was very powerful".[8]

Through the spring and summer of 1965, Warhol and Sedgwick were inseparable, but by the fall rumors of her association with Bob Dylan were beginning to strain their relationship, and Warhol asked Heide to write a screenplay in which she would commit suicide. Heide knew *Hollywood Babylon*, was a friend of Anger, and had the idea of using his account of Lupe Vélez as the vehicle for a suicide narrative. Though he disliked Warhol, Anger did not object, and Heide wrote *The Death of Lupe Vélez*, and gave copies to both Warhol and Sedgwick, and arranged to discuss the project with them. But when the playwright met Sedgwick (in Dylan's company) at the Kettle of Fish bar on MacDougal Street in the West Village, she told him that they had filmed it the previous afternoon. Later that day, Heide recalls, Warhol remarked to him, "When do you think Edie will commit suicide? I hope she lets me know so I can film it". Following Heide's script, the film opens with Lupe "curled up in bed wearing a negligee", but after that, few traces of his work recur. Nevertheless the motive for *Lupe* was clearly Warhol's desire to film Sedgwick's suicide, and the account of Vélez's death that Heide adapted from Anger's book provided a dramatic frame within which it could be improvised.

On the day in December 1965 Sedgwick mentioned, she, Warhol, and several others had gone to the Dakota at 72nd Street and Central Park West, to the apartment belonging to Panna Grady, a wealthy hostess who, according to Warhol, "put uptown intellectuals together with Lower East Side types – she seemed to adore the drug-related writers in particular".[9] With himself as the photographer and using his Auricon camera that recorded sound on an optical track during shooting, Warhol shot three 1,200' reels of 16 mm Ektachrome of

10 – "Apotheosis Into Tragedy": Catoptrics of Self in Andy Warhol's *Lupe*

Figure 1. *Lupe*: Reel One, Morning.

Sedgwick ostensibly playing Vélez on the last day of her life. He also shot at least two 100' rolls of her lying on the toilet floor with her head in the bowl and affixed them to two of the longer reels. *Lupe* is composed of two of these 1,300' reels.[10]

Perhaps with a nod to Warhol's first film, the first reel opens with an extended close-up on its star's sleeping face. After several minutes, a quick reverse zoom reveals that her bed abuts a mirror occupying the entire wall, whose edge vertically bisects the frame. Her face is reflected in it and for virtually the entire reel this mirror doubles her image, whether or not she looks directly into it (as she does later when she puts on her makeup). She awakens and sits up, displaying a short pink nightdress that leaves her arms, shoulders, and legs bare, and lights the first of many cigarettes. After a few minutes she answers the telephone, chatting briefly before Billy Name appears, playing a hairdresser as he had in Warhol's *Haircut No. 1* (1963) and other films. Wearing a blue shirt that echoes the blue of her pillow, he clips desultorily at her hair as they chat, though only odd remarks about going to church and vitamin B12 are audible. Promising to return at five in the afternoon with green dye for her hair, he leaves, and she continues with her makeup, until the reel suddenly cuts to her death scene, filmed in a single take.

Figure 2. *Lupe*: Reel Two, Evening.

In the second reel, Lupe enters a luxuriously furnished dining room, dressed in a long pale-blue Empire-styled nightgown, and places a vase of yellow flowers on the mantel over the fireplace. Alone there she smokes, drinks several glasses of wine, pops pills, and picks at a meal on the table. She turns the radio on and, wine glass in hand, dances drunkenly to songs that include "As Long As I Live", a swing tune written by Harold Arlen, composer of "Over the Rainbow". Again the scene ends with a cut to the footage of her body on the toilet floor, but this time it is comprised of a dozen or so shots with the zoom lens set at various focal lengths. The sound is of poor quality throughout, with only the fragments of dialogue between Lupe and her hairdresser from the first reel clearly audible, while the second is largely silent except for a period when she plays the radio. Until Warhol withdrew all his films from circulation in 1970, *Lupe* was distributed through the Film-Maker's Cooperative with instructions that it could be projected either as a single screen 72-minute, or as a 36-minute twin screen film, with reel 1, the morning, on the left and reel 2, the evening, on the right.

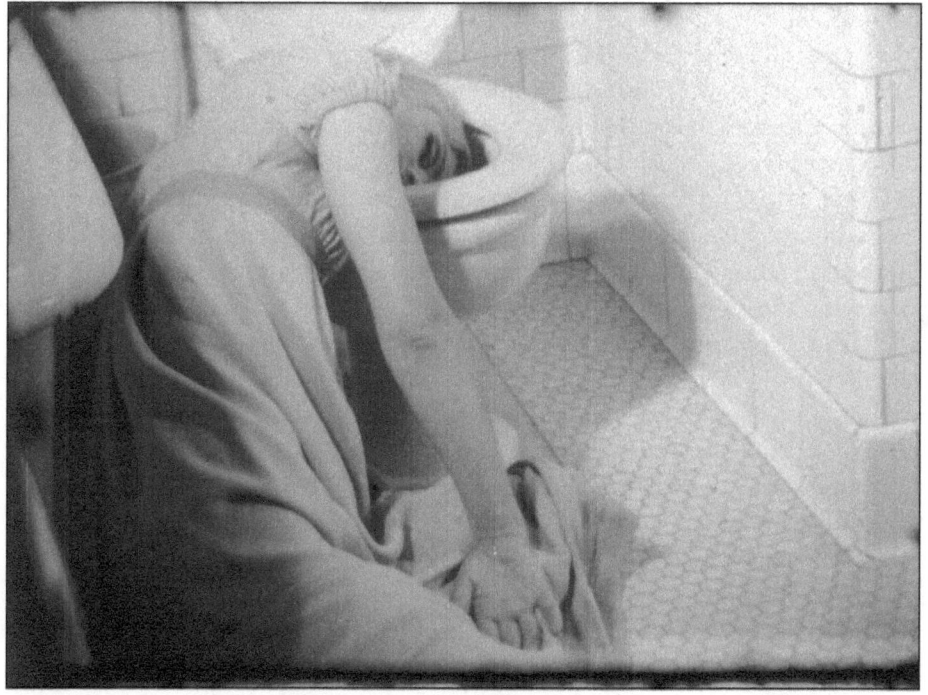

Figure 3. *Lupe*: Death Scene.

II

When his relationship with Sedgwick was at its most intense, Warhol articulated a radical cinematic project: "I always wanted to do a movie of a whole day in Edie's life", he began, and then elaborated on his dislike of selective editing, of "picking out certain scenes and pieces of time and putting them together, because then it ends up being different from what really happened – it's just not like life, it seems so corny". His ideal, he explained, was a film with no editing and no rehearsal: "I only wanted to find great people and let them be themselves and talk about what they usually talked about and I'd film them for a certain length of time and that would be the movie".[11] Many cinematic issues are involved here, but the prizing of minimally mediated documentary realism recalls both the remark attributed to Cesare Zavattini, "The ideal film would be ninety minutes of the life of a man to whom nothing happens", and more immediately the purely observational, "fly-on-the-wall" unobtrusiveness of Robert Drew's early conceptions of Direct Cinema.

But in fact, with the exceptions of *Sleep* and *Empire (1964)*, the fundamental tensions of Warhol's cinema as a whole are hinged on a dynamic interaction between the subject and the camera, aligning it rather with of Ricky Leacock's somewhat different formulations that, though still proposed as "uncontrolled cinema", implied the filmmaker's more active participation, as "an observer and perhaps as a participant capturing the essence of what takes place around him, selecting, arranging but never controlling the event".[12] Leaving aside Warhol's consistent eschewal of Direct Cinema's axiomatic handheld camera in favor of a tripod mount, his exploitation of the contradictions and impossibilities in Drew's ideal of an unselfconscious subject revealing him or herself for an unnoticed camera had been repeatedly displayed in the 472 *Screen Tests* he shot between 1964 and 1966, each of which documented a person simply being himself or herself alone in front of a 16 mm camera for the duration of a 100' roll film that was undefiled by editing. Nothing much happens in most of them, yet they are nevertheless full of the drama of their subjects' self-consciousness in their struggle to compose themselves against the camera's uninflected, unresponsive stare and to establish a persona that will stabilize them in its regard. In these ritual self-fabrications, the recording camera functioned as an implied mirror, but one that, until the film's screening, failed to provide a reflection in respect to which the construction of self could be negotiated. Even when Warhol's filmmaking more closely resembled the non-interventionist voyeuristic recording of innocent and unknowing subjects "being themselves", that impulse was inevitably undermined by an opposing recognition in both the humanist and the filmic registers: the implication that the self was never fully authentic and integral but rather elusive, unstable, and constructed; and that the intrusive material presence of the camera and other elements in the filmmaking process would always subvert the aspiration toward neutral representational transparency. These are the issues dramatized in *Lupe*. The notion of the self as constructed in social interactions – an idea introduced by Erving Goffman in *The Presentation of Self in Everyday Life* (1956) – had become axiomatic in contemporary sociology by the early '60s and been popularized by Susan Sontag in "Notes on 'Camp'" (1964) under the guise of "life as theater" and "Being-as-Playing-a- Role".[13] In the competitively theatrical social circle of Warhol's milieu, the self was provisional, a more or less artificial and constantly reconstructed persona, *performed* rather than revealed. It could only be improvised in contexts supplied by other performers, in the mirror of the filmmaking apparatus and, by implication, within the attention of the media apparatus as a whole.

In Warhol's art projects, this imaginary self-construction is staged in the two latter registers: self-dramatization in the medium of film and self-dramatization in cinema, or the mass media system, with the camera functioning as a metonymic connective pivot between these. Although the *Screen Tests* parodied their Hollywood references, nevertheless they and subsequent films always contained the possibility that, if successful, they might lead the sitter to prominence in the Factory – Warhol's travesty of the Hollywood studio system – and even open up the possibility of migrating beyond it and into the celebrity culture of the public media. For Warhol's own obsession with media icons who are enshrined in a halo of glamour and fame was reflected in its utopian inverse, the credo expressed by Kenneth Anger and his mentor, Aleister Crowley that "Every Man and Every Woman is a Star", who might shine in the media firmament. Since anyone who hopes to be famous, if only for fifteen minutes, must promote an image, many of Warhol's films revolve around the fabrication – and erosion – of personal identity in a media-saturated environment where the possibility of an autonomous selfhood has been colonized by publicity, advertising, and the movies, by the Spectacle.

The longer films for which Warhol commissioned scenarios did appear to offer his players the refuge of a consistent role, but he disrupted their security by all means available: by not providing the script until the last minute, by having crewmembers make hostile comments from off-screen, or by otherwise interfering in the shooting. Such reflexive interventions sacrificed transparent mimetic illusionism while maximizing his subjects' awareness of the camera, jeopardizing the stability of their roles, and provoking the crises that forced them into spontaneous, unscripted, and unexpected revelations of, as it were, their images' unconscious. "Pope" Ondine's attack on Rona Page in *The Chelsea Girls* after she calls him a phony is a pure moment in this cinema of sadism. Similarly, on the level of style, Warhol disoriented the films' observational transparency with a variety of ungrammatical effects: failure to focus the camera, inadequate lighting, arbitrary zooms and pans, seemingly haphazard in-camera cuts, and so on. Many of these "techniques" originated as accidents caused by his initial unfamiliarity with cinema technology; but their persistence as eruptions of willful or random infractions of standard film style, and especially his continued assertive display of unmotivated camera movement undercut both scenario and protagonist, as well as asserting the presence of the cinematic apparatus and procedures. Rather than enabling an illusionist representationalism, Warhol's ruptures of film grammar inserted a reflexive formalism into the core of his documentary realism that recalls Russian literary critic Viktor Shklovsky's notion of *ostranenie*, or defamiliarization, whereby the processes of art "make forms difficult [and] increase the difficulty and length of perception".[14] A parallel destabilization caught between the urge to promote and the urge to demote his stars' social profile occurred in his public utilization of them. What he had dramatized in film, he re-enacted in cinema.

III

Of all the Factory's inhouse superstars, Edie Sedgwick was the most promising candidate to become the real thing, and during the period of Warhol's closest involvement with her, each reciprocally used the other in generating their unprecedented celebrity. Earlier in 1965 Warhol and his entourage had been featured in prominent stories in the national press, including spreads in *Life* magazine and *Mademoiselle*, and on the occasion of the artist's first solo museum show at the Institute of Contemporary Art in Philadelphia, he experienced the frenzy of adulation firsthand. On 8 October 1965, two months before *Lupe* was shot, his show's opening night was all but preempted by a huge crowd of rowdy kids, estimated by Warhol to number four thousand, chanting "We want Andy and Edie". Afraid that the unruly youth would damage the art, the museum staff removed it from the walls with the result that, as Warhol realized, "we weren't just *at* the art exhibit – we *were* the art exhibit, we were the art incarnate".[15] That same month Edie and Andy appeared together on national television on the *Merv Griffin Show*, where the host introduced them as "the two leading exponents of the new scene". Sedgwick was clearly much the more comfortable with the media attention while Warhol spoke through her, whispering his comments in her ear and admitting that he had abandoned painting for full-time movie making.

By the time of *Lupe*, as well as appearing in nine *Screen Test*s proper, Sedgwick had appeared in more than a dozen of Warhol's films in 1965, starring in, among others, *Poor Little Rich Girl*, *Beauty # 1*, *Beauty #2*, *Kitchen*, and *Outer and Inner Space*.[16] The title, *Poor Little Rich Girl*, invokes a 1936 film of the same name that starred Shirley Temple as a rich girl who leaves an uncaring family and becomes a radio star, precisely paralleling the itinerary that Warhol envisaged for Sedgwick; and *Outer and Inner Space* anticipates the twin screen envisaged for *Lupe*. At the time of the Griffin show, her celebrity was so great that the move to Hollywood appeared to be a greater possibility than ever before. But now, only two months later, with Sedgwick and Dylan romantically linked and with Albert Grossman, Dylan's manager, expressing interest in taking her on as a client, the relationship between Warhol and his muse was strained. She was angry that he wouldn't pay her, while he felt abandoned by her. In *Lupe* he imagined her as a Hollywood star, but subjected her to a cruelly punitive and degrading death.

Lupe is a brief version of Warhol's ideal of "a movie of a whole day in Edie's life", but he sacrificed that documentary realism by projecting the role of Vélez on her and projecting onto both women Kenneth Anger's vicious account of the Mexican star's death. Precisely an instance of "picking out certain scenes and pieces of time and putting them together" the interpolated death scenes are a sensationalist dramatic eruption wholly anomalous in Warhol's cinema which, after *Sleep*, had abjured any other than in-camera editing, and whose narrative closure conclusively imposes shape on his usual uninflected temporal *durée*. Likewise, the mix of technical competence and formal restraint allows the portrait to be conventionally aestheticized and relatively accessible. Warhol photographed the film in a well-appointed apartment with proper lighting and the camera is in focus throughout, with the tripod mount allowing smooth zooms and pans. True, he sometimes strays from his subject to study the furnishings, and the second reel contains a sequence when Lupe's drunkenness is marked by frenetic camera activity suggestive of her delirium. But otherwise, *Lupe* differs radically from its companion pieces, *More Milk, Yvette,* and *Hedy*, whose narrative and technical irregularities filmicly reenact the violence that the narratives inflict on the heroines.

IV

The skeletal framework of a dramatic persona and the relatively transparent style of filming that maintains a coherent attention to the actress together allow thematic elements to emerge quite clearly. The private filmic event and the mass media resonances it metonymically subtends create a hall of mirrors. Draped over Sedgwick's everyday self-construction, the role of Lupe becomes a reflexive mantle of implications about her performance of an identity in the medium of film and its reverberations in the mass media. And observing Sedgwick in her looking-glasses, Warhol must have seen himself reflected back from her.

In the first reel, such mirroring is literal. Throughout, Warhol's alternates between wide angles and close-ups, but the wall mirror bisects the frame, continuously positioning Sedgwick alongside her reflection. As Billy Name clips at her hair, she brings a table mirror onto the bed, creating in the wall mirror an image of looking at herself in the table mirror, and the point when she drops it precipitates the most dramatic incident of the reel. These incidental uses of the wall mirror are matched by its functional use in the prolonged solo scenes in which Sedgwick looks directly into it while applying her makeup, constructing the face that sustains her image and celebrity. In the second reel, the large mirror hanging over the dining room fireplace is barely visible to the camera. Alone, bereft of a stabilizing reflected image or of the attention of her hairdresser, Sedgwick constructs herself in the figurative mirror of her role as Vélez, assuming her character's misery. Her eyes quivering nervously, her lips and face constantly in motion, popping pills, and with two glasses of wine on the go, she slips into abjection and several times seems to fall into unconsciousness. Whereas the events in the first reel merely supplied a frame for her *vérité* performance of her everyday routines, here Sedgwick is not acting drunk, but in reality getting drunk, itself an echo of Warhol's film, *Drink*, shot in January 1965, in which he filmed Emile de Antonio drinking himself into a stupor with whiskey. Although Sedgwick does not collapse, she appears to be at the end of her tether, as if actually on the verge of one of the many nervous breakdowns that had so often institutionalized her. Performing Lupe *in extremis*, the girl who fancied that the Rolling Stones' song, "Nineteenth Nervous Breakdown" was about her is also performing herself *in extremis*. Finally, as the perforations at the end of the reel meet the perforations at the beginning of the attached one-hundred foot, she reappears, flat on the toilet floor with her head in what Kenneth Anger had so archly termed "her last mirror". But the film provides yet another mirror: hung full-length on the bathroom door, it doubles the image of her body, just as had the wall mirror in the first reel. Here the different possibilities of the single and twin-screen version are most striking. In the two-screen version, with the first reel on the right and the other on the left, as she looks into the wall mirror, she is also looking across to the other screen so that her evening mirrors her morning. In this case the image of her death, already doubled in the bathroom door, is doubled again by the twin screens. But in the single screen version, the death scene that prematurely concluded Lupe's morning hangs proleptically over her final evening, foreshadowing the terrible conclusion of her descent into stupefied intoxication. The film stands in a similarly proleptic relation to Sedgwick's own life.

Though neither Warhol nor Grossman made her a movie star, half a decade after *Lupe* Sedgwick did star in a semi-autobiographical, theatrically released feature, *Ciao! Manhattan* (John Palmer and David Weisman, 1972). As Susan Superstar, she re-enacted her life after the Factory, her return to California, to hospitals and outpatient clinics, and to reckless promiscuity. A mentally-ill drug addict, she played a mentally-ill drug addict, and then, three months after finishing the shoot, died of what the Santa Barbara coroner who performed her autopsy described as "acute barbiturate intoxication".[17] Like Vélez, Sedgwick became a celebrity by playing herself, yet her role as Lupe was the apotheosis of her life and art in both of which she was a film star who died from self-administered drugs: in both, Edie and Edie-as-Lupe were players who held a mirror up to nature, and the nature they mirrored was their own, including ultimately their own deaths.

Many of the avant-garde films about "the mystique of Hollywood, the camp of it all" were made by gay men who identified with female stars of the classic era, Jack Smith's infatuation with María Montez being perhaps the most noteworthy.[18] But there's no evidence to suggest that Warhol's interest in Vélez specifically was fueled by anything other than Anger's account of her death. (By contrast, his interest in Hedy Lamarr that inspired *Hedy* began in a childhood infatuation with her; housebound after one of his several breakdowns, he had amused himself by copying the photograph of the star that had appeared in advertisements for Maybelline beauty products.) Nevertheless, his personal investment in Edie and in Edie-as-Lupe would seem to have reflected some deep if oblique personal psychic drive that made the mirrorings in the profilmic, before the camera, resonate in the events behind it, in the cinematic. In filming Sedgwick, Warhol was on some level filming himself – or an ideal version of himself.

When Andy and Edie were most closely identified, they emphasized their visual resemblance; they would dress in similar clothes, and at times she dyed her hair silver to match his wig. Poet René Ricard's comment that in this period "Edie was pasted up to look just like him – but looking so good! " pinpoints the fantasy projection.[19] It is supported by Truman Capote's observation, "I think Edie was something Andy would like to have been. He was transposing himself onto her *à la* Pygmalion … . Andy Warhol would like to have been Edie Sedgwick. He would like to have been a charming, well-born debutante from Boston".[20] In staging her death, not in Vélez's fake Mexican hacienda, but in the apartment of a wealthy Brahmin, he mobilized her there as his ideal self, while dramatizing his anxiety about losing her by brutally killing her off. The edge flares burning through the last frames of her body reflected in the toilet mirror bring to mind once again all the callous ironies of his comment on Anger's fiction of Vélez's death: "We thought it was wonderful".

Notes

1. Michelle Vogel's *Lupe Vélez: The Life and Career of Hollywood's "Mexican Spitfire"* (Jefferson, N.C.: McFarland, 2012) is the most reliable biography of Vélez.

2. Vogel, *Lupe Vélez*, p. 151.

3. Kenneth Anger, *Hollywood Babylon* (Phoenix, Az.: Associated Professional Service, 1965), pp. 234–235. In the more extended and lurid account in the later edition, Anger refers to Vélez as a "gyrating cunt-flashing Hollywood party girl": see *Hollywood Babylon* (New York: Dell, 1975), pp. 231–239.

4. Andy Warhol and Pat Hackett, *POPism: The Warhol '60s* (New York: Harcourt, Brace, Jovanovich, 1980), p. 127.

5. Beginning with *Harlot* (1964), Tavel wrote scenarios for eleven of Warhol's films, including *Poor Little Rich Girl* (1965), and *Kitchen* (1965), both also starring Sedgwick.

6. According to Callie Angell, *The Bed* "premiered at a benefit for the Caffe Cino at the Sullivan Street Theater in March 1965; the play reopened at the Caffe Cino on July 7, 1965, and ran for 150 performances. In the fall of 1965, Warhol and Dan Williams shot a double-screen film version of Heide's play. In 1966 Without using Heide's script, Warhol appropriated the basic idea of the play in 1966 for a three-reel film called *The John*, two reels of which, *Boys in Bed* and *Mario Sings Two Songs*, were included in *The Chelsea Girls*". Callie Angel, *Andy Warhol Screen Tests: The Films of Andy Warhol Catalogue Raisonné* (New York: Abrams, 2006), p. 193.

7. Personal correspondence. All information about Heide's relationship with Warhol and the *Lupe* project is from this correspondence and a telephone interview with Heide on 23 October 2013.

8. Quoted in Jean Stein, *Edie: An American Biography* (New York: Dell, 1982), p. 152.

9. Warhol and Hackett, *POPism*, p. 127.

10. At the film's premiere all three reels were projected side by side; the presently restored two-reel version is the one

distributed until Warhol withdrew all his films from circulation in 1970; see Callie Angel, *The Films of Andy Warhol: Part II* (New York: Whitney Museum of American Art, 1994), p. 25. The third reel, still unrestored, is rumored to include an appearance by Jason Holiday, who next year stared in Shirley Clarke's *Portrait of Jason* (1967). The poor sound in *Lupe* was a consequence of the fact that the Ektachrome optical track is compromised when the stock is processed for color rather than black and white.

11. Warhol and Hackett, *POPism*, p. 110.
12. Richard Leacock, "For an Uncontrolled Cinema", *Film Culture* 22–23 (Summer 1961): 25.
13. Susan Sontag, "Notes on 'Camp'" in *Against Interpretation and Other Essays* (New York: Dell, 1966), p. 281.
14. Victor Shklovsky, "Art as Technique", in *Russian Formalist Criticism: Four Essays*, eds. Lee T. Lemon and Marion J. Reis (Lincoln, Ne.: University of Nebraska Press, 1965), p. 12.
15. Warhol and Hackett, *POPism*, p. 133.
16. Callie Angel provided a definitive summary of Sedgwick's films in her, *Andy Warhol Screen Tests*, pp. 181–182. She notes, "Sedgwick nearly monopolized Warhol's camera for much of 1965, starring or appearing in every single sound film to come out of the Factory between late March ... and Labor Day Weekend" (p. 181).
17. Quoted in Stein, *Edie*, p. 343.
18. Among these is another, almost contemporaneous, film about Vélez, Jose Rodriguez-Soltero's *Lupe* (1966) that also starred Mario Montez.
19. Quoted in Stein, *Edie*, p. 152.
20. Quoted in Stein, *Edie*, p. 153.

Chapter Eleven Letter to Paul Arthur (Letter With Endnotes)

22 February 2011

Dear Paul,

I dreamed about you again last night. We were with some other people in a restaurant and I was quizzing you about your writing projects. Now that you had retired, what essays were you working on? Were you preparing a follow-up to *A Line of Sight*, since it was so well received?[1] You kept poking at your food, hedging my questions. Then you told me: you weren't retired, you were dead.

I have no illusions that you are somewhere reading this, but you do live in my mind. I want to tell you about a seminar on the historiography of the avant-garde that I recently attended in London,[2] where I talked about a couple of highly unusual events around avant-garde film that happened in Los Angeles last fall. Wishing you could have been there for them, I had mentally processed them – as I still often do with many events in my life – in the form of a letter to you. I think you would have relished them, for the films and the camaraderie, but also as a richly symptomatic object lesson in the way the avant-garde and its historiography in Los Angeles are now caught in the force fields of Hollywood, real estate, museums, the academy, and capital generally. Then, when I prepared to talk about these events at the London conference, I realized that the way it seemed spontaneously given to me to do so was as an extension of that letter to you. Pretty much all the film history I have written derived from either real or imagined dialogues with you and, as I wrote to you when you first told me you were so ill, "The fact that you have been there and willing to receive [my writing] made it possible for me to think and write".

The London conference call specifically requested a self-reflexive element in the papers, but to allow reflexivity to take such a personal form was a departure for me. Given that I had been invited back to my native country (where for many years I tried and failed to find employment) and that this conference was the only time in twenty years that I had been asked to give a paper in England, I was anxious that the other attendees would attack me for this infringement of scholarly decorum. But I wanted to get at the pressure of personal investment that underlies our scholarly writing. I suspect it's an issue that we all live deeply, but hardly ever talk about; at least I only ever talked about it with you. And now, as I approach retirement, I have little to lose, so I thought I'd take that chance. I'm glad I did. The other conferees were very kind, and Catherine Elwes and the other editors of the *Moving Image Review & Art Journal* (*MIRAJ*) were sufficiently receptive to my hybrid talk that they invited me to revise it for their inaugural issue. This is that revision. As then, I promise not to get maudlin and to do my best to pick my way among the competing demands of my own ego so as to minimize solipsistic projections.

When I began to think how I might make some useful contribution to the seminar, I noticed three points from the project statements that seemed particularly pertinent to my work, especially that on cinema in Los Angeles: the observation that "we should be thinking in terms of multiple histories – the canon forged in the art-world metropole might be constituted quite differently at the peripheries or in non-western contexts"; the second question related to the viability of ideas of medium specificity in a post-medium condition; and the third was an emphatic request for a self-reflexive element I just mentioned, specifically that we should "think about the nature of producing and publishing scholarship and criticism".

The organizers very generously agreed that my main contribution could be the essay "L.A.'s Hipster Cinema", a history of moving-image culture in Los Angeles in fall 2008, and that my actual presentation could consist of comments on that project. As I saw it, the essay clearly addressed the first two issues. The differences, but also the connections, between the histories of recent avant-garde cinema in Los Angeles and in London demonstrate such a multiplicity, even if it's not self-evident which is the metropole and which is the periphery. I had been asked to write the Hipster essay by Rob White who, from London, edits the journal *Film Quarterly* that is published in California. He suggested that I use as a model Nicky Hamlyn's terrific overview of the situation he described in London in 2006–2007.[3] There Nicky described what he saw in London as a plurality of practices dispersed mainly between galleries and theatres that had replaced the hegemonic singularity of the film-making associated with the London Filmmakers' Co-op through the mid-1990s; but to me, reading the essay in Los Angeles, the overall situation rather looked like a continuation of the austere aestheticism and its aspiration to autonomy associated with the Co-op. So, my *Film Quarterly* essay began with material that might well have appeared in Nicky's, a museum screening of films by conceptual artist Lawrence Weiner, but then shifted to much less formal social locations. Overall, I tried to describe a radically new vitality in experimental film in Los Angeles, especially in respect to screening events; its conspicuous difference from what it had been, say, fifteen years ago I attributed largely to the rise of digital media. What I found in the fall of 2008 was a spectrum of various degrees of experimental film's imbrication in industrial culture, advertising and real estate, but also in several kinds of grassroots, popular initiatives. To me, as you no doubt would have predicted, the evidence indicated that the historiography of avant-garde film had to include the history of its positions in relation to both subcultures, in this case to "hipsters" *and* to corporate capitalist culture.

That spectrum of practices also engages *the question of medium specificity*. Despite very small pockets where filmmaking is still oriented around its material properties, generally in Los Angeles it and all other forms of moving images are digitized so that once-important differences, like the one between film and video, have been subsumed in a general remediation. Since I'll return to it shortly, let me use as an example the place where I do my history writing, the University of Southern California's School of Cinematic Arts (USC, SCA), built from a 2006 $175 million donation from alumnus George Lucas's Lucasfilm Foundation. On the strength of his gift, George ordained that there be no film projection in the new building, everything was to be digital, and only desperate faculty pleas secured one room where film could be screened.

The ubiquity of digital media, in turn, transforms the social locations of cinema. Nicky's concern with the differences between theatre and gallery screening is difficult to imagine in Los Angeles, where now everything is available for projection on ubiquitous, inescapable screens that range in size from a cell phone, through the insides and outsides of buildings, to architectural environments bigger than the English village where I was born.

At the London seminar, I left these issues from my essay for general discussion and for the remainder of my time I turned to new material and the third topic, the reflexive element, that is, the two instances of how institutional events contribute to the writing of film history.

Last fall, quite fortuitously – if you believe anything is ever fortuitous – two extremely anomalous events took place in Los Angeles that proposed historiographies and canons for the avant-garde, but also very forthrightly exposed the institutional manoeuvres that subtend and so in some degree shape them. Since these contrast markedly with the array of state apparatuses that have been so important for artists' film in the United Kingdom,[4] I proposed my account of these as a meta-historiographical supplement to the hipster essay and tried, if in an anecdotal fashion, to bring them to bear on the tensions between the role of institutions and that of individuals in the production of historiography. Here's the story.

Last summer I was invited to participate in the corollary events attached to the mostly horrible Dennis Hopper exhibition curated by Julian Schnabel for the Museum of Contemporary Art (MOCA), the same museum – and in fact in the same room – in which I had seen Weiner's films. I gave a talk about Hopper's film *The Last Movie*, taking Jonas Mekas' 1964 statement, "American cinema remains in Hollywood and the New York Underground. There is no American 'art' film",[5] as a point of departure. (I'll be returning to that spatial and hierarchical binary: Hollywood and the New York Underground.) I disputed it, arguing that the New York Underground was never the only one; that art and the movies were variously intertwined in Hopper's life and work, and that *The Last Movie* was his greatest accomplishment and a classic American art film.

After my talk Jeffrey Deitch, MOCA's director as of June 2010 and whose first project the Hopper show was, introduced himself to me. He asked if I would be interested in curating a film festival with the New York Film-Makers' Cooperative (NYFC) and added that Jonas Mekas, Ken Jacobs, and Carolee Schneemann would attend. Flattered and still high from the talk, I agreed. Previously owner of Deitch Projects, the most successful contemporary art gallery in New York, Deitch is the first major art dealer to hold such a museum position. And many people thought his appointment breached the boundaries between museums and commercial galleries, between art and capital, which are already especially porous in Los Angeles.

From M.M. Serra, our friend and the Co-op's executive director, I later learned that the film festival was actually the project of Charles S. Cohen, a real-estate magnate, CEO of Cohen Brothers Realty Corporation and owner of several design centres. These include the Pacific Design Center (PDC), a complex of two huge buildings designed by Cesar Pelli on a 14-acre campus in West Hollywood, housing facilities for interior designers, architects and so on – and of course design and architecture are areas where the interaction between art and capital are especially direct. Cohen is also a film buff. He was the executive producer of *Frozen River* (Courtney Hunt, 2008) a well-received feature about impoverished single mothers, and he is the Co-op's most recent saviour. Learning that it was about to be evicted from its premises, early in 2009 he leased to it approximately 30,000 square feet in one of his buildings for $1 a year for five years:[6] a magnificent gesture by a very wealthy man.[7] And now he wanted to showcase the Co-op in his Los Angeles Design Center.

By this time, Deitch had e-mailed me to ask how much I would charge to curate the festival. Seeing it as a chance to help the Co-op, bring an interesting event to Los Angeles, and liberate some money from these capitalists, I asked for $1,000, which, I later learned, Cohen thought was too little. But there it was, I'd sold myself and even named my own price.

Los Angeles's celebration of the NYFC was to be held at the PDC's SilverScreen Theater and would be designated 'Counter Culture/Counter Cinema'. I wondered what interest either Deitch or Cohen could have in counter anything.[8] But M.M. reassured me that it would help the Co-op and that Cohen would fly Jonas Mekas, Ken Jacobs and Carolee Schneemann – surely the major survivors of the 1960s' avant-garde counter-cinemas – to Los Angeles in his private jet and put them up at a posh hotel. So in the next few weeks, M.M. and I put together a long weekend of seven programs of films distributed by the Co-op. Meanwhile I was called to a meeting at MOCA with assorted staffers and publicists, Cohen, Deitch and Cliff Einstein. Einstein is a noted art collector,[9] chair emeritus of the MOCA board of trustees and chief executive officer of Dailey & Associates, an advertising agency that achieves annual sales of between half a billion and a billion dollars and rents space in the PDC. The promotional ideas flew fast and furious. We would get John Waters to introduce George Kuchar. We would get Manohla Dargis to cover it in the *New York Times* and that would make the Los Angeles papers take note. And there would be a big party with art-world and especially Hollywood superstars. We would get John Baldessari and Ed Ruscha, Miranda July, Sophia Coppola, and Doug Aiken. Had he not been dead, Dennis Hopper would have been perfect, but Deitch reeled off the names of the young and famous "personal friends" who would be sure to show. Of course, it was understood that none of these would come to the films, only to the party. And vice-versa: the counter-cinema types would not be invited to the party but, I supposed, they would profit indirectly from the nimbus of glamour in which news about the party would shroud them.

Instructions were given and later e-mails sent to a representative from the Marshall Plan, a PR firm, self-designated as "a communications company specializing in luxury and lifestyle clients, with a clientele that's a virtual 'who's who' of the lifestyle, travel & spa industries".[10] But a week before the event they had done nothing; Dargis had not publicized it in the *New York Times*, and the only significant publicity came as a result of mailings sent by LA Filmforum's Adam Hyman;[11] one of them had been picked up by a freelance journalist for a local free paper, the *L.A. Weekly*, who on his own initiative got us a column in the place most likely to be seen by our constituency.[12] So, on the evening of Friday 15

Figure 1. Ken Jacobs, Charles S. Cohen, M.M. Serra, Carolee Schneemann, Jonas Mekas and Jeffrey Deitch at the Pacific Design Center, 15 October 2010.

October, after a cocktail reception (read cheap wine and expensive water) at the SilverScreen Lounge, Charles S. Cohen presented M.M. with a cheque for $25,000 for the Co-op and, on behalf of the City of West Hollywood, council member Lindsey Horvath presented Cohen, Deitch and Jonas Mekas each with a large illuminated commendation scroll. Our homage to the cinema of poverty and outsiders was launched in one of Mammon's satellite temples.[13]

The first programme was "Underground Classics": *Flaming Creatures, Lupe* and *Fuses*. Subsequently, Schneemann, Mekas, and Jacobs each had a dedicated screening: Mekas's film, *The Birth of a Nation* (1997), was disturbingly solipsistic, redeemed mainly by glimpses of a young P. Adams Sitney dancing down the street;[14] Jacobs's digital compositions, especially *Krypton is Doomed* (2005) and *The Pushcarts Leave Eternity Street* (2010), were sublime; and Carolee Schneemann's reworkings of documentation of her performances from the 1960s, especially *Snows* (1967), were very interesting, both in themselves and as historical records. M.M. and I had collaborated on a closing session, "The Art of Seeing: Underground Gems": classics from *Meshes of the Afternoon* (Maya Deren, 1943) to *Chumlum* (Ron Rice, 1964). Together with a Spanish historian, Juan Suárez, M.M. curated a program of mostly queer, but all pretty transgressive, films based on the body, including her own *Chop Off* (2009), a film about a man who for kicks is progressively cutting off his fingers and toes – Ken Jacobs had warned me it was tough, and he was right! And I curated a programme of 1960s counter-cultural films made in California from the 1971 Co-op catalogue, several of them political-agitational works: Lenny Lipton's 1965 classic, *We Shall March Again*, about an anti-war march in Berkeley, for example, and Jerry Abrams's *Be-In* (1967), a psychedelic documentary with music by Blue Cheer about the January 1967 "Human Be-in" in Golden Gate Park that kicked-off the Summer of Love.

And a great success it was. Though the party never happened and the celebs never appeared, to my surprise experimental film audiences did. The PDC has little history as a venue for avant-garde film (and a massively unsuccessful but costly Warhol retrospective there in the mid-1990s had put LA Filmforum out of business for a season), still between 75 and 100 people came for each program and the discussions were very lively.

Given the festival's title and the fact that the films and personages were so closely associated with the 1960s, many of the debates revolved around the ironies of celebrating oppositional cultures at a time when a contemporary equivalent for them appears impossible. An audience member and avant-garde aficionado Mark Skoner first broached the issue by remarking that watching the films in my political counter-culture programme seemed weird: usually avant-garde films have a banal content and an interesting form, he said, but through advertising and other forms of capitalist culture's appropriations we have become familiar with what were then radical stylistic innovations. Now it's their social content – the possibility of contestation – that is abstract and theoretical. The issue recurred in the response to my panel, when film-maker Lenny Lipton expressed wonderment that his film could be really understood at the present time. And it came up again in the Q&A for Carolee Schneemann, who talked about the censorship around *Fuses* (1967) and the fact that only a Mafia-run porn emporium would print it. When someone asked Carolee why political action was possible then but not now, filmmaker Morgan Fisher chastised her (the audience member) for what he called "misplaced nostalgia" for the 1960s, arguing that young people should direct their attention to their own historical moment. He was of course on some level right, though he entirely overlooked her implication that the possibility of social action is itself a social and historical condition, not just an individual option.

But no one raised the issue that was foremost in my mind: the disjunct between the programme's overall political thrust and the fact that the event, like the Co-op itself, was sponsored by a maverick capitalist and held in his emporium. Did this mean that our historiography had become part of capital's legitimizing apparatus, connected to it (like art history) by an "umbilical cord of gold"?[15] Or was the event an instance of contradictions and disjunctions in the system that we had successfully exploited, and thereby sustained some degree of cultural difference in an otherwise flattened environment? Then I remembered that this event was not anomalous in the history of the Co-op, and that in fact Jonas was doing what he had been best at doing for fifty years: Charles S. Cohen was only the latest of the rich people he had found to sustain the New York Underground.

"Counter Culture/Counter Cinema", Los Angeles's celebration of the heritage of the New York Underground, was sponsored by the museum/real-estate complex; the second event, "Alternative Projections: Experimental Film in Los Angeles, 1945–1980", Los Angeles's celebration of its own history, was sponsored by the museum/academic complex.

In 2007 the Getty Foundation in Los Angeles – big oil money with an annual operating budget of $27.8 million – announced a competition for nearly $2.8 million in grants around a project that was eventually called "Pacific Standard Time: Art in L.A. 1945–1980". With delirious hubris, Adam Hyman and Stephanie Sapienza, respectively executive director and board president of LA Filmforum, applied for one. Taking my history of Los Angeles avant-garde film as their point of reference,[16] their project would continue the historical excavation of experimental filmmaking in Los Angeles. Along with virtually all the corporate and academic behemoths in southern California from LACMA to MOCA,[17] they were one of the fifteen winners. A David and Goliath victory by any count for an entirely volunteer organization with an annual budget of $20,000 to be awarded $118,000 for research and planning, with another $65,000 awarded later for exhibitions and publications. I reluctantly came aboard, and with a small committee we shaped "Alternative Projections: Experimental Film in Los Angeles, 1945–1980", an archival research project consisting of more than thirty videotaped and transcribed oral histories; a research symposium to include panels, presentations and a screening series as part of the "Pacific Standard Time" exhibitions in 2011–2012; and some form of publication.

Filmforum went ahead with the oral histories and with me as the connection we landed another $20,000 from "Visions and Voices", a humanities initiative at the University of Southern California (USC), a private university, with additional support from its School of Cinematic Arts (SCA), now resplendent in its kitschy new premises, not only donated by Lucas but also designed by him: *Star Wars* cash and *Star Wars* taste made manifest. We announced that a three-day symposium would be held at USC over the weekend 12–14 November 2010, and our calls for papers returned around 35 proposals, totally confounding my expectation that no one would be interested. Three days before it began, we closed the pre-registration at 500, and in the event some 350 people attended all or part. So, the opportunity to revisit Mekas's assertion that there had never been any cinema in Los Angeles but Hollywood took place in the film school most signally associated with the business.[18]

SCA's Dean, Elizabeth Daley, made an opening address, reminding us of some of the school's relations with the avant-garde that none of our PR material ever mentions: the period in the mid-1940s when Gregory Markopoulos, Curtis Harrington, and Kenneth Anger were all students; the period in the late 1940s when Slavko Vorkapich was department chair; students in the 1960s including Thom Andersen and Morgan Fisher as well as George Lucas; the work of more recent graduates, including Adam Hyman; and faculty members with interests in the avant-garde.

Over the weekend, several kinds of historical reconstruction were mounted. Terry Cannon, the founder of Filmforum, filled six vitrines with memorabilia about the series of avant-garde screening organizations Los Angeles has more or less continuously sustained since the early 1950s, and John Whitney Jr's *Side Phase Drift*, an abstract three-screen performance projection piece initially realized in 1965 on a mechanical analogue computer system, was digitally recreated.

The scholars' panels included sixteen 25-minute papers, of which I thought fifteen were potentially publishable. The Q&As were delightful and productive, reflecting the mix of artists who had been there at the time and done it and younger generations eager to find out about it. Perhaps the high point of the interaction between scholars and makers came in the last panel, Paul, in which a very promising young scholar, Carlos Kase, used your essays on structural film[19] in analysing the films of Grahame Weinbren and Roberta Friedman; Friedman was in the audience, but Weinbren was on the same panel, giving a paper on Pat O'Neill, who was himself in the audience. In preparation for the panels we screened full versions of many of the works that were discussed – some of them even on film in the one room equipped to do so – several of which had long been unseen and two of which turned out to be real gems. I'll give one example, since it so clearly demonstrates how conferences like this can rediscover history.

Wanting to participate but having no appropriate topic in hand, Ken Eisenstein, a young Hollis Frampton scholar, searched through the Co-op catalogue and found a film that seemed to be connected to Los Angeles, but which had not been rented for many years: *Shoppers Market* (1963) by John Vicario. It turned out to be a fascinating, lyrical and yet weird documentary about a Santa Monica supermarket, but nothing was known about Vicario, other than that he had been a student at UCLA with Francis Ford Coppola and had a credit as camera operator on his *Dementia 13*.[20] Eisenstein found Vicario alive, though frail, in the San Fernando Valley, and also discovered that *Shoppers Market* had screened at the 1963 Third International Experimental Film Competition at Knokke-le-Zoute, along with such masterpieces of the U.S. avant-garde as *Scorpio Rising* (Kenneth Anger) and *Mothlight* (Stan Brakhage). Vicario, who had himself not seen the film for forty years, was warmly welcomed, and his film has now been restored.

One evening was devoted to the recently reconstituted 1960s lightshow, Single Wing Turquoise Bird; they screened the only extant film record of the original show, films by each of the six current members, and a recorded, in-studio improvisation made by the resurgent Bird Ensemble.[21] And the final afternoon was given over to a reunion of the Los Angeles Independent Film Oasis, the film-makers' screening collective, which from 1976 to 1981 kept the flame of something like structural film alive in Los Angeles (and which incidentally had connections with the London Filmmakers' Co-op circle of the time). Since you, Paul, were of course an Oasis member, had you not died, you would have been welcomed to the reunion. Seven films made by members during the collective's life from 1976 to 1981 were screened, then moderator Terry Cannon introduced the ten film-makers who had been reassembled, and the discussion among them elicited some interesting revelations, including Beverly O'Neill's anecdote about Oasis's opening night, when Jonas Mekas's *Journey to Lithuania* had brought a SRO crowd of incensed Lithuanians who blamed the film's pixilation on an incompetent projectionist, and Morgan Fisher's recollection that a show curated by Grahame Weinbren titled 'The Naked and the Nude' had attracted a crowd of silent, solitary raincoated men. So overall the reunion was both an occasion for a communal public oral history of Oasis itself and a debate about the differences between the cinematic possibilities of Los Angeles 35 years ago and at present.

So, Paul, throughout this I was wearing many hats, not all of them well fitting. As one of the organizers, and especially as the USC organizer, I was responsible for making sure that all the meals arrived on time, that the various technologies worked, and that the events kept to a reasonable schedule. If the attendance at "Counter Culture/Counter Cinema" had been as spotty as I expected, I could have blamed the dysfunctional corporate PR; but here, the 500 pre-registrants had me concerned about too many people showing up rather than too few. But in the event, the collaboration among the Getty, LA Filmforum, SCA, and USC – the museum, the screening organization, the cinema school and the university – worked well, guided as it was by the diligence and commitment of the

Filmforum committee, the SCA support team and all the participants. History was written, both in the minds of the people present and in the papers, for which we are now looking to find a publisher.[22]

But my ego issues ran far deeper. During the panels, my desire to be recognized and cited, pain when I was not, and embarrassment when I was were all intertwined with the pleasure in the event's overall success, the excellence of the papers, and especially seeing several of my students doing such excellent historiography. But beneath all these, the event seemed the summary of such a very large part of my life, not just of my activity but also of my value system and sense of identity, that thinking seriously about it as I now approach retirement is fraught with psychological and metaphysical demons. I promised you and the London people that I wouldn't get maudlin about these, so I'll make a couple of remarks and end.

Whatever historical knowledge was produced and shared in these events was done so communally, in the dialogues among filmmakers, scholars and audiences, between images and words, between the past and the present. Within these lies a process, articulated by our friend and collaborator, Michele Pierson,[23] who in a letter to me countered my (Althusserian) attempt to displace responsibility and agency onto larger social forces; she conversely emphasized that, no less than in avant-garde film-making, in cinema historiography, as individuals we are not simply the bearers of history, but also its makers. She wrote: "In the midst of these powerful force fields, individuals, and the writing, research, pedagogical and curatorial/organizational activities that they initiate are still essential catalysts for getting avant-garde work seen and talked about. For all that they don't/do control, it still takes individuals – people with vision and energy and commitment – to put new ways of doing/seeing things into motion",[24] individuals with as disparate agendas in these cases as Charles S. Cohen and Adam Hyman.

And so finally, in my London talk, I proposed that the work we do as historians is framed by many forces, but their limits are on the one hand social and economic, the institutions through which we live and work, and on the other personal and libidinal, the various desires that fuel our writing. But as I was saying this, I realized that a third term linked these together: the notion of community. I thought that someone would point this out; no one did, but still the strongest element in my experience of the seminar and of the two events I described was a sense that the people present felt themselves to be members of a community. As an outsider to the London event, I was of course ignorant of the jealousies and hostilities there that even the best communities contain. But, for the next few days, I felt that I had come home to a community, which has been such an integral, if distant, part of my life: David Curtis, whom I first met at the London "Festival of Independent Avant-Garde Film" in 1973, who over the years has helped my research in many ways, who contributed to the collection of essays on Jonas Mekas, and whose history of British artists' film is a classic in our field; A.L. Rees, whom I met at a Warhol conference in 1989 and whose book, *A History of Experimental Film and Video*, has been a mainstay of my seminars; Nicky Hamlyn, whose essay on Stan Brakhage was one of the very best pieces in the Brakhage book; Julia Knight, with whom I've had extended correspondence about *The Miners' Campaign Tapes*; Lucy Reynolds, who wrote such a generous review of my book on the Los Angeles avant-garde; and a student in the seminar I taught at NYU in 1989, when you and I were able to spend so much time together.[25] Of course I may well be deluding myself in the trite and also solipsistic way I promised to avoid, but I felt that with these and the several new friends I was for a time part of a community, a sensation that, for me at least, has been so fugitive in Los Angeles and which made the two festivals so anomalous. And I am grateful that what you once termed our absolutely essential friendship allows me still to share that community with you.

Your friend,

David

Notes

1. Paul Arthur, *A Line of Sight: American Avant-Garde Film Since 1965* (Minneapolis and London: University of Minnesota Press, 2005).
2. "Rewriting History: Interrogating the Past and the Question of Medium Specificity", Graduate School, CCW, University of the Arts, London, 19 January 2011. This seminar was the first in a series of AHRC-funded international events, convened by Catherine Elwes and Pratap Rughani to provide a discursive platform for the development of the *Moving Image Review & Art Journal (MIRAJ)*.
3. "London Avant-garde Round-up", *Film Quarterly* 61, no. 2 (Winter 2007): 46–55.
4. See David Curtis' *A History of Artists' Film and Video in Britain* (London: British Film Institute, 2008).
5. *Movie Journal: The Rise of a New American Cinema, 1959–71* (New York: Collier Books, 1972), p. 120.
6. "'I was in a position to help, and I thought that I should', Mr. Cohen said. 'They are a wonderful group doing important work, and there is no other place to go and see this kind of thing. They needed a storage space for their archives, and this meets their needs.'" See Larry Rohter, "Avant-Garde Film Group Gets New Home, Cheap", *New York Times*, 27 May 2009, www.nytimes.com/2009/05/28/movies/28film.html?_r=1&scp=3&sq=Charles%20S%20Cohen%20FilM.M.akers&st=cse. Accessed 15 November 2010.
7. The PDC also houses a branch of MOCA where, among the shows I've seen there, two were especially interesting, if in differently complicated and contradictory ways: "Superflat" in 2001 and "Black Panther: The Revolutionary Art of Emory Douglas" in 2007. "Superflat" was the show that essentially introduced to the United States Takashi Murakami, perhaps the name now most associated with the collapse of art into capital. The show was funded by Cohen, who provided both the space and all operating expenses. See www.artnet.com/Magazine/features/drohojowska-philp/drohojowska-philp1-18-01.asp. Accessed 15 November 2010; and in 2007 Murakami had a full-scale retrospective at MOCA that became notorious for, among other matters, including a Louis Vuitton Boutique.
8. A limit of Deitch's dedication to the contemporary counter-culture was demonstrated early in December 2010. As a gallery owner, he had been a long-time supporter of street art, and in his new position at MOCA he co-organized a survey of graffiti art, "Art in the Streets", commissioning an Italian artist, Blu, to paint a mural on the side of the museum. On discovering that the mural consisted of coffins draped with dollar bills (presumably a comment on

11 – Letter to Paul Arthur (Letter With Endnotes)

recent U.S. imperialist wars), he immediately ordered it painted over. Local graffiti artists responded by projecting protests on the blank wall; see Deborah Vankin, "A Message in their Graffiti", *Los Angeles Times*, 5 January 2011, section D, pp. 1 and 8.

9. For Einstein's philosophy of art collecting, see Barbara Isenberg, "What Makes a Great Collection?", *Time*, 29 March 2007, www.time.com/time/magazine/article/0,9171,1604930,00.html#ixzz15TkDDehX. Accessed 15 November 2010.

10. www.themarshallplan.com/team.htm. Accessed 15 November 2010.

11. Founded in 1975, the Los Angeles Filmforum is the city's "longest-running organization dedicated to weekly screenings of experimental films, documentary, animation and video art"; see www.lafilmforum.org/index/Home.html. Accessed 15 November 2010.

12. See Todd David Schwartz, "Best Films Guaranteed Not To Be Showing At A Theater Near You", www.laweekly.com/2010-10-07/calendar/best-films-guaranteed-not-to-be-showing-at-a-theater-near-you/. Accessed 15 November 2010.

13. An excellent account of the screenings appeared in cinemawithoutborders.com/notebook/2420-looking-back-at-counter-culture-counter-cinema-an-avant-garde-film-festival.html. Accessed 6 February 2011.

14. Another paean to the New York Underground, *The Birth of a Nation*, contains clips of 160 of Mekas's film-maker friends and acquaintances. Finished just after the period when the most vital American cinema was produced by sexual and racial minorities, it implies that the "nation" of film-makers contains no people of color and only one or two women.

15. In his investigation of the relationship between avant-garde art and bourgeois society, Clement Greenberg pointedly concluded: "No culture can develop without a social basis, without a source of stable income. And in the case of the avant-garde, this was provided by an elite among the ruling class of that society from which it assumed itself to be cut off, but to which it has always remained attached by an umbilical cord of gold." See "Avant-Garde and Kitsch", in *Pollock and After: The Critical Debate*, ed. Francis Frascina (New York: Harper and Row, 1985), p. 24.

16. David E. James, *The Most Typical Avant-Garde: History and Geography of Minor Cinemas in Los Angeles* (Berkeley: University of California Press, 2005).

17. They included the Los Angeles County Museum of Art, the Museum of Contemporary Art San Diego, the Orange County Museum of Art, the Santa Monica Museum of Art, Pomona College Museum of Art, the Hammer Museum, the Long Beach Museum of Art, the University of California at Santa Barbara Art Museum – and MOCA.

18. For more information, see the Los Angeles Filmforum website at www.lafilmforum.org/index/Symposium.html.

19. Paul Arthur, "Structural Film: Revisions, New Versions and the Artefact", *Millennium Film Journal* 1, no. 2 (Spring 1978): 5–13, and "Structural Film: Revisions, New Versions and the Artefact. Part Two", *Millennium Film Journal* 4–5 (Summer/Fall 1979): 122–134.

20. For more details, see www.lafilmforum.org/index/Symposium-Presentations-Eisenstein.html. Accessed 15 November 2010. For a review of *Shoppers Market* by Robin Menken, see cinemawithoutborders.com/notebook/2456-best-film-of-2010.html?p=6. Accessed 10 February 2011.

21. Ironically, the same evening, MOCA was celebrating with "The Artist's Museum Happening", a gala envisioned by Doug Aitken that raised more than $3.2 million for the museum and featured red carpet arrivals of Hollywood celebrities. The press release continued, "Many thanks to Doug Aitken for his extraordinary vision which brought together the worlds of art, design, Hollywood, and music in support of MOCA, said MOCA Director Jeffrey Deitch. Doug is one of the most visionary artists working today and we thank him for the once-in-a-lifetime, collective experience, in which the sounds of iconic performers and the visual fabric of works by Los Angeles artists met to present Doug's vision of the West." (www.google.com/search?client=firefox-a&rls=org.mozilla%3AenUS%3Aofficial&channel=s&hl=en&source=hp&biw=1189&bih=1051&q=%E2%80%9D+The+Artist%E2%80%99s+Museum+Happening%2C%E2%80%9D++press+release&btnG=Google+Search. Accessed 20 December 2010.)

22. Together with other material pertaining to avant-garde film in Los Angeles, the papers were in fact published in David E. James and Adam Hyman, eds., *Alternative Projections: Experimental Film In Los Angeles, 1945–1980* (London: John Libbey Publishing; Bloomington: Indiana University Press, 2015).

23. We three collaborated on Michele Pierson, David E. James, and Paul Arthur, eds., *Optic Antics: The Cinema of Ken Jacobs* (New York and London: Oxford University Press, 2011).

24. Letter from Michele Pierson to David E. James, 21 November 2010.

25. These books are respectively, David E. James, ed., *To Free the Cinema: Jonas Mekas and the New York Underground* (Princeton, N.J.: Princeton University Press, 1992); David Curtis, *A History of Artists' Film and Video in Britain* (London: BFI Publishing, 2007); A.L. Rees, *A History of Experimental Film and Video* (London: British Film Institute, 1999); David E. James, ed., *Stan Brakhage: Filmmaker* (Philadelphia: Temple University Press, 2005); and David E. James, *The Most Typical Avant-Garde*.

Chapter Twelve Agricultural Revelation: Land, Labor and Voice in Three Films About Laxton

for Cynthia and David Day

A fair feld ful of folk fond I.
William Langland, *The Vision of Piers Plowman* (c.1370–1390)

At the same time there was an Agricultural Revelation which was caused by the invention of turnips and the discovery that Trespassers would be Prosecuted. This was a Good Thing too, because previously the Land had all been rather common, and it was called the Enclosure movement.
W.C. Sellar and R.J. Yeatman, *1066 And All That*

I.

The Nottinghamshire village of Laxton is unique in that only there has survived the common – or open – field system of farming, with its substantial elements of community participation and control. Developed by Anglo-Saxon tribes who brought it to England after the departure of the Romans in the fifth century AD, it was once prevalent over large areas of the Midlands, Eastern, and Southern England, as well as across Europe. It was based, not on enclosed, individually farmed fields, but on the division of the village land into several, usually three (as in Laxton), very large open fields that were subdivided into many strips. Tenant families inhabiting the nucleated village at the centre of these fields were each assigned a number of the strips scattered across them so as to ensure an equable division of good and bad, close and distant, land. Originally, each strip was of a size that a team of oxen drawing a mould-board plough could till in one day, a task that typically involved the cooperation of several workers. The fields were subject to a strict rotation, one being winter-sown wheat, another spring-sown crops, and the third left fallow. Outside these strips lay the 'sykes', meadowland too damp for grain farming, and undeveloped heaths, both held in common for hay (which was auctioned annually) and for grazing oxen, sheep and cows. The overall system, the farming year, and especially each tenant's observance of the edges of his strips were administered by a Manorial Court Leet, empowered to punish infractions by the imposition of fines.[1]

Everywhere except Laxton, these open fields and the untilled commons have been divided and enclosed by hedgerows into separate fields. More or less continuous since it began in the thirteenth century, the process of enclosure accelerated in Tudor times and again during the Industrial Revolution, especially between 1761 and 1845, the year of the first of the nineteenth century General Inclosure Acts. Over the centuries, enclosure of common land by landlords, other putative agricultural improvements, and diverse forms of privatization, dispossession, and theft have supplanted communal activity and control. The consequent social dislocations have been recognised since at least 1516 when Thomas More's *Utopia* denounced the nobility who "leave no ground for tillage, thei inclose al into pastures", devastating the peasantry: "what can they els doo but steale, and then justly pardy be hanged, or els go about beggyng".[2] The widespread unrest caused by subsequent sixteenth century enclosures culminated in 1549 in Kett's Rebellion in which more than 12,000 peasants occupied Norwich before being routed by an army sent by Edward VI. A contemporary verse dialogue between Jack of the North and Pyrse Plowman and several other peasant speakers expressed support for Jack's defiance:

> For common to the commons again I restore
> Wherever it hath been yet common before.
> If agayne they enclose it never so faste
> Agayne asondre it shall be wraste.[3]

Two hundred and fifty years later William Cobbett inveigled against enclosure in terms similar to More's, arguing that it could not generate higher food productivity but only dispossess the labourers from the common land – what he called the "the blessing and the ornament" of the kingdom – and cram them "into the stinking suburbs of the towns amidst filth of all sorts".[4]

Despite such advocates, the common-field farmers have, like other working-class and peasant communities, generally been unable to record their experience of communal farming and its destruction; if they have been represented at all, it has been by others. So, in his classic *The Making of the English Landscape*, W.G. Hoskins lamented "the entire absence of any poetry associated with the open fields, any lament in literature for their passing … . It was above all a peasant world and the peasant was inarticulate". Consequently, he proposed, "of what it felt like to live in such a world we are, and must for ever remain, entirely ignorant".[5] The one exception, he correctly noted, was John Clare, "the Northamptonshire Peasant Poet", who was in fact for a time employed in planting the hedgerows around the new fields in his home village of Helpston – less than sixty miles from Laxton – during its enclosure, which was completed in 1820 when he was twenty-seven. Clare's eloquence evoked not life within the common-field community but its destruction. In his poem "The Mores" he wrote,

> Inclosure came and trampled on the grave
> Of labours rights and left the poor a slave
> And memorys pride ere want to wealth did bow
> Is both the shadow and the substance now
> The sheep and cows were free to range as then
> Where change might prompt nor felt the bonds of men
> Cows went and came with evening morn and night
> To the wild pasture as their common right.[6]

Laxton escaped the ravages of enclosure by a series of historical accidents.[7] Lexingtune, as it was originally known, prospered before the 1066 conquest, and by the time of the Domesday book, the thirty-five adult males mentioned in it represented a total population of approximately 120. Under the Normans it became the major administrative centre of the Royal Forests of Nottinghamshire and Derbyshire, and its substantial motte and bailey castle, perhaps the finest in the county, welcomed royalty from Henry II to Edward I. A hereditary sequence of the de Everinghams and other important families oversaw the manor, a large church dating to 1190, and an increasingly populous village. But in the mid-fourteenth century the Black Death precipitated an economic decline that eventually obliged the last of the hereditary lords to sell the manor. In 1635 it was bought by a London merchant, Sir William Courten, who commissioned a surveyor, Mark Pierce, to map his possessions and also to produce a "terrier", a record of all the village's tenants and the by-now substantial number of freeholders, together with details of their holdings – in sum, 3,333 parcels of land.[8] Much enclosure has taken place since, and of the 1,894 acres in the open fields divided into 2,280 strips that Pierce mapped, only 483 divided into 164 strips remained in 1988. Around 1730, four separate farms were laid out on the periphery of the village, and complete enclosure was considered for the first time in 1810, and again in the 1840s and early 1900s. However, the village's prosperity, the costs of enclosure, and disagreements among sellers and potential buyers saved it until its uniqueness became a public issue. Since 1906 Laxton has been recognized as a museum; but it is a working museum. The three open fields, their division into strips, the rotation of crops, and the villagers' jurisdiction over themselves by means of the Court Leet still function as a living example of an otherwise lost form of collective social organization. A combination of academic, journalistic, and popular interest has supported efforts to preserve it, and in several instances cinema has made some contribution.

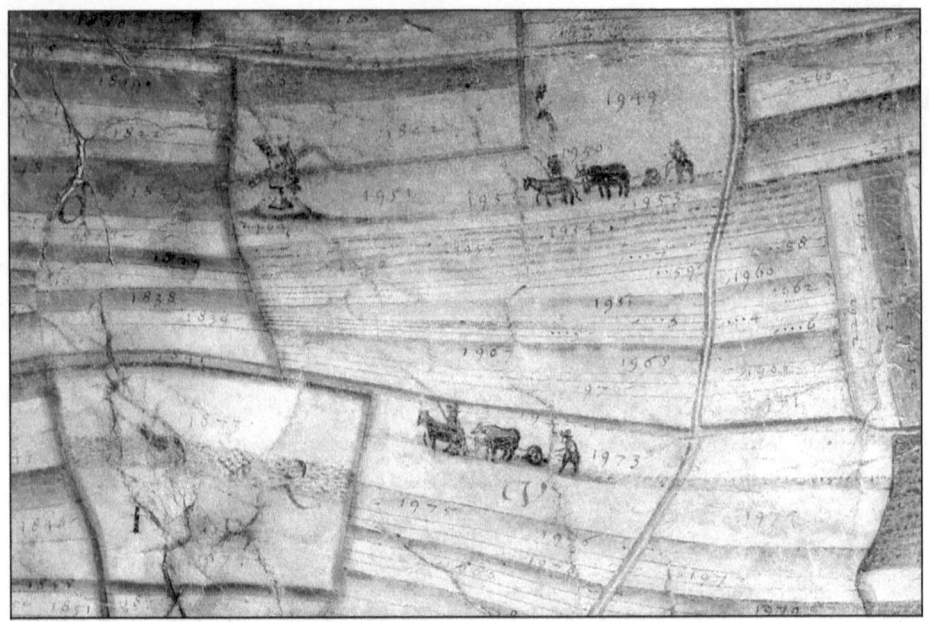

Figure 1. Ploughing at Laxton in the early seventeenth century; illustration from Mark Pierce's map (1635).

In addition to numerous segments in various newsreels and television shows, three films have been made for general distribution: *Mediaeval Village* (1935), *Laxton* (1975), and *Heritage for Sale* (1981). Since all were made to document and preserve a culture fundamentally unchanged for more than a thousand years, they are inevitably broadly similar, addressing the history of the village, its unique agricultural system, including the farmers' work and the operations of the Court Leet that regulate it, and evaluating its anomalous survival. All are between twenty and twenty-five minutes long, and all are constructed around the commentary of an omniscient narrator.[9] However, the respective historical moments of their composition, the diverse modes of cinematic production employed, and their producers' specific interests in the village together produce different mobilizations of their shared commitments. Overall, they display elements of the progressive democratization that was one component of twentieth-century mass media.

Like other visual representations of Laxton's history, these films benefited from the written historical legacy, but especially from Pierce's map. Drawn on sheepskin with a scale of eight inches to the mile, it showed every building in the village and the location of every strip in the fields. It also contained simple drawings of the farmers working at their routine tasks, their livestock, and hunting and hawking by the ruling classes, similar to the illustrations of peasant life two centuries earlier in the nearby Lincolnshire village of Irnham that decorated the

Luttrell Psalter.¹⁰ The conjunction on Pierce's map of a quasi-aerial view of the village and its vignettes of peasant life anticipates two of the signal motifs of the films: on the one-hand, extended views from the air that reveal the topography of the village and its surrounding landscape, showing both the remaining open fields and the hedgerow patterns of those parts that have been enclosed; and on the other, cameos of the villagers and their work. Since the social and topographic survivals intersect around the issue of agricultural labour, the figure of the ploughman and the activities that arable farming entailed – ploughing, sowing, and harvesting – have been the crucial motifs in the representations of Laxton's significance.

II

Released in 1935, exactly three hundred years after Pierce's map, the first was a 35 mm black-and-white educational documentary, *Mediaeval Village*. Made by the Gaumont-British Instructional production company, it was directed by J.B. Holmes, photographed by Frank Bundy and Frank Goodliffe, and written by H.L. Beales and R.S. Lambert, the last being two solidly left populist authors who had recently collaborated on the book, *Memoirs of the Unemployed*.¹¹

Accompanying a map of Nottinghamshire and surrounding areas illustrated with simple drawings, the voice-over announces that the people of the central part of England have always been known for their "independence of character", adducing as examples the pilgrim fathers of nearby Scrooby and Robin Hood, who "preferred to become an outlaw in Sherwood Forest rather than submit to the tyranny of the nobles". Signalling Laxton's significance between these by a drawing of a peasant ploughman, the narrator turns to the farmers who have "clung stubbornly to the customs and methods that their forebears used centuries before Robin Hood … [and] resisted the tides of economic change that have swept away others less stubborn". Shots of the earthworks that remain from the castle, now dotted with luxuriantly foliaged trees, are followed by a pan from its mound to West (Top) Field.

Illustrating his account with a photograph of a castle keep superimposed over a present-day shot of its location, the narrator sketches the village's history, moving to the church and the tombs of the de Everingham family, Lords of the Manor in the period of Laxton's importance, and noting a later aristocratic family, the de Rooses, whose descendants, the Roses, are now "simple village people". A copy of Pierce's map is introduced and corresponding aerial shots show the unchanged plan of the village's houses. So far, the film's structure has been a conceptual zoom-in, from Laxton's ancient history marked by the remnants of its major institutions – the castle, the manor house and the church – then descending with

Figure 2. *Mediaeval Village*: aerial view of Laxton; ploughing with moldboard plough; sowing and harrowing; pegging the strips; Mrs. Clark feeding her chickens.

the fortunes of the de Rooses to contemporary farmers. Finally, one such farmer is shown watering his cattle in the stockyard in front of New Bar Farm, opening the way to the central topic, the farmers' activities in the open fields. The voice-over describes the size and location of the fields, and their essential properties: their division into scattered strips, the rotation of crops, the fallow field, the access roads, and the untilled sykes of meadow among them. His account is illustrated with both contemporary photography and vignettes from Pierce's map, documenting the system and its continuity over the centuries.

12 Agricultural Revelation: Land, Labor and Voice in Three Films About Laxton

The key central sequence depicts arable farming. A series of beautiful low-angle shots show the "fair feld ful of folk": three farmers on adjacent strips, each managing his plough behind a two-horse team, silhouetted against the sky. Three weeks after ploughing is done, the farmers again walk through the fields, scattering the grain with the "old fashioned two-handed broadcast", immediately followed by horse-drawn harrows. Further illustrated by a drawing of a virtually identical scene on Pierce's map, labour and land are idyllically united. Their work in place, the farmers proceed to their complementary responsibility, their obligation to administer the system by the proceedings of the Court Leet and its fines for ploughing over strip boundaries. Identically dressed in white shirts with black waistcoats and trousers that the-black-and-white photography integrates into the landscape, the men of the jury tour the fields and hammer in wooden stakes to mark the correct boundaries, as the narrator notes, "juries have been pegging out Laxton fields for centuries and each new juror inherits the traditional knowledge of his predecessors".

Within this enduring system, however, two things have changed. Until recently a large unenclosed area to the northeast known as "the common" was used for grazing beasts. However, the motorists who now drive along the road through it often neglect to close the gates on its borders, and stray cattle have so overwhelmed the village pinfold that free grazing is now confined to the open fields themselves. The mill pictured on Pierce's map has fallen down and, since it is no longer integral to the village economy, it has not been rebuilt. Otherwise the past continues into the present. Briefly recalling the de Everinghams, now silent in their tombs, *Mediaeval Village* concludes with cameos of two villagers, for the first time individualizing and naming them, though not giving them voices of their own: Mr. Morton, the wheelwright, and Mrs. Clark, dispersing wheat to her chickens with a gesture reminiscent of the earlier shots of sowing. Shots of the harvest, the horses drawing the mowers, and the sheaves of freshly-cut wheat stooked to dry in the clear summer sky bring the film and its argument to a close: "a living example of English life going back through the ages to days so remote that they are lost in antiquity".

III.

No significant new enclosure had taken place by the time of the second film, but crucial developments in administration, farming, and historiography had impacted Laxton: the estate had been sold; mechanization had replaced the oxen and horse teams used for a millennium to till the land; and three editions of the first major study of the village, C.S. and C.S. Orwin's *The Open Fields* (1954) had been published.

The Open Fields was immediately recognized as a classic of agricultural writing. Its two parts respectively reconstructed the method by which open field villages in general had been created out of the prehistoric woodland and surveyed the history of the one such remaining village. Some of the book's arguments, especially that the system's communitarian elements resulted from economic necessity rather than ethical principle, were controversial; but as a whole it became the seminal reference for all subsequent writing on Laxton. Its central demonstration that the nature of mould-board ploughing generated the strip-structure and the communal farming practices and so justified the economic and social value of the system as a whole contradicted and rebuked the several centuries of agricultural writing that had presented enclosure as synonymous with improvement.[12] For the Orwins, Laxton was not an anachronistic, obsolete survival, only sustained as *Mediaeval Village* had proposed by the stubbornness of the farmers, but rather the model of a utopian social order:

> Laxton has retained something which has been lost everywhere else in the process of the inclosure of the Open Fields. Its people control their own affairs in the daily incidents of their work, by a scheme of voluntary administration maintained by public opinion without recourse to the law of the land and without the expenditure of a single penny ... [All disputes] are settled here by the community at its own court.[13]

Whether or not the nature of Laxton as an independent, semi-autonomous work unit was recognized, control of the village was still in the hands of the people. After World War II, economic hardship obliged Earl Manvers to sell both the open field farms that his family had owned continuously since Stuart times and the individual farms on the village's periphery. On 28 February 1952, after two years of negotiations, the Ministry of Agriculture acquired 1,761 acres and the lordship of the manor.[14] The next film reflected these developments.

Though in colour rather than black-and-white and in 16 rather than 35 mm, *Laxton* (1975) is structurally similarly to *Mediaeval Village*.[15] It too is an illustrated lecture, but this time, the voice-over was not by God, but rather by one of the nation's most distinguished Marxist labour historians, one born moreover in a Lincolnshire village only twenty miles from Laxton: John Saville, Professor of Economic and Social History at Hull University, a member of the Communist Party Historians' Group, and one of the editors of the remarkable ten-volume *Dictionary of Labour Biography* that began publication in 1972.

Saville begins by announcing the village's uniqueness: "though remnants of the open- field system survive elsewhere, Laxton is the only common field village still in existence where cultivation of the open fields is inseparably bound up with the life of farmers who work them". Recapitulating the earlier film's historical survey but at a more sophisticated academic level, he first locates the village on the edge of Sherwood forest, again invoking Robin Hood, and then turns to the remains of thirteenth century monuments, the castle and its fall into disuse, the manor house and the church. An aerial survey together with Pierce's map documents the survival of the ancient village structure and its buildings, and accounts of the open field system are followed by the historical evolution of the agricultural methods that "changed remarkably little down the years before the Second World War": the creation of the four peripheral farms, the piecemeal enclosures in the 1860s and again in 1904-07 that reduced the fields from 847 to 534 acres, and the 1,162 strips to 240, and finally the 1952 transfer of the manor to the Ministry of Agriculture, when "The Nation in effect bought Laxton". Along with the much superior historical detail, several elements display Saville's Marxist assimilation of the Orwins' work, especially their account of the determination of the entire system by the mould-board plough and a more detailed account of the Court Leet that they celebrated.

Using simple animations, the film explains how the operation of the plough produced the ridge and furrows that shaped the strip and its drainage patterns, and the collaboration among the peasants in the use of the oxen that pulled it. Again referencing Pierce's illustrations, Saville provides footage of a farmer operating the plough with a two-horse team. But while in *Mediaeval Village* the documentation was of current practice, here it is of a re-enactment, staged specifically for the film by one of the few farmers who retain the old skills. By the late-1950s, tractors, combine harvesters, and other mechanization had made horse-drawn tillage obsolete and, with that the determining agricultural and social centrality of the mould-board plough disappeared. Though Saville does not show a modern, tractor-pulled plough with the multiple shares that would soon eradicate the ancient ridge and furrows and replace the communitarian if not communal tillage, he does show one of the new harvesters that 'combine' in a single operation the previously discrete activities of mowing, stooking-up, transporting the wheat back to the farms, and thrashing.

Though the practices of Laxton farmers had been transformed, the essential component of the Orwins' conception of the village's social significance remains: the Court Leet. Shifting his focus to the present, Saville inquires into "the working life of the people of Laxton in this mediaeval survival", and his answers come via the present instance of the de Roos lineage whose descent *Mediaeval Village* had traced: bailiff Edmund Rose. Saville may regularly speak for or interrupt him, but in both voice-over and *vérité* footage Rose dominates the remainder of the film. The open-field peasant has at last become articulate and able to represent himself.

Introduced driving his incongruous red car into Bottom (South) Field, Rose

Figure 3. *Laxton*: combine harvester; Edmund Rose, Bailiff; swearing in the jury; Jury Day.

appropriates Pierce and Saville's authority, speaking of his own history in the village and describing the jury's work and the Court Leet where the famers gather to evaluate its findings. The jurors are seen climbing aboard the tractor and trailer – "in the old days this used to be the horse and cart", Rose announces, "but horses and carts are in short supply these days". Together, they investigate the strips, insert new boundary stakes where necessary and return to the Dovecote Inn for lunch. A week later, still in *vérité* sync-sound footage, the farmers again assemble to debate the fines and the next year's twelve jurors kiss the bible as they are sworn in.

The film continues with other issues, especially recent changes in the village administration and discussion of the reason for Laxton's survival, until both Saville and Rose offer their final conclusions on its social significance. Saville reaffirms the Owins' celebration of "the unique survival of this self-governing village community" and "the working farmers themselves" who maintain the Court Leet. And Rose announces the farmers' commitment to its continuation: "This is done with the good will of the tenants, and I feel the majority of the tenants of the Laxton Estate will continue to farm according to the open fields' rules. The majority of us are Laxton born and bred. And the last thing we should like to see would be the disappearing of the open fields". But four years later, the nation that had bought Laxton wanted to sell it.

12 Agricultural Revelation: Land, Labor and Voice in Three Films About Laxton

In November 1979, the tenants gathered for their annual rent dinner, expecting as usual to meet their Lord of the Manor, the Minister of Agriculture. Instead Lord Ferrers, recently appointed as Minister of State when the Conservatives were returned to power under Margaret Thatcher, greeted them with the announcement that the estate was to be sold. There is no reason to suppose that Thatcher, though born only thirty miles away, had any interest in local history and certainly not in the idea of community that the village represented. Compared with her administration's shredding of fundamental national assets, the privatization of Laxton might have been a distinctly minor affair, overlooked amidst the epochal depredations; but a chorus of public protests joined with villagers and academics to bruit in local and national media the need to save the open fields.[16] In this context public television took up the cause, and did so via a singularly appropriate farmer-broadcaster.

IV

Written and presented by David Richardson, *Heritage for Sale* was made by Anglia Television, since 1959 the ITV franchise holder for the East of England, and broadcast on 12 February 1981 as part of its 'About Britain' series.[17] In 1960 at sixteen, Richardson had left school to work his own farm and, having gained some reputation as a member of Norfolk Young Farmers Club, he was recruited to be a writer and presenter for a farming section on a new magazine programme, *About Anglia*. In the intervening twenty years, alongside his work as a farmer, he had turned this opportunity into a media career as a presenter for ITV and the BBC, and a journalist for the *Financial Times*, *Farmers Weekly*, and other national publications that gained him a reputation for his understanding of agricultural issues. His programme again begins with an aerial view of the village, over which he himself announces the current affair prompting it:

> The only surviving system of open field farming administered by a mediaeval manorial court is up for sale. Its owner since 1952, the British Government, and its Lord of the Manor, Ministry of Agriculture, say it's a necessary economy. But historians regard the sale as a major disaster, which could destroy a living working museum, and the tenants who voluntarily farm the strips of land around this village of Laxton in Nottinghamshire fear a new owner might amalgamate their holdings into bigger units and that they would lose their livelihood.

Richardson's first witness to the government's treachery are those very tenants, interviewed on camera, identified by name in subtitles, and speaking in their own voices: Edmund Rose again argues that "we kept our part of the bargain" and "we feel let down by the ministry offering it for sale", and Bill and Robert Haigh, farmers both father and son, add, "we are very disappointed, very shocked as well. The original plan was to preserve it for posterity". Richardson moves to Oxford

University, where Joan Thirsk, Reader in Economic History and a foremost agricultural historian (who had written the preface to the 1967 edition of the Orwins' *The Open Fields*), supports them, ironically complaining, "Surely we're not so poor that we have to sell a precious piece of our historical heritage for a few million pounds. To me it's like dismantling Stonehenge for the sake of the building material".

To generate debate and justify his programme, Richardson questions whether this pessimism is exaggerated: "Are we really in danger of losing this last example of manorial government", one that, he asserts (without mentioning the Orwins' vision of its political significance), is "like a tiny self-governing republic raising and spending its own taxes and keeping the peace". To display this republic in operation, Edmund Rose again takes center stage; he is seen calling the Court Leet to order and swearing in the jurors, each individualized as he kisses the Bible. Interiors of the church show the de Everinghams' tombs and a plaque that lists the succession of the lords of the manor down to its acquisition by the Ministry of Agriculture, "supposed to be in perpetuity", whose representative, Peter Evans, begins the account of the agricultural history.

Here the film reverts to the structure of the previous educational documentaries: shots of the village and an aerial view of the fields followed by a map that illustrates their diminishment and accounts of the rotation of crops, culminating with a collage of shots of the ploughmen from *Mediaeval Village*, preserved in the nostalgic beauty of 35 mm celluloid. But while in 1935 these images documented a current reality, reproduced nearly fifty years later both the agricultural practice and the medium of its depiction have become archaic. And Richardson's recognition that "the old film shows that there have been more changes since the 1930s than in the previous thousand years" is illustrated by an abrupt cut from the ploughmen filmed in black and white to Edmund Rose on his red tractor moving the huge circular straw bales that the combine harvester produces, as in voice-over he asserts: "I along with practically all the tenants are quite happy to farm along the old fashioned lines, given the good-will of the tenant and landlord. It's far from an economic way of farming – but it's the Laxton way of life". The Haighs, one seen harvesting with a red combine and the other spreading manure with the red tractor, appear again and concur with his emphasis on the economic insecurity of their lives; and a sequence with Colin Cree, the only farmer to reintroduce sheep after a 1967 outbreak of foot and mouth disease, shows him and his daughter feeding their flock.

Having documented Laxton and given voice to its farmers – but also recognizing the irony of the "struggle to see modern machines working their way across a mediaeval landscape" and admitting that this farming "couldn't carry on without an element of paternalism" – the film returns to its focus on the present crisis. At the 1980 Harvest Thanksgiving Dinner, a year after the proposed sale had been announced, Richardson somewhat aggressively interviews the ill-favoured Jerry Wiggin, Parliamentary Secretary to the Agriculture Ministry, who explains the government's decision as economic exigency: "Above all we need the money".[18] His accent revealing the huge class and regional gulf separating him from the tenants, Wiggin protests that every effort will be made "to choose the right purchaser who will guarantee to sustain the system". His manifestly unconvincing claims are immediately swept aside by brilliant reiterations of the previous documentaries' motifs: jury day and the sale of the commons grass that display the villagers' self-governance. In group shots of them in the fields and in close ups in the public-house discussions, the farmers are themselves made convincingly present and real, with their facial expressions, the grain and accent of their voices, and their rustic, unfashionable clothing echoing the topography, colours, and textures of the landscape.

With this dramatic escalation of the living reality of the motifs of Pierce's map, academic expertise ratifies its continuing significance. In the Bodleian library in Oxford, Joan Thirsk shows us, not a copy of it, but the nine stitched rectangles of sheepskin of the original two-and-a-half by two-foot map itself. The camera pans over its colours, all the more exquisite for their fading, and picks out the drawings of animals, trees, and workers, the castle and the church and, of course, the strips themselves, each marked to identify their tenants, much as the film has itself identified their descendants. Originally made for a new lord of the manor this, the first visual representation of Laxton, has become a major instrument in the defence of the tenants, a national treasure like the village itself. Although Thirsk's reference to it authorizes her elegant re-affirmation of the importance of "the only surviving example of common field farming we have in this country", she also admits that its survival is contingent on the famers' pride and determination to preserve it. A return to William Haigh provides the necessary reassurance: "We are proud of it. We've got something that the Americans would give their back teeth for". Accompanying the final aerial shots of the village street, the houses that edge it and beyond them the expanses of green and brown fields, Richardson asks the summary question: "The open fields and the ancient customs by which they are governed are as important to Britain as any national monuments. Once lost, they could never be replaced. Should our heritage really be up for sale?" When his programme was broadcast, the question was still moot.

In *Mediaeval Village* and *Laxton*, the combination of the open-field system's survival and the educational documentary format allowed their respective omniscient narrators to command history and to adduce the present-day farmers as witnesses. *Heritage for Sale*'s situation was contrary in both respects. At the time, when the government was systematically privatizing the nation's assets, and replacing cooperation with competition and exploitation in social relations, any parallel certainty about Laxton's future was not available to Richardson. His inconclusiveness corresponded with the obligation of privatized television to present both sides of any argument, especially the government's. But though Richardson did allow the government's spokesman his moment, his film overwhelmingly supports his own contention that "Laxton and its tenants are surely too important to be subjected to such risk". The serendipity that allowed him, accomplished as both a farmer and a communicator, to write and present this programme created a televisual discursive regime in which subject and object, the presenter and his concerns were unprecedentedly linked. Like open-field farming, public affairs broadcast television was ideally a community cultural practice, but one that ironically has itself been made increasingly subject to neoliberal market forces. Together with Richardson's own experience as a farmer and a broadcaster, his production team of two researchers, three cameramen, and three sound recordists supplied his authority; and even if the structural role of his voice ultimately enclosed those of the farmers, his knowledge and sympathy, and his incorporation of live interviews and other demotic *cinéma vérité* techniques allowed the peasants to transcend their socially-constructed inarticulateness and speak for themselves. No longer may we be ignorant of "what it felt like to live in such a world".[19]

Richardson's programme may well have played a role in the survival of this signal heritage of communal agricultural self-governance. Unable to find a buyer for Laxton, in 1981 the Ministry of Agriculture relinquished it to the Crown Estate, the British monarchy's "public estate", distinct from both the government's and its own holdings, whose portfolio is managed by a public body headed by the Crown Estate Commissioners. Since then the Crown Estate Commissioners have been the Lords of the Manor and, according to a notice in the Laxton Visitor Centre, they "are committed to continuing this unique example of our heritage". Given the present U.K. government's apocalyptic combination of incompetence and neoliberal avarice, how long they will be able to do so is now in doubt. The village faces a crisis more severe than those traced in the three films, one that causes many tenant farmers again to fear for the survival of the open fields.

While one tenanted farm still belongs to the family that purchased the manor in Stuart times, the Crown Estate owns the other fourteen farms in Laxton with strips in the open fields. Forming the Court Leet, the fourteen farmers are now on average aged sixty-four, with three of them over eighty.[20] Only six of them work their own farms, and the remainder effectively sub-let their land to other farmers, six of them living in Laxton and two in neighbouring villages. The consolidation gives these farmers a financial viability impossible today for those with only a hundred acres; but it also necessitates the depletion of communal involvement, especially in maintaining a quorum for the Court Leet. Even with the intrinsic subsidy of their own arduous labour, the farmers depend on the Crown Estate that keeps rents below market value, at present only £6,000 a year for both the house and land. They are additionally assisted by support from the U.K. government and European funds that amount in total to around £220,000 per annum. Some of this money is for stewardship of the land and includes maintenance of the fallow field that supports birds and other wildlife. This support is unlikely to continue at the present level when Britain leaves the E.U.

V.

At the time of writing, while Brexit looms, negotiations between the villagers and the Crown Trust are struggling to resolve the incompatibility between the latter's commitment to maintaining the system and its obligation to maximise financial returns to the U.K. Treasury. As the spirits of the men and women who for a millennium and a half sustained a self-governing agricultural and ecological community fade into the evening mists over the Top Field streams and sykes, the future of Laxton is again in crisis.

Notes

1. On the open fields generally and Laxton specifically, see C.S. and C.S. Orwin, *The Open Fields*, 3rd edition with preface by Joan Thirsk (Oxford: The Clarendon Press, 1967). See also J.D. Chambers, *Laxton: The Last English Open Field Village* (London: H.M. Stationary Office, 1964); W.E. Tate, *The English Village Community and the Enclosure Movement* (London: Victor Gollancz, 1967); and J.V. Beckett, *A History of Laxton: England's Last Open-Field Village* (Oxford: Basil Blackwell, 1989). A very useful introduction to enclosures, Simon Fairlie's "A Short History of Enclosure in Britain" (2009), is available online: http://www.thelandmagazine.org.uk/articles/short-history-enclosure-britain. Nottingham University maintains a collection of research materials about Laxton: https://www.nottingham.ac.uk/manuscriptsandspecialcollections/learning/laxton/introduction.aspx. Though it does not mention Laxton, Ian Waites's *Common Land in English Painting, 1700–1850* (Woodbridge, Suffolk: Boydell Press. 2012) is an invaluable survey of eighteenth and nineteenth century representations of the commons and their enclosure.

2. Thomas More, *Utopia*, first English ed., trans. R. Robinson (London, 1551), quoted in Tate, *English Village Community*, p. 64.

3. Quoted in Charles Henry Cooper, ed., *Annals of Cambridge* (Cambridge: Warwick and Co., 1843), vol. 2, p. 42.

4. Quoted in John M. and James P. Cobbett, eds., *Selections from Cobbett's Political Works* (London: Anne Cobbett, 1883), vol. 4, pp. 255–263. The *Political Register* of 28 July 1813 was comprised entirely of arguments against the pending General Inclosure Bill. Karl Marx drew on More, Cobbett, and of course many others in summarily surveying the role of enclosures, the theft of the common land, and the usurpation of the rights of free peasant proprietors in creating the pre-conditions for the development of industrial capitalism; see Marx, *Capital*, English trans. S. Moore and E.B. Aveling (London: S. Sonnenschein, Lowrey, 1887), vol. 1, ch. 27, "Expropriation of the Agricultural Population from the Land".

5. W.G. Hoskins, *The Making of the English Landscape* (London: Hodder and Stoughton, 1977), p. 194. Unacknow-

ledged by Hoskins is a largely forgotten late medieval tradition of what James M. Dean has termed "Plowman Writings" which, given the priority of the ploughman in medieval agriculture, inevitably reference the common fields; see James M. Dean, ed., *Medieval English Political Writings* (Kalamazoo, Mich.: Medieval Institute Publications, 1966). Jack of the North's verse dialogue ("see note 3 above") is a late contribution to this tradition, with Edmund Spenser's *The Faerie Queene* (1590–1596) its culmination.

6. John Clare, *Major Works*, ed. Eric Robinson and David Powell (Oxford: Oxford University Press, 2004), p. 168. Other poems in which Clare denounced enclosure as a disaster for both the social and natural worlds include "To a Fallen Elm" and "Remembrances".

7. Beckett summarily addresses this question in the Epilogue to *History of Laxton*; see esp. pp. 313–320.

8. Pierce's map may be downloaded from:
http://bibliodyssey.blogspot.co.uk/2007/12/laxton-open-field-survey-map.html. Parts of it are also available to view at: http://digital.bodleian.ox.ac.uk/. Accessed 2 April 2017. In 1939, two members of the University of Nottingham color-coded the strips to indicate their tenants on the six-inches-to-the-mile 1921 Ordnance Survey map of Laxton; it may be seen at: http://www.nottingham.ac.uk/"anuscriptsandspecialcollections/exhibitions/online/laxton/mapoflaxtonfarmsc1939.aspx. Accessed 2 April 2017.

9. A further film, *Laxton: England's Last Open-Field Village* (Nottingham University Engineering Faculty Workshop, 1988) may be seen at the Laxton Visitor Center. Written and directed by J.V. Beckett, Laxton's foremost historian, it follows the basic structure of the other films, but it is distinguished by rich details of land management that Beckett derived from the archives of the Earls Manvers (Lords of the Manor 1640–1952), including the enclosures in the early twentieth century.

10. *The Luttrell Psalter Film* (Nick Loven, 2010) dramatized these illustrations: it includes shots of Laxton's Top Field.

11. H.L. Beales and R.S. Lambert, *Memoirs of the Unemployed* (London: Victor Gollancz, 1934). The first editor of *The Listener*, Lambert was a successful writer and broadcaster who worked for the BBC in the 1930s. Beales had published historical accounts of the Industrial Revolution (1928) and early English Socialists (1933). Holmes made documentaries for Gaumont and other companies, notably *The Mine* (1936), and continued with socially responsible projects after the war. Considered an historical educational film, *Mediaeval Village* received favorable reviews in two of the most popular film journals of the time, *Sight and Sound* and *Monthly Film Bulletin*: respectively, H.L. Beales and R.S. Lambert, "Living History", *Sight and Sound* 5, no. 18 (Summer 1936): 18–20, and History Committee, "Mediaeval Village", *Monthly Film Bulletin* 4, no. 38 (February 1937): 22–23. Both emphasized that the continuation of the ancient system into the present obviated the need for historical reconstruction or reenactment and while praising the film, focused on the village itself and the agricultural system it maintained. The film is available on BFI Player: http://player.bfi.org.uk/britain-on-film/map/#/53.19964400/-0.7436283162/11/Laxton//. Accessed 7 April 2017.

12. "The evolution of the Open Fields was the natural and inevitable consequence of the common experience and the common technique of communities who had settled down to till the soil with the mould-board plough" (Orwin, *Open Fields*, p. 170).

13. Orwin, *Open Fields*, p. 173.

14. Beckett, *History of Laxton*, p. 309.

15. It too is available online through BFI Player: http://player.bfi.org.uk/britain-on-film/map/#/53.19964400/-0.7436283162/11/Laxton//. Accessed 7 April 2017.

16. See, for example, R.I. Muir, "Ploughing Up History", *Observer Magazine*, 18 June 1980, 22–25.

17. The programme is available at the East Anglian Film Archive in Norwich. Richardson was a Fellow of the Royal Agricultural Societies (FRAgS) and the recipient of an award from the Royal Norfolk Agricultural Association for promoting public understanding of farming and the countryside. His autobiography, *In at the Deep End* (Cromer: Poppyland Publishing, 2016), does not mention the television program. Since then, further short pieces on Laxton have appeared on television, most recently on the BBC's *Countryfile* (14 June 2015). It featured Edmund Rose's nephew, Stuart Rose, explaining the village as his uncle had done in previous documentaries. In 2004, Laxton's Jury day and Court Leet were featured in the first episode of the BBC's *Terry Jones' Medieval Lives* that argued that mediaeval peasants had a considerable degree of autonomy: https://www.youtube.com/watch?v=Yg3YDN5gTX0. Accessed 8 April 2017.

18. Dubbed "Junket Jerry" by the satirical magazine, *Private Eye*, Wiggin was a far-right Conservative MP who became embroiled in a "cash for amendments" scandal in 1995 when it was revealed that he had tabled an amendment to a motion in which he had a financial interest in the name of – but without the knowledge of – a fellow MP.

19. Since 2008, past and present members of the village have organized a history group to produce their own account of Laxton: see http://www.laxtonhistorygroup.org.uk/about_us.htm. Accessed 8 April 2017.

20. Information on Laxton's present situation was supplied in conversations with several villagers, especially Mr. Mike Jackson, himself a tenant farmer.

Index

7 Dudley Cinema 163

A
Adada (Im Kwon-taek, 1988) 10, 20, 31, 33, 36
Adorno, Theodor 99, 100, 175
Ahmad, Aijaz 47, 49, 66
Aiiieeeee! An Anthology of Asian-American Writers (eds., Frank Chin, Jeffery Paul Chan, Lawson Fusao Inada, and Shawn Wong, 1974) 72, 74
Airshaft (Ken Jacobs, 1964) 176
Alexander, Thomas Kent 159
"Alternative Projections: Experimental Film in Los Angeles, 1945–1980" 224-27
Amateur filmmaking 78, 101, 106, 112-13, 162, 169, 171, 192
"Amateur Versus Professional" (Maya Deren, 1959) 112-13
Anger, Kenneth 113-14, 126, 159, 164, 181, 204-06, 214
Anker, Steve 164
Arledge, Sara Kathryn 129, 212, 215, 226
Arthur, Paul 217, 226

B
Baby Maker, The (James Bridges, 1970) 140-42, 149-50
Baldessari, John 167, 221
Ballet mécanique (Fernand Léger, Dudley Murphy, and Man Ray, 1924) 113
Banham, Reyner 107, 114-15, 125
Baudrillard, Jean 107, 169
Be-In (Jerry Abrams, 1967) 223
Biggers, Earl Derr 72
Billboard Wars 171
Black Dice 168

Blade Runner (Ridley Scott, 1982) 124, 170
Blake, William ix, 91, 102
Blaxploitation 117
Bless Their Little Hearts (Billy Woodberry, 1983) 119
Brakhage, Stan 113, 122, 167, 181, 188, 192, 203, 224, 228
Bridges-Go-Round (Shirley Clarke,1958) 195
Brooklyn Bridge 177, 180, 192-98
Buchanan, Nancy 172
Buddhism 11-27, 82
Burkhardt, Rudy 195-96
Burnett, Charles 75, 114-20

C
Caldwell, Ben 119
Cannon, Terry 225, 226
Capote, Truman 215
Center for Visual Music (CVM) 166
Chihwaseon (Im Kwon-taek, 2002) 31, 34, 38-40, 54
Chilsu and Mansu (Park Kwang-su, 1988) 55-58
Chin, Frank 69, 73, 80, 81
Chinatown (Roman Polanski, 1974) 109
Chong Il-song 33
Chop Off (M.M. Serra, 2009) 222
Chu, Louis 72
Ch'unhyang (Im Kwon-taek, 2000) 21, 33, 34-37
Ciao! Manhattan (John Palmer and David Weisman, 1972) 214
Cinefamily 173, 165-66
Cinematheque 108 163
Cinematheque 16 131, 137-38
Cinespia Cemetery Screenings 170

Clare, John 232-33
Clark, Larry 119
Carke, Shirley 195
Class ix, 2, 8, 10-11, 20, 27, 33, 39, 57, 62, 69, 74, 76-77, 81, 100-01, 105-06, 116, 148-50, 232
Clavilux (Thomas Wilfred) 129
Clay Walls (Kim Ronyoung, 1987) 75
Cobbett, William 232
Cohen, Charles S. 220-22, 227
Come, Come, Come Upward (Im Kwon-taek, 1989) 13, 22-27, 43
common field system of farming 231-245
Conditions in Los Angeles (Los Angeles Workers Film and Photo League, 1934) 106
Country of Dreams and Dust (Russell Leong, 1993) 69, 81-84
Creative Film Associates 114
Cultural Studies ix, 100-101
Cumberland Mountain Film Company 139, 143
Curtis, David 228
Cybernetik 5.3 (John Stehura, 1965) 133, 142

D
Dash, Julie 119
Debord, Guy 99
Deitch, Jeffrey 220-22
Deren, Maya 113, 180, 203, 222
Diary of Anne Frank, The (Anne Frank, 1947) 181-83, 190-91
Diary of Anne Frank, The (George Stevens, 1959) 182-83
"Diary of Madman" (Lu Xun, 1918) 47
Direct Cinema 210

E
Eat a Bowl of Tea (Louis Chu, 1961) 72
Echo Park Film Center (EPFC) 156, 162, 168

Eisenstein, Ken 225
Elwes, Catherine 218
Ethno-Communications Program (UCLA) 75, 118, 147
Expanded Cinema 129, 137, 145-47

F
Festival (Im Kwon-taek, 1996) 5, 10
Filmforum 114, 161-62, 165, 221, 223-26
Fischinger, Oskar 129, 130, 166, 168
Fisher, Morgan 223
Floating World, The (Cynthia Kadohata, 1989) 83
Fly High, Run Far (Im Kwon-taek, 1991) 1
Francis, Sam 136, 139-40
Frank, Anne 178, 181-184, 190-92
Friedman, Roberta 225

G
Genealogy, The (Im Kwon-taek, 1978) 6-8, 10, 31
geo-cinematic hermeneutic 105, 111-15
Gerima, Haille 119
Gershfield, Burton 130, 131, 133, 138
Good Men, Good Women (Hou Hsiao Hsien, 1995) 4, 52, 60-65
Graduate, The (Mike Nichols, 1967) 108
Greene, Jon 131, 135-36, 140
Groupe Dziga Vertov 49
Gunga Din Highway (Frank Chin, 1994) 69, 73

H
Hagedorn, Jessica 69
Ham, Bill 131
Hamersveld, John Van 130, 133
Hamlyn, Nicky 218, 228
Han Yong-un 1
Han 7-14, 23, 33
Hangul 32, 45
Hanji (Im Kwon-taek, 2011) 29, 39-43

Hardy, Scott   131, 135
Hartshorn, Helena   131
Heat (Paul Morrissey,1972)   203
Heide, Robert   205
Heritage for Sale (David Richardson,
    1981)   241-44
hipster   159, 219
His Wife's Lover (Sidney M.
    Goldin, 1931)   178
Hock, Louis   170
Hog Farm   131
Hollywood (corporate entertainment
    industry)   4, 40, 55, 71, 73,
                         94-99, 101, 106-11,
                         119, 124-25, 140,
                         149-51, 162, 164,
                         203, 205, 212, 217
Holmes, J.B.   235
Home is Where the Heart Is (Yun
    Yong-gyu, 1948)   1
Hopper, Dennis   143, 148, 219
Hoskins, W.G.   232
Hou Hsiao Hsien   4, 5, 52, 60-66, 165
Hwang, David Henry   73
Hyman, Adam   162, 221, 224, 227

I

Im Kwon-taek   1-30, 31-46
immigration into Los Angeles   71, 110, 116
In the Heart of the Valley of Love
    (Cynthia Kadohata, 1992)   75
*Invocation L.A.: Urban Multicultural
    Poetry* (eds., Michèlle T. Clinton,
    Sesshu Foster, Naomi
    Quiñonez, 1989)   81
iotaCenter   166

J

Jabès, Edmond   192
Jacobs, Flo   178, 180-81, 191
Jacobs, Ken   178-98, 220-22
Jameson, Fredric   47-48, 170
Janss, Larry   140
Joy Luck Club, The (Amy Tan, 1989)   74

Juliet (Man Ray, 1943)   112-14

K

Kadohata, Cynthia   74-75
KAOS Network   163
Kase, Carlos   225
Keefer, Cindy   166
Keesling, Alan   131, 140
Killer of Sheep (Charles Burnett,
    1977)   116-121
Kim Dong-won   105
Kim Ronyoung   75
Kim, Elaine   74
King, Rodney   76, 79, 84
Kingston, Maxine Hong   69, 73, 83
Knight, Julia   228
Kruger, Barbara   174
Kuchar, Mike   170, 192

L

Lane, Bruce   130
Last Movie, The (Dennis Hopper,
    1971)   143, 220
Late Spring (Yasujiro Ozu, 1949)   81
Lawrence, Noel   170
Laxton (John Saville,1975)   238-241
Laxton   231-244
Lebrun, David   130-31, 134
Lhevinne, Isadore   175, 178-92
Lipman, Ross   167
Lippincott, Charles   132
Los Angeles Abstract Movie
    Workshop   167
Los Angeles Free Press   131, 137, 147
Los Angeles Independent Film
    Oasis   123, 226
Los Angeles, social and urban
    structure of   70-71, 75,
                         82, 92-96, 112-13,
                         106-12, 115-17, 125,
                         155, 217, 219, 220, 224
Lu Xun   47, 52-56
Lullaby (Boris Deutsch,1929)   181

Lupe (Andy Warhol, 1965) 203-15

M
MacDonald-Wright, Stanton 129
Man Ray 112-13
Mandala (Im Kwon-taek, 1981) 5, 10, 11-21
Manhatta (Charles Sheeler and Paul Strand, 1921) 180, 194
Marr, Lisa 156
Mayakovsky, Vladimir 198
Mays, Peter 130-32, 139-43
means of film production 106, 114
Mediaeval Village (J.B. Holmes, 1935) 235-37, 239, 243
mediating apparatuses (cinema) 112
Mekas, Jonas 140, 145, 159, 176, 191, 203, 220-22, 226
Meshes of the Afternoon (Maya Deren and Alexander Hammid, 1943) 112, 222, 180
Mills, Mike 172
Minjung Movement 2, 11, 22, 34, 57, 60, 65, 105
MobMov (MOBile MOVie) 170
mode of film production 60, 109-11, 113-17, 203
Mogul, Susan 162
Mohr, Bill 81
More, Thomas 232
Moritz, William 136, 138, 144
Movies 'Round Midnight 131
Moving Image Review & Art Journal (MIRAJ) 218
Mr. Motorboat's Last Stand (John Flory, 1933) 180
Murphy, Dudley 113, 129
Murrow, Rol 132, 135, 136, 139-40
Museum of Jurassic Technology 167

N
New American Cinema 159, 191
New Korean Cinema 33-34, 45, 55, 105

New York Film-Makers' Cooperative (NYFC) 208, 220
Newsreel 148, 150
NewTown Pasadena 163
Nin, Anaïs 137
No-No Boy (John Okada, 1957) 70
Nokia Theatre 172-73
Nothing to Lose (*Niets Ann Verloren*, Lawrence Weiner, 1984) 155

O
O'Neill, Pat 115, 121-26, 130, 139, 141, 160, 225
Okada, John 72
open field system of farming; see common field system of farming
Open Fields, The (C.S. and C.S. Orwin, 1954) 237
Orwin, C.S. and C.S. 237-39, 242
Ozu, Yasujiro 81

P
Park Chung-hee (Pak Chonghui) 2
Park Kwang-su 3, 55-60, 64
Passing Through (Larry Clark, 1977) 119
Perkins, Jeff 128, 138
Phantom Galleries L.A 172
Pierce, Mark 233-35, 237, 239, 243
Pierson, Michele 226
Pinnacle Productions 128, 130, 134
Poetry Loves Poetry: An Anthology of Los Angeles Poets (Bill Mohr, ed., 1985) 81

R
Ramond, Harald 204
REDCAT Theater 163-65
Rees, A.L. 228
Reynaud, Bérénice 163
Reynolds, Lucy 228
Ricard, René 215
Richardson, David 241-44
Roebling, John 192-93

Romero, Elias 131
Rose, Edmund 239-42
Ruscha, Ed 167, 221

S

Sa-I-Gu (Dai Sil Kim-Gibson, Christine Choy, and Elaine Kim, 1993) 69, 76-80, 84
Sanggye-dong Olympics (Kim Dong-won, 1988) 105
Sapienza, Stephanie 224
Saugus Series (Pat O'Neill, 1974) 121
Saville, John 238-40
Schneemann, Carolee 162, 220-23
Scopitones 156-57
Scroggins, Michael 132, 135-36, 143
Sedgwick, Edie 205-09, 212-15
Seoul Film Group 55
Serra, M.M. 220, 222
Shiri (Kang Je-gyu, 1999) 2, 38
Shoppers Market (John Vicario, 1963) 225-26
Single Spark, A (Park Kwang-su, 1995) 1, 50, 55-58, 62
Single Wing Turquoise Bird 127-152, 168
Sins of the Fleshapoids (Mike Kuchar, 1965) 170
Sister Midnight (Peter Mays, 1975) 143
Sitney, P. Adams 137, 181, 222
Sky Socialist, The (Ken Jacobs, 1965) 175-198
Smith, Jack 189, 191, 214
Socialism xi, 48, 51, 59, 66, 79, 95, 176-77, 193
Socialist Realism 45-68
Sopyonje (Im Kwon-taek, 1993) 2, 3, 8
Star Spangled to Death (Ken Jacobs, 2004) 175-76
Star Wars (George Lucas, 1977) 148, 224
Stehura, John 133, 142
Steinkamp, Jennifer 168
Story of Ch'unhyang (Ch'unhyang'ga) 8
Suderburg, Erika 156

T

Tan, Amy 74
Thater, Diana 168
Thirsk, Joan 242-43
Thomas Edison Lighting Company 130, 132
Toscano, Mark 167
Trips Festival 131
Two Stage Sisters (Xie Jin, 1964) 2, 52-55, 59

U

Un chien Andalou (Luis Buñuel and Salvador Dalí, 1929) 112, 122, 144
Under the Brooklyn Bridge (Rudy Burkhardt, 1953) 195
University of California, Los Angeles (UCLA) 116, 125, 130-36, 148, 163
University of Southern California (USC) 108, 116, 131, 163, 169, 219, 223-24, 226

V

Vanderbeek, Stan 145, 150, 172
Vélez, Lupe 203-07, 212-15
Vicario, John 225-26
Visual Communications 75, 90, 163

W

Wang, Wayne 69
Warhol, Andy 192-215
Water and Power (Pat O'Neill, 1988) 105, 115, 121-26
We Shall March Again (Lenny Lipton, 1965) 223
Wedlock House: An Intercourse (Stan Brakhage, 1959) 113
Weinbren, Grahame 225, 226
Weiner, Lawrence 155, 158, 218
Whitney, John 225
Wieland, Joyce 178
Wilfred, Thomas 129

Wilson, David	167	**Y**	
"Women on Tano Day" (Sin Yun-bok)	8	Yallasong Film Studies Group	55
Woman Warrior, The (Maxine Hong Kingston, 1976)	69	Yamamoto, Hisaye	74
		Youngblood, Gene	137, 144, 146
Woodberry, Billy	118	Yun Yong-gyu	1
Worker Photography Movement (*Arbeiterphotographen*)	106		
Workers Film and Photo League	106, 180	**Z**	
		Zornes, Milford	195

X

Xala (Ousmane Sembène, 1973)   147

www.ingramcontent.com/pod-product-compliance
Lightning Source LLC
Chambersburg PA
CBHW032003220426
43664CB00005B/124